ADVANCE PRAISE FOR
BANANA CAPITAL

"This is an eye-opening and engaging exploration of one of the world's most popular fruits. Brisbois exposes the social and ecological consequences of the modern industrial banana." —LENORE NEWMAN, author of *Speaking in Cod Tongues*

"*Banana Capital* is more than an extraordinarily engaging look at why bananas are produced under toxic and unfair conditions—and what it means for people on the ground in Latin America. It is also a deeply thoughtful exploration of global change, and what it might take to transform one of the most unjust industries in the world." —STEVE STRIFFLER, co-editor of *Banana Wars*

"*Banana Capital* upends North American notions of bananas as a 'healthy' snack by revealing to readers the precarious lives of farm labour in Ecuador—the world's leading exporter of bananas for more than half a century—whose work is marked by social inequalities and exposure to hazardous pesticides. What's more, the author compels readers to find ways to achieve meaningful changes that go beyond virtuous consumption." —JOHN SOLURI, author of *Banana Cultures*

"Weaving together the science of banana production with realities of pesticides and poison, *Banana Capital* is a timely critique of the social, public health, political, and economic realities of the contemporary banana industry." —KEES JANSEN, editor of the *Journal of Agrarian Change*

"A grim reminder of how plantation ecologies reverberate in human bodies in devastatingly unequal ways." —JULIE GUTHMAN, author of *Wilted: Pathogens, Chemicals, and the Fragile Future of the Strawberry Industry*

"*Banana Capital* comprehensively explores the exploitation of Ecuadorian banana workers through power dynamics, environmental impacts, and history." —CARLOS LARREA, Universidad Andina Simón Bolívar

BANANA CAPITAL

Science, Stories, and Poison at the Equator

Ben Brisbois

University of Regina Press

© Ben Brisbois, 2025

All rights reserved. No part of this work covered by the copyrights hereon may be reproduced or used in any form or by any means—graphic, electronic, or mechanical—without the prior written permission of the publisher. Any request for photocopying, recording, taping, or placement in information storage and retrieval systems of any sort shall be directed in writing to Access Copyright.

Printed and bound in Canada. The text of this book is printed on 100% post-consumer recycled paper with earth-friendly vegetable-based inks.

COVER ART: "bunch of green bananas on background" By Kurapy / AdobeStock.
COVER AND TEXT DESIGN: Duncan Noel Campbell, University of Regina Press
COPY EDITOR: Kelly Laycock
PROOFREADER: Ryan Perks
INDEXER: Judy Dunlop
PHOTO CREDIT: All photos in the text were taken by the author.

Library and Archives Canada Cataloguing in Publication

TITLE: Banana capital : science, stories, and poison at the equator / Ben Brisbois.

NAMES: Brisbois, Ben, author.

SERIES: Digestions (Regina, Sask.)

DESCRIPTION: Series statement: Digestions | Includes bibliographical references and index.

IDENTIFIERS: Canadiana (print) 20240457226 | Canadiana (ebook) 20240457250 | ISBN 9781779400352 (hardcover) | ISBN 9781779400345 (softcover) | ISBN 9781779400369 (PDF) | ISBN 9781779400376 (EPUB)

SUBJECTS: LCSH: Banana trade,—Health aspects,—Ecuador, History. | LCSH: Banana trade,—Environmental aspects,—Ecuador,—History. | LCSH: Pesticides,—Health aspects,—Ecuador,—History. | LCSH: Public health,—Ecuador,—History. | LCSH: Political ecology,—Ecuador. | LCSH: Ecuador,—Environmental conditions. | LCSH: Ecuador,—Social conditions. | LCSH: Ecuador,—Economic conditions.

CLASSIFICATION: LCC HD9259.B3 E28 2025 | DDC 338.7/63477209866,—dc23

10 9 8 7 6 5 4 3 2 1

University of Regina Press, University of Regina
Regina, Saskatchewan, Canada, S4S 0A2
TEL: (306) 585-4758 FAX: (306) 585-4699
WEB: www.uofrpress.ca

We acknowledge the support of the Canada Council for the Arts for our publishing program. We acknowledge the financial support of the Government of Canada. / Nous reconnaissons l'appui financier du gouvernement du Canada. This publication was made possible with support from Creative Saskatchewan's Book Publishing Production Grant Program.

CONTENTS

Figures vii
Preface ix
Introduction 1

PART 1: 1870–1960
    CHAPTER 1: *El pulpo* 15
    CHAPTER 2: Race to the Equator 21
    CHAPTER 3: Bananas, Environments, and Histories 31
    CHAPTER 4: Beyond Its Control 39
    CHAPTER 5: The Very, Very Tropical Equator 45
    CHAPTER 6: The Parakeet in the Plantation 51

PART 2: 1961–2000
    CHAPTER 7: An Insult 59
    CHAPTER 8: Cavendish Ecologies 67
    CHAPTER 9: Empire's Guinea Pigs 77
    CHAPTER 10: *El fruto del neoliberalismo* 85
    CHAPTER 11: Healthy Resistance 97

PART 3: 2001–2023
    CHAPTER 12: *A la costa* 107
    CHAPTER 13: Twenty-First-Century Socialism
        and Contemporary Forms of Slavery 115
    CHAPTER 14: A Question of Culture 121
    CHAPTER 15: The Illness of the Century 129
    CHAPTER 16: *El gringuito* 137
    CHAPTER 17: Same Joke, Different Clown 145
    CHAPTER 18: *Plagas* 153
    CHAPTER 19: The Bananthropocene 161

PART 4: GREEN FUTURES
    CHAPTER 20: Stories 177
    CHAPTER 21: Evidence I: Regulating and Litigating Toxics 187
    CHAPTER 22: Evidence II: Epidemiology
        and "Developing Countries" 201
    CHAPTER 23: Shopping 215
    CHAPTER 24: Noticing 229
    CHAPTER 25: Plotting 241

Acknowledgements 253
Glossary 257
Notes 261
Bibliography 287
Index 321

FIGURES

2.01 Mural adorning Chiquita's office in Machala 27
9.01 Alejandro Bananahands 78
12.01 Pesticide brands available in coastal Ecuador 111
19.01 Anti-Chevron pipeline graffiti on the highway to *el oriente* 163

PREFACE

The engine died and the truck rolled to a halt at the side of the road. In the moments before the driver announced that we had run out of gas, I took in the shadowy rows of banana plants as tall as trees, extending as far as the headlights allowed us to see. The light crept along the bare ground between rows of plants before dying out in the plantation's interior, illuminating the plastic bags that covered the growing banana bunches. We stood at the side of the road, and I recalled stories of violent muggings on local highways that I had heard over the preceding months—what locals referred to as *la delincuencia*. Meanwhile, Hector[1] called back to the community we had just left to ask if someone could bring us *un galoncito*, turning a gallon of gas into an object of affection by adding *-cito* at the end to downplay the favour he was asking.

It was late 2011. Several hours earlier, I had met Hector and a man he knew with a truck at a gas station in Machala. The city is the capital of El Oro province, located towards the southern end of Ecuador's Pacific coast (a region known as *la costa*). Reflecting Ecuador's perennial leadership of global banana exports, Machala calls itself "the banana capital of the world." Weeks previously, Hector had sought me out at the downtown hotel where I was renting an apartment while I carried out my PhD fieldwork on reducing the health effects associated with pesticide use in banana production. He had invited me to visit the nearby community where he worked as a teacher, in the midst of banana fields and with a name suggesting hope for a better future.[2] I had made a preliminary visit with Hector and Ramón, a local physician I had gotten to know. Ramón had driven us on that initial trip, stopping first to drop off his young children—whom he affectionately referred to as *cholitos*,[3] a derogatory term for uncouth mixed-race *mestizos*—at his gated home in one of Machala's middle-class neighbourhoods.

On that first visit we observed fumigation planes spraying the banana plantations that surround the community and learned that both planes and drifting pesticides would frequently stray over the inhabited area, including when children were at play during recess. We observed plastic bags that had been taken off banana bunches hanging to dry on clotheslines, a practice that Ramón explained would expose the women who washed the bags to hazardous insecticides (typically one called *chlorpyrifos*, whose numerous impacts include impaired nerve function). We also discussed my anticipated return to the community to carry out interviews, and I explained to Hector that I was unable to offer participants any gifts or compensation, based on the terms of my ethics approval. While I usually bent the rules by bringing a small packet of cookies to share, Hector suggested that I instead offer participants vitamins to compensate for their poor diet.

Weeks later when we met again at the gas station, I was preparing mentally for the strain conducting interviews in Spanish would entail for me, even after months of ethnographic fieldwork in *la costa*. Despite being the foreign researcher who was apparently expected to help improve health-related behaviours in the community, I ended up in the back of the pickup truck while Hector sat in the cab with the driver. After a nerve-wracking trip at highway speeds, we arrived just as the equatorial sun was setting. I was introduced to Efraín, a community leader who asked me what my profession was—a common question in Ecuador, where people are often referred to by their professional titles. For example, President Rafael Correa, who was then attempting to transform the country via a political program termed *twenty-first-century socialism*, was often referred to as *el economista*, reflecting his PhD training in economics. I struggled to explain that I was being trained in a faculty of medicine but was not a physician. Efraín promptly retired to a public address system from which I heard his voice echo tinnily across the village's central soccer field, announcing to everyone in town that "the Canadian physician (*médico*) invites you to a meeting."

As about a dozen local men trickled into the community centre, I tried repeatedly to explain the nature of what I was doing and my consent form's material on possible risks and benefits of participating. I explained that those "benefits" might involve some future, vaguely defined but definitely research-informed improvements to community health in relation to banana production, also invoking a larger action-research project my doctoral supervisor and his Ecuadorian colleagues were about to undertake.[4] Each time I neared the end of that carefully crafted spiel, more men would arrive and I would have to get them up to speed. I realized I would not be carrying out my intended one-on-one interviews (which could take up to an hour each) and set about conducting an impromptu focus group. I still relied on the laboriously refined interview guide that was supposed to help me divine "the culture of the coastal region." Figuring this out, my research proposal maintained, would suggest some transcendently equitable solution to the problem of pesticide-related health impacts in and around banana plantations.

This self-imposed quest had originated three years previously, at the start of my PhD in population and public health at the University of British Columbia (UBC). A course assignment led to me learning about—and then rapidly being consumed by—stories of unfair and dangerous working conditions on Ecuador's banana farms. A hard-hitting 2002 Human Rights Watch report was particularly eye-opening, describing low-paid and precarious workers who were prevented from unionizing by farm owners.[5] A variety of dirty tricks helped foil their labour-organizing efforts, such as keeping workers in a perpetual temporary state so they would not count towards the minimum thirty permanent employees legally required to form a union. Even more alarming were interviews with children as young as eight, who worked long days in hazardous conditions with pervasive exposure to toxic pesticides such as chlorpyrifos and the fungicides constantly applied with backpack sprayers and fumigation planes. These children were often not allowed to exit the fields when planes passed overhead, instead hiding under banana leaves or cardboard boxes and using shirts or their hands to hold off the falling *veneno* (poison—a local term for pesticides).[6]

Spurred on by such accounts and enabled by the Ecuadorian research collaborations of my PhD supervisor, Jerry Spiegel, I had proposed to fix the problem by translating public health science on toxic pesticides into actual policies and control practices. A growing body of knowledge had accumulated by that time criticizing naive attempts at using "evidence-based policy" to remedy social and environmental injustices and their health consequences.[7] And so I laboriously designed a project that would try to bring about real change by valuing the lived experiences of pesticide-affected banana workers and farmers, and by being realistic about the political and economic power relations affecting coastal Ecuador. This trajectory meant that when I arrived in Ecuador to carry out fieldwork, I was in the midst of an ambitious attempt to make the world a better place through applied research—but was far from confident about how exactly to do so.

"I'm not complete," declared Efraín. He had responded with "bad" to a "how would you rate your health" question I asked early on in every interview. "I've been operated on."

"They gave him the caesarean," joked one of the other men enigmatically, leaving me to wonder to this day what specific body part Efraín was missing. This internal disharmony appeared to be one cause of Efraín's severe manner, but another was more external, having to do with the village's lack of unity. The community had been founded decades earlier by poor migrants from Ecuador's Andean plateau, or *la sierra*, who had moved in response to the country's land reform initiatives, often pushed out by drought and the concentration of land ownership in their home regions. They had pursued employment opportunities in the coastal region, where, they told me, *serranos* like them were sought out for their reputation as hard-working. Consistent with Andean traditions of communal labour (*minga*, in Kichwa, Ecuador's dialect of the Indigenous Quechua family of languages), Efraín's neighbours had in those early decades frequently come together to complete community-improvement projects. Now, he said angrily, people rarely attended meetings (such as the one he had convened on my behalf), and "wouldn't contribute even a single cent" towards purchasing communal improvements such as water and sanitation infrastructure.

The need for such infrastructure, as well as for adequate health services, was a common refrain as I moved the group through the interview guide. In response to several questions about health and pesticides, the men painted a picture that was depressingly consistent with those hard-hitting reports that had initially drawn me to Ecuador. Rather than reflecting ignorance or lack of education, health hazards such as poor diets and exposure to pesticides stemmed from pervasive injustice. Compounding the careless aerial pesticide applications I had already observed was the fact that precariously employed and non-unionized workers would often not be allowed to leave plantations while they were happening. While the law forbade the practice of leaving workers in the field, it wasn't "convenient" for owners and managers to let their workforce lose a half-hour of work time. Some of the men also combined wage labour with work on their own small banana or cacao farms. They observed that staying afloat in brutally competitive global banana markets was made almost impossible by large plantation owners who seemed to want small producers to disappear. And the government whose responsibility it was to fix such problems, all in attendance agreed, would not intervene because they were corrupt. As one man put it, "you can say it, but because you're not the farm owner ... they buy justice, buy the authorities. It's difficult. The rich have the power."

It took about two hours to get through the interview guide. The chaotic environment and long day meant that I was thoroughly exhausted by the end and having trouble making sense of the conversation. Like the truck I again climbed into for the trip home, I had very little left in my tank. This sense of exhaustion was compounded by the sinking feeling that I had been experiencing for weeks as interview participants repeatedly voiced needs and priorities—such as health clinics or sanitation infrastructure— that were far removed from even the supposedly enlightened, social science–informed vision of evidence-based pesticide policy I had brought with me to Ecuador. Still, I managed to perform one last feat of research when the truck ran out of gas. When a younger man from the community pulled up on a motorcycle with the *galoncito* in a soft drink bottle, the driver was initially stumped on how to get it in the gas tank. Drawing on the full power of UBC's behavioural research ethics board, I rolled up one of my project's unused consent forms into a makeshift funnel and successfully poured the contents of the bottle into the tank.

Once back in my apartment in Machala, and later as my fieldwork gave way to analysis and writing and eventually postdoctoral research, I would continue my efforts to understand and then help address the unfair situation I had encountered in Ecuador. What could be done in response to the poisons that pervade daily life in banana-producing parts of *la costa*? How could the overwhelming power dynamics I had observed—in both global banana markets and Ecuadorian politics—possibly be challenged? What was I to make of the desires of professionals such as Ramón and Hector to educate or improve their less-educated compatriots, not to mention the regional and sometimes racist stereotypes that swirled around such conversations? And what was my role in a situation where I could arrive in the back of a truck but also be *el médico canadiense*, entreated—though frustratingly not able—to help Ecuadorians acquire basic health and sanitation infrastructure?

INTRODUCTION

This book grew out of the difficult questions generated by my involvement with the problem of pesticide-related health impacts in the areas surrounding Machala, Ecuador, the self-described banana capital of the world. That initial impetus for a Canadian public health graduate student to do something helpful in relation to a country at the equator has persisted for a decade and a half of research, teaching, and activism. That period has seen both important advances but also major setbacks in the situation facing farmers, workers, and communities who live far from and near banana farms in Ecuador and elsewhere. The use of subcontracted labour on banana farms was made illegal in 2009, but disguised forms of the practice and other means of evading worker protection laws persist to the present day.[1] The country belatedly banned the highly toxic herbicide *paraquat* in 2018, but exposure to dozens of other pesticides with worrisome impacts continues largely unchecked.[2] Ecuador's banana industry remains the site of massive *environmental injustice* (a term describing the disproportionate concentration of environmental risks in racialized, poor, and other marginalized communities).[3] Workers continue to toil in low-paid, precarious, and hazardous jobs; small banana farmers still face cutthroat competition in markets dominated by giant corporations; and a toxic soup of pesticides continues to permeate banana plantations, their surrounding environments, and their inhabitants.[4]

Even more ominously, addressing banana-related injustices is complicated by flaws in the agro-industrial food system that export bananas have always exemplified, with its impacts ranging from obesity and malnutrition through income inequality and increased pressures on the ecosystems from which diseases such as COVID-19 tend to emerge.[5] In fact, the environmental destructiveness of the banana industry, with its enormous carbon footprint, is generating questions about whether export banana production has—or should have—a future. That future is also threatened by banana production's fragility in the face of plant diseases such as the TR4 fungus, roughly a century after the related Panama disease began its disruptive spread through the banana-producing world.[6]

Of relevance to the challenge of addressing the pesticide-related health impacts of Ecuadorian banana production in the first decades of the twenty-first century are a handful of epidemiology studies that have documented such effects (epidemiology is the study of health and illness, and their causes, in human populations).[7] While suggesting numerous worrisome impacts, these studies have tended to raise as many questions as they answer, for reasons involving limitations at the heart of environmental health sciences. For example, even determining the scale of the problem is complicated by the notoriously uncertain health effects of complex chemical mixtures such as the evolving "cocktails" of different pesticides used in banana production. It's hard to figure out if conditions such as cancer, neurological impairment, depression, birth defects, or even coughs or rashes are due to one pesticide, multiple pesticides, pesticides in combination with other factors, or just the many physical and social insults lived on a daily basis by the impoverished—and hard-to-study—populations who make up the banana workforce.[8]

Cutting-edge environmental health science is confronting these methodological challenges. Communities lacking access to the resources required to carry out sophisticated studies, however, continue to be exposed to toxic chemicals in ways that merit noticing, and demand action. But even were definitive evidence on the scale of the problem to be obtained, the ability of the banana industry to sidestep challenges to unrestrained profit-making is legendary, complicating hopes of holding it to account.[9] When governments or unions have threatened to require a living wage and respect for worker rights, banana companies have nimbly moved their sourcing to cheaper and less-protected jurisdictions. Ecuador has been the main such "safety valve" destination for over sixty years now, raising the question of where the banana industry would go if meaningful protection of workers and farmers was finally achieved in that country. The rapidly restructuring global pesticide industry is similarly notorious for defusing the threat that countries will ban highly hazardous pesticides. It has successfully steered policy and science over decades towards ineffectual "safe use" educational programs that erroneously blame pesticide exposures on individual ignorance or carelessness among agricultural workers.[10]

Perhaps not surprisingly, then, people living and working in coastal Ecuador have repeatedly pushed me to look beyond the impacts of pesticides to account for broader economic inequities that also have real and major health consequences. As social science research on toxic chemicals explains, "an emphasis on bodily harm risks ignoring the ways in which toxicity ramifies beyond the individual to socioecological relationships."[11] In fact, explaining the societal causes of pesticide exposures implicates factors—such as hazardous working conditions, precarious employment, and structurally determined poverty—that themselves generate enormous burdens of illness through modification of the social determinants of health ("the circumstances in which people are born, grow, live, work, and age"[12]). That is, in Ecuador as in other countries, occupational pesticide exposure attests to, or is an epidemiologic "proxy" for, numerous additional contributors to poor health: lack of education, low and precarious income, and unhealthy housing and neighbourhoods, among others.[13]

When initially deciding how to approach banana-related environmental injustice in Ecuador, therefore, I determined that throwing another epidemiology study at the problem would likely be ineffective in terms of achieving environmental justice. I instead needed to learn from the stories people in *la costa* told about pesticide risk, about the toxic social circumstances giving rise to it, and about what should be done in response.[14] In swimming through the literature on pesticide risk perception to its anthropological deep end and beyond, I arrived at work on "illness narratives" showing how the stories people tell about health and disease reflect their social worlds, and also the large-scale colonial and capitalist power relations that shape them.[15] For example, in *The Devil and Commodity Fetishism in South America*, Michael T. Taussig argues that devil stories among Bolivian tin miners and Afro-Colombian residents of sugarcane-producing regions reflect the encounter of pre-capitalist ways of knowing with the health-destroying violence of capitalism and its mystifying ideologies.[16]

In using such theories to guide my research, I sought to discover how *costeños'* interpretations of pesticide risk aligned with their broader ways of making sense of the world—and therefore with the complicated notion of "culture" and its shaping by political and economic power.[17] Then, I reasoned, within those perceptions I could find the core of resistance to capitalist ideology and help to amplify it in designing progressive public health interventions. While this plan hasn't exactly worked as originally envisioned, the lessons learned along the way turned out to hold relevance for future attempts to address social and environmental injustice in relation to banana production (and possibly more broadly).

This book has therefore had to evolve in order to relate the health-damaging toxicity experienced by people in Ecuador's banana-producing regions to interacting political, economic, cultural, and environmental forces—and to explore how it might be addressed. While Ecuador is at the centre of the story, explaining how it got there and with such distressing results for people and the environment requires a broader focus. The banana industry is a particularly vivid example of global interconnectedness, with complex transnational flows of fruit, money, people, pathogens, ideas, and dynamics of the global climate. Trying to make sense of the situation currently facing the banana capital of the world has therefore required tracing the history of banana production in multiple parts of the Americas back into the late nineteenth century. Piecing together this story has also required integrating knowledge on things like the health effects of specific toxic chemicals, the agroecology of banana farms, the agency and feelings of people exposed to both pesticides and corporate power, the inequities of banana markets, blind spots in environmental and occupational health sciences, and colonialism's ongoing legacies in terms of racism and huge economic disparities.

For help with that analysis and storytelling challenge, the book draws on a research approach known as *political ecology of health* (PEH). PEH traces how health is shaped by political and economic power (the political economy) and its interaction with the environment.[18] It takes epidemiology, toxicology (the experimental study of how health is affected by controlled doses of toxic substances), and related health sciences seriously but is itself a primarily social scientific approach. Political ecologists examine the role of gender, race, ability, age, class, and caste in interactions of political and economic power with the environment, and how the resulting impacts are interpreted and embodied in people's experiences of health and well-being.[19] They also challenge artificial distinctions between external environments and those found within human bodies, documenting—for example—how having one disease (e.g., HIV) changes the body's "internal ecologies" as it confronts others (e.g., tuberculosis).[20] Especially relevant for the quest to apply public health sciences to solving environmental injustice is PEH's focus on how scientific knowledge on health and the environment is shaped by often disturbing power relations (e.g., colonialism, patriarchy, or simply capitalism).[21] The story that this approach has led to synthesizes health, agricultural, environmental, and social science into what is hopefully a well-rounded analysis with implications for action.

"So what sort of bananas should I be buying?"

Such questions have emerged frequently when I talk about bananas, which are among the world's most consumed fruits. As anthropologists Steve Striffler and Mark Moberg put it in their introduction to the illuminating edited volume *Banana Wars: Power, Production and History in the Americas*, "one tropical fruit has transformed more of Central America, the Caribbean, and South America than any other commodity."[22] One crowd-pleasing device for conveying this importance is my insistence that pretty much any significant historical event in the last 150 years in the Americas can be linked to the banana trade—what I started calling "six degrees of bananas." For example, the 1959 Cuban Revolution triggered the (failed) Bay of Pigs invasion, in which Cuban expats were assisted by both the notorious United Fruit Company (UFC, today known as Chiquita) and the oil company Zapata Petroleum, owned by later US president George H.W. Bush. A few years earlier, the initial meeting between Cuban revolutionary leaders Fidel Castro and Ernesto "Che" Guevara took place in Mexico, where Che had fled after the 1954 CIA-backed coup in Guatemala ended his political work organizing UFC's banana workers in that country.

In such conversations I can't help but stray into the academic considerations that have guided my research, but it doesn't take long for many listeners to bring the conversation back to something with more personal traction: their grocery shopping and eating decisions. People can be forgiven for viewing banana-buying as a fun, healthy, and possibly world-saving thing to do, especially in light of banana labels that claim to ensure environmentally friendly or socially just production. Fairtrade America, for example, urges consumers to buy fairtrade-certified bananas to ensure a living wage for banana workers, and to "protect the fundamental rights and freedoms of banana farmers in the workplace, including health and safety, gender equity, acceptable working hours and the right to bargain."[23] My own fieldwork was helped enormously by the leadership, staff, and farmers of the Machala-based fairtrade, organic banana and cacao producer co-operative UROCAL (Regional Union of Peasant-Farmer Organizations of the Coast). After emerging from a process of labour organizing against UFC in the 1950s and '60s, UROCAL's members now survive as small farmers due to international solidarity they have actively cultivated, including by encouraging European consumers to buy certified bananas. The banana worker organization ASTAC (Union Association of Agricultural and Peasant Workers), which has also helped me find resources and research participants, is similarly involved in campaigns to educate banana consumers and thereby put pressure on transnational corporations to improve worker rights.

So while I was and am uncomfortable with the idea of trying to remedy environmental and social injustice with better purchasing decisions, both my research collaborators and my own social world have forced me to take that idea seriously. As a result, I learned that the cultural identities of bananas and their consumers have long been cultivated by the banana industry at least as carefully as have bananas themselves.[24] In 1944, UFC gave the world Miss Chiquita, a singing cartoon banana patterned on Brazilian star Carmen Miranda, with her fruit-bowl hat.[25] Miss Chiquita helped to consolidate the fruit's identification with the sultry and (apparently) silly global South, in a famous TV jingle explaining that "Bananas are accustomed to the very, very tropical equator."[26] The stickers that adorn today's bananas bolster this identification with a vaguely defined but definitely warmer part of the world. Display labels in produce sections will read "Bananas: From" and then a country name such as Guatemala or Ecuador or Honduras or Costa Rica. The country name will sometimes match the one on the banana stickers, but often not. I have also seen a revealing catch-all as stores give up in the face of the industry's restless sourcing practices: "Bananas: From the Tropics."

The tropical aura surrounding bananas also evokes an interestingly checkered past, as in the name of the upscale Banana Republic clothing chain.[27] Despite the fact that UFC came to be identified with the worst tendencies of US imperialism in twentieth-century Latin America, popular representations of bananas often have a light political touch. As a summer camp counsellor in Ontario in my early twenties, I sometimes led campers in the rallying cry "Bananas of the world, unite!" This tongue-in-cheek callback to militant labour organizing—a play on the closing lines of *The Communist Manifesto*—is followed by a series of banana-related "tasks" that evoke the factory-farm character of agro-industrial banana plantations:

> Pick, bananas. Pick, pick bananas.
> Peel, bananas. Peel, peel bananas.
> Smush, bananas. Smush, smush bananas.
> Eat, bananas. Eat, eat bananas.

An accompanying assembly line of hand gestures culminates in a kind of workers' emancipation in which kids dance wildly: "GO! BANANAS! GO, GO BANANAS!" I can confirm that this is a fun song to sing but now can't help linking it to the Ecuadorian child labourers interviewed by Human Rights Watch, whose repetitive work tasks were all too real and whose ability to "unite"—along with their adult co-workers—had been systematically suppressed. The contrast between the reality of bananas and their popular representation becomes especially poignant, verging on horrifying, if you populate the song with those Ecuadorian child workers taking shelter under cardboard boxes or banana leaves while fumigation planes mist them in fungicides.

It is ironic, then, that bananas have also long been invested in the global North with healthy connotations in relation to growing children.[28] UFC recruited doctors in the early twentieth century when popular awareness of healthy diets was in its infancy, having them develop nutrition advice meant to brand bananas a health food, especially for kids.[29] The famous 1944 jingle sung by Miss Chiquita Banana, for example, advocates including bananas in infants' diets. And while cartoon singing bananas were cutting-edge marketing in the 1940s, they are eclipsed by today's animation studios (and nutrition advice). Chiquita now provides numerous recipes on its website, generally healthy ones.[30] The site also features images of its remarkably colourful promotional campaigns, such as banana stickers that enlist (banana-yellow) Minions from the *Despicable Me* films, a hugely popular franchise with children. The website of another banana giant, Dole, similarly provides numerous recipes with ingredients that are elaborately low-fat, gluten-free, or vegan—hitting the main dietary trends of the twenty-first century.[31] These recipes also link to fun occasions such as Halloween and a large cast of characters drawn from several Disney/Pixar films, including *A Bug's Life*, *Toy Story*, *Monsters Inc.*, and *Inside Out*. These characters are woven through the website's substantial kid- and parent-oriented content and can also be found on the stickers that adorn Dole bananas in stores.

As you scroll down to the bottom of Dole's site, though, you encounter a less kid-friendly link reading simply "DBCP Facts." Clicking on this link leads to a very *uncolourful* page discussing legal action in relation to a pesticide known as dibromochloropropane (DBCP, a nematicide, meaning a pesticide used for killing soil worms known as nematodes).[32] In response to accusations from banana workers in Latin America, among other places, the page flatly states, "we can tell you that there is no credible scientific evidence that Dole's use of DBCP on banana farms caused any of the injuries claimed in any of the DBCP lawsuits, *including sterility*" (emphasis added).[33] More details about the multiple lawsuits follow as does Dole's assertion of their groundless nature, despite which the company states that it has "entered into a number of worker programs whereby male banana workers who can demonstrate that they worked during the time when DBCP was used, that they suffer from impaired fertility, and meet other minimal criteria are fairly compensated." So while characters such as *Toy Story*'s Woody the cowboy and Buzz Lightyear and the female leads of "Disney's Ultimate Princess Celebration"[34] hold down the fort on Dole banana stickers and the Dole-Disney page, lawyers and "credible scientific evidence" guard a darker and more grown-up corner of the company's site, where they fend off accusations that *Dole sterilized people*.

Jarring pairings such as those involving beloved Disney characters and denials of responsibility for human sterilizations illustrate how compelling and disturbing the stories surrounding bananas can be. The power of those stories has steered me away from producing a conventional academic book that builds on existing knowledge in a particular field by addressing some errors or shortcomings in it. This book instead has stories and characters whose unexpectedly moving ties to its intellectual content are at least as important as the results of its analysis or argument.

This analytic focus on stories ultimately grew out of a deeper attention to political power and the environment than is found in most public health scholarship. The book nevertheless still aims at public health's desire to concretely change the world for the better. In this it is preceded by numerous committed scientists and health professionals who have worked hard to protect agricultural workers' health from pesticides.[35] Such engaged researchers and practitioners have assiduously generated scientific knowledge using methodological rigour within epidemiology and related sciences. As they learned, however, and as countless marginalized communities can confirm, forcing efforts at environmental justice to jump through evidence-based hoops and other state structures is generally a losing battle.[36] Belying the story of evidence-based public health, those sciences and structures have largely evolved to do the opposite of fight injustice, and they perform poorly when they start biting the invisible hand that feeds them.

Giant corporations of the kind that feature prominently in the story of bananas and pesticides, in contrast, have historically achieved their goals through tactics that are less constrained by rules such as epidemiology's methodologies. UFC's early twentieth-century manipulation of Latin American governments or payments by Chiquita, Dole, and Del Monte to Colombian right-wing paramilitary groups around the turn of this century vividly illustrate this fact.[37] If public health scholars use their customary strategies to take on powerful interests that can employ such tactics—not to mention Buzz Lightyear, Princess Merida, Minions, and a large number of highly trained public relations professionals, scientists, and lawyers—they seem likely to lose. The emotionally appealing story in which science automatically makes the world a better and fairer place has therefore come to seem less and less credible.

This book asks why we get into some stories about bananas and toxics and not others—and how we can get into *better* stories. My ongoing learning about the vivid, disturbing, fascinating history of banana production has changed me in ways that go beyond just the intellectual. Stories affect us emotionally, which seems relevant at a time of particularly discouraging global environmental and social crises. North-South relations, racism, food, the natural world, scientific progress, advocacy, and capitalism all look and feel different when viewed through the lens of banana stories. By focusing on the affective dimensions of how people make sense of these inequities through story, rather than focusing on the existing, worn avenues of activism and social change, we are ultimately led to new strategies and unexpectedly hopeful possibilities for confronting environmental injustice.

This book draws frequently on other stories that I have encountered in researching and writing it. Some of these come from poems and novels, while others emerge from less obvious places such as epidemiology and other scientific articles or the plots of those animated films used to advertise bananas. Also in the book are stories I encountered by living them, especially during the years in which I've had the privilege of travelling in Ecuador and other banana-producing countries. Drawing on my personal experience is consistent with the practice of some very good social scientists whose work I encountered and learned from while conducting the academic research that informs this book. While scientific journal articles often strive to convey an image of objectivity through the use of third-person voice, passive verb tenses, and other time-honoured scientific writing conventions, such pretending to be observing reality "objectively" from a vantage point outside of or above it is just that: pretending.[38] While I do my best to report scientific evidence in an accurate and unbiased way in this book, I don't attempt to minimize my own role in the story. Including the observer telling a story is more honest than pretensions at objectivity—and usually more fun to read.

The long-standing injustices I first observed in Ecuador in 2009, and their continuation across the banana-producing world to the present day, represent the conflict that drives this story. Part 1 of the book explains why Ecuador has been the world's leading exporter of bananas since the 1950s, and why those bananas are produced in such toxic and unfair conditions. This part draws on existing studies by historians and social scientists on the vivid and disturbing history of banana production in the Americas, which in its early decades occurred mainly in Central America and Colombia. It covers the period from approximately 1870 to 1960, and prominently features the infamous UFC. Part 2 picks the story up in the 1960s, with a major transformation of the industry from the original Gros Michel to the new Cavendish banana variety, and a new pesticide-intensive and contract-based approach to producing it. I again rely on secondary sources by historians and others, but also integrate my own analyses of the Latin American "travels" of health and agricultural sciences in this period and the troubling scientific stories that have guided them.[39] Part 3 follows the story into the twenty-first century while narrowing to focus specifically on Ecuador, integrating secondary sources with results of my fieldwork in the country.[40] Parts 1 to 3 of the book therefore attempt to explain its central conflict, a task that also uncovers various lessons for how it might be resolved.

Some such lessons are hinted at along the way, oriented towards people concerned with the health and well-being of people living in the shadow of banana production—so potentially towards anyone who has ever bought or eaten a banana. A more sustained look at possible solutions is found in Part 4, which revisits the question of being helpful in relation to bananas and the people and places who produce them. It looks carefully at some of the main strategies that have been envisioned in response to environmental injustice in banana production. These strategies, from the everyday to the revolutionary, represent possible denouements or resolutions to the conflict driving this book. Those possible resolutions are Ecuador-focused, but global interconnections in the causes of the problem mean that the possible solutions are also often transnational in scope.

One such category of solution involves strengthening and working with regulatory and legal mechanisms for protecting communities from environmental injustice, especially featuring the discipline of toxicology. Another involves documenting pesticide exposures and other determinants of poor health using the discipline of epidemiology and the resulting "evidence" to change policy. A third strategy entails "conscious consumption" and other forms of market-based solidarity with banana farmers and workers (and environments). Nuanced social scientific study (*noticing*) of lived experiences of toxicity represents a fourth strategy. Finally, the word *plotting* is used to explore three interrelated strategies—food sovereignty, political organizing, and living better stories—that go beyond standard responses to social and environmental injustice within existing societal structures.

Part 4 makes some pointed suggestions regarding the costs and benefits of these strategies but acknowledges that definitively figuring out how to proceed towards a fairer and more environmentally grounded banana industry—and world—is a work in progress. This book is an attempt to make sense of a broad swathe of reality and scholarship about it, in ways that are generally more exploratory than authoritative. I am not a historian or an agronomist or a toxicologist. I am not a researcher from or based in Latin America, although I have attempted to learn from and represent such work in this book (the deficiencies that inevitably remain are my own). Sometimes I consider myself barely a social scientist, and I know enough epidemiology to know I'm not an epidemiologist. Most importantly, I am not a banana worker or farmer but still find myself in the somewhat uncomfortable position of trying to share their stories and be helpful in relation to their problems.

Reflecting such limitations, the humility I have tried to bring to the stories in this book therefore leads to something other than an argument culminating in a single, unassailable truth, famously described by Deleuze and Guattari as an oppressive "root-book" in which the various branches lead to a central, all-powerful trunk.[41] Deleuze and Guattari instead propose "rhizomatic" thinking, writing, and doing, referring to plants whose underground tangled roots have no central tendency (argument) to which they funnel nutrients. Rather than a single towering tree, such rhizomes send up multiple "lines of flight." Bananas plants, for example, are not trees, but rather herbs that grow from rhizomes.

Consistent with this model, this book represents my attempt to "get the right answers" to the questions that drive it—but I recognize that those answers are often diverse and at least a little bit uncertain, especially when viewed from my partial perspective. As a result, this book is less a towering edifice of truth about how to solve a problem than an invitation to engage, together, with that challenge in the future.

PART 1:
1870–1960

CHAPTER 1
EL PULPO

One common entry point into the story of bananas and their human impacts focuses on a single company. "When the trumpet sounded," explains Pablo Neruda in his poem *La United Fruit Co.*, "everything was prepared on earth" and God distributed the world to American corporations. UFC, however, "reserved for itself the most juicy piece."[1] Neruda is referring here to Central America, where UFC "rebaptized these countries Banana Republics." This poem gives a sense of how central Chiquita's original incarnation, UFC, is to the broader origin story of agro-industrial banana production—and, by extension, to the history of the Americas. The company controlled so many different aspects of life in such countries that it became known in the region by the Spanish word for octopus: *el pulpo*. This control was never complete or uncontested, though, complicating simplistic stories of monolithic corporate power. Both UFC's dominance and the cracks in that edifice help to explain how Ecuador eventually came to dominate global banana exports.

North American shipping companies such as Lorenzo Dow Baker's Boston Fruit Company began buying bananas from Jamaica in about the 1860s. Jamaican peasant farmers were particularly active in growing bananas in the aftermath of slavery's official end in the British Empire in 1834, when recurrent crises in sugar markets freed up land and labour on the island.[2] Importing such bananas to North America was a lucrative trade whose profits would lead to rapidly increasing quantities of bananas being grown and purchased from the 1870s onwards, especially of the hardy and good-tasting Gros Michel variety.[3] As the export banana trade developed, however, smallholder (Afro-descended) growers in Jamaica found themselves priced out of the market for land in banana-growing areas close to port facilities, moving onto increasingly marginal or mountainous lands farther from the ocean where production in the export banana trade was largely impossible.

Plantations (and people with the wealth to own and run them) soon came to dominate the production of bananas, as vertical integration with shipping and distribution networks served to control access to consumers in large markets in North America and smaller ones in Europe.[4] The emerging banana trade had initially been characterized by numerous competing growers, shippers, importers, and sellers. On the eve of the twentieth century, for example, seven banana-growing districts of Honduras were farmed by an estimated 1,000 different banana growers, many of whom organized in co-operative organizations to jointly ship bananas to North American markets.[5] Such early initiatives were commercially risky due to factors such as unpredictable wind patterns, which frustrated attempts to bring bananas to market on sailboats. The perishable nature of bananas favoured companies with enough access to capital to coordinate the production and prompt, reliable shipping of bananas to North American markets via emerging railroad and steamship networks.[6] Gros Michel was robust enough to best withstand the trip north and matured predictably in ways that American fruit transporters and ripeners (*jobbers*) could standardize their procedures around.

Such advantages, and concerted efforts to shape North American tastes by banana companies, eventually led to Gros Michel being preferred by consumers, for whom it came to represent "the" banana rather than just one variety of many.[7] The initial diversity of firms in the banana sector would also be substantially consolidated in the twentieth century, most notably through an 1899 merger involving the Boston Fruit Company and a US-owned company specializing in building railroads in Costa Rica. That railroad company was led by an entrepreneur named Minor Keith, to whom the Costa Rican government had previously given a large land concession in exchange for a commitment to build the country a major railroad.[8] The bananas produced on Keith's land concession would combine with Boston Fruit's shipping and marketing capacity to help make UFC one of the early twentieth century's most dominant and notorious corporations—one synonymous with the worst tendencies of US imperialism towards Latin America.⁹ UFC would use its political and economic clout, as well as technological innovations such as steamships and refrigeration, in creating a highly profitable business over the first few decades of the twentieth century and swallowing up most of its competitors.¹⁰ The company would establish major divisions in Costa Rica, Guatemala, and Colombia, among other countries in the Caribbean basin.

Driven by UFC as well as smaller competitors such as Standard Fruit and the Cuyamel Fruit Company, banana production would profoundly reshape the physical and cultural geographies of Latin America over the first half of the twentieth century. The emergence and consolidation of the export banana trade was accompanied by major changes to life in banana-producing countries.¹¹ Between 1910 and 1925, for example, the population of the principal banana-growing departments in Honduras rose from 65,000 to 200,000, while UFC and its competitors also built huge amounts of infrastructure, including railroads, hospitals, banks, and factories. Life was also changing dramatically in banana-*consuming* countries. An emerging infrastructure of large grocery stores and rail networks within North America joined up with the shipping and distribution networks monopolized by UFC to make bananas available and affordable year-round. Concurrent marketing campaigns by UFC played up the fun and tropical identity of bananas (capped by Miss Chiquita's fruity hat), while emphasizing their health benefits—especially for children.¹²

UFC's growth also occurred under the protective umbrella of a thoroughly imperialist US foreign policy towards the region. The concept of manifest destiny and economic greed, among other factors, made Latin America a major target of US attention by the late nineteenth century, building on its occupation of Mexico between 1846 and 1848.¹³ This interventionist role intensified over the first half of the twentieth century: "by 1930, Washington had sent gunboats into Latin American ports over six thousand times, invaded Cuba, Mexico (again), Guatemala, and Honduras, fought protracted guerrilla wars in the Dominican Republic, Nicaragua, and Haiti, annexed Puerto Rico, and taken a piece of Colombia to create both the Panamanian nation and the Panama Canal."¹⁴ UFC was a common beneficiary, and instigator, of such military interventions, inspiring the pejorative term *banana republic* (a country, usually Latin American, under the sway of a large, usually US-based, foreign corporation).¹⁵

Despite its reputation as *el pulpo*, UFC's dominance was never complete or monolithic. For a variety of reasons, the company never completely consolidated production under its own ownership. Sometimes it was deemed more profitable for UFC to buy bananas from independent producers than to grow them all itself, and in other cases US anti-trust worries or formal rulings prompted the company to sell off or refrain from taking over smaller companies. For example, the Cuyamel Fruit Company of New Orleans entrepreneur Samuel Zemurray had initially partnered with and received investment capital from UFC to operate plantations in Honduras. UFC sold its stake in Cuyamel to placate US regulators worried it was monopolizing the industry, and Zemurray competed with the much larger UFC before eventually being purchased by it in 1928.[16] Simplistic portrayals of banana republics in which US companies controlled all aspects of life in banana-producing "enclaves" while contributing virtually nothing to broader national economic development have similarly been challenged.[17] Careful historical analyses show that US banana companies always relied on alliances with local elites, who would actively pursue their own interests and economic activities as best they could.[18] However, while challenging the idea of monolithic US dominance of Latin American places and peoples, such complex interactions generally furthered the extraction of value from Latin American workers and territories by elites, both foreign and domestic.[19]

A particularly well-storied episode illustrates the dominance of UFC in Latin America, as well as the ways in which that dominance was both buttressed and challenged by Latin American actors. Early twentieth-century banana production in Colombia's Magdalena region on the Caribbean coast saw local elites selling substantial quantities of bananas to UFC. By the 1920s, the region was the third-largest banana-exporting zone in the world. The organization of production was contentious, though, as UFC brought the largest share of profits home to the United States. Workers were exploited via mechanisms such as the use of labour subcontractors, which UFC used to evade responsibilities to adequately pay workers and provide them with protections outlined in Colombian law (one day off per week, for example).[20]

When workers organized and threatened to strike in late 1928, the United States raised the possibility that it would invade to protect UFC's interests, and Colombia quickly passed legislation restricting freedom of assembly and press freedoms.[21] The workers' demands largely involved holding UFC to Colombia's labour laws, eliminating the use of labour subcontractors, establishing health services for workers, and having workers paid regularly so they could avoid buying goods on credit from UFC's expensive stores. Despite these less-than-revolutionary demands and a request from the region's governor, UFC refused to negotiate with the workers, who in turn went on strike. Troops made mass arrests while the governor summoned the strikers to the city of Ciénaga to negotiate an end to the strike. In parallel, though, the Colombian government in Bogotá passed a legislative decree imposing a state of siege (*estado de sitio*) in the Magdalena region, which General Cortéz Vargas (in charge of government troops in the area) interpreted as requiring his forces to "strictly comply with this decree, firing at the multitude if necessary."[22]

On December 5, the workers congregated at Ciénaga's train station in a makeshift amphitheatre created by parked rail cars, where one of their leaders urged them to disperse as he felt they were being set up by the military. They didn't, however, and troops arrived at the station shortly after midnight. After reading both the legislative decree and Cortéz Vargas's interpretation of it out loud (likely to steel reluctant troops for the unpleasant task of firing on their compatriots), the captain in charge gave the workers five minutes to disperse, and then one more minute before ordering the troops to open fire on the unarmed workers. According to some official accounts, the number of deaths was as low as nine, which was the number of dead workers the soldiers left on the ground at the train station after working through the night to load garbage trucks and a freighter with bodies for mass disposal in the ocean (nine is also the number of demands the workers had made). The UFC representative in the area would later report over 1,000 deaths, some of which occurred in scattered conflicts as the dispersed workers resisted the end of the strike. Nobel Prize–winning novelist Gabriel García Márquez, who was born a year later in the area and grew up with stories of the strike, would arrive at a significantly higher figure. In his beloved novel *One Hundred Years of Solitude*, over 3,000 people die in the confrontation at the train station.[23]

Subsequent chapters show how the story of US-based banana companies in Latin America, notably UFC, helps to explain Ecuador's emergence as the world's leading banana exporter. The example of UFC also speaks to the challenge of confronting corporate power in relation to well-being in banana-producing countries, explored in more detail in Part 4. Public health researchers alarmed at the negative influence of corporations on health and well-being in the twenty-first century have been chided for their frequent "anti-corporate, adversarial stance" and for portraying industry as a "homogeneous entity."[24] Indeed, while UFC would dominate banana production over the first half of the twentieth century and remains important today in its current incarnation, Chiquita, the company was never comfortable in its dominance, which was resisted by a variety of interests in both North and Latin America.

Nevertheless, such struggles often had predictable results for Latin American workers and small farmers. For example, a 1920 strike by workers on the Vaccaro brothers' plantations in Honduras (the Vaccaros would later become Standard Fruit, which is today known as Dole) prompted competitors UFC and Cuyamel to threaten to lock out their workers in solidarity and help break the strike. Competition between companies was then temporarily suspended in order to intervene in a labour dispute that the American consul described as a "class struggle."[25] The following chapter explores such dynamics of class struggle in terms of the diverse workforces that were involved, devious but never-complete corporate control of that diversity, and the neocolonial structures of thought and feeling at work underneath it all.

CHAPTER 2
RACE TO THE EQUATOR

UFC's machinations represent what historian James Martin terms *corporate colonialism*, as the resulting extraction of profits from a global South region was facilitated by the corporation's manipulation of neocolonial attitudes concerning people of colour and Southern settings.[1] More generally, racism both helped provide the land on which bananas are grown in the Americas and contributed to an arms race between banana companies and their diverse workforces that would eventually drive the industry to Ecuador. Understanding racism's historical role helps explain contemporary environmental injustice in the banana industry and holds implications for what to do about it.

Ecuadorian author and bureaucrat Luis Martínez's classic 1894 novel *A la costa* tells the story of Salvador Ramírez, the beleaguered descendant of a formerly wealthy highland family at the time of Ecuador's Liberal Revolution in 1895.[2] The highly educated Salvador is imbued with impractical upper-class Conservative sensibilities that the omniscient narrator spends a considerable portion of the novel ridiculing. After fighting ineffectually on the side of the losing Conservative forces, Salvador emigrates to *la costa* to work on a cacao plantation, where he encounters violent and uncouth *costeño* co-workers and eventually dies of a tropical fever. His more robust Liberal (prominently *mestizo*) friend Luciano, in contrast, becomes a successful entrepreneur after deflowering, then discarding, Salvador's younger sister Mariana. Several of Mariana's more troublesome characteristics and her disastrous decision to surrender her virginity are attributed by the narrator to the presence in the family's past of a Black ancestor, based on the assertion that "blood has its effect": "vulgar blood apt for bloody insults. Rage disfigured the young girl's face, eyes swollen like a wild beast's, contracted lips through which words escaped like lashes of a whip, indicating black lineage, ardent and vengeful, that after a century revived in this girl who had grown up in a different environment from the shack of the slave martyred by the whip and coarsened by alcohol and lust."[3]

A la costa was written in the years immediately preceding the founding of UFC, at a time when co-founder Minor Keith had already purchased large tracts of land to grow bananas in Central America and Colombia, just one country to the north of Ecuador. While export-based banana production in Ecuador would take until the 1930s to get going in the coastal region where Salvador meets his end, the novel's racial stereotyping illustrates key aspects of the Latin American social dynamics that, when exploited by North American and elite Latin American interests, would shape the industry's evolution and eventual prioritization of bananas grown on the Ecuadorian coast.

The centrality of racism to the history of bananas began early. The wild ancestors of bananas and numerous edible varieties bred by non-European farmers were originally found in South and Southeast Asian regions.[4] After a pre-colonial transcontinental migration in which bananas and peoples travelled together as far as Africa, several varieties were eventually introduced to the Americas by slave-holding European plantation owners. In this way, before the establishment of the first plantations by UFC and its competitors and suppliers, racist narratives and imperialism played a central role in the "prehistory" of bananas in justifying European colonization of the Americas. Later, numerous US military interventions in Latin America in the nineteenth and twentieth centuries operationalized racist logics while paving the way for and later protecting the banana industry.[5]

Another subsequent precursor to the establishment of banana production was the granting of massive land concessions to US interests by Latin American governments in exchange for promises to build rail lines. Liberal elites in Latin America in the nineteenth century (romanticized in the form of *A la costa*'s Luciano) generally viewed such concessions and the foreign capital and technology they were aimed at bringing to the region as essential for modernization and progress.[6] The lands in question were often the traditional territories of Indigenous peoples,[7] and the Latin American elites in question often whites or "cultured" *mestizos* who held racist views regarding their Indigenous, lower-class *mestizo*, and Afro-descended compatriots.[8] Viewing Indigenous peoples as sub-human allowed the violent expropriation of their territories, and the subsequent transfer of that land to foreign corporations that would profit enormously from it. For example, UFC at the turn of the twentieth century obtained concessions for huge tracts of land in the Bocas del Toro frontier region of Costa Rica and Panama, using a variety of tactics to expel pre-existing inhabitants such as the Bribri people. One such technique involved the Costa Rican government allocating Bribri territory to non-Indigenous Costa Ricans, who promptly signed it over to UFC in exchange for small amounts of money.[9]

In general, such actions of Latin American elites emerged from their own priorities but also involved power-laden interactions with global North interests. Beyond helping to explain the industry's eventual prioritization of Ecuadorian bananas, this turbulent dynamic shows the profoundly but complicatedly racist origins of banana industry profits (whose implications for fairness today are explored in Part 4 of the book). Prior to UFC's founding, the concession granted to Minor Keith by Costa Rica was motivated by that nation's indebted financial state, which hindered its modernizing railroad project. Costa Rica initially borrowed from British lenders, reflecting an international distribution of wealth created by colonialism. A ninety-nine-year lease on the national railway and a land concession amounting to approximately 7 percent of the entire country was the price Costa Rica subsequently felt it made sense to pay Keith for finishing the railroad and renegotiating the country's debt with British creditors. In this way the disadvantageous financial position of Costa Rica, coupled with the (racist) modernization impulses of its leaders, led to the allocation of infrastructure and territory that would eventually enable the advent and profitability of UFC.[10]

A revealing parallel is pointed out by historian Jason Colby between the Costa Rican railroad and the infamous railroad built by King Leopold of Belgium in the Congo. Both Keith and Leopold sought funding from British financiers for their projects, and both railways became notorious for having "a black body buried beneath each rail tie."[11] Prior to helping form UFC in 1899, Minor Keith experimented with migrant workers imported from a range of locations, especially the West Indies, to build the railroad. While the blatant coerced labour practices employed by Leopold were not seen in Costa Rica, Keith was not above calling on the government to force labourers to work, or even employing brutal violence to discipline his workers. Indeed, Keith became known as the "Cecil Rhodes of Central America," after the infamous white supremacist mining magnate and colonial leader in British South Africa.

The dynamics linking racism to the establishment of a banana industry in Ecuador were more indirect, but nevertheless firmly oriented around ideals of white supremacy. As illustrated by *A la costa*, banana production in Ecuador was preceded by a "cacao boom" from 1860 to approximately 1920, which motivated massive clearing of forests in the coastal region and entrenched the country's colonial role as an exporter of primary commodities to feed appetites in the global North.[12] The boom drove massive demographic and biophysical changes, both decimating the spectacularly biodiverse country's coastal forests and helping pull huge waves of migration from *la sierra*.[13] The push for such impoverished and landless Indigenous and *mestizo* migrants included economic depression, the inequitable concentration of agricultural land, and the repression of resulting social conflicts by the wealthy *serrano* landowners.[14]

Once again, racism played a major role in justifying the exclusion of Indigenous peoples and poor *mestizos* from land ownership in *la sierra*. Specifically, racist narratives explained away poverty as resulting from such people's supposed tendency to make poor choices, or their lack of *cultura* (culture, best understood as refinement or education). *Cultura* also supposedly served to distinguish "more Indigenous" poor rural *mestizos* from urban, educated, or landowning ones with more refined habits. The waves of migrant labour that would work in the cacao boom and eventually bananas were therefore impelled by Ecuador's particular version of *mestizaje*, amounting to a complex hierarchy of racialized discrimination.[15] As Part 3 of the book documents, this hierarchy continues to persist in the twenty-first century and contributes to ongoing environmental injustice in *la costa*.

While Ecuador's coastal region was still planted in cacao (with the first "banana boom" not starting until 1948), the banana industry was operating in Central America and Colombia in ways that relied on racist strategies of labour control—and in ways that would contribute to the industry's eventual massive arrival in Ecuador. An estimated 300,000 West Indians were recruited to Central America between 1850 and 1914, where they worked on French and American efforts to build the Panama Canal, railroad projects, and eventually banana plantations. The official abolition of slavery in the British Empire in 1834 had not substantially threatened the economic dominance of British and other white or European interests through meaningful redistribution of wealth in the West Indies.[16] Black Jamaicans and other West Indians therefore presented a pool of underemployed and land-poor workers available to American government or commercial interests in need of labour.

In Minor Keith's early railroad projects, workers were primarily West Indian in origin.[17] Keith observed the well-developed ability to grow bananas (especially Gros Michel) of West Indian workers, mainly Jamaicans, in his railroad projects, and so he encouraged planting in land cleared adjacent to the rail line. By encouraging or organizing the scaling up of these banana plots, Keith was able to provide substantial fruit to market in the United States. After Keith co-founded UFC in 1899, the company also brought in large numbers of Jamaican and other West Indian labourers to work on its plantations in the Bocas division and elsewhere in Central America.[18] These workers were highly sought-after—though not well-paid—because of their pre-existing knowledge of banana farming, which typically outstripped the agricultural expertise of UFC's white American managers.[19] Despite this superior knowledge, however, West Indian workers would play subservient roles to those managers.[20]

Race would also play a part in major capital-labour conflicts on banana plantations. The 1928 Ciénaga massacre in Colombia is often cited as the classic example of UFC's tactics of labour control in Latin America, with the involvement of Colombian governmental and commercial actors demonstrating both local resistance and co-operation with such imperialist practices and the economic dominance they furthered. Intersecting with such North-South and class dimensions was the company's active use and promotion of racial divisions on its plantations as a way of controlling labour.[21] The white North American management lived in luxurious enclaves, while UFC assigned Black West Indian, *mestizo* Central

American, and Indigenous workers to different categories of work and encouraged them to identify with other members of their racial group through employee housing and recreation programs provided by the company. This management practice deepened divides between English-speaking West Indian workers and Spanish- or Indigenous language–speaking Central Americans. Labour disputes were handled with the same divide-and-conquer tactics. When Jamaican workers began to organize and demand better pay and working conditions, the company brought in strike-breakers from Barbados and St. Kitts. During the 1934 Great Banana Strike in Costa Rica, the company also published a racist petition with the forged signatures of the *mestizo* strike leaders, then founded a West Indian organization and had it denounce the petition in public.[22] UFC's racial micromanaging, which went as far as assigning Panamanian Indigenous workers from the Ngäbe (Guaymí) and Kuna Nations to different job tasks, helped the company keep its workforce divided and therefore less likely to organize for better pay or working conditions.

The complexity of race relations in UFC divisions is further illustrated by the presence of *ladinos* (another term for *mestizos*) as workers on Guatemalan plantations and in local police forces.[23] Guatemalan *ladinos* such as those working for UFC were told by the white and *ladino* elites who ruled the country that they were a superior race to the country's Indigenous majority. The company nevertheless viewed *ladinos* as lower on the racial hierarchy than their white North American managers and incorporated them into the hierarchical system of segregation on plantations—but always in ways that kept them separate from and unlikely to organize together with Black West Indian workers. *Ladinos* in Guatemala generally held a similar sense of racial superiority to such Afro-descended peoples, but with the added wrinkle that such West Indian migrants—whose presence in the country was often due to UFC—were viewed as a sign of American domination. The company did not discourage such racial animosity, and in fact used it to its advantage. When *ladino* workers were recruited to fight in World War I, for example, the company promoted many West Indian workers to junior managerial roles where they were on the front lines facing *ladino* resentments that stemmed from hazardous working conditions or low pay.[24] Such use of racialized differences in labour management represents one key aspect of how UFC fought labour organization among its workforce and thus protected the company's profitability. This strategy from the past has implications for what fairness looks like in the future and helps to explain the specific trajectory the industry took to ultimately delegate labour management largely to independent farmers under contract, especially in Ecuador.

The ideas of racial superiority motivating actions such as those of UFC are a familiar aspect of colonialism and imperialism.[25] In justifying the wholesale appropriation of territories and peoples around the world, they have generally expressed a "civilizing mission" in which European knowledges, technologies, and practices would be used to lift up or improve such non-European peoples.[26] These narratives were part of broader "imaginative geographies" that expressed a skewed

Figure 2.01: Mural adorning Chiquita's office in Machala

kind of common sense about the regions where bananas were grown, and the envisioned role of white Northerners with respect to them.[27] As historian John Soluri puts it, early twentieth-century English-speaking commentators with ties to UFC typically "depicted the expansion of export banana production as a process of bringing modernity to 'pestilential' tropical regions via industrial capitalism, medicine, and science."[28] The gendered nature of such narratives and their persistence into the twenty-first century are illustrated by the unassuming Machala office of Chiquita, UFC's current incarnation. The office bears no external distinguishing features except a colourful tile mural in which an impassive woman with bare legs and an unbuttoned shirt sits amidst bananas and other local agricultural products.

Such stereotypes held by Northerners resonated with internal racial hierarchies stemming from Spanish colonialism in Latin America,[29] and were accompanied by related imaginative geographies internal to specific banana-producing regions. For example, the Ecuadorian regions from which cacao and eventually bananas would be exported are the subject of stereotypes that developed in Guayaquil and other Ecuadorian cities about the rural people of the coastal region. Such stereotypes about rural *costeños*—pejoratively termed *montubios*—hold them to be inherently violent, promiscuous, disease-ridden, lazy, and childlike (thus "explaining" both Salvador's brutish co-workers on the cacao plantation and the tropical fever he dies of in A la Costa).[30] They combine discursive elements of stereotypes concerning low-class *mestizo* and Indigenous populations who migrated from *la sierra*, and of Afro-Ecuadorian coastal populations who migrated from Colombia after escaping slavery during Spanish colonial rule.[31] Such imaginative geographies, which incorporate various racist and class-based rhetorical elements, have helped to justify the extraction of wealth from rural Ecuadorian coastal agricultural areas by urban centres for over a century.

In general, the profitable exploitation of Latin American and Caribbean territories and bodies by UFC and its competitors was interpreted using racist narratives and imaginative geographies, providing a justification that transformed exploitation into benevolent and dynamic improvement. The use of racism was always part of a provisional or fragile labour control strategy, however; workers were frequently manipulated and dominated, but they nevertheless employed forms of resistance such as unionizing and demanding better wages and working conditions. For example, West Indian workers pursued a range of strategies to fight back against UFC and make better lives for themselves and their families, including frequently going on strike, working their way up the ranks to more technical and managerial roles on plantations (albeit not upper management), and acquiring land to grow their own crops so they would be less dependent on the company.[32] And while sometimes displaying deferential attitudes that reflected a complex relationship to British and later American imperialism, Black West Indian workers also terrified the company with their growing mobilization against racial oppression and use of Black empowerment ideas to fight harsh working conditions and low pay. In the years after World War I, for example, the company established a network of spies to keep tabs on the activities of the Universal Negro Improvement Association (UNIA).[33] Such expensive and repressive labour management practices would eventually make less sense than simply delegating conflicts with workers of various racialized identities to contract-based producers.

Another unlikely example of resistance to UFC's racism was provided by the British consul in Guatemala during the labour dispute involving West Indian workers, when he counselled Guatemalan troops against using violence except as a last resort. The British vice-consul later conducted an investigation into working conditions and treatment of West Indian workers (who were still legally British subjects), noting the company's manipulative payroll practices, as well as frequent violence, racial slurs, and intimidation. While British diplomats can certainly not be considered early practitioners of anti-oppression, their frequent role in speaking up to protect UFC's West Indian workers from abuses attests to the presence of variations, resistances, and cracks in the white-supremacist structures that enabled both British colonialism and US (UFC-centred) imperialism.[34] Together with the constant problems UFC faced from its racialized workers, variations and resistances within racist patterns of exploitation (even paternalistic or self-interested resistances) provide important detail regarding how the banana industry evolved over the first half of the twentieth century. This escalating conflict between racialized workforces and UFC would help to make non-unionized locales—especially Ecuador—increasingly attractive to the industry as the twentieth century progressed, eventually leading to Ecuador's emergence in the 1950s as the world's perennially leading exporter.

The challenges posed by systemic racism to the protection of public health have come to the fore in recent years.[35] Rather than simply noting and lamenting the fact that racialized groups tend to have worse health outcomes, some of the most perceptive scholarship explains such differences in terms of the workings of *racial capitalism*, a term that conveys how capitalism operates through the exploitation of socially constructed racial differences or processes of racialization.[36] In general, capitalism has always allowed some people—already-wealthy white men, to take the most obvious and common example—to make money in ways that are enabled by racism and its devaluing of the humanity of people of colour.[37] As this chapter has documented, the history of banana production makes it a particularly vivid example of racial capitalism, carrying major implications for what might constitute fairness in the twenty-first century for banana farmers and workers exposed to pesticides and other facets of social and environmental injustice. However, as this chapter has also demonstrated, the racist workings of corporate colonialism in Latin America were always heterogeneous and resisted by numerous diverse groups of people. The next chapter follows resistance to banana imperialism across the human–more-than-human divide, where banana corporations, farmers, and workers found unexpected and influential opponents and allies.

CHAPTER 3
BANANAS, ENVIRONMENTS, AND HISTORIES

The diverse and uneasily coexisting ethnic groups on UFC farms show the incredible diversity of the human characters who have populated the story of bananas. Even more varied are the "more-than-human"[1] inhabitants of banana plantations and the regions they are found in, inhabitants such as soils, forests, fungi, and insects, not to mention bananas themselves. The influence of such lively entities on historical events is just as non-monolithic and unpredictable as that of corporate power and racism, and often helps to round out explanations of such social dynamics.[2] That is, nature never behaves exactly as human organizations such as giant corporations expect or want it to, and it is always present and consequential in the struggles of marginalized peoples against such powerful forces. Complex interactions of banana history with the natural world therefore form an important part of the explanation of how the banana industry arrived at pesticide-intensive production and a leading role for Ecuador.

In *Viento Fuerte*, Guatemalan novelist Miguel Ángel Asturias paints a picture of banana production in the early twentieth century as involving massive and irresistible human transformation of nature:

> The terrain where some [workers] were sitting and others lying down seemed totally dominated by them. Everything [was] dominated except the humid, immobile, blinding heat of the coast. The will of man had been

imposed. Human hands and mechanical equipment modified the earth.³

Although massive environmental changes due to banana production were indeed hugely damaging to Latin American environments, such transformations were more than just a unilateral imposition of "the will of man." Banana production, like agriculture more generally, is "environmentally rooted" in that it is always shaped by complex agro-ecological dynamics involving crops, soils, moisture, and an enormous range of other organisms and substances.⁴ For example, Boston Fruit's Jamaican banana suppliers had their crops decimated by a hurricane in 1898, making the Costa Rican bananas controlled by Minor Keith more valuable. By March of the following year, Keith had merged his operations with those of Boston Fruit to form UFC. In this way corporate jockeying for profitable products and markets—enabled by US imperialism and colonial legacies in both Costa Rica and Jamaica—was given a push in a particular direction by an "act of God" in the form of the 1898 hurricane.⁵

Such environmental rootedness of bananas leads to predictable problems when the fruit is produced in large monocultural plantations (which it usually is). Gros Michel bananas, and the Cavendish variety that would eventually replace them, reproduce asexually from existing banana plants. While the human participants in the story of bananas are incredibly diverse, the bananas themselves are not.⁶ The numerous large plantations that UFC and its smaller competitors rapidly established across Central America, the Caribbean, and Colombia in the late nineteenth and early twentieth centuries therefore featured little to no genetic diversity.⁷ Plantations (then and now) are physically organized to maximize production by packing bananas into every available square metre of soil. Pests that prey on bananas can rapidly devastate farms, unimpeded by other species, physical obstacles such as trees, or genetic hurdles such as bananas with greater natural resistance.⁸

Fungi are among the most successful organisms at exploiting the highly managed environment of a banana plantation, as they breed quickly in hot, humid environments. One in particular proved so troublesome to banana companies that it is often promoted from micro-organism to "force of history" in accounts of Latin America's past.⁹ Beginning in the 1890s, banana farmers in Central America observed recurring discolouration and wilting of their plants' leaves, often followed quickly by loss of the fruit and collapse of the entire plant.[10] The infection became known as Panama disease after its first apparent identification in that country, and would be scientifically identified in 1915 as the *Fusarium oxysporum* f.sp. *cubense* fungus. Panama disease had a devastating impact on the banana industry in the first half of the twentieth century, leading to the abandonment of an estimated 100,000 hectares of infected banana plantations (and the deforestation of a comparably large area of tropical forest in efforts to evade the fungus).[11]

Illustrating the complexity of human-environment relations surrounding Panama disease are ties between such ecological dynamics and the influence of racism on banana production. In its early decades, UFC relied on the agro-ecological knowledge of its imported West Indian workers, who often had experience growing Gros Michel bananas in their home countries, especially Jamaica.[12] For example, West Indian workers employed manual techniques to remove or isolate plants infected with Panama disease. This knowledge could only help so much, though, in the face of the ecological niche that the dramatic scale-up of banana production was creating.

Despite the role of monocultural "scientific" agriculture in creating the problem, the company itself soon came to deride their West Indian workers' disease-control methods as "primitive." Like many American corporations—though not many agricultural ones—UFC established its own in-house research department in the 1920s, including new experimental farms within its Latin American landholdings. It then undertook more modern and centralized disease control and agricultural decision-making, albeit without much success. Company scientists in the '20s and '30s tried to identify and replicate features of farms that appeared more resistant to Panama disease. Observing that such farms were in relatively dry regions, UFC undertook massive earth-moving operations to improve drainage and dry out farms in Central America.[13] They also conducted soil science surveys that might identify soil conditions that impeded the progress of *Fusarium* epidemics, and then attempted to replicate those conditions on existing farms or—more commonly—just start new farms. UFC also undertook similarly massive—and ecologically destructive—earthworks to flood infected fields under a metre of water for extended periods and, theoretically, eliminate the fungus by starving it of oxygen. For example, a total of 4,000 hectares in Panama and 6,100 in Honduras were submerged between 1945 and 1955.

While initially claiming to see hopeful results with these strategies, UFC scientists ultimately had to admit that they didn't work.[14] Even well-drained irrigated farms eventually developed Panama disease, as did farms with theoretically healthy soil parameters. The flooding strategy did drown the *Fusarium* fungus, but also drowned many competing organisms. Flooded farms were then rapidly re-infected after they were drained and replanted. As their resource-intensive scientific efforts to control the disease on existing farms failed repeatedly,[15] UFC instead reacted to Panama disease by abandoning plantations and clearing forest for new ones (competitors such as Standard Fruit also ran from Panama disease into new territories in the 1920s and '30s[16]). Ominously, however, the fungus would typically arrive soon after due to the movement of people and equipment across transnational corporations' geographically integrated divisions.

As John Soluri's illuminating environmental history explains, banana companies had already cut down massive swathes of tropical rainforest in Latin America to establish the industry, while attracting waves of workers and other economic migrants to the resulting banana zones.[17] When Panama disease hit, consumer preferences were deemed so unchangeable by the company that it could not seriously consider replacing Gros Michel with a disease-resistant variety. And so UFC undertook a strategy that would transform even greater quantities of tropical rainforest into plantations, and then—once Panama disease inevitably arrived—into abandoned plantations.[18] The strategy UFC arrived at was especially ironic in light of their contempt for the supposedly primitive disease-control strategies of their West Indian workers. UFC's practice of abandoning farms and felling more forest for new monocultures essentially amounted to slash-and-burn agriculture—the much-derided stereotype of pre-modern farming. UFC thus scaled up the environmental destruction typically attributed to the practice to hemispheric levels, enabled by the constant threat of US military intervention and allied Latin American governments.

Comparable irony is found in Soluri's explanation of the research strategies undertaken by American and British plant pathologists (*phytopathologists*, or scientists who study plant disease) in response to Panama disease, especially their appropriation of the banana-breeding efforts of supposedly primitive peasant farmers. Britain's banana-producing colonies in the Americas had relatively small landmasses, so their Panama disease-resolution efforts focused on finding disease-resistant banana varieties via bioprospecting trips to British colonies in wild bananas' territories of origin, such as Samoa, Queensland (Australia), Papua New Guinea, and Malaysia.[19] UFC took much longer to commission similar bioprospecting expeditions and experiment with the resulting varieties in their research farms, and longer still to actually consider replacing the Gros Michel banana.

The ready access to new Latin American territories enabled by US imperialism in the region, in Soluri's reading, essentially eliminated the urgency for UFC's scientists to find real solutions to Panama disease. A disease-resistant banana variety would be one such effective solution, and both British and eventually American scientists looked hard for suitable candidates across the tropical world. The banana varieties collected on these bioprospecting trips—carried out by numerous scientists who felt they were bringing the light of scientific progress to the world's uncivilized places and peoples—were first developed by Indigenous farmers in places such as Papua New Guinea and Malaysia. The science of phytopathology, and agro-industrial banana production, essentially advanced by appropriating such traditional knowledges and then claiming them as scientific discoveries.[20]

Neocolonial imaginative geographies also enabled such scientific "advances," especially celebratory narratives of progress in which UFC and its scientists brought progress to the backwards, disease-prone tropics— narratives that persist today.[21] Reflecting back on the emergence of Panama disease, a 2005 review article by a leading American banana phytopathologist tellingly recounts a story of heroic Northern scientific investigation into *Fusarium*'s spread by phytopathologists studying Panama disease and other threats to banana production.[22] The article identifies several white Anglophone or European men of science who made phytopathological discoveries in "primitive" countries where "early banana plantations were hewn out of virgin rainforest." The "positive impact" of banana agroindustry on Latin America is linked to such efforts, notwithstanding the sordid history of US interventions. As this scientist puts it,

> Although the trades corrupted governments and caused considerable social upheaval and hardship, they also had a positive impact. They dramatically improved transportation and shipping infrastructure in the western tropics. They were major employers who paid relatively high wages. They provided decent homes, schools, and hospitals for

their employees, and initiated aggressive programs to combat malaria, dengue fever, and other tropical diseases. Despite their unsavory reputation in many quarters, the trades improved the lives of many."[23]

Such triumphalism recognizes but then dismisses the exploitative history of banana production as a mere "unsavory reputation" and provides a cover story for scientific progress (in this case of phytopathology) to occur on lands made available by imperialism in the Americas.[24]

Comparable racist-scientific dynamics occurred with respect to another disruptive more-than-human actor, the *Plasmodium* malaria parasite. By pushing back the agricultural frontier in Latin America in the early twentieth century, UFC brought its workers into frequent contact with disease-transmitting mosquitoes. UFC's Medical Department occupied itself with the maintenance of a healthy workforce in the face of the risks involved in clearing tropical rainforests for banana production, especially malaria and yellow fever.[25] The Medical Department "saw as the central component of its work transforming a backwards, disease-ridden society into a modern productive workforce through improved healthcare and education."[26] The struggle against malaria enabled the Medical Department to extend its paternalistic reach into all corners of life in UFC's divisions, and to generate "scientific" knowledge about non-white workers, generally foregrounding their supposed cultural and behavioural tendencies towards carelessness and ignorance. This knowledge would in turn reinforce and justify the company's racist exploitation of those workers and the privileges afforded white employees in the tropics.[27]

While UFC preferred West Indian labourers for their reputed ability to withstand tropical diseases (and many West Indians had indeed been exposed to yellow fever as children), for example, the Medical Department came to associate malaria with "backwardness" among its workers of colour. Workers and their alleged poor hygiene were particularly targeted by the Medical Department through a mixture of moral and hygienic education. But while the reputation of science played a key role in the Medical Department's civilizing mission, actual sound public health science did not. While the supposed individual behavioural failings of West Indian, *mestizo*, and Indigenous workers were often targeted by the company's doctors, worker health was in reality overwhelmingly compromised through environmental conditions that were largely out of workers' control, such as the substandard housing and workplace hazards they endured.[28] In this way, both fungal and protozoan micro-organisms, and the scientists who studied and managed them, featured in a self-serving fabricated story of Northerners bringing progress and civilization to the primitive tropics.

Public health science has increasingly sought to account for animals, ecosystems, and planetary dynamics such as climate change as they affect human health.[29] The interactions of banana production, hurricanes, fungi, malaria, and even the mules used to bring bananas from fields to ports in the industry's early years vividly illustrate the wisdom of this holism, but also the ways in which corporate power, racism, imperialism, and other disturbing political and economic factors shape such complex systemic dynamics.[30] One final encounter of corporate power with racism, fungi, and workers illustrates how such interactions helped drive the industry to prioritize Ecuadorian bananas by the mid- to late twentieth century. After Panama disease had thoroughly infested Central America's banana fields, UFC decided to close entire divisions on the Atlantic coasts of Costa Rica (1940) and Guatemala (1955).[31] The company opened up new divisions on both countries' Pacific coasts, but their national governments requested that the West Indian workers who had been brought in by the company to work Caribbean coastal divisions be denied employment in the new divisions. The company complied, leaving their West Indian workers largely unemployed.[32] Once again, racism interacted in complex ways with the challenges posed by workers and more-than-human threats to banana company profits. UFC could in fact only maintain its profitability by retreating from an implacable fungal disease fostered by its monocultural production model into new territories (increasingly Ecuador), while manipulating ever more combative workers using an exhausting assortment of repressive and racist strategies. The next chapter shows that, like bananas, this strategy had a limited shelf life.

CHAPTER 4

BEYOND ITS CONTROL

The preceding chapters have demonstrated the intersecting roles played by corporate machinations, racism, diverse workers, and the unruly more-than-human world in shaping how banana transnationals made large but precarious profits, while the industry gravitated steadily towards Ecuador. While such dynamics were prominent in the first half of the twentieth century, they came to a climax in 1954 as the Cold War deepened, also involving related public anxieties in North America over the Soviet threat. Importantly, such banana industry dynamics would be profoundly shaped by the role of US investors and their changing willingness to finance UFC's Latin American operations. An especially infamous episode in banana history paradoxically shows both the egregious dynamics of Northern and Latin American elite domination in Guatemala, and how the underlying fragility of such strategies led to Ecuador's emergence as the world's leading banana exporter.

Guatemala is one of the western hemisphere's poorest and most Indigenous nations in terms of population makeup. When a new and progressive government in the 1950s sought to stand up to UFC and alleviate the poverty of the country's Indigenous majority, one of banana imperialism's most emblematic outrages took place. That episode would signal the beginning of the end of UFC's dominance of the industry and advance banana production's transformation towards the contract-based, pesticide-intensive, and often Ecuadorian form it takes today.

UFC began producing bananas in Guatemala early in the twentieth century, first on the country's Atlantic coast with imported West Indian labour and later—after Panama disease infested the original division—in the Tiquisate region west of the capital city, with the original West Indian workforce expressly excluded at the request of the Guatemalan government.[1] By the mid-1940s the country represented more than a quarter of UFC's entire production. The country's then-dictator Jorge Ubico, who ruled with the aid of extrajudicial killings, secret police, and torture, had previously given UFC very generous land concessions. Ubico was forced from office by popular protest in 1944, as was his hand-picked successor by October of the same year. During the following ten-year period (known as the October Revolution), a new president named Juan José Arévalo, a former professor, attempted to raise living standards for the country's peasant population and Indigenous majority. Arévalo used a mix of paternalistic and redistributive measures to achieve such goals, and also came into frequent conflict with the militant banana workers of UFC's Tiquisate farms.

In 1951, Arévalo was succeeded by the democratically elected Jacobo Árbenz, who took his predecessor's sometimes-progressive policy platform further left and came into more direct conflict with UFC. Shortly after Árbenz's election, a hurricane decimated UFC's plantations on the country's Pacific coast. The company laid off 3,746 workers without pay in apparent retribution for a previous strike and claimed that re-establishing the farms would be too expensive, also sending a clear message to the new president over how it would handle organized labour. And so the more-than-human world (a hurricane and the banana plantations it levelled) once again threatened UFC's profits in parallel with troublesome workers; the company, in response, used nature's intervention as a pretext for attacking the power of those workers.

Undeterred by this flexing of UFC's muscles, Árbenz took aim at Guatemala's hugely inequitable distribution of land and wealth, especially among the country's Spanish-origin and other Euro-descended elites, poor *mestizo* peasants, and the even poorer Indigenous majority.[2] In 1952 he initiated agrarian reform legislation, nationalizing unused agricultural lands and redistributing them, a move that came into direct conflict with the company and its uneasy relationship to the *Fusarium* fungus. Since UFC's strategy for dealing with Panama disease had settled on running away from it and planting new farms, the company had accumulated large amounts of unused land. In Tiquisate, for example, UFC had approximately 72,843 hectares at the beginning of the October Revolution and therefore lost a large amount of land to nationalization. After it was compensated $1,185,000 for its losses over the entire country—the value of the land that it had declared on its tax returns—UFC then shamelessly admitted that it had intentionally underestimated the land's value and it was actually worth $19,355,000.[3] Árbenz stood firm, however, and the company registered a sizable loss on its balance sheet.

UFC was led at this time by Samuel Zemurray, a larger-than-life figure whose actions attest to both the terrible power and the vulnerability of US corporate imperialism in banana-producing lands.[4] Zemurray had begun his career selling overripe or rejected bananas in the US South for a small margin, before taking over the Cuyamel Fruit Company in 1905 and growing bananas in Honduras. That country, at that time considered the stereotypical banana republic and the inspiration for the short story by O. Henry coining that pejorative term, had given Zemurray very favourable concessions and tax or customs arrangements. He stood to lose these when Honduras's out-of-control foreign debt led to a US-imposed plan to give control of the country's finances to a US bank. Rather than submit to the plan, Zemurray conspired with a Honduran general and American mercenaries to organize a successful coup, overthrowing the government of Honduras in 1911 and avoiding the loss of profitability that government was about to impose on him.

This story certainly attests to the unconscionable and self-interested nature of US interventions in banana-producing Latin America, but also to their unpredictable character and the fact that they were never fully under the control of corporations or other powerful actors. At the time of the coup, Zemurray was under active surveillance by the US government, which both suspected and opposed his plans. Additional heterogeneity is found in the fact that Zemurray was representing a competitor of the giant UFC, although he had partnered with the company earlier in his career. UFC had in fact been legally prevented from eating up Cuyamel by the US government and its anti-trust enforcement, although eventually the merger was allowed and even encouraged. After UFC acquired Cuyamel in 1929, however, the upstart Zemurray continued to provide unexpected resistance to the company's corporate dominance. He had received substantial UFC stock in the acquisition, which he then leveraged to take control of the much larger company.[5]

The man at the helm of UFC at the time of Árbenz's land reform was therefore both an illustration of and an unexpected complication to stories of banana imperialism. In 1954, Zemurray would again apply the instincts that led him to overthrow the government of Honduras in 1911 in straightforward support of UFC's interests. Reports by the Mexican ambassador suggest that UFC had been plotting behind the scenes from before the start of the October Revolution. For example, the company had been helping Ubico's successor with propaganda efforts.[6] After Arévalo came to power, the ambassador reported that UFC was attempting to promote civil unrest in Guatemala with the help of its dictatorial allies in El Salvador, Honduras, and Nicaragua, thereby creating the pretext for a US invasion. After the land reform, such behind-the-scenes plotting intensified and bore "bitter fruit"[7] for the company, which used its numerous ties to the Eisenhower administration—notably Secretary of State John Foster Dulles and his brother, CIA director Allen Dulles—to make that US intervention a reality.

An American-trained, -supplied, and -funded army thus invaded Guatemala in 1954, with the support of both the CIA and Guatemala's "petty bourgeoisie," whose democratic instincts, in the words of historian Cindy Forster, "had by that point been overcome by their racism toward the indigenous majority."[8] US government and public support for the intervention was bolstered by a slick UFC public relations (PR) campaign portraying Árbenz as an alarming new front in the Red Menace of international communism. The PR campaign also helped intimidate the Guatemalan army, which eventually refused to fight the numerically inferior invasion force. US support was a decisive factor in what would become a successful coup to oust Árbenz and reverse his redistributive measures, especially the land reform. Repression after the coup was especially brutal in banana-growing Tiquisate, where "an estimated one thousand campesinos and workers were machine-gunned at Finca Jocotán" in an early episode of the decades of state-sponsored and genocidal terror that Guatemala has seen since the 1954 coup.[9]

The CIA-backed coup and the events leading up to it show how UFC's corporate strategies to control the risks posed by workers, governments, and the natural world entered the Cold War era in which international communism was increasingly invoked as a threat justifying US intervention.[10] But while the Cold War was new, the racism that fuelled the coup of 1954 was anything but. The agrarian reform that threatened the company's balance sheet was targeted at redistributing land to the country's Indigenous majority, while the decades of genocidal repression that followed the 1954 coup would take thousands more Indigenous lives—operationalizing the racism of the Guatemalan elites involved with the CIA in deposing the democratically elected Árbenz.[11]

UFC had previously used racialized workforces and race-based labour relations strategies to impede unionization and strikes throughout Central America; the coup in Guatemala shows how it could pull strings in Washington[12] to exploit racism at the level of entire nations and further its destructive war with Panama disease, with horrific results that preserved the company's profitable ability to grown bananas—even if the ground they were grown in was increasingly blood-soaked.

The Guatemala coup and the agro-ecological, labour-organizing, cultural, and geopolitical forces that led up to it marked the approximate end of an era for UFC, transforming banana production into something that resembles today's industry practices. While the 1954 coup shows that obstacles such as nationalist Latin American governments weren't insurmountable, even the reliably imperialist US government began cracking down on the company soon after. Anti-trust rulings compelled UFC to sell off its Guatemalan land holdings to Del Monte, which would join Chiquita (UFC's re-branded identity) and Standard Fruit (Dole) as the major players in the banana trade after the 1950s.[13] The elaborate PR campaign UFC had used to build support for the coup, and concurrent flexing of its political and economic muscles, was also a pretty costly effort to maintain business as usual. It was expensive in terms of corporate reputation as well, as not all Americans were convinced that the coup was justified, in spite of the sophisticated propaganda effort to portray it as a victory against the Red Tide of communism.[14]

The story of the coup in Guatemala shows how the dominance of even the notorious UFC was subject to threats from Latin American people and places, but also from those at home on whom the company depended. Modern stock markets had enabled UFC and competitors such as Standard Fruit to finance their dramatic expansions into Latin America and accompanying flight from Panama disease.[15] However, as business historian Marco Bucheli has shown, the possibility of disrupted profits that the

Guatemala coup raised was worrisome to investors, who exerted considerable influence over UFC's subsequent strategies.[16]

Even before Árbenz came to power, UFC had observed in its 1951 annual report to shareholders that "banana production in Guatemala has been declining due to frequent windstorms, inroads of disease, and the absence of conditions conducive to the planting of new plantations. At the same time labor costs have been rising sharply."[17] Moody's Investors Service subsequently observed Árbenz's actions in Guatemala with concern, speculating that such nationalist governments might become the norm in Latin America and put UFC's profitability at risk. Even after the coup showed UFC's ability to violently remove a democratically elected Central American leader from power to protect its interests, Moody's reported that "Unfortunately ... the company's operations are subject to natural and foreign political hazards *beyond its control* (emphasis added).[18]

Such investor and corporate worries over interacting human and more-than-human risks to profitability prompted UFC's new director to announce in 1960 some major changes to how the company would do business: a wholesale transition to the Cavendish banana that Standard Fruit had successfully tried out as a replacement for the Panama disease–susceptible Gros Michel (Cavendish banana plants are also shorter, and thus less vulnerable to wind damage and toppling, for example in hurricanes[19]); an increase in purchases of bananas from independent producers under contract, and especially from Ecuador; and a general diversification into products other than bananas, with accompanying sell-offs of major chunks of land, consistent with the company's transition to more of a banana marketer than a banana grower.[20]

Bucheli has pointed out that UFC could probably have acquired fruit more cheaply, and realized larger profits, by simply continuing to grow its own bananas in the Cavendish era. Pressure from investors and Moody's, however, led it to adopt a less profitable but also less risky approach. The decision to prioritize purchases from Ecuador helped to cement that country's status as the world's leading exporter of bananas, a place it first occupied in the mid-1950s and—with the exception of a handful of years—has occupied to the present.

CHAPTER 5
THE VERY, VERY TROPICAL EQUATOR

UFC's 1960 announcement that it would be prioritizing Ecuadorian bananas continued the banana industry's decades-long retreat from human and more-than-human challenges—and augured a continuation of the enormous environmental and social changes associated with agro-industrial banana production. That continuation would display unique Ecuadorian characteristics, however, as the country's physical and cultural geographies altered the subsequent trajectory of the banana industry, with its increasingly precarious contract-based and pesticide-intensive production model. From this point onwards, Ecuadorian landscapes, workers, peasants, and elites experienced and shaped a toxic spiral converging on Machala, the self-declared banana capital of the world.

As the ignoble death suffered on a cacao plantation by *A la costa*'s protagonist Salvador illustrates, Ecuador's coastal region was inducted into global agro-export commodity markets decades before bananas would be produced in significant quantities. After the late nineteenth-century cacao boom generated fortunes for a privileged few and spurred mass migration westwards from the Andes for many impoverished others, a global crash occurred in the cacao trade by the 1920s. Due to price declines in global markets and the "witches' broom" fungus, plantations were rapidly abandoned.[1] The land that had been cleared for cacao was still there, however, as were the fortunes that had been made by agricultural capitalists based in Guayaquil and other urban centres. Also present were migrant workers and their families who had uprooted their lives in *la sierra* to seek livelihoods in the cacao boom. Meanwhile, concentration of land ownership in *la sierra* and the racism that underwrote it continued to limit the ability of expanding poor populations to make a living, fuelling continued migration.

Taking advantage of this available land, labour, and capital, Ecuador's first "banana boom" began in 1948 but was preceded by experiments in export banana production by several corporate interests.[2] These included the Fruit Trading Corporation in the northern coastal province of Esmeraldas, a German group of companies called EFE-UBESA, and the Chilean company Frutera Sudamericana. Among the largest early Ecuadorian banana plantations, however, and certainly the best studied, was UFC's Hacienda Tenguel in the central coastal province of Guayas. As the company scoured the hemisphere for places where it could evade resistance from workers, governments, fungi, hurricanes, and other natural hazards, it began producing bananas on a dozen properties in Ecuador's coastal region in 1933 while also buying and exporting bananas from numerous independent producers. UFC would have 3,017 hectares planted with bananas by 1957, aided by support from Ecuadorian president (and former UFC functionary) Galo Plaza.[3]

Hacienda Tenguel had been the largest cacao farm in the world before the bust, after which former workers occupied it to practise subsistence farming. UFC acquired the property and violently evicted most of these farmers, although holdouts in the hacienda's less-productive regions in the Andean foothills foreshadowed larger problems to come for the company.[4] Hacienda Tenguel began free of the *Fusarium* fungus that UFC was confronting throughout Central America and Colombia, while workers in the region appeared to lack the unionizing impulses that were giving the company such difficulties elsewhere. Building on the cultural legacies of Ecuador's semi-feudal *huasipunaje* system of labour in *la sierra*, from where many of its employees or their parents had migrated, the company carefully cultivated both bananas and what was meant to be a docile workforce.[5]

To accomplish this, UFC paid relatively high wages (compared to the low Ecuadorian average) and created an extensive social infrastructure on the hacienda intended to stave off the threat of unionization.[6] While the largely *mestizo* workforce meant that it could not manipulate obvious racialized distinctions as it did in Central America,[7] the company nevertheless carefully fostered distinct identities across categories of worker through the construction of separate recreational and social facilities and clubs. It created a pro-management worker organization to preclude the formation of a real union, then backed two factions supposedly fighting for control of it. Undercover "labour leaders" would loudly denounce the company and make easily satisfied demands that would give workers a sense of having successfully fought the giant company. UFC also tended to hire married men who would bring their families, under the theory that this would make them less likely to risk losing their jobs—and their homes and new sense of community—by organizing for higher pay or better working conditions.

This approach worked but was fragile. Panama disease eventually arrived on the hacienda and dramatically reduced yields, and the company began laying off workers.[8] These workers undertook land occupations, extending the previous invasions that had followed the end of the cacao boom. UFC had successfully expelled subsistence farmers from the hacienda's more productive and flat coastal lands, but had never completely obtained control over the entire property that legally belonged to it. Landless workers would simply begin clearing and farming land that belonged to the company, and they befriended local authorities who would in turn drag their feet when enforcing orders from Quito or elsewhere to back up the company.

After UFC made mass layoffs in the late 1950s and early '60s, unemployed and hungry former workers used a similar strategy in occupying the more central areas of the hacienda in 1962. As Striffler has documented, the "family man" strategy that the company had used to promote worker docility backfired, and men no longer able to provide for their families occupied the hacienda, with significant encouragement and leadership from their wives. In addition, Ecuador's populist leader, José María Velasco Ibarra (Galo Plaza's successor), appeared unwilling or—in the remote coastal region—unable to violently repress labour unrest on UFC's behalf. The company thus withdrew from direct production of bananas in Ecuador, a move that reinforced its 1960 decision to reduce its landholdings throughout its corporate empire and buy more bananas under contract from independent producers.

It had been struggles with fungi, labour, and nationalist governments that steadily drove UFC towards Ecuador, and away from producing the majority of the bananas it sold. The occupation and subsequent abandonment of Hacienda Tenguel represented an extension of the Central American and Colombian dynamics that had transformed the banana industry over half a century. The loss of Hacienda Tenguel also represented additional evidence that Gros Michel banana production could not be sustained—not even through the constant exploitation of new territory that had brought the company into deadly conflict with Guatemala's Árbenz and led to its prioritization of bananas from Ecuador. Ominously (at least with respect to the precarious and dangerous employment dynamics prevailing in the twenty-first century), UFC's abandonment of direct production after the occupation of the hacienda also helped build momentum for an industry-wide move to contract-based banana production, in which independent producers sell to the transnationals and assume the risky responsibility of managing labour-related and agro-ecological threats to profitability.[9]

Although productivity per hectare tended to be lower than in Central America and bananas typically had to travel farther to reach markets—through the Panama Canal—Ecuador had moved into top spot among banana-exporting nations by 1954.[10] The competitiveness of Ecuadorian bananas in global markets has been attributed to Ecuador's relative poverty and lack of organized labour, which kept wages low in comparison to Central America. Hurricanes were also not a factor and—as previously discussed—Panama disease was absent, at least initially. Standard Fruit had become the country's leading exporter by 1964, followed by the Exportadora Bananera Noboa (an Ecuadorian firm discussed in more detail later), with UFC in third place. The flows of wealth generated by banana production in Ecuador were less externally oriented (i.e., northwards) than in Central America. While UFC was certainly prominent in the origins of Ecuadorian banana production, the strength of Ecuadorian elites is generally cited as a reason why production in the country has always been relatively dispersed, without the giant foreign-owned enclaves seen in Central America.[11]

Many of the most powerful economic groups in Ecuador either formed or strengthened during the 1948–65 banana boom, notably those centred around the Exportadora Bananera Noboa, which began operations in 1954 and has played an enormous role in the country over the following seven decades.[12] Grupo Noboa would eventually grow to include companies producing or importing supplies for bananas such as cardboard boxes and pesticides, but also companies producing flour, plastics, cooking oil, and cars, and significant banking and investment interests.

The successes of Noboa and other Ecuadorian banana entrepreneurs such as Segundo Wong have been lauded as triumphs of Latin American ingenuity over Northern dominance such as that of UFC.[13] While compelling, such narratives conspicuously avoid the role of workers in driving and experiencing transformations in the industry.[14] For example, Striffler's exhaustive analysis of the resistance of workers to UFC on Hacienda Tenguel credits it with not only helping to drive UFC out of direct production in Ecuador, but with playing a pivotal role in moving the banana industry—and possibly agribusiness more generally—towards contract-based production.[15] As this part of the book has illustrated, worker resistance compounded by assertive Latin American governments, fungal diseases, and investor anxieties did indeed lead to the situation sometimes attributed to heroic Ecuadorian entrepreneurs. Those entrepreneurs were essentially delegated the dirty work of being on the front lines against the numerous risks that threaten profitable banana growing. Ecuadorian political economist Carlos Larrea points out that eight companies controlled 90 percent of banana exports in 1964 with six of these foreign-owned, leading to at least 25 percent of the added value generated by banana sales leaving the country. In general, the vast majority of profits from Ecuador's industry have still flowed to exporters, with farmers and workers receiving a much smaller share.[16] The long-standing banana industry pattern of banana profits accruing to interests in the global North and to Latin American elites was thus reproduced in Ecuador.

CHAPTER 6
THE PARAKEET IN THE PLANTATION

The story of how banana production became largely contract-based and centred around Ecuador explains much of the unfair situation found in that country in the twenty-first century. The specifically *toxic* nature of that injustice requires additional explanation. The expression "canary in the coal mine" stems from the historic use of canaries to detect carbon monoxide in coal mines before levels of the deadly gas became toxic to human miners, based on the tiny birds' heightened susceptibility.[1] A vivid episode from the closing decades of the Gros Michel period in Central America provides comparable "avian" foreshadowing for the toxic onslaught of synthetic pesticides that would enter banana plantations in the second half of the twentieth century.

Panama disease was not the only fungus that took advantage of the opportunity UFC and its competitors created with their giant monocultures. A fungal disease known as "sigatoka" (*Mycosphaerella musicola*, since renamed *Pseudocercospora musae*) was first detected in Trinidad in 1934 and then in Central America shortly after.[2] Sigatoka (or yellow sigatoka, since a black variety has been identified) attacks leaf surfaces and dramatically reduces yields, or sometimes causes plants to bear bananas that look fine when harvested but taste off when they arrive at market. Like Panama disease, the sigatoka fungus would present major obstacles to banana company ambitions and shape historical events. But in addition to fungi and other more-than-human constituents of agro-ecosystems, the story of banana agroindustry's battle with sigatoka features another actor: the chemicals that would become increasingly central to such battles. Those chemicals in turn compromised worker health, making the illnesses experienced by such bodies and the professionals mandated to care for them increasingly central to how banana production would be conducted and fought over in the second half of the twentieth century and beyond.

Historian Steve Marquardt observes that UFC's Central American operations in the mid-1930s "offered the pathogen almost fifty thousand hectares of susceptible plants, growing in massive, uniform blocks of three hundred to six hundred hectares."[3] In this welcoming environment, the airborne sigatoka fungus could colonize monocultural banana plantations even faster than could *Fusarium*.[4] It posed such a threat to UFC's operations that the company undertook control efforts on a comparable "pharaonic" scale to their futile attempts to re-engineer plantations to dry out, or drown, the Panama disease fungus.[5] Still, the company's response to sigatoka differed in some ways from how it was concurrently approaching Panama disease. The sigatoka fungus proved more susceptible to control strategies than did *Fusarium*, and so UFC embarked on massive operations to spray Bordeaux mixture (named after its origins controlling fungal pests in vineyards), a fungicide consisting of copper sulphate mixed with quicklime in water.[6]

Bordeaux mixture would be pumped from a centralized location on a given plantation through a network of iron pipes connected to heavy hoses that had to be laboriously carried throughout the farm to spray infected plants. The massive scale of UFC's operations meant that the company's workers applied 100 to 150 kilograms of copper annually per hectare of banana plants, and an estimated seventy thousand litres of Bordeaux mixture over the period from 1938, when spraying began, to its end in 1962 with the advent of synthetic fungicides.[7]

UFC's hiring practices in relation to sigatoka control followed its usual pattern of racialized segregation. The workers who undertook the spraying, in Marquardt's analysis of the Pacific division of UFC's Costa Rican operations, were often drawn from that country's central plateau, which tended to dominate national economic life and be considered "whiter." The workers who migrated to UFC farms to work, however, were drawn from the lower classes of the region and often ended up in the undesirable—though relatively well-paid—spray-worker position. The undesirable nature of the sprayer's job related to the physical challenges of lugging heavy metal hoses over the rough surface of a banana plantation, but especially to the fact that a fair amount of the chemical that flowed through them would end up on the spray workers. This would lead to them physically turning blue from the copper sulphate in Bordeaux mixture and sweating blue liquid long after their usually short stint in that job had ended—earning them the name "parakeets" (*pericos*).

Exposure to Bordeaux mixture would by 1970 be shown to cause a deadly condition named "vineyard sprayers' lung," based on its detection among Portuguese grape workers: "a chronic, often fatal condition . . . [involving] cavernous regions of cellular breakdown, much like those produced by coal miners' black-lung disease."[8] Not surprisingly, then, Marquardt's interviews and popular culture representations of spray workers emphasize their sickly and tubercular nature. In the Bocas division, the task of spraying Bordeaux mixture fell largely on Ngäbe (Guaymí) workers. Philippe Bourgois reports that these workers were not provided protective goggles and could later be seen begging in the streets after going blind, apparently from burns to their retinas caused by the chemical.[9]

Despite such vivid impacts, health services for workers on UFC farms did not properly document what was going on in the spray workers' lungs (among other organ systems) and often misdiagnosed them with tuberculosis (TB).[10] Another plausible interpretation is that spray workers experienced the impacts of both Bordeaux mixture and TB, with the toxic exposure creating an especially susceptible internal ecology for the TB bacillus to colonize in the lungs.[11] Misdiagnosing the spray workers in a way that ignored workplace hazards was in keeping with the approach to worker health employed by UFC's Medical Department, another important locus of interaction between banana-related labour relations, corporate strategy, racism, and the more-than-human world.

Ignoring the occupational roots of worker health conditions such as lung impairment among sigatoka spray workers and focusing on their alleged origins in worker ignorance or carelessness fit with the generally paternalistic and management-friendly approach of the Medical Department, and with UFC's scientific practice more generally (as documented in Chapter 3). For example, Marquardt documents how UFC scientists pursued research informed by the view that worker carelessness or ignorance was the source of the sigatoka problem. They also repeatedly attempted to find mechanized (though not very effective) solutions such as overhead spray towers that would control the fungus without needing spray workers at all.[12]

The Bordeaux mixture episode exposes how, after UFC repeatedly created tropical agro-ecosystems in which pathogens such as malaria and sigatoka could flourish, it applied ineffective and paternalistic scientific "solutions," and washed its hands of the damages evident in workers' ravaged bodies.

Marquardt highlights the crisis caused for the company by the failure of its ongoing battle with Panama disease, at a time of increasing unionization and repeated strikes among workers in Central America. With the concurrent difficulties caused by sigatoka, labour responses in the face of Bordeaux mixture's impacts compounded grievances related to low salaries and UFC's controversial use of piecework pay to help control work processes. Although sigatoka spray workers were clearly suffering at the hands of the company and working in settings with constant labour unrest, they were initially not active participants in labour organizing or strikes.[13]

Bourgois's account of tensions between different ethnic groups, and UFC's use and manipulation of them, helps to explain why the Ngäbe spray workers were not more militant in the Bocas division.[14] In the Pacific plantations of Costa Rica, where the spray workers were actually among the phenotypically whitest (non–North American) workers on the plantation, things were differently complicated.[15] Hiring a specific ethnic group for a specific job task again meant that UFC helped to avoid solidarity based on regional or ethnic identity. The often young spray workers were typically viewed as less masculine by the other *mestizo* workers from Honduras, Nicaragua, or the Costa Rican province of Guanacaste, who also characterized them as unhygienic and weak. The term *perico* was used to ridicule them. The spray workers' use of hoses instead of the machete wielded by more "manly" field workers was similarly a powerful symbol of the lack of respect accorded them.

Over time, though, the spray workers were sought out by their more militant co-workers and the threat of sigatoka became part of labour organizing tactics. Since the fungus could devastate plantations and any interruption in control efforts could render them unproductive for quite some time into the future, the spray workers eventually became key players in strike actions and threats. They were often reluctant, as spray workers would report being told to stop work by their colleagues, and were not among the more militant originators of strikes. When the spray operators did eventually walk off the job, UFC was forced to develop additional innovative worker control tactics. The company repeatedly used the threat of production stoppages due to sigatoka in getting the Costa Rican state to intervene in declaring strikes illegal, and often violently intervening to break them up. The escalating and Ecuador-bound arms race involving fungi, organized and racialized labour, Latin American governments, and banana corporations now included novel elements in the form of toxic chemicals—but displayed familiar dynamics in terms of union suppression.

The story of the *pericos* illustrates how workers and more-than-human actors have always shaped the course of banana history through their mutual, but often unexpected, interactions—with the presence of toxic chemicals among the more-than-human participants foreshadowing the pesticide-intensive banana production methods used in Ecuador and elsewhere in the twenty-first century. Massive monocultures in Latin American settings generated predictable threats to profitability such as the sigatoka fungus, which UFC attempted to address through top-down solutions involving mass application of toxic chemicals. The equally predictable morbidity and mortality among the devalued workers who applied those chemicals was also filtered through processes of racialization, interpreted by the company as the result of individual negligence, and eventually mobilized in labour disputes—patterns that would repeat again and again, up to the present day.

But while Bordeaux mixture was developed via a relatively slow process of experimentation with inorganic chemicals to control fungi in places like vineyards, the synthetic fungicides that ultimately replaced it in the banana industry's sigatoka control efforts would be invented and introduced into farms (and surrounding ecosystems and workers' bodies) by the post–World War II chemical industry at a significantly higher pace. As Part 2 of the book details, this enormous process of experimentation on the bodies of banana workers exposed to synthetic pesticides would continue the interaction of tropical ecosystems with Northern corporate ambitions, governments, oppressive narratives, workers, and—increasingly—health scientists whose reactions to the health effects of pesticides would reproduce but also sometimes resist the colonial mindset of UFC's "civilizing mission."

PART 2: 1961-2000

CHAPTER 7
AN INSULT

"That, for me, is an insult," exclaimed one of the men in the interview. "Nobody here is asking you for anything." My ethics approval indicated that I had to tell people they would not be getting any incentive to participate in interviews (such as a small amount of money or other gift), although I still brought a packet of Nestlé Amor wafers to share. It wasn't the wafers or their corporate agribusiness origins that this banana farmer and co-op president objected to, however; it was the idea that he might be looking for anything in exchange for his time. "Listen," he continued heatedly, "please. I don't know about elsewhere, but here it wouldn't even occur . . . what you're talking about is for others. I don't accept it for me." As I struggled to explain the university requirement that I communicate the absence of a participation incentive, he continued rapidly.

> You're from an industrialized country. There are products [pesticides] that you yourselves have evaluated, that you produce in the North, no? They're products that shouldn't come out, shouldn't be sent here to South American countries where, whether due to ignorance or greed, human health doesn't matter. For example, the carbamates. The carbamates! They've been evaluated in your countries, but here they're still applied. They're products that have been demonstrated to be carcinogenic, mutagenic, to cause VERY serious problems in the liver, the pancreas. And mutations at the moment of reproduction, no? But here they're still applied. Guilty! Our authorities here in this

country, very guilty, complicit with all this. But also guilty are these lying companies ... And with indiscriminate use of these chemicals, biological control has been broken to the point where there are species of fauna that control other species, and they've disappeared.

Once he grasped the fact that I only mentioned an incentive to participate as a formality, he congratulated me on being "very ethical" and things got less tense. Still, I would remember the forceful commentary on North-South relations I had absorbed, which was only one of many incidents during my fieldwork where my presence evoked the sordid history of Northern adventures in Latin America. Further clarifying the implications of this history, a participant in a subsequent interview (in the community referred to in this book's introduction) gave me instructions on how I might best leverage my North American privilege: "Listen, I think that it would be more practical if you would take this message direct to your government. And, in turn, your government would have contact with the Ecuadorian government, so that the two parts—one selling and the other exporting—so then we'd see a better exchange of ideas, to improve these things."

These encounters with Ecuadorian banana farmers and their understandings of North-South relations bring up important dimensions of the history of banana production, both before and after the introduction of Cavendish bananas and Ecuador's arrival as the world's perennially leading exporter. Northerners, their money, their values, their scientific ambitions, and their technologies (of which pesticides are a relatively recent form) have been shaping—and shaped by—Latin America for centuries. Part 1 followed the banana-producing period of this history from its origins to approximately 1960, as the industry and the story gravitated towards Ecuador. The processes by which this equator-ward movement took place involved imperialism and corporate domination in Latin America, with racism playing a key role in enabling both. The powerful actors driving such exploitation, however, were never comfortable or unopposed in their efforts to extract value from workers and the land. Diverse workforces fought back through labour organizing and countless everyday acts of resistance; Latin American governments that had previously welcomed UFC and its North American competitors began to assert themselves and place limits on such companies' actions; investors, competitors, British diplomats, North American regulators, and the wives of UFC employees complicated the company's ability to continue its dominant role in the industry; and fungi, malaria parasites, and hurricanes meant that Latin American territories and workers' bodies were rarely docile factors of production. These complex interactions culminated in the industry's increasingly southward flight to the equator.

The story next moves into the period beginning in approximately 1960 and ending at the turn of the twenty-first century. This period began with UFC's loss of centrality in the corporate "ecology" of banana production as well as its decision to prioritize purchases from independent producers, especially in Ecuador. After the initial banana boom of 1948–65, Ecuador soon settled into a role as reserve supplier to the transnationals.[1] The transition from the Panama disease–prone Gros Michel banana to the Cavendish banana seen in stores today was another key change at this time. While Standard Fruit had begun replacing Gros Michel bananas in Central America with Cavendish in the '50s, it would take until 1960 for United Fruit to decide to make the transition and as late as the mid-'60s before the new variety took over Ecuadorian farms.

Plantations of Cavendish bananas produced almost double the yield per hectare as did Gros Michel, leading to a reduction in production costs in Central America, and a reduction in area planted in bananas in Ecuador. The higher productivity and lower prices of bananas from Panama, Guatemala, Costa Rica, and Honduras meant that Ecuador's abundant production often served as a surplus or second-rate supply of bananas that would satisfy excess demand created by seasonal patterns in Central America or go to less-demanding markets.[2]

Another major impact of the transition to Cavendish was the increase in technology required to produce bananas, as the new variety was susceptible to both bruising and several fungal or other plant pests (just not Panama disease). Innovations in this period included the use of cardboard boxes to transport bananas, mechanical irrigation systems, drainage canals, overhead cable systems for transporting bunches of bananas to packing facilities, and the on-farm packing facilities themselves. These technological changes required capital that was less available to smaller producers, as did the chemical pesticides and fertilizers that were increasingly considered key to productivity. Land ownership concentration in Ecuador thus worsened as increasing technification of production squeezed out producers with smaller farms and less access to credit or technology. Over the 1965–76 period, numerous small and medium-sized farms were pushed out of business.[3]

The lower workforce requirements created by both Cavendish's superior yields and mechanization on increasingly large farms (though never so large as UFC's giant Central American plantations) also threw huge numbers of workers out of work, with the Ecuadorian banana workforce dropping from an estimated 60,000 workers in the 1960s to approximately 32,000 by the late 1980s.[4] Even those remaining workers saw stagnation or decreases in wages and purchasing power. Larrea calculates that the average wage for workers, adjusted for inflation, decreased by almost half between 1952 and 1976 (from 770 sucres, in constant 1965 terms, to 415). This was accompanied by major increases in the cost of living, such as a 55 percent increase in the price of food between 1965 and 1976. As a result wages for banana workers dropped dramatically in the early 1960s, and even further in 1976, with the cost of living rising more or less constantly.[5] Although the support Ecuadorian exports provided for workers decreased over the second half of the twentieth century, they remained world-leading. Exports surpassed one million metric tons in 1964 and stayed that way for the next several decades except for a handful of years.[6] Western Europe and the United States accounted for the majority of sales, while smaller markets such as Japan, Eastern Europe, and Southern Cone countries (Chile, Argentina, and Uruguay) played smaller and varying roles over the decades. The total value of exports came to over $460 million (US) in 1990, putting Ecuador ahead of its nearest rival, Honduras (at approximately $365 million in exports). By 2000 Ecuador's exports had increased to over $809 million, with Costa Rica in second place among banana-growing countries at almost $570 million.[7]

Transformations of the banana industry that maintained these world-leading exports occurred against the backdrop of a troubled national process of land redistribution. The invasion of Hacienda Tenguel had initially fed hopes for a national agrarian reform process, comparable to the one Árbenz had attempted in Guatemala, that would address the country's massive inequalities by redistributing land to the impoverished majority.[8] Shortly after workers occupied the hacienda in 1962, however, the first of what would be two military governments over a twenty-year period took power in Ecuador and immediately sent troops to Tenguel to quell the uprising. While the dictatorship did subsequently begin a national process of agrarian reform in 1964, which would be followed by another in the early 1970s, both reforms are widely viewed as incomplete or ineffective at actually redressing land concentration and inequality.[9]

Such half-hearted land reforms stemmed in large part from the hemispheric fear of communism that helped motivate the 1954 coup in Guatemala. In the aftermath of the 1959 Cuban Revolution, John F. Kennedy's "Alliance for Progress" attempted to promote modest economic and land reforms in Latin America as a way of averting more revolutionary changes. Governments such as Ecuador's military dictatorships were encouraged to pursue mild versions of land reform in which (some) large estates would be broken up to provide (some) peasant farmers with land.[10] In *la costa*, land reform did go some way towards breaking up extreme land concentration, at least initially. In El Oro, four families had controlled at least 14,000 hectares of banana farmland (or 50 percent of the province's total) prior to the reform but emerged controlling one-seventh of that amount. Many landless workers did receive land or title to land they had occupied, as occurred with many of the former UFC workers on Hacienda Tenguel. Power imbalances in negotiating with the military government, however, ensured that this was often less-productive mountainous land in the Andean foothills.[11]

In contrast, powerful owners of large plantations employed a variety of strategies to escape the land reform with much of their wealth intact, or even increased.[12] Many large landowners convinced the military government that their operations were indispensable to the national interest and should remain untouched. Some even took advantage of the break-up of neighbouring properties in the reform to expand, either eating up newly available lands or recruiting their new (poor) inhabitants as workers. One final wealth-preserving strategy was for large properties to be divided up among members of families and thereby escape the breaking up of large properties, while effectively remaining a single enterprise for the purposes of decision-making and agricultural—often banana—production. The lasting impacts of this strategy are illustrated by the fact that the Noboa group of companies—including Ecuador's largest banana company—controlled over 22,000 hectares of land in 1983.[13] And so Ecuador's land reforms were not the unqualified emancipatory success the occupation of Hacienda Tenguel had led some to hope for, consistent with the nature of comparable reforms throughout Latin America as a lopsided compromise among impoverished majorities, local elites, and foreign (especially US) interests.

In addition, Ecuador's land reform incorporated peasant farmers into agricultural commodity markets that would reward large-scale, technology-intensive production, especially for export.[14] Former Hacienda Tenguel workers and other poor Ecuadorians who received small parcels of land did not receive corresponding support in the form of credit or agricultural inputs to make investments and improve productivity. These farmers nevertheless faced the challenge of competing against large agribusinesses in cacao and banana markets. They often had to subsequently sell to those larger landowners, rejoining the ranks of the landless poor, vulnerable to exploitation on the farms of others.[15] Alternately, they sometimes left land to their multiple children by inheritance, splitting ten- or twenty-hectare pieces into fragments as small as one or two hectares. This fragmentation process compromised productivity, at least with respect to maximizing a single crop for export, and contributed to reconcentration of land, with increasingly small and uncompetitive farms often being swallowed up by larger and wealthier interests.

Banana production in the Cavendish period also became increasingly reliant on synthetic chemical pesticides produced by Northern corporations and subjected to safety evaluations of questionable adequacy before being exported to Latin America. The resulting havoc wreaked on ecosystems generated major human health issues that "lying companies" and complicit Latin American governments would do far too little to address. These decades also saw Latin America transformed by new forms of US intervention oriented towards a neoliberal model of development in which pesticide toxicity both reflected broader societal toxicity and was ideologically attributed to the inherent deficiencies of individual workers and farmers.

The resulting turmoil in these decades triggered grassroots and other forms of resistance, including from epidemiologists bringing Northern scientific techniques and priorities to bear on the health of Latin Americans involved with banana production. As the varied and sometimes hostile reactions my own presence in Ecuador elicited in the twenty-first century suggest, such involvement was always freighted with the weight of inequitable histories linking Latin America to banana-consuming Northern countries. While such scientific efforts took place largely in Central America, the resulting knowledge and its fate in political struggles would shape the evolution of the entire industry and its interactions with workers and farmers. The disturbing situation documented on Ecuadorian farms in the twenty-first century, and prospects for addressing its health consequences, therefore resulted from political, ecological, and scientific interactions linking Ecuador and the remainder of the banana industry over the second half of the twentieth century.

CHAPTER 8
CAVENDISH ECOLOGIES

Former Bordeaux-mixture applicator (*venenero*) Ramón Amaya Amador published his classic novel *Prisión Verde* (Green Prison), about life in UFC's Honduran plantations, in 1950. In the novel, the *veneneros* (poisoners) represent a kind of labour vanguard, educating themselves in preparation for an eventual strike with the help of left-wing literature from urban organizers. The foe they were organizing against was dramatically described by Amaya Amador as a "giant green monster"

> whose heart was the pump, that machine of superhuman potency, tamed as if it were a beast ... Impelled by its mechanical force, the blue blood—mixture of sulphur and copper, lime and water—exited the giant tanks through the enormous principal artery to flow to the farthest branches, where the field workers connected the hoses and took up the battle against *sigatoka*. The men were human appendices of the inhuman clockwork of the circulatory system of *espray* [spray]. The life of the peons melted into the life of the bananas and the force of the machines, against the backdrop of land that demanded pain in order to bear fruit. Blue blood of sulphate, through long pipes. Reddish black blood of men with Koch's bacillus [the tuberculosis bacterium] impelling them towards death. Bananas. Machines. Men. The Company accumulating gold. The workers chasing their daily bread.[1]

While written at the tail end of the Gros Michel era, this passage and the labour politics it is linked to in *Prisión Verde* foreshadow how changing agroecologies in the Cavendish period would reverberate through interactions among corporations, workers, and the health of their bodies. Sociologist Kees Jansen explains that "the efforts of growers to combat pests and diseases in banana monocultures are in themselves a battleground, which tends to have a significant impact on the other wars between capital and labour and between capital and capital."[2] Understanding such new and violent ecologies of banana production and its impacts yields important insights for the task of responding to those impacts today.

The abandonment of direct production in Ecuador after the occupation of Hacienda Tenguel, coupled with UFC's 1960 decision to prioritize contract-based production throughout its empire, came at the same time the company was being forced to accept competition from its main rivals. An antitrust ruling in the United States responding to UFC's near-monopoly and negative publicity over the coup in Guatemala forced the company to sell off major holdings to Standard Fruit (Dole) and Del Monte, putting an end to its six-decades-long reign as the unchallenged leader of the banana industry.[3] Standard Fruit had piloted Cavendish production in the 1950s while UFC slavishly stuck with Gros Michel and employed shifting cultivation to avoid Panama disease.[4] Standard's innovation helped move it into an industry leadership role, and UFC eventually followed in its footsteps in adopting the Cavendish.[5]

The strengthened role of Standard Fruit and Del Monte in the 1960s and beyond would also be accompanied by the entry into the banana world of other transnational corporations such as Dow, Shell, DuPont, and other manufacturers of the pesticides that were rapidly becoming central to banana growing. Such shifts in the "corporate ecology" of bananas paralleled major changes to the actual agricultural ecologies (agroecologies) of banana farms—and to the internal ecologies[6] or health of the men and women working on them.

The Cavendish banana variety is more fragile than Gros Michel and is therefore shipped in cardboard boxes, requiring new work routines such as banana-packing days by dedicated teams of workers in special on-farm facilities. After being marginal to the industry in the Gros Michel period, women would also finally join the Cavendish banana workforce in significant numbers in packing tasks, which are deemed appropriate for them as they require nimble fingers and attention to detail, but not the brute strength or macho machete-wielding skills of fieldwork.[7] The packing process also allowed application of stickers to the bananas, and therefore branding with specific company names in the competitive corporate ecology of the post-1960s banana industry.

The Cavendish is not vulnerable to the original Panama disease, but it is still grown in pathogen-friendly monocultures employing year-round production, making it highly susceptible to fungal diseases and a host of invertebrates.[8] One case study of pesticide use on banana farms owned by the three transnationals in Costa Rica found an estimated eighty-nine different kinds of insects that could threaten banana production.[9] As in global agriculture more generally, the post-1960s era has seen synthetic pesticides—petroleum-based organic chemicals—become increasingly central to Cavendish banana growing, in a kind of arms race with the pathogens who predictably exploit the monocultural ecological niches the industry continues to create.[10] In response to nematode damage, for example, nematicides from the same chemical classes as common insecticides have been applied using a variety of methods, such as mixing them into the water sprayed from overhead irrigation systems or injection directly into the soil using pogo-stick-like applicators.[11] Additional chemical use in the Cavendish era also takes advantage of the availability of herbicides that can control vegetation in between the rows of banana plants without labour-intensive use of machetes (also avoiding the tendency of the people holding machetes to organize into unions).

Consistent with Jansen's battleground metaphor, the American and European industries that manufactured such pesticides evolved over the early and mid-twentieth century in close connection with military interests, with products developed as chemical weapons in wartime often finding profitable use in a parallel war against nature. Pesticides were developed, approved, and introduced into markets with increasing speed after World War II, building on the successful use of DDT to protect American troops in the Pacific from insect-borne diseases.[12] Revealingly, then, banana company managers studied by political ecologist Lori Ann Thrupp in Costa

Rica in the 1980s would describe pest control in the shadow of demanding yield and cosmetic standards as a kind of "war-front or chemical battle."[13]

As Thrupp documented, when and how to apply pesticides on large Cavendish plantations came to involve a mixture of top-down decisions at the transnational corporate level, company scientists' input into them based on experimental farm plots, and locally specific inputs from farm managers and technicians employing agricultural sampling procedures.[14] Pesticide manufacturers' technicians and representatives also provided input, cemented by testing of new chemicals on banana farms and banana pest control managers' attendance at pesticide company information sessions. Another overwhelming influence comes from stringent quality standards for bananas creating an atmosphere of "fear"—to the point where multiple managers described to Thrupp a kind of "psychosis" or "paranoia"—over the prospect that yield reductions or cosmetic damage to the fruit would cause rejection and economic losses.[15]

The more-than-human inhabitants of banana ecosystems, however, have not taken such chemical assaults lying down. The phenomenon of pesticide resistance occurs when pests—with their typically short reproductive cycles—rapidly evolve the ability to survive specific chemicals. Indeed, this phenomenon began in the waning years of Gros Michel production. Prior to the 1950s, thrips—a kind of insect that damages banana peels—and the banana corm weevil were the only insects known to cause occasional problems on banana plantations, but these were usually kept in check by natural predators.[16] UFC's 1954 aerial fumigation of over 12,000 hectares of bananas for thrips using the organochlorine insecticide dieldrin in its Golfito division in Costa Rica disrupted this equilibrium (dieldrin granules and spray were also simultaneously applied to the base of plants to control the corm weevil). While the dieldrin treatments did eliminate the thrips, they were rapidly followed by damaging outbreaks of previously unimportant pests such as the banana stalk borer (*Castniomera humbolti*) and another pest from the order Lepidoptera (which contains moths and butterflies), *Platynota rostrana*. The first of these novel pests weakened banana plants by boring through the trunk, while the second fed between the banana fingers. Both caused major crop losses.

In response to the problems caused by the dieldrin spraying, UFC experimented with more pesticides, most of which are now recognized as hugely destructive to health and the environment. Chemicals such as DDT, endrin, malathion, heptachlor, diazinon, and dieldrin were applied in increasing amounts and frequencies, according to "calendar spraying" schedules (conveniently) recommended by pesticide companies, with little or no attention to actual sampling from affected fields. The predictable result of this approach was an explosion of new insect problems as the chemical assault destroyed "natural enemies" that had previously kept populations in check. UFC-sponsored entomological research also revealed that insects were developing resistance to the pesticides being sprayed, meaning that evolutionary pressure caused resistance genes to become progressively more widespread in each successive generation of the rapidly reproducing pests.[17] Frequent and widespread fumigation exerted such strong selection pressures by killing off non-resistant insects and increasing the proportion of resistant ones in subsequent generations. Chemical companies had been aware of the potential for such problems based on previously published scientific studies but did not communicate these risks to UFC in their application recommendations. The chemicals thus lost most, and often eventually all, of their effectiveness. UFC made adjustments in the 1960s by introducing new chemicals (which also then lost their effectiveness due to resistance) and reducing overall pesticide usage by tolerating more insect damage to plants.

While insects and nematodes were prominent targets of the chemical assault that accompanied the switch from Gros Michel to Cavendish, some of the largest volumes of pesticide use were—and are—related to yet another fungus. After Panama disease transformed the industry and the Americas over the first half of the twentieth century and yellow sigatoka prompted UFC's first major foray into chemical pest control using Bordeaux mixture (and the spray workers, or *pericos*, it would turn sickly and blue), a related fungal threat made the jump to the western hemisphere. The black sigatoka fungus (*Mycosphaerella fijiensis*, since renamed *Pseudocercospora fijiensis*) was detected in Honduras in 1972 and had reached Costa Rica by the end of the decade.[18] Black sigatoka attacks the banana plant's leaves and results in premature ripening, necessitating early harvests of smaller bananas that do not meet the standards of exporters and supermarkets.

As the fungus spread through Central America in the 1970s, the fungicide benomyl was used to control it and the frequency of applications—again using calendar spraying recommended by pesticide manufacturers—increased from the 12 to 16 cycles per year that had been used in the early 1960s to 30 to 35 in 1975–76 and even 40 to 45 on some farms before the fungicide was deemed to have completely lost effectiveness by 1977–78.[19] As this increase suggests, the same type of evolutionary pressures that had selected for insects resistant to dieldrin and other insecticides helped the black sigatoka fungus develop resistance to the chemicals used to fight it. That is, resistance genes rapidly become more prevalent in fungal populations as regular and frequent fungicide applications kill off non-resistant fungal cells.[20] While attacking sigatoka fungi with pesticides does not necessarily result in the proliferation of different fungi—as was the case with insects such as the banana stock borer when dieldrin was used to control thrips—regular fumigation with fungicides drives birds from plantations, reducing the degree to which they can control caterpillars. The use of herbicides to control weeds similarly reduces populations of natural predators.[21]

Banana production was therefore an early site of the "pesticide treadmill," in which intensive chemical use leads to pesticide resistance and surges in new pests. The result is a perceived need for even more, and more varied, pesticide use. When the problem of black sigatoka's resistance was belatedly recognized by UFC, for example, a number of strategies were employed, such as rotating fungicides and spraying with a variable chemical cocktail to prevent the development of resistance to any single product; more precise spraying using on-field sampling and finely tuned fumigation equipment; and complementary practices such as manual trimming of diseased leaves and removal of fallen leaves from the plantation floor to reduce the overall amount of fungus. In spite of these innovations, however, control of black sigatoka continued to be enormously difficult, with control costs estimated to have increased by 400 percent from the late '70s to the mid-'80s.[22] Over 40 percent of total pre-production variable input costs (including labour) in 1984 were estimated by Thrupp to be accounted for by pest or disease control, of which at least half was devoted to controlling black sigatoka.[23]

The changing ecologies on pesticide-intensive Cavendish farms also compromised ecosystems *outside* the boundaries of plantations. Because bananas tend to be grown in lowland tropical areas with heavy rainfall, the pesticides used to produce them are washed off quickly and must be reapplied frequently.[24] Plantations typically feature drainage systems to control moisture levels, promoting runoff of pesticide-laced waters into downstream aquatic ecosystems. This toxic soup is also "enriched" with chemical fertilizers and soil erosion from farms whose soil-stabilizing undergrowth is systematically removed, often with herbicides. Since Cavendish bananas are washed and then treated with special fungicides to prevent crown (stem) rot before shipping, these chemicals are also part of the cocktail that banana plantations serve to downstream waterways and the lives—human and more-than-human—that depend on them. Research in aquatic ecosystems downstream from banana plantations has shown numerous negative impacts on organisms as small as benthic macroinvertebrates (a common indicator of aquatic ecosystem health) and as large as black caiman (a member of the same taxonomic family as alligators).[25]

Beyond such ecosystem disruptions external to plantations are disruptions *internal* to the banana workers who apply and are most exposed to pesticides. As foreshadowed by the rotted lungs of UFC's Bordeaux mixture sprayers, chemical pest control has led to a wide range of health effects among banana workers and others exposed to fumigations. Some of the most obvious and identifiable such effects have involved serious acute poisonings with substances such as the herbicide paraquat, as well as with organophosphate and carbamate pesticides, which disrupt neurotransmission. Carbamates and organophosphates, which came into widespread use after bans on DDT and other organochlorines, are much more acutely toxic and can cause immediate "intoxication" and even death. Chronic low-dose exposure to them also has several long-term effects, including neurobehavioural impacts such as delayed reflexes, reduced mental capacity, and depression. Additional impacts of the various classes of pesticides used in banana production include skin irritation and rashes; eye irritation and vision problems; respiratory problems; and serious long-term effects such as reproductive impacts and cancers.[26]

An early indication of such health consequences came from Costa Rica.[27] In one hospital in the country's Atlantic banana zone, 374 people were hospitalized for pesticide-related problems in 1981, an estimated 90 percent of them banana workers. An estimated 800 pesticide poisonings per year were formally reported in Costa Rica in the mid-1980s, although there were at least 113 unreported cases in one small clinic in the southern Pacific banana zone in 1981, suggesting massive underreporting.

The interaction of these different ecologies—on-farm, corporate, and internal to workers—is vividly and infuriatingly illustrated by the story of a pesticide known as dibromochloropropane (the nematicide featured in the "DBCP Facts" portion of Dole's website along with assertions of that company's innocence in relation to related human sterilizations). Compounding threats from insects and fungi, monocultural banana production suffers from vulnerability to soil-borne nematodes (a kind of worm of the phylum Nemata) that attack banana plants' roots.[28] Nematodes can promote the growth of fungal or bacterial pests in the plants whose roots they are burrowing into.[29] In addition to having ample genetically identical plants planted close together to maximize yields, the agroecology of producing bananas for foreign markets makes them especially vulnerable to nematodes. Specifically, pruning banana plants' "son" and "grandson" generations allows them to concentrate nutrients in the main stalk and produce larger, more attractive bananas, but also leaves the plant more vulnerable to nematode damage in the remaining roots. A resulting risk is toppling of plants when their truncated and infested roots prove unable to stabilize them in strong winds.[30]

The banana transnationals eagerly welcomed DBCP when it was developed by Shell and Dow Chemical in the 1950s, then used it in conditions that led to massive worker exposure.[31] On some plantations in Honduras and Nicaragua, for example, the chemical was sprayed aerially from fixed towers, with workers who had to clean or fix the turbines and "guns" on these towers frequently coming into prolonged contact with it. Since these aerial applications left liquid on the banana plants themselves, workers who passed under the leaves or put plastic bags around the bunches to protect them from insects would experience drips, or more sustained wetting. Pesticide drift from the aerial applications also exposed people other than workers, such as their families or others living in housing near or on plantations. DBCP would also pool in puddles on the ground or in the foot-deep holes left by poles used in planting young banana plants, which meant that unsuspecting workers (often barefoot) could find themselves up to their ankles or even their knees in a mix of DBCP and water.

Other ecological conditions led to additional routes of exposure. Regular rainfall on Costa Rican plantations meant that irrigation systems were unnecessary. A granular form of the chemical was mixed by hand and loaded into "guns" that were used to inject the nematicide into the ground near or around the roots of the banana plants. Workers who mixed and applied the pesticide in this way also found themselves exposed to it in ways that were not anticipated by safety labels on pesticide containers. Those safety labels thus proved largely ineffectual, as did the idea that adequate personal protective equipment (PPE) could be worn in the hot, humid, fast-paced environment of a Central American banana plantation.[32]

The consequences of these massive worker exposures would emerge in the 1980s, when workers in DBCP manufacturing plants in the United States would be found to have been sterilized by the chemical, a result that—infuriatingly—animal toxicology studies conducted decades earlier by Dow and Shell had anticipated. The banana transnationals would nevertheless continue to use the chemical for years after it was banned in the US, with UFC (renamed United Brands by that point) moving faster than Dole (owned by Castle & Cooke at the time) to eliminate it. Thousands of Latin American and Filipino banana workers would eventually report being unable to have children, with additional impacts documented epidemiologically, including several forms of cancer and an elevated risk of mortality.[33]

The story of DBCP is discussed in more detail in Chapter 21, including its racial capitalist dimensions and implications for the pursuit of environmental justice through legal and other state structures. For now, it illustrates interacting changes to the corporate, on-farm, downstream, and internal ecologies associated with banana production in the pesticide-intensive Cavendish era that help explain how people such as Ecuadorians living in *la costa* experience toxicity in the twenty-first century. The specific patterns of exposure, however, have been shaped by more than interacting corporations, chemicals, and pests. As discussed in the following chapter, the US imperialism that drove the complex evolution of banana production early in the twentieth century would—like plant pathogens on banana plantations—adapt to and, in turn, shape the changing toxic circumstances of the century's closing decades.

CHAPTER 9
EMPIRE'S GUINEA PIGS

While the changing ecologies prompted by the innovation of Cavendish banana production help explain the presence of pesticides in contemporary banana farms, the specific forms of toxicity experienced in banana-producing countries have been shaped by two additional "experimental" processes. Late twentieth-century assaults on Latin America—both chemical and military—would shape the increasingly globalized banana industry, and the broader terrain on which twenty-first-century battles for environmental justice take place.

The mechanized, chemical-intensive, and largely contract-based Cavendish banana production model that took root in the 1960s remains in place to the present. It was on my first trip to Ecuador in 2009, in the second year of my PhD, that I first experienced such a banana plantation, accompanied by a group including my supervisor, Jerry Spiegel, and another member of my committee named Alejandro Rojas. Alejandro was a professor of land and food systems who held a deep respect for the diversity—biological and epistemological—associated with small-scale, agro-ecological farming. In his class on participatory research, he had often quoted Vandana Shiva's famous phrase capturing the homogenizing tendencies of agro-industrial production: *monocultures of the mind*.[1]

When we stepped onto a conventional (not organic) banana plantation in El Oro to conduct a field visit, however, Alejandro maintained his sense of wonder. He marvelled at the imposing banana plants and the way

Figure 9.01: Alejandro Bananahands

in which successive generations could be seen emerging from the base of an adult plant. He picked up two hands of bananas that were lying on the ground and posed for a picture with them covering his own hands. This was not the denunciation of agro-industrial farming I had expected; Alejandro was having *fun* in a monocultural plantation.

In hindsight I have come to link Alejandro's playful response to toxic agriculture to his earlier experience of toxic social transformations in Latin America. I had been inspired in class when Alejandro described his political activities in his native Chile, for example, conducting literacy and political education campaigns in the countryside with the revered Brazilian educator Paulo Freire. Earlier on that trip to Ecuador he had also told me about his experience in the Unidad Popular movement of Chile's president from 1970 to 1973, Salvador Allende. Alejandro explained that he and his *compañeros* in the Allende years thought they were at the dawn of a new world—a better society based on justice and freedom from imperialism. In addition to the rural campaigns with Freire, Alejandro was a frequent participant in Allende's public events, such as one rally with Cuban leader Fidel Castro. He was on the stage during Castro's characteristically lengthy speech on Cuba's success at managing peak electricity demand, or what he termed *el pico eléctrico*—a term that sent the audience into gales of laughter because it translated into Chilean slang as "the electric penis."

It was during Castro's speech that Alejandro locked eyes with his eventual second wife, Elena, at the time part of a delegation of students seated in the front row of the audience. Historical events slowed the romance, though. Allende's policies threatened Chile's elites and the American interests they tended to ally with, such as the Anaconda Copper Mining Company he nationalized.[2] The United States conspired with such elites to sabotage the country's already-troubled economy and defuse any risk that its economic model would result in a dangerous success story for socialist policies. Then on September 11, 1973, a CIA-backed coup brought General Augusto Pinochet to power and resulted in Allende's death. The coup ushered in decades of radical free-market (neoliberal) economic reforms, guided by several University of Chicago–trained Chilean economists ("the Chicago Boys"). The reforms were also enforced by state-sponsored terror, involving killings, torture, and "disappearances" of opponents of Pinochet—or just anyone with a reputation for being an intellectual or progressive thinker.[3] This category included Elena's father, who was detained and tortured before the family was able to escape to Honduras and eventually Canada.

Having been elected a Unidad Popular representative for Santiago in the country's Chamber of Deputies in 1972,[4] Alejandro faced dark prospects if captured. He lived in hiding and then in the Finnish embassy for over a year before being taken to the airport in the trunk of a car and flown to Europe. When he landed, he quickly called Elena in Toronto. Elena had needed her wisdom teeth removed and—as the family had little money—had relied on free care provided by dentistry students. When Alejandro called, after his months in hiding and dramatic escape from the horrors of Pinochet's rule, Elena could come to the phone, but her recent oral surgery meant she couldn't make anything more than inarticulate tearful noises. Her mother had to take the phone to convey Elena's joy and relief. Elena would join Alejandro in Europe soon after, where they started a family before ending up in Canada among the ranks of the Chilean intellectuals who have subsequently made enormous contributions to progressive scholarship and activism in Canada.

Alejandro had to step down from my committee soon after that trip to Machala and later passed away in 2018 of cancer at age seventy-three (and after forty-eight years of marriage to Elena).[5] Alejandro's experience escaping Pinochet's Chile to a career centred on marginalized ways of knowing and of farming captures some of the key dynamics that would shape the Americas over the final decades of the twentieth century and into the twenty-first. These transformations would bring about specific forms of toxicity whose impacts are still present on Ecuadorian banana farms in the twenty-first century.

The outcomes of Ecuador's Alliance for Progress–inspired land reform are important for understanding the specific health outcomes currently being experienced by the descendants of those land reform beneficiaries. Accompanying the Alliance for Progress in the 1960s and beyond was a parallel US initiative that would strengthen the movement towards large-scale, mechanized, and pesticide-intensive agriculture begun by half-hearted land reform efforts across Latin America. Once again, the real or perceived threat of communism was among the major driving forces. According to sociologist Douglas L. Murray, "The United States emerged from the Second World War with a mission."[6] The *international development* mission sought to improve living conditions in "developing countries" through modernization, and especially modern industrial agriculture steered by (Northern) science and technology. It was asserted that increasing yields of agriculture using pesticides, fertilizers, high-yield seeds, and other "Green Revolution" agricultural technologies would alleviate hunger and make restive and growing Latin American populations less susceptible to revolutionary ideology.[7]

Murray documents the massive promotion of pesticide-intensive agriculture in Central America—especially of "non-traditional" export crops—by the United States Agency for International Development (USAID) in the 1970s and '80s, justified by such Green Revolution narratives (similar initiatives took place in other "developing" regions of the world). Murray describes this promotion of pesticide-intensive agriculture as a process of "cultivating crisis" in Central America, for its health, environmental, and economic impacts.[8] The environmental impacts included massive disruption of ecosystems, consistent with the "pesticide treadmill" of escalating organochlorine use and rampant ecological disruption observed on UFC's farms in the '60s. Economic disruptions followed from this ecological upheaval, as peasant farmers found their livelihoods compromised by unreliable yields and increasing agrochemical input costs, belying the promise of the Green Revolution cover story.

The health effects of Green Revolution agriculture were the third—predictable—component of the crisis cultivated by USAID and related development efforts. Murray describes how pesticide-intensive development created an enormous burden of pesticide-related illness among farmers and farm workers in Central America, essentially turning the isthmus into a "natural experiment" that has served as the raw data for countless pesticide-health studies over a period of decades. This experiment evokes the title of an early twentieth-century book, *100,000,000 Guinea Pigs* (based on the approximate US population at the time), reflecting the unpredictable impacts of introducing massive quantities of new chemicals into society without adequate knowledge of their health impacts.[9]

The health effects of the pesticides introduced into Latin American ecosystems and bodies in this way would motivate a substantial investment of money and human energy in the practice of pesticide epidemiology in the region. Accompanying this scientifically "productive" use of countries in the Americas and the people living in them was a parallel effort that would use those people as involuntary experimental subjects in a different way. Agricultural productivity enhancements represented a kind of "carrot" approach to ensuring that the region remained hospitable to American geopolitical and commercial initiatives. Latin American leaders nevertheless displayed a worrisome tendency to stand up to the United States and attempt to retain more of the region's wealth in the countries where it was generated. Examples of such assertiveness included Árbenz's attempts at land reform in Guatemala and Allende's nationalization of Chile's copper mines. Such nationalist leaders also included Omar Torrijos of Panama, who led the 1974 formation by several countries (but not Ecuador) of the Union of Banana Exporting Countries (UPEB, from *Unión de Países Exportadores de Banano*) to impose a tariff of one dollar on every case of bananas exported.[10]

The United States supplemented the carrot of agricultural intensification with a definite stick. This took the form of both overt and covert military actions to destabilize uncooperative (often democratically elected) Latin American leaders and replace them with more co-operative ones (often dictators).[11] In particular, the US tended to replace left-leaning leaders with right-wing ones who would implement a distinctive package of economic policies.[12] Historian Greg Grandin describes Latin America in this period as "empire's workshop," in which the US refined tactics of military-economic interventionism that would subsequently be used in the 1990s (as in Iraq) and twenty-first century (Iraq again, and Afghanistan).[13]

As piloted in Pinochet's Chile, the neoliberal economic model that such experiments would help to refine and reproduce included privatizing state businesses, reducing state spending, deregulating finance and other sectors of the economy, weakening or crushing organized labour, and generally promoting unfettered profit-making by big business, prominently including foreign interests.[14] Naomi Klein explains that such economic "shock therapy" is far too brutal to be accepted by democratically empowered populations, necessitating violent tactics such as those horrifically employed by Pinochet to shut down popular resistance and create docility in the face of enormously damaging policy measures.[15] Both Klein and Grandin point out how the Chilean experiment in pushing through neoliberal economic policy packages would serve as a source of data and experience as the US worked to help install and support repressive regimes elsewhere in the Southern Cone, namely Argentina and Uruguay. Subsequent interventions in the 1980s destabilized Central American governments such as the revolutionary Sandinistas in Nicaragua, or bolstered repressive regimes fighting leftist revolutionary movements, such those of Guatemala and El Salvador.

Complementing and extending the illicit American military interventions, multilateral organizations and bilateral treaties subsequently helped to entrench neoliberal economic policies throughout the world, leading to the Washington Consensus regarding the overall global economic model that should be followed—or enforced—at the end of the twentieth century. US experiments in the imposition of neoliberalism thus paralleled pesticide-intensive Green Revolution agricultural development in using Latin American bodies as involuntary experimental subjects. In a suggestive parallel, the toxicology methods that would be used to deem pesticides "safe" for use in Latin America in this period were significantly shaped by researchers at the "Tox Lab" of the University of Chicago, who would use a diverse army of animals as experimental subjects to refine methodologies in the post–World War II years, helping to professionalize the discipline of toxicology before spreading out to establish toxicology departments at universities across the United States.[16] Just as pesticide-intensive agriculture enabled by University of Chicago toxicologists tends to reduce agro-biodiversity and eliminate livelihood alternatives to monocultural farms, violent American imposition of the Chicago Boys' neoliberal economic thinking tended to eliminate dangerous examples of alternative, more collectivist economic development models.

This history helps explain why Alejandro devoted his life after escaping Pinochet's Chile to scholarship and action confronting such monocultures—both those on farms and those "of the mind." The disillusionment that he described feeling after the promise of Allende's government gave way to the violent neoliberalization of Chile and the Americas attests to the overwhelming nature of the forces promoting dominant economic and agricultural models. The sense of humour he exhibited in the midst of a monocultural banana plantation was one response to such oppressive forces. As described in the following chapters, toxicities of neoliberalism in the Americas would do enormous damage to banana workers, environments, and communities but would always take unique forms in different settings, responding to local particularities.[17] Such particularities, which would force various concessions and contortions on the part of would-be neoliberal architects in governments and industry, would also include diverse forms of resistance. Like Alejandro's bananahands, such unpredictable responses to politico-economic transformations on the part of both humans and more-than-humans connected to the banana trade suggest hope in the face of oppressive forces.

CHAPTER 10
EL FRUTO DEL NEOLIBERALISMO

Ecuador's specific trajectory in the last three decades of the twentieth century illustrates how the large-scale collection of practices and ideas termed *neoliberalism* has evolved in context-specific ways to account for local circumstances and the diverse forms of resistance its dehumanizing impacts have almost inevitably engendered.[1] Such local nuances nevertheless form part of an overall trajectory that began in the Gros Michel era with Ecuador's emergence as a kind of safety valve for the banana industry. The extension and transformation of that role in the neoliberal period would shape life prospects for both Ecuadorian workers and farmers, and for those throughout the banana-producing Americas.

"Globalization" is frequently said to elevate the power of corporations in relation to the state. More accurately, neoliberal globalization (i.e., the kind of globalization that actually exists) still typically involves major state intervention in economies and societies but reoriented to prioritize corporate interests. The banana industry, however, was globalized before globalization existed. UFC exercised major power over banana-producing states of the early twentieth century and toppled the government of Guatemala in 1954. The industry has also had the ability to purchase bananas from the most convenient jurisdictions since at least the early twentieth century, foreshadowing the neoliberal period's widespread reductions in the power of organized labour and an increasing ability of industry to relocate to avoid unions and inconvenient social or environmental regulations.[2]

The banana industry's conflicts with its workers nevertheless took on a qualitatively different character in the neoliberal period, enabled by the violent US imperialism of the '70s and '80s.[3] Assertive Latin American governments in this period had increasingly sought to use bananas as a vehicle for national economic growth after the transition to the Cavendish variety and contract-based production. Since UFC and its competitors were moving away from direct production, a niche was created for domestic Latin American elites to profit more from banana production. And so they advocated—often successfully—for state support in the form of credit, infrastructure, subsidies, and favourable taxation and export rules. By providing this support, and especially infrastructure such as highways, states created conditions for an exploitable banana "proletariat," with landless workers often migrating to the new banana zones to work on the farms of local elites selling bananas under contract to the transnationals. These workers, in turn, found themselves in conflict with their employers over wages and working conditions, with those employers and their state backers often responding with violence.

Efforts by economically nationalist governments to retain more of the profits of banana production had included the 1974 Union of Banana Exporting Countries (UPEB), but this intended cartel never succeeded in controlling banana prices, especially when undercut by Ecuador. As a result, the banana industry saw a "race to the bottom" in terms of wages, working conditions, and other factors of production that could give specific jurisdictions a comparative advantage.[4] This race quickened in the 1990s when the archetypal institutions of globalization solidified. The European Union's preferential treatment of bananas from its former colonies was deemed to violate international trade rules laid out by the General Agreement on Tariffs and Trade and its successor, the World Trade Organization (WTO). Chiquita and other banana transnationals—enthusiastic donors to both Democrats and, especially, Republicans in the United States—successfully mobilized the US (on whose soil no bananas were actually produced for export) to lead a WTO challenge, backed by Ecuador and several other Latin American countries.[5] As a result, major obstacles to the complete globalization of the banana industry were eliminated, increasing the ability of transnational corporations to source bananas from whichever jurisdictions could provide the lowest production costs.

The role of cheap, abundant bananas produced by largely non-unionized Ecuadorian workers in undercutting the bargaining power of banana worker unions in Colombia and Central America arguably makes bananas "the fruit of neoliberalism" (*el fruto del neoliberalismo*).[6] The non-unionized and vulnerable banana workforce in Ecuador has helped to keep labour in line throughout the Americas by providing a perpetually cheap option for the banana transnationals when they seek to source bananas and their Central American or Colombian farms are experiencing too much labour strife. Ecuador's arrival at this pressure-valve role in relation to labour organization and other threats to corporate profits similarly illustrate how unique experiences of imperialism and neoliberalism in one country have in turn helped to shape the overall trajectory of globalized banana production.

The dramatic ascendancy of Noboa as a major producer of bananas in the 1970s, which took place while technological changes and related economic dynamics squeezed out small producers and workers, is a consequential Ecuadorian wrinkle in the neoliberalization of the banana-producing Americas. Grupo Noboa increased its share of Ecuadorian production from 15.8 percent in 1964 to 46.6 percent in 1977.[7] It simultaneously lobbied successfully with other exporters for an abolition of export duties on bananas, reflecting what Carlos Larrea terms banana elites' "large influence on state policies."[8] Indeed, Noboa was routinely consulted by the Ecuadorian government about any regulatory decision affecting the banana industry, and was able to exert significant influence, including through a revolving door between government and its corporate empire.[9] Ecuador's decision not to join UPEB in 1974, which thereby undermined the power of the organization by providing a competing source of cheap bananas, was largely taken as a result of Noboa's lobbying. Another example was the decision by the government—again following opposition by Noboa—to cancel a contract it had signed with Del Monte in 1978, which would have seen the state participate in purchasing and exporting bananas while Del Monte ensured quality control.

Similarly, Noboa was consistently able to obtain substantial financial concessions from the Ecuadorian government.[10] A consortium of foreign companies had struck oil in the country's Amazon region in 1967, and Ecuador rapidly became an oil-producing country after 1972, with Texaco (later purchased by Chevron) leading extraction. This development took place under the rule of the country's second military dictatorship, which took power in 1976 and pursued some nationalist and redistributive policies that were largely financed by oil revenues. The influx of revenues to the central government allowed it to invest in a national fleet of banana boats (Flota Bananera Ecuatoriana, which had been founded in 1966), which it leased primarily to Noboa even while operating at a loss. In addition, Noboa's boats qualified for subsidized fuel at "internal" prices whereas the transnational companies had to pay higher "external" fuel costs. Enabled by such support and by substantial foreign investment, Noboa also employed flexible strategies such as occasionally supplying bananas to Chiquita, as well as pursuing non-traditional markets in socialist countries and the Middle East.[11]

Ecuador's role as reserve supplier began to change as the transnationals perceived various categories of risks to their operations in Central America over the 1970s and '80s, many of them stemming from the forced neoliberalization processes described in the previous chapter.[12] More-than-human threats in this period included the rapid spread in Central America and Colombia of the black sigatoka fungus. The cost of controlling black sigatoka rapidly came to represent a large proportion of total production costs, estimated at $900 per hectare in 1983, corresponding to approximately 10 percent of the total price paid by exporters. Hurricanes also continued to threaten Central American production, such as Hurricane Fifi, which devastated plantations in Honduras in 1974. Beyond workers and nationalist leaders, revolutionary Central American movements and the Sandinista revolution in Nicaragua in 1979 would also be a factor in the renewed focus on Ecuadorian bananas, as would the massive violence, militarization, and destabilization of the region caused by US reactions to those movements in the 1980s. Similarly, guerrilla movements in the Philippines (operating in 63 of the country's 75 provinces) began to disrupt the transnationals' production of bananas for Japanese markets, which had begun in the Philippines in 1970.

Responding to such threats, Standard Fruit in 1976 established an associated producer program in Ecuador that gave some producers medium-term contracts, credit, and technical assistance in exchange for giving the company almost total control over production decisions, including implementation of a technological package.[13] This allowed for production of higher-quality fruit for the primary international markets, as Standard Fruit increased its share of exports from 18 percent in 1977 to 37 percent in 1984. Larrea suggests that compliance with labour legislation and other regulations was relatively high on Standard Fruit's farms in this period. The technification of production that Standard Fruit imposed on its associated producers drove a general transformation of Ecuadorian banana farming, to which chemical fertilizers and pesticides became increasingly central. Del Monte soon followed suit in promoting standardized, technified production methods while increasing its share of exports to approximately 10 percent, although its control over production decisions was less absolute than Standard Fruit's.[14]

A marked decline in need for labour on farms during the Cavendish era continued after 1976 as many of the low-skilled tasks that had formerly been done by workers were taken over by machines or other technologies.[15] As a result, after the banana boom in the 1948–65 period had brought about within-Ecuador migration that Larrea describes as unprecedented in the history of the global banana industry, many of those workers became redundant. Larrea also observes that workers tended to be young and generally left the workforce after the age of forty to acquire land or—more frequently—join the "marginal urban population."[16] These conditions were also not conducive to unionization. Larrea estimates that only 10 percent of the national banana workforce was unionized in the mid-1980s, and these tended to be only on large farms with collective bargaining agreements that would ensure fulfillment of labour legislation. On most farms, workers would end up prematurely aged by back-breaking work for low pay, and then summarily fired without compensation.

A democratic election was held in Ecuador in 1979 after decades of what were largely dictatorships, but the newly elected and progressive-seeming president Jaime Roldós Aguilera died in a mysterious plane crash early in his mandate. An accelerated parade of governments followed Roldós during Ecuador's turbulent 1980s and '90s, with both internal and external pressures keeping the country's political and economic dynamics in flux.[17] Despite such turbulence—indeed, helping fuel popular resistance that worsened it—governments in this period instituted neoliberal macroeconomic reforms that would have major repercussions for banana farms and the people working them, and for the country as a whole.[18] Beginning in 1982, these reforms involved liberalization of the exchange rate and interest rates; dismantling of tariff protections; opening of markets; elimination of subsidies; and partial deregulation of the financial system and labour markets.[19] This package, much of which was pushed through using an International Monetary Fund (IMF)–designed structural adjustment program, led to even greater inequality in the already-unequal country, and helped to generate the underemployed mass of poor, uneducated workers who largely supply banana farms' labour needs today.

Consistent with the austerity dimension of neoliberalism, social spending in Ecuador fell from 7.5 percent of GDP to 5.2 percent between the beginning of the 1980s and 1996.[20] Larrea estimates that real social spending per capita in 2001 was less than half of its 1981 value.[21] The role of external lenders in both requiring and benefiting from neoliberal reforms is illustrated by the fact that debt payments would rise to be 40 percent higher than social spending by 2003, putting the country in second-last place for social investment among twenty-one Latin American countries.[22] Commodity production–oriented reforms in the 1990s included policies to increase petroleum extraction and agro-industrial exports such as bananas, shrimp, and cut flowers, and changes to the country's mining code designed to promote large-scale mining. By 2001, 88.1 percent of Ecuadorian exports were of primary commodities, the third-highest figure in Latin America.[23] Agricultural reforms tended to involve reductions in state support for small-scale agriculture, including the abolition of official minimum prices to be paid for agricultural commodities and reductions in tariffs designed to protect domestic producers. The general result was a reduction in support for small-scale domestic-oriented agriculture (although these supports were already minimal) and a further-increased emphasis on large-scale monocultural (pesticide-intensive) agroindustry for export, of which bananas are the dominant Ecuadorian example.

These reforms also served to intensify the processes of land reconcentration that had been advancing since the (incomplete, ineffective) agrarian reforms of 1964 and 1973. Ecuador's neoliberal reforms therefore accelerated the transformation of small farmers into landless and precarious labourers, a position they shared with increasing numbers of Ecuadorians—especially young people—made under- or unemployed by the austerity measures imposed over the '80s and '90s.[24] With respect to labour protections, a series of laws made it easier for foreign capital to operate in the country, and generally accomplished *flexibilization* that reduced financial obligations or risks of employers. The laws made it easier for employers to terminate employees by facilitating the practice of contracting temporary workers and eliminating compensation for untimely or arbitrary firings. They also made it easier to employ subcontracted labour, eliminating or avoiding the need to observe whatever remaining protections were owed by employers to their own employees. Finally, the new laws were not supportive of, and in many cases were actively detrimental towards, the functioning of unions or other worker organizations. The number of collective bargaining agreements in the country fell from 315 to 206 between 1987 and 1996, and the number of unions fell from approximately 1,800 in the 1970s to about 500 at the start of the twenty-first century.[25]

In response to the harsh impacts of neoliberal austerity measures in 1980s and '90s, but also to centuries of marginalization of Indigenous peoples, the latter decade saw nation-wide *levantamientos indígenas* (Indigenous uprisings), which effectively shut down national economic activity for periods of protest. The *levantamientos* were a major part of larger popular protests against the neoliberalizing and often corrupt governments of the 1990s, with the rapid exit from power of several presidents building Ecuador's increasing reputation as "ungovernable."[26] Then, in 1998, Hurricane Mitch devastated Central American banana plantations and prompted multinationals to purchase additional bananas from independent producers in Ecuador.

As sociologist Henry Frundt explains, this improved bargaining position allowed Ecuadorian producers Bonita (Noboa's label) and Favorita (controlled by Ecuadorian banana tycoon Segundo Wong) to bypass the large banana transnationals and negotiate contracts directly with multinational supermarket chains (which by then had increasingly begun to dictate terms in the banana industry).[27] In addition to establishing itself as a major player in the international banana market, Bonita was largely successful, with Ecuadorian government support, in suppressing unions on its plantations while taking advantage of the opportunity created by Mitch's devastation of Central American banana harvests. Further illustrating more-than-human dimensions to banana's identity as "the fruit of neoliberalism," Del Monte, Dole, and Chiquita also used Hurricane Mitch as a pretext for laying off unionized workers in Central America and sourcing more bananas from Ecuador and other countries with non-unionized plantations.[28]

Ecuador's economic situation entered an acute crisis in the twentieth century's final years. Larrea holds the causes of the crisis to include a border war fought by Ecuador with Peru in 1995 (the second of these in the twentieth century), the global financial crisis that began in Southeast Asia in 1997, the accompanying fall of global prices for petroleum (Ecuador's main source of foreign exchange) in 1998 and '99, and the economic impacts of the strong 1997–98 El Niño–Southern Oscillation, which caused massive flooding in the coastal region and reduced banana yields.[29] Rapid withdrawal of capital from the country, hyperinflation, and the failure or nationalization of the majority of the country's banks were the immediate interlocking causes of the resulting crisis, which led to the replacement of the sucre with the US dollar in 2000 (Ecuador still uses the dollar today) and still more civil unrest that ended yet another short-lived presidency, that of Jamil Mahuad.

Similarly, the growth of the Grupo Noboa to become the fourth-largest producer of bananas in the world shows context-specific responses to changing Northern politico-economic power dynamics, in the form of local elites who could both ally themselves with foreign companies and compete with them under the right circumstances.[30] Of course, such successes for Noboa and other Ecuadorian elites were not typically reflected in benefits for smaller banana producers, and even less so for workers. Writing in 1987, Larrea observed that working conditions on Noboa's farms were worse than those on Standard Fruit's associated farms, and also worse than those of most other exporters' associated farms. The Ecuadorian example shows real and effective resistance to the power of transnational corporations, but not in ways that substantially benefited workers or small farmers. The counter-intuitive role of Hurricane Mitch in helping to consolidate Noboa's position globally, at the expense of banana worker rights in Ecuador and throughout the Americas, further shows the (unpredictable) centrality of more-than-human actors to societal transformations such as those set in motion by the architects of neoliberalism.

The transnational impact of Ecuador's trajectory from the 1970s to the end of the century is illustrated by concurrent developments in its neighbour to the north, Colombia. In that country, the state had financed the opening up of the Urabá region to banana production in the 1960s and beyond, through measures including the building of a major highway and the provision of credit and other infrastructure. Migrants from other parts of Colombia subsequently swelled the region's population and banana workforce. In the final decades of the twentieth century, banana workers in the region were often unionized, participants in strikes, and therefore targets of repressive violence.

Another local particularity—the 1928 massacre of striking workers—would continue to shape the fate of Colombia's banana workers through the end of the century. The massacre was drawn upon by politician Juan Eliécer Gaitán in making fiery speeches in parliament in mid-century. Gaitán's 1948 assassination was the spark that set off *la violencia*, a bloody period of civil war during which several guerrilla armies emerged. The ongoing violence that would characterize Colombia in the second half of the twentieth century was among the major forces pushing migrants out of areas such as the primarily Afro-Colombian Chocó region, from where they would migrate to Urabá and often work in bananas.[31] These workers lived and worked in appalling conditions and were both participants in and frequent victims of ongoing political violence whose roots prominently included the 1928 massacre conducted on UFC's behalf. Local circumstances in Urabá thus included persistent worker attempts to organize in spite of the violent region's identity as a "neoliberal paradise" lacking virtually all forms of state protection for workers and communities.[32]

The Revolutionary Armed Forces of Colombia (FARC, from *Fuerzas Armadas Revolucionarias de Colombia*) and other left-wing guerrillas had a significant presence among the banana workers' unions, while wealthy landowners often used violence to consolidate their properties by expelling previous users of the land. Violence involving banana workers intensified as those elites began supporting and arming right-wing paramilitaries, who tended to target unarmed but politically committed members of left-wing movements—especially banana union leaders. As paramilitary violence purged Urabá and its banana worker unions of left-wing leaders, the major union eventually allied itself with the paramilitaries and toned down its demands for higher wages and other redistributive measures. This right-wing drift of some of the world's most militant banana unions was shaped by the emerging globalized banana market, as union leaders began to use the threat of job losses—often to sparsely unionized Ecuador—as a way to argue against the need for strikes or other more radical actions.[33]

The banana companies themselves, however, had responded to more militant union demands of previous decades by making major concessions, and also by beginning to provide some infrastructure and services for workers and communities via corporate social responsibility (CSR) efforts. In another corporate response to the violent contexts of Urabá and Santa Marta, Chiquita's Colombian subsidiary was found to have paid almost $2 million to the brutal paramilitary group AUC (*Autodefensas Unidas de Colombia*, or United Self-Defense Forces of Colombia), which framed the payments as an exchange for protection of the company's workers from the FARC—although the AUC was at least as likely to attack the company's workers if not paid off. Chiquita subsequently sold off its Colombian subsidiary (while contracting to buy bananas from the new local owners) and sought to defend itself from US regulators, lawsuits, and reputational damage.[34]

When increasingly globalized banana markets undercut the bargaining position of Colombian unions by increasing the threat of complete plantation closures if labour organizing made Colombian bananas too expensive, workers next responded by attempting to organize at the level of the entire Latin American banana industry, in the form of the regional organization COLSIBA (*Coordinadora Latinoamericana de Sindicatos Bananeros*, or Latin American Organization of Banana Unions). In this way Colombian labour politics—themselves shaped by Ecuador's role as safety valve for the banana transnationals—ramified outwards to shape regional and global structures.

The Ecuadorian and Colombian examples demonstrate the importance of local context in shaping particular place-dependent forms of neoliberalization, and in assessing the prospects for resistance in the future. For example, the neoliberal model settled over Ecuador without such dramatic interventions as the Chilean coup or the US-backed Contra war against Nicaragua's revolutionary Sandinista government, but still generally cohered with the macroeconomic prescription that the United States "refined" through its bloody interventions in Latin America in the '70s and '80s. Ecuador's path to this policy climate was markedly different, however, as the country mostly avoided the most vivid excesses of brutal dictatorships and US intervention. Its left-wing insurgent movements were also brutally repressed by its own military dictatorship, but never with the same level of violence as in the Southern Cone, Colombia, or Central America. The comparatively peaceful Ecuadorian context would nevertheless arrive at neoliberal domestic policies that would in turn help to discipline banana labour in settings more obviously transformed by (US-backed) imperialist violence, such as Colombia and Central America.[35] As the following chapter details, additional context-dependent reactions to the toxicity of neoliberal banana production would take place in Central America, with implications for the role of health concerns and health science in banana futures.

CHAPTER 11
HEALTHY RESISTANCE

In *Mamita Yunai*, Costa Rican novelist Carlos Luis Fallas uses the travels of a labour leader through the banana zones in the far south of the country to recount a story of workers' exploitation at the hands of UFC ("la Yunai"). In one scene he depicts the workers in a moment of repose, when emotional responses to life in the plantations emerge vividly: "The workers loved the music and the songs with riotous rhythm. The youngest were most excited and fiery, especially when in love. But they also loved the sad and lugubrious songs, telling of unfortunate loves, lives cut short and deep pain. That was when they most connected with themselves, getting lost in the dark vagaries of memories or letting the birds of their dreams flutter their wings against the bars of their enslaved existence, in search of distant hope."[1]

A prominent labour leader himself, Fallas would later explain to a labour solidarity gathering how affective reactions to that "enslaved existence" eventually led to the massive Costa Rican banana workers' strike of 1934: "And if we add to such monstrous maltreatment the exploitation in the commissaries, the lack of medical attention, the pigsties they were forced to live in, etcetera, we can understand how much human desperation and how much righteous anger was building up day after day in those terrible times, in the banana plantations of the Atlantic zone."[2]

The righteous anger of the Costa Rican workers and its ultimate expression in labour strife illustrates how supposedly all-powerful forces such as colonialism or imperialism invariably spark resistance from communities and the environment, and in turn are forced to adapt, compromise, and contort themselves.[3] This dynamic persisted into the neoliberal period,[4] as the military-chemical assault on Latin America mounted by US Cold War imperialism and pesticide-intensive agriculture provoked pushback from banana workers and other affected Latin American communities. For example, fungi and insects became resistant to the chemicals intended to kill them, as the more-than-human world literally evolved strategies for circumventing and surviving synthetic pesticides.[5] DBCP-related lawsuits against banana and chemical companies also emerged from the struggles of banana workers caught in the chemical crossfire of banana companies' war on nature, and were among the factors that prompted banana companies to undertake extensive CSR efforts to protect their battered images (these lawsuits are discussed in more detail in Chapter 21).

While pushback from workers and nature had been a feature of banana production in the Gros Michel era, it was joined in the late twentieth century by a novel and specifically "healthy" form of resistance. This new reaction to the military-chemical onslaught surrounding banana production would increasingly involve health sciences and scientists—both Latin American and Northern—in struggles for environmental and social justice. While such health-focused resistance largely occurred in Central America, the globalized nature of bananas, the pesticide industry, and public health science means that it holds important implications for understanding and addressing the challenges facing Ecuadorian banana farmers and workers in the twenty-first century.

One major pole of health science resistance to imperialism and its chemical infrastructures was Nicaragua, where the Sandinista revolution overthrew the dictatorial Somoza regime (a US ally) in 1979. The Sandinistas then introduced a range of redistributive measures as well as innovative and scientifically sound public health and agricultural programs—with a major focus on reducing indiscriminate pesticide use and related health effects through integrated pest management (IPM).[6]

In spite of such progressive programs—or possibly because of them—the US and Nicaraguan elites predictably mobilized to try to remove the Sandinistas from power. Their efforts included economic sabotage, as had been wielded against Chile's Allende administration prior to the 1973 coup. For example, Castle & Cooke (which acquired Standard Fruit / Dole in the 1960s) had banana plantations in the country in the 1970s—the same ones where thousands of workers were exposed to DBCP. The company abruptly withdrew from the country in 1983 because, as one Standard Fruit official later informed anthropologist Philippe Bourgois, "We wanted to make an example of the Sandinistas. We wanted them to fall flat on their faces."[7] Such economic attacks were accompanied by actual military ones in the infamous Contra war waged out of bases in Honduras and Costa Rica, with funding, equipment, and training from the US Reagan administration. The Contras waged a bloody long-term conflict, one component of which was attempting to discredit the Sandinistas and compound economic sabotage (including a stifling US embargo) with literal sabotage of their health, agricultural, and social initiatives.

Against this backdrop, the broad Nicaraguan social movement that had brought the Sandinistas to power was joined by numerous North American and European volunteers who flocked to the country in the 1980s to support the revolutionary government and its health and agricultural programs—volunteers who were often enraged by thinly disguised US support for the Contras.[8] Such *internacionalistas* or *sandalistas*—as their customary footwear prompted Nicaraguans to affectionately call them—were supported by a range of Northern religious, civil society, and governmental organizations. These volunteers supported programs such as those implementing the Sandinistas' "revolution in pesticide policy," which sought to both reduce pesticide use in agriculture through IPM and document and reduce pesticide-related health impacts.[9] For example, *sandalista* (US-based) epidemiologists and their Nicaraguan colleagues from the National Autonomous University in the city of Léon (UNAN-Léon) visited fifteen plantations owned by a major banana exporter in 1987–88 and examined the lungs of workers who sprayed the highly toxic herbicide paraquat, finding them to have lower lung capacity and greater incidence of self-reported respiratory symptoms than the control group.[10]

International volunteers working in the Nicaraguan pesticide program included North American physicians who would play a major role in a subsequent Swedish-funded program to strengthen Nicaragua's epidemiology research and public health capacity, especially with respect to the health of workers.[11] This program was one of two main contributors to subsequent Central American initiatives oriented around the use of epidemiology in controlling occupational and environmental pesticide risks. The other main source of expertise and lessons for such regional initiatives was Nicaragua's neighbour to the south. As a more intensively banana-producing nation than Nicaragua, Costa Rica had many more banana workers who would experience and mobilize against pesticide-related health impacts, while the nation's well-developed national health and social security systems enabled such impacts to be readily studied.[12]

In the early 1980s, while Nicaragua was under a revolutionary government and constant assault from the Contras, Costa Rica defaulted on its external debt and was subsequently inundated with foreign loans (with strings attached). Part of the service Costa Rica provided in exchange for loans was serving as a base for Contra attacks into Nicaragua, while jumping through economic policy hoops that followed a classical neoliberal formula of "fewer public expenditures, increased exports, and labor discipline."[13] In particular, the country's strong banana unions were systematically undermined by legislation reducing protection for collective bargaining rights, while an organizing model known as *solidarismo* was promoted as a management-friendly alternative to real unions, backed by conservative sectors of the Catholic Church.

The resulting company-controlled *solidarista* associations offered certain benefits such as sports programs and low-interest loans to workers but failed to meet International Labour Organization standards for genuine freedom of organization.[14] Additional moves to weaken Costa Rican unions included closure of the entire Pacific coast Golfito division of the United Brands Company (UFC's name as of 1970) in 1984, nominally due to black sigatoka infestation but also conveniently ridding the company of a combative and unionized workforce.[15]

Against this backdrop, Costa Rican workers had launched the first lawsuit seeking damages for DBCP-related sterilization in the mid-1980s. They would simultaneously engage in public protests and also seek assistance from scientific experts and some parts of the Catholic Church.[16] In the early 1980s a new bishop, Alfonso Coto, joined the Vicariate of Limón and became concerned about rapid expansion of banana production in the province's banana-producing Atlantic coastal region (the country's only export banana zone after the closure of Golfito).[17] The impacts of past DBCP use and ongoing use of additional pesticides had become more visible in the mid-1980s, while the banana transnationals had driven major clearing of tropical forests in the country to expand banana production in anticipation of getting greater access to European and Soviet Bloc banana markets through progressive market liberalization.[18]

After the vicariate conducted a study of living conditions in the province in 1987–88, the bishop published a pastoral letter in 1989 expressing a desire for the church to help mitigate the negative impacts of rapidly expanding banana production.[19] The letter expressed Christian "liberation theology" themes of solidarity with the poor and specifically questioned the church's support for company-controlled *solidarista* organizations. It is generally thought to have raised national attention regarding problems in the banana-producing Atlantic region, with occupational and environmental pesticide exposures prominent among them. It sparked a process of organizing, beginning in 1992, involving a wide range of groups affected by the industry, including unions struggling to stay relevant in the *solidarista* era; farmers; Indigenous and environmental groups; and other Christian denominations. After a meeting in the Casa Emaús (a church building in the city of Limón), the *Foro Emaús* (Emaús Forum) was formed.[20]

In an example of grassroots globalization, Foro Emaús obtained funding and other forms of support from European activists and organizations such as BanaFair, the German office of the Bread for the World charitable organization, and the Swedish Society for Nature Conservation.[21] They also mounted campaigns in Europe to show the reality of how bananas are produced, which helped motivate such European involvement. The Foro is thought to have contributed to a general "greening" of the banana industry in the late 1990s and beyond, when companies began to institute—and aggressively advertise—a variety of CSR efforts such as Chiquita's creation of a certification system with the formerly independent non-governmental organization (NGO) Rainforest Alliance.[22] However, Costa Rican environmental health researcher Douglas Barraza and his colleagues pointed out in 2013 that companies had not actually reduced their overall pesticide use, or altered specific application practices involving highly hazardous pesticides on banana farms.[23]

One distinctive accomplishment of the Foro involved cultivating relationships with scientists—especially public health scientists—at the Universidad Nacional in Heredia, near the capital of San José.[24] For example, Foro and SITRAP (Agricultural Plantation Workers' Union) members observing massive fish kills after pesticide applications would send dead fish for analysis in the university's pesticide residue analysis laboratory.

The laboratory was associated first with the university's Pesticide Program with its focus on "Environment, Health and Development," and later with its successor, the Central American Institute for Studies on Toxic Substances (IRET, from *Instituto Regional de Estudios en Sustancias Tóxicas*). IRET researchers partnered with Foro Emaús and especially its banana worker union members to conduct and publish numerous pesticide epidemiology studies,[25] functioning as "scientific experts that could counteract official versions of the environmental and health situations on banana plantations."[26] Accordingly, IRET researchers also advocated at the national level for stricter controls on highly toxic pesticides and better protection for banana workers and surrounding communities.

One encouraging result of this collaboration involved a DBCP-related 1997 complaint to Costa Rica's Office of the Ombudsperson (DHR, for *Defensoría de los Habitantes de la República*, which translates loosely as Defender of the Inhabitants), which led to a commissioned review of the health effects of DBCP by Universidad Nacional researchers. Somewhat unexpectedly, banana workers and their organizations were able to choose scientific experts to sit on the review panel.[27] In Bohme's account, the review by Drs. Wesseling and Monge of the Universidad Nacional eventually helped support a decision by the Costa Rican government to provide compensation to banana workers sterilized or otherwise affected by DBCP. But while workers were able to enlist the Costa Rican state in their struggles and shape the scientific processes through which it would operate, the compensation provided by the government was orders of magnitude less than amounts received by US chemical plant workers who had been sterilized by DBCP. In addition, the transnational banana and chemical companies completely avoided contributing financially to these Costa Rican compensation programs, which were instead funded by the indebted country's already-stretched public budget.

The role of public health scientists in resistances to the joint chemical-military assault on Latin America over the 1980s and '90s would mark an important new element in the ongoing battle between corporate strategy and the human and more-than-human members of banana-producing communities. Such Nicaraguan and Costa Rican scientists and health professionals, and their allies in Europe and North America, eventually created broader regional training programs aimed at "solving the pesticide problem in Latin America,"[28] by generating evidence and then translating it into policies. These efforts underscore the increasing importance of health concerns—and transnational health research networks responding to them under the aegis of international development—to the story of banana production.

Solidarity among Northern and Latin American epidemiologists and social movements in Nicaragua and Costa Rica shows the increasing presence of health concerns in battles over the toxic injustices of banana production. The story of Foro Emaús shows how such solidarity could contribute to real advances in the protection of human (and more-than-human) life from toxic exposures and the broader patterns of exploitation they reflect in banana production. Such health-focused resistance has built a growing body of scientific knowledge on the human impacts of pesticides used in banana-producing regions, while helping motivate corporate responses in the form of CSR programs. Whether the wins obtained by social movements and their epidemiologist allies were an adequate payoff for the scientific and grassroots energy that went into them is discussed in more detail in Chapter 23. In any case, the results of such health-focused resistance would become part of the story of attempts to address pesticide toxicity in places such as Ecuador.

CHAPTER 12
A LA COSTA

Like the historical pathway through which this book arrived at the banana capital of the world, physical roads to Machala are often winding and unsettling. The Andean plateau that is home to Quito is linked to *la costa* by highways that lose over two kilometres of altitude in a short westward distance while traversing numerous switchbacks. The views of the Andes are spectacular, such as from the interprovincial bus linking Bolívar province to Guayas, where connections to Machala can be caught. The bus seems to be fleeing from the volcano Chimborazo, whose top is the farthest point on earth from the planet's centre. The snow-capped giant appears through windows on alternating sides of the bus and sometimes looms directly behind, appearing to shrink and grow with changing lines of sight. Such transcendent beauty is often jarringly accompanied inside buses by the playing of violent Hollywood movies. On one trip I marvelled at Chimborazo while, inside the bus, a stripper emerged topless from a cake on a US navy ship in a Steven Seagal movie.

Such contrasts evoke the conflict between Andean lifeways centred on reverence for *Pachamama* (the Kichwa term for the earth-mother deity) and the violence of Northern imperialist interventions in Ecuador, such as the land dispossession that has fuelled mass migration to the agro-industrial coastal region. Indeed, such bus trips recapitulate the physical route of such journeys that have so shaped *la costa*'s geography. Many such journeys pass through the coastal metropolis of Guayaquil, whose bus terminal features a food court with fancy coffee outlets, along with North American and Ecuadorian fast-food chains. The wealth found alongside grinding poverty in Guayaquil reflect the city's identity as the country's economic capital, where profits from banana production disproportionately concentrated over the twentieth century and up to the present. The major beneficiaries of the banana booms were Guayaco (meaning "from Guayaquil") banana-exporting elites as well as large landowners, capitalists, and bankers or investors, who largely spent or invested their money in the city. Larrea describes the emergence and strengthening of this class of elites, observing that "the influence of this medium bourgeoisie, with its origins in agro-exportation, has been very significant in the historic constitution of the country's dominant classes."[1]

Cultural (racist) underpinnings of such extraction of wealth from specific regions and bodies are suggested by one of the fast-food chains present in the bus terminal. Las Menestras del Negro specializes in a coastal staple involving beans with rice and meat (*menestra* means "stew"; *negro* is the direct origin of the same word in English but is generally considered less offensive in Spanish). When I began my fieldwork, the chain's logo featured a smiling, big-lipped cartoon black face, a fork stuck through his Afro mimicking the bone through Pebbles's hair in the Flintstones.

Coastal highways such as the one linking Guayaquil and Machala generally date back to the banana boom of 1948–65, which saw the Ecuadorian state invest significantly in infrastructure that would help transform the physical geography of the region.[2] As buses to Machala leave the terminal and clear Guayaquil's suburban outskirts, the landscape becomes agricultural, featuring sugarcane, rice, and large rectangular aquaculture ponds. As the coastal plain narrows towards the south of Guayas, the Andean foothills loom to the east, sometimes a vague outline shrouded in clouds and other times breathtakingly clear, at which point bare deforested patches can be seen. Houses alongside the highway include large fenced-in haciendas as well as small wooden shacks on stilts. The contrast between Guayaquil's gleaming bus terminal and the more rustic housing encountered on rural highways reflects factors such as the historical city-oriented flows of wealth from Ecuador's banana booms. Reinvestment of banana boom profits supported a diversified portfolio of money-making activities in industry and finance in Guayaquil, leading to what Larrea terms an amplified "breach between the countryside and the city."[3]

Buses pass through numerous small towns, with roadside stalls selling packaged foods, fruits and vegetables from the country's amazing agricultural abundance, impressive fish from the nearby Pacific, large purple crabs tied in stacks, and prepared foods such as *chicharrón* (fried pork fat).

Various vendors climb on the bus at stops to sell food, drinks, or cheap consumer goods. I once heard one describe himself as part of an *ejército de chicos* (army of boys) eking out a living on buses across the country, one 25-cent chocolate bar or bag of peanuts at a time. Others climb on to share a story, asking for support with the costs of chronic illness, child-raising, or surgery. These requests sometimes enlist divine help and use visual aids such as—once, memorably—an attached, full colostomy bag. Billboards and messages stencilled on cement walls surrounding roadside properties highlight political candidates or specific government programs. During my time in the country these largely promoted the Alianza País government of Rafael Correa (2007–17) and his successor Lenín Moreno (Alianza País was voted out of office in 2021). The Correa period saw Ecuadorians frequently informed via such media of the exciting progress of the government's "Citizens' Revolution": *La revolución ciudadana avanza!*

Commercial billboards are also common, a large proportion related to banana production. Ads for pesticides often feature violent or sporty English-language names, such as Killer, Rugby, or Volley, that evoke what Vandana Shiva has termed "the violence of the Green Revolution."[4] The gendered nature of such violence also comes through, as in a fertilizer billboard featuring a sexy silhouetted woman looking out over a verdant green field. Some ads belong to Ecuadorian chemical and agricultural companies such as Ecuaquímica or Agripac and others to pesticide transnationals such as BASF, Syngenta, and Dow. As in the Andes, the relationship of such scenery to the films that play inside buses is jarring. In a vivid linkage of cinematic violence and petroleum-fuelled Green Revolution violence, I once tore my attention away from *Furious 7* (in the long-running *Fast & Furious* series of car-racing action films) to glance outside at a pesticide billboard. The chemical being advertised was named with a verb, *Balear*, meaning to spray with bullets. Almost simultaneously, the movie reached its climax in a seemingly endless car chase with constant gunfire: *balear*.

As the bus distances itself from Guayaquil, land uses change to feature more cattle grazing, wooded lots, increasing amounts of cacao, and, eventually, mile after mile of banana plantations. Such farms feature rows of plants as big as trees, with leaves that flop diagonally up and out or point straight upwards to conserve moisture in the midday heat. Translucent plastic bags in green, blue, or red mark the banana bunches. Familiar names and logos adorn structures or signs at such plantations: Dole, Chiquita, Del Monte, the Ecuadorian-owned Bonita (Noboa's brand), and less-familiar labels such as Bonanza (formerly Russian, sold to the Japanese company Sumifru in 2015). Workers in the fields carry out tasks such as cutting down heavy mature bunches of bananas, with another worker catching them on a large, cushioned pad held on one shoulder. Workers can be seen on smaller farms with backpack sprayers and a variety of protective gear, from full biohazard-style suits with facemasks and gloves to flimsier masks, pants, rubber boots, and long-sleeved shirts. Fumigation planes can often be seen in the distance, sometimes passing over houses or schools near plantations, and sometimes close enough that they leave a perceptible odour and taste of fungicide lingering within the bus.

As the bus nears Machala the frequency of plantations seems to increase, as if in response to the strengthening gravitational field of the world's banana capital. Before the construction of the city's new bus terminal, interprovincial buses would drive directly into the centre of town. The route passes the approximate dividing line between banana plantations and Machala's urban frontier not far from the city's mall (*El Shopping*), and a roundabout with *el bananero,* a monument to a nameless, shirtless man with a machete in his hand and a bunch of bananas hoisted on his shoulder. Out of eyesight north of the road are informal settlements resulting from past land invasions of disused banana plantations, with rudimentary houses and patchy access to municipal services.

Closer to the road are plazas with stores such as pricey supermarkets and upscale clothing shops. Larrea notes that the dramatic growth of Machala and regional markets for goods and services needed by the influx of banana workers during the 1948–65 period helped to establish a "regional bourgeoisie" in the city.[5] Such agricultural roots of Machala's wealth are reflected in the proximity to *El Shopping* of a fertilizer store, next to billboards such as ones showing Bobcat or RYC tractors operating amidst banana plants. A receiving facility for bananas to be exported by Grupo Noboa is found nearby, along with facilities for producing cardboard, plastics, and other inputs required for modern banana production. Finally, the area contains Ecuaquímica's office, its outside bearing logos such as Monsanto's folksy branch-and-leaves insignia, as well as those of pesticide multinationals such as Syngenta, the Belgian company Janssen Pharmaceuticals, and the Dutch company Cerexagri.

As the bus continues west into downtown on Avenida 9 de Mayo, it passes shops, numerous restaurants, pharmacies, lone sidewalk vendors,

Figure 12.01: Pesticide brands available in coastal Ecuador

and open-air market stalls selling food (increasingly "healthy" options), clothing, electronics, and other consumer goods. Also for sale are natural medicines, from modern nutritional supplements to traditional remedies such as dried snakes and a plant named *sangre de drago* (dragon's blood) from Ecuador's Amazon region. Peppering this commercial mixture are several agricultural input stores with backpack sprayers and pesticide containers displayed in welcoming storefronts, with pesticide company logos on posters.

Toxic agricultural chemicals are thus embedded in Machala's streetscapes, alongside health-promoting foods and medicines. Similarly in the city's athletic stadium, which buses on 9 de Mayo pass as they traverse downtown on their way to the city's port, Puerto Bolívar. Early mornings see upper- and middle-class *machaleños* walking or running around the track, taking advantage of one of the few places in the city where such forms of exercise can be safely and feasibly accomplished. A *bailoterapia* (dance therapy) class sees mostly women moving energetically to sped-up versions of already up-tempo popular Latin songs. I remember one trip to the stadium when those frenetic movements and the more sedate weight- and blood-pressure-controlling efforts of the walkers and joggers on the track were presided over by two giant billboards advertising Fumipalma, a company specializing in aerial fumigations to control the black sigatoka fungus on banana farms.

Once a year, 9 de Mayo is taken over by a parade in which the competitors for the title of Banana Queen of the World make their entrance into the city. The industry-financed *Feria Mundial del Banano* (World Banana Fair) takes place every September, celebrating and helping shore up Machala's identity as the world's banana capital. When I observed the parade in 2011, the candidates for queen, *las reinas*—over a dozen young, attractive women from mostly banana-producing countries[6]—glided through downtown standing next to soldiers with rifles in the backs of slow-moving pickup trucks, waving and wearing pageant dresses with sashes displaying the names of their home countries. Another key stage is a swimsuit competition on the beach at Jambelí, a mangrove-covered group of islands separated from Puerto Bolívar by waters from which banana boats depart for Europe and North America. The day after the swimsuit competition, local newspapers publish centrefolds showing *las reinas* posed together in their bikinis. In an especially objectifying parallel, the flyer for one year's *Feria* featured the previous year's smiling queen on the panel opposite a giant *racimo* (bunch) of bananas with a crown on it—the Banana King, or the largest and most valuable *racimo* grown in the region.[7]

As Ecuadorian geographers have shown, the unsettling landscapes of banana-producing coastal Ecuador reflect the inequitable history of banana production over the twentieth century and its extension into the twenty-first—in ways that ultimately shape the health of the people who inhabit those territories.[8] The contradictions written into such landscapes are many: the routine permeation of living and working spaces by toxic chemicals and the companies who make them, surrounded by both modern and traditional efforts to promote health; warlike portrayals of pest control in agriculture, along with "armies" of boys attesting to a giant pool of exploitable labour; incredible cultural and culinary diversity coexisting with monocultural banana agroindustry, transnational chemical companies, and pervasive American popular culture; extremes of wealth bordered by grinding poverty; revolutions both Green and Citizens'; and routine racialized stereotyping of different social groups and objectification of women. This part of the book attempts to make sense of such dynamics and their implications for the health of people connected to bananas. It extends the history told in Parts 1 and 2 by drawing on my own ethnographic data collection in the twenty-first century and an extended focus on one specific context: the banana capital of the world and the rural regions that surround it.

CHAPTER 13

TWENTY-FIRST-CENTURY SOCIALISM AND CONTEMPORARY FORMS OF SLAVERY

The twenty-first century began with an extension of Ecuador's role as the non-unionized leader of the banana industry's globalized "race to the bottom," as documented in the influential Human Rights Watch (HRW) report of 2002 and other sources.[1] The consequences of this "leadership" for worker health and the environment would trigger specifically Ecuadorian types of resistance in the form of social movements and related public health research.

In a development that took place too late to be documented by HRW, 1,400 workers on Noboa's seven-plantation Hacienda Los Álamos in Guayas province sought to unionize in 2002, asking for basic rights such as the legally required minimum wage and enrolment in Ecuador's social security system.[2] The company immediately fired more than 100 workers, including the labour leaders, and declined to renew the temporary contracts of many more. The workers then went on strike, before being beaten and threatened by an estimated 400 masked and armed men who also invaded and robbed their homes. One worker shot in the confrontation lost his leg, while the police assisted with the eviction of the striking workers' families from company-owned housing and the replacement of workers with strikebreakers. In response to the strike and international solidarity actions such as a campaign by the US Labor Education in the Americas Project to pressure Noboa via a major banana purchaser, Costco, Noboa promised to improve health services and personal protective equipment for workers and address the problem of unpaid overtime hours. Still, the union was never recognized, and its organizers were never re-hired.[3]

Despite the notoriety of his company's operations, Álvaro Noboa—Ecuador's richest man at the time—felt confident enough to run multiple times for president of Ecuador. In the 2006 presidential election, Noboa won the first round of voting but with insufficient votes to avoid a runoff. His main rival was a young US-trained economist from Guayaquil named Rafael Correa, whose campaign had included vehement attacks on the exploitative labour-management practices of the banana industry. In a statement that clearly indicted Noboa, Correa vowed that he would not allow Ecuador "to be converted into a banana plantation."[4] The runoff election would bring victory to Correa's Alianza País coalition of labour, Indigenous, environmental, and other civil society groups. Correa's "twenty-first-century socialism" promised a new era in which Ecuador's wealth would be both reclaimed from foreign imperialism and redistributed to the country's poor.[5] His economic reforms accordingly strengthened redistributive social programs and state capacity to deliver them, thereby countering decades of neoliberal gutting of public services.[6]

Correa's government also expressed substantial rhetorical support for nature and Indigenous rights and launched a national constituent assembly to develop a new Ecuadorian constitution.[7] The 2008 constitution was lauded globally as a model of respect for social justice, Indigenous peoples, and the environment, the latter reflecting its groundbreaking inclusion of the right of nature (*Pachamama*, in Kichwa) to be protected. The constitution assumed a special relevance in banana-producing regions via its inclusion of a right to health and a right to live in a healthy environment.

Rights for workers were operationalized soon after through measures such as Mandate 8, which outlawed the practice of banana farm owners dodging legal responsibilities to their employees by subcontracting to *capitanes* (captains) who supplied them with workers.[8] A new requirement to affiliate workers to Ecuador's social security system similarly promised to improve banana workers' standard of living. Policies invoking the concept of food sovereignty (a concept discussed in more detail in Chapter 25) were also promised by Correa, including overtures towards land reform.[9] Nevertheless, a 2010 complaint by the Ecuadorian worker rights organization ASTAC sparked an investigation by the UN special rapporteur on contemporary forms of slavery. The investigation found that forced labour practices were indeed ongoing in Ecuadorian banana production, despite measures such as Mandate 8.¹⁰

Such labour rights abuses are incentivized by the contract-based model that came to dominate banana production in the Cavendish era, especially in Ecuador. It allows exporters (transnational or Ecuadorian) to avoid the risky business of banana growing but maintain control over the profitable sales end of the supply chain.¹¹ Control over shipping and marketing are key components of how transnational corporations—fruit and increasingly supermarket companies in recent decades—maintain their market share, and the lion's share of profits.¹² Exporters sign contracts for certain quantities of bananas with large farm owners or small producer co-operatives, but typically need more fruit than is contracted for. They can then pick up the rest of what consumers demand at wildly fluctuating market rates, whether from their contracted farms or from farmers without contracts.

The precarity and downward risk-shifting of contract-based banana production is passed on by farmers to workers, and, through pesticide contamination, to the more-than-human communities that populate and surround plantations.¹³ Producers facing uncertain demand for their bananas tend to avoid financial commitments to workers whenever possible, often hiring by the day or for longer periods but with no contractually guaranteed job security. Production decisions on farms, moreover, have been largely controlled via contracts and their stringent quality requirements for perfect fruit. The typical result is a mandated heavy use of pesticides that reduces farmers' risk of having shipments rejected but increases the health risks of workers and more-than-human communities such as downstream aquatic ecosystems. Even fairtrade-certified Ecuadorian banana farmers in the first decade of the twenty-first century were found by a Fairtrade Foundation–commissioned examination to have problematic relationships with their workers, although in less egregious ways than on larger plantations.¹⁴

In addition to outright violent union suppression such as at Hacienda Los Álamos, farm owners on medium- and large-scale farms have historically used a variety of tactics to keep unions from forming, such as (illegal) worker blacklists that make labour organizers unemployable. Ongoing violations of banana worker rights have been enabled by the presence of a huge underemployed pool of landless and exploitable workers in the coastal region (also explaining the *ejército de chicos* or "army of boys").[15] The availability of this pool of labour reflects histories of dispossession and land concentration stretching back to the Spanish conquest, continuing through the agribusiness-promoting policies of twentieth-century Ecuadorian governments and their intensification with neoliberal reforms of the 1980s and '90s.[16]

Banana producers lacking guaranteed contracts, or fearing the loss of their contracts in hyper-competitive globalized banana markets, are incentivized to cut corners on worker health and safety. This often compromises training of workers; time for them to wash their hands before eating lunch; provision of PPE such as gloves, overalls, and facemasks; or observance of re-entry periods following pesticide application. By not observing the required waiting time after a pesticide is applied, producers can often squeeze a bit more labour out of their workers. The extreme example occurs when workers are not actually allowed to leave the field during aerial fumigation and are bathed in fungicide (as in the heartbreaking accounts of the children interviewed by Human Rights Watch).

As in Central America, such health risks caught the attention of health researchers, though largely without the presence of Northern epidemiologists. Several studies originated in a Quito-based organization called IFA, led by a physician named Raúl Harari and facilitated by the workers' organization FENACLE (Federación Nacional de Trabajadores Agroindustriales de Campesinos e Indígenas Libres del Ecuador) before it lost strength in the Correa years.[17] IFA studies on the health effects of pesticides in banana production were published as early as 1989 and a small study of DBCP-exposed workers was carried out in 1998, with additional studies conducted over the following decade. Such studies revealed unacceptable toxic exposures and related health impacts, using techniques such as biological sampling and fluorescent tracers that cause skin exposed to pesticides to dramatically light up under UV light.[18]

Another epidemiologic account of the health effects of pesticides emerged from a 2004 conflict around aerial fumigations, involving banana workers and residents of the community of Las Ramas in Guayas province, which drew in the Quito-based environmental organization

Acción Ecológica.[19] The resulting study, led by a physician named Adolfo Maldonado, found higher rates of cancer and much higher rates of congenital malformations in Las Ramas than in a control community (14 children compared to 1). Sampling and analysis of well water and soil in the community showed the worrisome presence of several pesticides with known serious impacts.

At approximately the same time, a group of fumigation pilots (which would eventually crystallize into ASTAC) made a formal complaint about pesticide-related health impacts to Ecuador's Defensoría del Pueblo (Office of the Ombudsperson).[20] In response to symptoms listed in the complaint such as nausea, blurred vision, and abnormal heartbeat, the Defensoría commissioned a study by Dr. Jaime Breilh of the Universidad Andina Simón Bolívar in Quito, also involving Acción Ecológica's Adolfo Maldonado and another Quito-based NGO, CEAS (Centro de Estudios y Asesoría en Salud). The study confirmed the existence of worrisome health impacts potentially related to pesticide exposure among the pilots, as well as in communities near plantations.

But while such studies showed that working and living conditions associated with banana production were clearly conducive to massive and worrisome toxic exposures (among other health hazards), conclusive "proof" of health harms did not emerge in this period. Likely reflecting funding and time constraints, the studies that were conducted were exclusively "cross-sectional" ones measuring outcomes and exposures at a single point in time. These—it was drilled into my head during my own epidemiology training—are viewed by epidemiologists as providing preliminary or exploratory insights that can motivate further research, but as incapable of generating proof of a causal effect.[21]

As I realized when planning my own research in 2009 and 2010, more conclusive epidemiology studies were prevented by reasons previously identified by epidemiologists studying pesticide-exposed banana workers in Central America: poor quality data in resource-poor countries; uncooperative employers creating a climate of secrecy and fear; "confounding" of pesticide-health relationships by numerous possible alternative causes of ill health among impoverished worker populations; and complex, changing chemical mixtures that would tax even well-funded epidemiologists' abilities to detect cause-and-effect relationships.

Beyond such methodological limitations were epistemological and political ones. In the theorization of Jaime Breilh, Northern epidemiology focuses on supposedly independent risk factors and neglects the upstream forces (especially capitalism and imperialism) driving or "socially determining" whole constellations of health outcomes.[22] In addition, the limited victories obtained for banana workers using epidemiology in Costa Rica were not reproduced in Ecuador, despite the existence of the Central American studies and the fact that the same chemicals and even more dangerous working conditions were present in Ecuador.[23] But while epidemiologic evidence remained incomplete or largely powerless, toxic exposures were ongoing and left other forms of "evidence," in the embodied experiences, stories, and ways of life of banana farmers, workers, and communities.

CHAPTER 14
A QUESTION OF CULTURE

The shortcomings of environmental health sciences when it comes to protecting marginalized communities from environmental injustice are well known to social scientists, who now view specific chemical exposures as symptoms of a more generalized and metaphorical toxicity in the form of inequitable power relations.[1] A few decades ago, comparable insights were drawn by anthropologists who researched aspects of such communities' culture—especially the stories they told about health and illness—as responses to the unfair workings of capitalism those communities were experiencing.[2] But when I looked for *la cultura de la costa* (the culture of the coastal region) in an effort to be in solidarity with such responses to injustice, I arrived at another set of complications. What I found would link the racism that built the banana industry in the early twentieth century with the Green Revolution ideologies and individualizing ("victim-blaming") narratives that guided it into the pesticide-soaked Cavendish era, and that continue to perpetuate situations of injustice in the banana industry and beyond.

I initially tried to find the culture of the coastal region by reading about it. One previously mentioned epidemiologic effort by the Quito-based organization IFA on banana worker health justifies its use of fluorescent tracer methods to show pesticide exposure by saying that such visual approaches "speak much more than words, especially in peasant areas where there is a strong oral, but not reading, culture."[3] In keeping with the focus of much anthropologic work on illness narratives, I also found some references to "traditional" medical practices and beliefs such as the folk illnesses *susto* (fright) or *mal de ojo* (evil eye).[4] When I actually started talking to people, however, I found that their understandings of health did not actually reflect the violent tendencies, promiscuity, or superstition pejoratively attributed to *costeños* by widespread stereotypes (although one university-educated woman did explain to me that going to traditional healers was good for problems such as *susto* that are not amenable to modern medical treatments). People instead largely relied on modern medical terminology to describe health and illness, including the impacts of pesticides.

Similarly belying stereotypes of *costeños* as lazy, my interviewees generally defined health as an ability to work. As one person told me, "Health is the primary thing, it's the basic thing for a human being. Without health, there's no progress, there's no work. The body needs to be full of health to develop all of its potential to work." I interpreted this to reflect the fact that, for farmers and workers in El Oro, survival and social reproduction largely depend on their ability to participate in the labour-intensive process of banana cultivation. I therefore decided that the dangerous uncertainty inherent in contract-based banana production was behind another tendency I observed, for health to be portrayed as precarious. Several respondents described their health as good but hastened to add that they did not know what long-term conditions (cancer, for example) might be lurking within: "I'd say [that my health is] good, because if I say 'excellent,' you never know. You never know what problems are sick inside. You don't know the hour, or the day, when you'll get sick and go to the other side."

I also detected the resistance to structural inequities I was looking for, in the form of power-conscious explanations many people gave for pesticide exposures and other health hazards, which clearly indicted the Ecuadorian elites and transnational interests who control banana markets. As one banana worker informed me, "When the airplane fumigates, people are inside the plantations. You have to leave for an hour or a half-hour, but it's not being observed. Why? It's clearly related to the interests of the owners of the plantations—especially the plantations that fumigate with airplanes. It isn't convenient for the boss that his people lose an hour or two, so they have to stay in the plantations when the airplanes are fumigating."

The situation was just as bad, I was told, for workers housed on plantations:

> People live in the banana farms. I'm telling you in the case of my friends, they can't say anything to the boss because they're living on his land. So if they're living on his land then they have to tolerate it, because—all the same—they're working for him, to live . . . so, because there's not work and this is what they know how to do, then, they have to put up with it . . . they have to know how to survive this . . . where they are . . . so they can't say anything, because if they do they'll be kicked off.

But while narratives portraying *costeños* as hard-working and conscious of the inequities of banana production fit with the resistance-to-capitalism motif the illness-narratives literature led me to expect, I soon ran into themes that not only did not fit such an interpretation but actually seemed to directly conflict with it. Instead of—or in addition to—expressing resistance to the hugely unfair dynamics of agro-industrial capitalism that shape life in coastal Ecuador and other banana-producing regions, for example, many people I interviewed began to point fingers at their fellow *costeños*. As one university-educated small banana producer put it when asked to explain pesticide exposures,

> Some people don't want to protect themselves. There are people who don't like it, including workers. You say to them, "Look, you're going to fumigate, put on this hat, put on these goggles to protect your vision, put on gloves, boots." They say, "No, no, no, no, it doesn't affect me, I'm a strong man." You say, "Put on this mask," and they say, "No, I can't breathe, it's too hot." The pesticide applicator, if we're going to fumigate for the black sigatoka, doesn't want to [protect himself]. It bothers him, suffocates him, is uncomfortable with the goggles or the protective clothing, so some go uncovered [*pelado*]. So, it's a question of culture [*una cuestion de cultura*] as well, no?

So after showing up looking for *la cultura de la costa*, I appeared to have found it—or at least a version of *cultura* that reappeared with disturbing regularity when *costeños* with some money and education, usually urban, described their poorer, usually rural, compatriots. In fact, many such people described their own health and well-being as shaped by inequitable power dynamics, but also described the poor health of less-privileged, rural landless others as *their own fault*. In such explanations, health was attributed to behaviours such as healthy eating and avoiding alcohol or cigarettes, while pesticide exposure was attributed to carelessness, including improper use of PPE such as gloves and facemasks.

Complementing such explanations, many urban *costeños* involved in banana production described their rural counterparts in ways ranging from being "apart from society" and lacking motivation, to being inbred and engaging in superstitious or folkloric explanations of the resulting congenital abnormalities. Attribution of the poor health of such rural peoples to individual behaviours and characteristics then flowed smoothly into recommendations for better education. As another university-educated small farmer explained, "There are people who eat anything and think that filling their belly more means they're better fed, when that's not the case. It's not a question of eating a certain quantity of food, but rather quality. So, it's *something cultural that we need to change* little by little."

I hadn't shown up in Ecuador with the naïveté to think I would be straightforwardly "saving" anyone, but I was disconcerted that many of the people I encountered there had such ambitions themselves. What's more, such aspirations often flowed directly out of individualizing or victim-blaming narratives of pesticide risk and health that seemed to echo ineffective and oppressive "safe use" approaches to pesticide safety pushed by the chemical and agribusiness sectors and their academic apologists. As I related my findings to ethnographic pesticide risk perception studies done elsewhere in Latin America and around the world, however, I found comparable patterns in how people of different social backgrounds understand pesticide risk. In such studies, some people do indeed indict powerful interests such as "the rich" and multinational corporations, but many others blame pesticide-exposed workers and farmers, in ways that reflect their position in agricultural supply chains (or put differently, their position in relation to the means of agricultural production).[5] In a study done in Chiapas, Mexico, for example, pesticide-exposed farmers, agricultural extension agents, and health professionals interpreted the causes of pesticide exposures in diametrically opposed ways, generally pointing fingers at one another.⁶ Workers interviewed in a study of highland Ecuadorian potato production described pesticide exposure as an occupational hazard, and suicide via pesticide ingestion as an act of desperation; employers, in contrast, attributed pesticide exposures to worker carelessness, and suicide using pesticides to insanity.⁷ In short, the trend I was observing in coastal Ecuador cohered with numerous studies showing how the people most vulnerable to pesticide risk—who are generally the least successful in agricultural market structures—are frequently blamed for their own exposures and poor health, in ways that leave out the structural causes of such vulnerabilities.⁸

I have since learned to recognize likely origins of such ways of making sense of poverty and its toxic impacts. Histories of Northern environmental and occupational health sciences document the exaggerated belief of many toxicologists and the chemical industry that pesticides can be used safely in real-world conditions, a belief grounded in laboratory-scale evidence showing supposedly "safe" thresholds of exposure.⁹ Green Revolution stories in which industrial agriculture solves the problems of "developing countries" readily incorporate and amplify such beliefs. The neoliberal ideology that was forcibly imposed on Latin America, together with enormous quantities of toxic pesticides in the Cold War period, has in turn only strengthened such fictions blaming the problems of poor people on individual failures while exonerating societal structures.

I also learned that the *cultura* people were talking about in relation to pesticide exposures (i.e., something that was lacking in their poorer, less healthy compatriots) did not specifically refer to some anthropologically noteworthy set of characteristics such as folkloric beliefs, kinship structures, or traditional dress and foods. It translates, rather, as "refinement" or "education," and has disturbing historical resonances in Ecuador that cohere neatly with the individualizing focus of neoliberal and (some, problematic) health science perspectives on pesticides. Ecuador's agricultural development policy decisions have been historically guided by racist narratives in which modern, productive agriculture could be best managed by white immigrants or by the kinds of Ecuadorians—typically urban, white(r) ones—who did not lack *cultura*. Such agricultural ideologies extended racist explanations of Ecuador's "Indian problem" in the 1930s and '40s, when Indigenous poverty was widely attributed to lack of *cultura*, with accompanying social ills such as alcoholism, poor nutrition, and poor hygiene—all to be addressed through education.¹⁰

In that the poverty of Ecuador's Indigenous peoples has clear roots in colonial and post-independence racist exploitation, their supposed culture (and its identification with a lack of refinement or *cultura*) has also functioned to make exploitation vanish and to replace it with something far less sinister and more amenable to repair through paternalistic state intervention.[11] Like faith in the benefits of pesticides and other agricultural technologies, such racism in Ecuador's past has meshed readily with Green Revolution narratives imported into the country under the guise of development.[12] Indigenous and Afro-descended Ecuadorians have been the groups most consistently said to lack *cultura* and therefore suitability as agents of agricultural development in such narratives, but the elaborate system of racial hierarchies in Ecuador—summarized using the concept of *mestizaje*—has made the situation especially complex. *Mestizaje* in Ecuador blends racialized categories based on Indigeneity and blackness or whiteness with class (and *cultura*) and geographic location, including status as urban workers or rural peasants.[13] Thus the expansive racial category of *mestizo* has numerous subdivisions, with whiter *mestizos*—in terms of skin tone but also behaviours (*cultura*), wealth, and urbanity—generally afforded higher status than physically darker *mestizos* with less refined, implicitly Indigenous or African, behaviours and characteristics.[14]

The stereotypes concerning rural residents of *la costa* I had previously read about also turn out to bear a complex relationship to such racial hierarchies and to the political economy of banana production—and by extension to how its health impacts are distributed and experienced across social groups. Such stereotypes, which reach as far back as the late nineteenth century, when migration to the region responded to the cacao boom, have originated as much—or more—in the city of Guayaquil as in *la sierra*.[15] The Indigenous or poor, rural *mestizo* roots of Andean migrants, combined with the substantial presence of Afro-Ecuadorians in the coastal region, have tinged regional stereotypes about *costeños* with elements of white supremacy. Such stereotypes function as a rhetorical resource that both *serranos* and urban *costeños* can use to explain rural poverty in *la costa*. This kind of "explanation" leaves out the enormous wealth generated by rural areas—especially through agro-industrial cacao and later banana production—and the ways in which that wealth has accumulated in cities such as Machala, Guayaquil, and Quito.

And so my search for culture as it related to pesticides and health uncovered uses of *cultura* that drew on intersecting class and racial hierarchies in

Ecuadorian society and the agricultural peoples and practices that figure so prominently in it. While the *costeños* I interviewed might themselves be called *monos* (monkeys) by residents of *la sierra*, their frequent tendency to blame toxic exposures and ill health on the inherent carelessness and lack of *cultura* of poor, rural banana workers resonated with common essentializing narratives making skewed sense of urban-rural disparities in *la costa*.

I would eventually publish interpretations of such results that contextualize them in light of Ecuador's complex racial and regional hierarchies, and well-established relationships between class position and interpretations of pesticide risk.[16] Such findings also reflected my lack of success at doing deep ethnographic research with the banana workers most vulnerable to pesticide exposures, as my interview sample ended up disproportionately including small banana producers with some property and post-secondary education (the fact that relatively privileged populations who hold middle- to upper-class sensibilities are the easiest to study is a truism of ethnographic research). One major discomfort stemming from the interpretations that have culminated in my academic publications, however, relates to the risk of unfairly judging people for their understandable reactions to the inequities of banana production, and then publishing about them in international peer-reviewed journals. What's more, these were often people who had been quite helpful in facilitating my research (either as individuals or through their co-operatives), and with whom I got along quite well. They also had the most in common with me in terms of education and even sometimes work or travel experiences and relatives in North America and Europe. The next chapter therefore takes a more explicitly compassionate approach to understanding how such people experience their position within globalized commodity chains.

CHAPTER 15

THE ILLNESS OF THE CENTURY

One of the more pleasant interviews I conducted took place near the end of my primary fieldwork period in 2011, outside the semi-rural office of a fairtrade banana producer co-operative. The four women who participated in the interview comprised two small farmers, as well as an agricultural engineer and an accountant employed by the co-op. In talking with them I started to gain a sense of the important ways in which the inequities and uncertainties of banana production are lived and viscerally experienced through people's feelings.[1] And while it was women who were most forthcoming about the emotional dimensions of life in the chemical and social toxicity of Ecuador's banana regions, such an affective lens also helps make sense of men's experiences—and, ultimately, of prospects for challenging the power structures generating that toxicity.

The women's no-nonsense outfits belied the sexualized image portrayed by the Banana Queen competition and Chiquita's Machala mural. The women did, however, display familiar tendencies to attribute the poor health of rural members of the landless banana workforce to individual deficiencies such as alcoholism and lack of education. While I had become accustomed to such individualizing perspectives by that point, I was surprised at the rich details that emerged. As one of the women explained,

> I've noticed that the people who work near where I live, it's
> full of banana farms and the people live there, no? That's

the zone—pure delinquency. I'm telling you, you pay them their week, but people don't know how to make use of their money, and they just devote themselves to drinking. They drink, they drink too much. And their children, also, end up drinking. There's a guy there who works with my father, the son drinks already, the other brother as well. You learn what you see. And they don't pay attention to feeding themselves. And also, they don't protect themselves, because it's necessary to use certain chemical products, right? Over time, this affects your health. And they're thin, not taken care of. But it's not because they're not getting paid, but because they don't use their weekly pay like they should. You see this a lot there. There are a lot of these people. They don't take care of themselves. You give them gloves and everything, but they don't, it's their way, how do you say, of being. *Because of their ignorance*, they don't protect themselves.

The progression from individualizing explanations to educational aspirations I had learned to recognize was especially striking in this interview: "Well, you have to teach them, right? I don't know, design some talks so they can be guided, told that if they keep drinking, alcohol can give them cirrhosis. Talks to motivate them to have better health. And these talks would be, practically speaking, *for people in the countryside*. Lots of times people don't listen to the advice you give them. They say: what's this got to do with me, why are you interfering in our lives? So I don't know how to arrive at these people, *to save them*, no?"

But while stereotypes about "people in the countryside" that blame them for their own misfortunes have a sordid history in Ecuador and a tendency to naturalize social inequities around the world, I couldn't just dismiss these kind and thoughtful women as dupes of capitalist ideology and its various essentialisms. The very real stresses they were facing in their lives pointed to a reality that was anything but comfortable. While a mission to "save" the rural poor is definitely associated with positions of privilege, the fragility of that privilege was belied by comments about mental health that emerged when I asked health-related questions. As one woman explained in reference to the ongoing crisis caused by low banana prices in late 2011, "We also should have mental health, psychological health. Because with such a crisis, one ends up in turmoil [*trastornada*]. The illness of the century is stress." Another woman elaborated on the dual pressures of fast-paced work in the banana sector and women's disproportionate share of household labour: "Imagine, I get up at five in the morning, I make the [family's] lunch, then at seven I come here [to the co-op office], really quickly ... Imagine, living an accelerated life ... Right now, there's a deadly stress [*un estrés fatal*]."

The woman who was most vocal on the "pure delinquency" of the countryside and the alcoholism and ignorance of the banana workforce also shared her own stress-related health challenges:

> Although I'm diabetic, I've always considered myself a healthy, happy, stable person. I always viewed life—you have to keep pressing on, I would say, but always okay. Some months ago, there was a change. I felt stressed, preoccupied, every day the same. And the bus [between her home and the co-op office] was robbed twice that week. Thankfully my son didn't have to go that time, but he tells me that sometimes he gets on and immediately gets off. There are robberies [*asaltos*], it's a danger. My other son lives in Guayaquil. I have to be waiting, on eggshells [*pendiente*], calling him, but if he doesn't answer—things like that. So I walk around so stressed. It's almost too much. I've had to do therapy but didn't find a solution.

So while these women did reproduce problematic "victim-blaming" narratives in which rural *costeños* lack *cultura* and are prone to carelessness, alcoholism, and violence, such narratives appeared to play a role in the lives of people who were themselves frequently struggling. They were struggling with things like the very real risk that they or their children would be the victim of an armed robbery, or that they would lose their farm if banana prices dropped too low or their co-op lost a key contract in the "accelerated life" produced by the neoliberalization of Ecuador's economy.[2] The weight of banana production's twentieth-century history, culminating in Ecuador's poverty- and crime-generating neoliberal reforms, was falling on their shoulders in ways that were embodied through experiences of "deadly stress" and threats to relationships that were important to them, such as with their families.

If individualizing narratives help relatively privileged groups in society duck responsibility for their complicity with the structures creating privilege and poverty, then it doesn't seem like those narratives always do such a good job. A banana farmer who voiced what could be termed *neoliberal narratives*[3] about the individual personal failures of people in the countryside—alcoholism, ignorance, violence—was herself, poignantly, on the verge of collapse while "pressing on" as a diabetic single mother working to keep a family safe and a banana farm afloat.

Such stories illustrate how people in *la costa* experience and react to inequitable circumstances in ways that involve their feelings, bodies, and interpersonal (or even human-environment) relationships.[4] And as with the oppressive conditions generating "the illness of the century" (i.e., stress), so too were supportive and helpful circumstances filtered through the emotions and social relationships of Ecuadorians (male and female) embedded in the banana industry.[5] Positive affective reactions frequently stemmed from experiences of social support through banana producer co-operatives and the transnational solidarity associated with fairtrade and organic contracts. Indeed, the same women told me that, in the face of uncertain banana markets and the stress they engendered, talks by foreign experts organized by their fairtrade co-op helped motivate them to "keep fighting." As one put it, "The fact that we sell our fruit through fairtrade, that's a lot, because it motivates us, and not only ourselves, but also for our community through the premium" (a supplement to the price of every case of bananas that goes to social projects among fairtrade producers and their communities). They even urged me to return to share the results of my research with them once they were available, making me feel that I was part of relationships that might help mitigate the impacts of being small, isolated individuals in vast, competitive arenas dominated by larger players.

When I started to look, I found comparable—but varied—patterns in how other farmers, workers, and community members emotionally and relationally experienced the unfair and toxic world of banana production. One male agricultural engineer in charge of pesticide applications on a large plantation, for example, mused that his decades of working with agrochemicals might leave him with long-term impacts, then smiled wryly as his wife joked from the kitchen that he might "end up sterile." However, in contrast to this fatalistic response to the uncertainties of pesticide risk and its entanglement with his family relationships was the dream he described of retiring to farm bananas organically. Such organic ambitions were in fact quite widespread and illustrate the fact that relationships with the more-than-human world also often emerged as sources of hope or concern. The four women discussed above added that talks from foreign experts in the fairtrade co-op's office helped them "be more organic." Another female small farmer (from a different co-op) movingly described her transition to organic farming and the entanglement of health and environmental concerns with emotional reactions to banana markets:

> In the time when we were conventional, *we suffered a lot*. The small producer is always last. The big producers always got the exports and when there was extra demand, the small producers would get it. Apart from this, chemical products can affect your health. So we heard of [an organic co-operative], and we decided to start like that. But even when we were conventional, we never used nematicide because it always damages the earth. The earth dries, the bacteria, fungi, everything dies.

Similarly, one young banana worker who also carried out part-time health promotion work for a local foundation lamented the fact that pesticides "damage my land, where I'm going to live." This individual urged me to "incentivize" his banana co-workers so that "they could work their own land in a way that's more productive, more ecological, so also helping the environment." Another female fairtrade farmer who had migrated from *la sierra* expressed sadness at banana production's apparent decimation of the coastal region's biodiversity: "When I was little, you didn't need any chemicals. You could pick a banana wherever you wanted, or a fruit, and it was healthy. Now, because of the sigatoka, if you plant an orange tree over here, the airplane fumigates it and you get pure chemical. In the water, there were lots of fish, all the micro-organisms [*animalitos*]. There were little birds, butterflies. Now with the chemicals, they've gone away."

While this farmer's memory of pesticide-free production was likely not representative of the majority of banana plantations in her youth, it nevertheless attests to the emotional power of relationships with (particular corners of) the more-than-human world. But these kinds of sustaining more-than-human relationships and social supports such as fairtrade certification were not evenly available to all, as illustrated by negative affective responses to the injustices of the banana trade. In another group interview with small banana farmers—mostly men, and not fairtrade or organic certified—the difficult market conditions of late 2011 were linked with a palpable sense of anger and exhaustion to family dynamics:

> Because, you know, let's say, a well-fed child: good health, for sure. But if a child isn't well fed, what can you hope for? There's no way. This is what we lack. Because it's not fair, it's not doable, that peasant farmers are out of breath, working, there's not even a free hour to say, "I'll work until that hour and then rest." Not what's proper to have. Rain or shine, you have to be there, working and working. I can't even say I'm content as father of a family, arriving at my house, I produced so many cases of bananas and I'm going to collect my money for them, and I have to buy you kids milk, buy bread, buy you some shoes, some clothing, stuff like that. If you arrive with a little bit, to buy four little things to eat, and also to pay the worker, to give the things that help, buy bags [to protect growing bunches of bananas from insects] and what have you. I have to fumigate, I have to go buy the products [pesticides], I have to irrigate. And it's not enough. So, you end up buying not enough food, no? And because of this they're in poor health. Their health is bad.

The same farmer colourfully expressed hopelessness at the power relations of banana production, dominated in Ecuador by both transnational and local large companies. In his view, small farmers were

> at the mercy of whatever company buys what we're producing. *Now we're suffering,* now we're ruined . . . If you don't have money, how can you care for your life? You could be really half-sick, in bed, because there's no money to get cured. And this is the situation of us banana farmers. At times, one loses hope. Some deceive themselves,

> say that next year will be better. We get excited. Then the next year it's the same bullshit [*pendejada*].

Another man in the same interview expressed a sense of inevitability at toxic contamination: "We live surrounded by banana farms. Here there's one, and another on the other side, and our house is in the middle. And there's a lot of chemical, and it's affecting our health. There's not time. The plane passes and it gets you, even if you run to the house it still gets you. It bathes you." Another interview with a banana worker and labour leader, this one in the border region of Guayas and Los Ríos provinces, provided a similarly bleak portrayal of the precarity of contract-based banana production and its health consequences.

> My salary is $200 [per month]. Sometimes I don't get even that much because the plantation doesn't get a fixed price [per case of bananas]. There are days I earn ten, days I earn twenty, days I earn eight, but more or less I earn $200 monthly. I don't get enough for even the basics. Imagine if my wife or I get sick. With $200, when you get sick, how can you pay the doctor? And if we all get sick at the same time, *we'll just have to die*. Sometimes you want to complain but, out of fear or timidity, you put up with it because you have to feed your children. If you complain, they fire you.

In contrast to such negative emotions, though, were themes of resistance and hope, echoing the four women who had talked about their co-operative as a source of relief and motivation. As one male small producer put it, finding hope in a difficult situation, "Christmas is coming and every year we say, 'Happy New Year,' brother, how happy. Instead we should say, 'damn new year' [*maldito año*], because instead of being better, it's worse! This year, three months were better, and then nine months of getting screwed [*nueve meses de joda*]. But at least we have the co-operative that's giving us the same [price per case of bananas]. At least we're eating."

Looking carefully at the very human reactions of people affected by banana production in coastal Ecuador shows how forces such as neoliberal globalization and its oppressive sense of inevitability are experienced and navigated by individual people entangled in specific and emotionally mediated relationships to others. Those others included people as close as their own households and as far away as banana-consuming countries, and numerous facets of the more-than-human world. This insight suggests hope that might counter the depressing ubiquity of individualizing or victim-blaming narratives of health and pesticide risk. That is, by realizing that legitimate human emotions and needs help people (including me) to live but also sometimes to reproduce situations of injustice, we can start to see such emotional responses as understandable and possibly even temporary. In *la costa*, moreover, these affective dynamics prominently involve relationships to the global North, whether in the form of appreciation for fairtrade and organic solidarity or less conciliatory reactions to Northern control or paternalism. This realization suggested to me a need to look more carefully at my own role in such North-South entanglements.

CHAPTER 16
EL GRINGUITO

It is by now a truism of ethnographic research that the researcher's positionality—gender, age, racialized identity, class, ability, etc.—shapes the knowledge that is generated. My identity as a Canadian in Machala did indeed affect the data I collected, but also led me to disturbing realizations about the potential for research by me or other Northerners to be helpful with respect to pesticide toxicity in banana production or other socio-environmental problems in Latin America.[1]

The Ecuadorian film *Qué Tan Lejos* tells the story of a bus voyage from Quito to Cuenca taken by an Ecuadorian university student and a Spanish travel agent vacationing in the country in the 1990s. The journey is disrupted by one of the Indigenous uprisings (*levantamientos indígenas*) that rocked Ecuador in the last decade of the twentieth century. Subsequent detours taken by the travellers illustrate the country's physical and cultural diversity. One scene, for example, involves a night spent drinking around a campfire on a beach in *la costa*, ending with the travellers being robbed by their seemingly cool *costeño* host. I watched the film in the Quito apartment of my Ecuadorian friend and banana-health research colleague Pati. Pati was not there, but her mother was, talking on the phone. At one point in the film, the Spanish traveller offers sweets to a young Indigenous girl on the bus, whose mother instructs her to say thank you to *la gringuita* (the affectionate and female version of *gringo*, a word most commonly used to refer to North Americans). The Spanish woman protests that she is no *gringuita*. At the same time and seemingly independently, Pati's mother informed the family member on the other end of the line that she was in Pati's apartment with *el gringuito* (i.e., me).

Like the Spanish travel agent in *Qué Tan Lejos*, I went to Ecuador thinking *gringos* were some other category of person, not me. I soon learned that the term can encompass US residents but also more or less all Euro-descended foreigners, and thus suggests a privileged class position. One implication of this identity emerged in an interview I conducted with members of a small banana-producer co-operative, including an elderly female farmer who had migrated from *la sierra* and her son. As the son put it,

> I have an idea, now that you're here. You come from another country. We want to have a factory here. If you support us, the small producers, so much the better! With machinery, we could make juice, sweets, so many things, and give them to the schools. I always tell the friends who come from other countries, other *gringos*. *Gringos*, that's what we call you. Since you come from another country, you have more sense of these things, or better than us. *Sí o no, compañero?* [Yes or no, friend?] You should give some support here. We're also supporting you!

I had undertaken my fieldwork with the goal of finding solutions to environmental injustice, in solidarity with those most affected. I had read postcolonial and feminist theory telling me of the dangers of pretensions at objectivity, and also that the knowledge of researchers from the global North is in no way "better" than the knowledges of farmers and farm workers in banana-producing countries. In spite of this, I was being told that I had "more sense of these things, or better than us". Rather than solidarity-focused policy and structural change, this man saw my likely usefulness to him in an imagined ability to provide badly needed capital for money-making endeavours that would circumvent the 2011 banana crisis. Another small farmer in the same interview similarly set me straight regarding the real usefulness of my pesticide-focused research:

> All these chemicals are harmful. We have lots of knowledge about this. But the situation in our country is critical,

with the lowering of the price of the fruit, all the time. So we Ecuadorians, we who live from banana, we live marginalized. Because I tell you, sincerely, the government should first focus on work, on agriculture. Because from that comes the food of a whole people, and exports also. When there's good production, there's enough for everyone, enough to eat. If we focus anywhere else and forget that then the whole thing's messed up, no? And that's what's happening to us. Here the banana-exporting companies do whatever they feel like. They pay, they don't pay. They raise the price when they want to, when they feel like it. There's no respect for our signed contracts. They don't pay the official price, which is in the contract. And the government can't do anything, because they're millionaires. And they pay money under the table, and the poor people, we're always screwed [*jodidos*].

While resonating with my understanding of power dynamics in the banana industry, this not-so-subtle redirection of my focus on pesticides pinned me down as a stereotypically out-of-touch *gringo*, complete with upper-class academic and environmentalist impracticality. There was, in fact, sound public health reasoning behind challenges to my focus on pesticides, as pesticide exposures in coastal Ecuador are a symptom of broader toxicity in the form of health-damaging power relations that govern the banana trade, and life in the region more generally. In my interviews I would frequently see similar redirections away from the health effects of pesticides to broader questions of economics and inequity, sometimes before I even got through the informed consent process explaining what my study was about.

These subtle forms of pushback against the stereotypically Northern framing of my research would add to more direct challenges, such as the co-operative leader in Chapter 7 who interpreted my ethics spiel as insulting paternalism and put me in my place with a scientifically dense lecture on Northern arrogance and corporate malfeasance (but also complicit Latin American governments). But whether it led to requests to provide diplomatic or material support or anti-imperialist resentment of the idea that I might try, my identity as a *gringo* seemed to be the first, and usually the most important, thing people saw about me in *la costa*.

When I arrived in Machala in September of 2011 to begin fieldwork, I took over the apartment rented by my friend Kendra while she conducted her own fieldwork. The hotel sat one block from Machala's municipal building and the fountains and paved paths of Parque Montalvo, where resident iguanas move slowly and strolling couples move only slightly faster. It lacked hot water or an elevator but was considerably more expensive than the accommodations Ecuadorian researchers such as Pati have rented while in *la costa* (although well within what my doctoral fellowship's research and travel allowance could cover).

My discomfort at being a comparatively well-resourced foreign graduate student in hard-working Machala, with nothing more useful to do than the "deep hanging out" that is ethnographic fieldwork, was informed by feminist and science and technology studies literature about pernicious attempts to observe society from an imaginary privileged position detached from and above it (the "god trick" that enables pretensions to objectivity and disavows the racism, patriarchy, and class differences that have historically enabled the practice of science).[2] Ironically, I found myself literally above Machala society, as I looked down on it from the balcony onto the busy street corner with its open-air market and constant street noise.

Even my attempt at ethnography, involving numerous excursions on foot or by bus to conduct fieldwork, came across as leisure activity to the staff at the hotel. My constant trips up and down the stairs to my apartment led one of the staff to joke that I would always *sube y baja, sube y baja* (go up and down repeatedly). As he saw it, I was always leaving to do fun recreational things while they were always working: *usted paseando, nosotros trabajando*. But while ethnography does often resemble recreational activity (albeit with furious scribbling into little notebooks), and generally signals a social location that does not have to "work for a living" in the sense of carrying out menial labour, it did not feel very relaxing to me. I was working to a compressed schedule in which a complicated, multi-stage research project had to progress from ethics approval through preliminary observation through finalization of my interview guides to actually carrying out a respectable number of in-depth interviews. After all, I had set out to find *la cultura de la costa* and put it to work in a public health quest to make a difference.

The self-directed nature of my project meant that I was usually on my own in my travels, causing the hotel staff to ask with concern if it wasn't difficult and lonely to walk around *solito* (alone) as I was doing. It was. After a month in Machala I retreated to the highland city of Cuenca for a week of Spanish language training. My status as a semi-tourist there unexpectedly enabled a glimpse into the darker side of banana production. A fellow student connected me through her homestay family to a banana farm owner, Laura (a pseudonym), living in Cuenca and commuting regularly to her plantation in *la costa*. During our interview, Laura described her employees' tendency to misuse PPE—for example, by wearing facemasks on top of their heads instead of over the mouth and nose. She also informed me that they were frequently too drunk to work. In a logical leap that barely registered with me, she moved from such deficiencies of her banana workers to her Indigenous maid's difficulties in understanding the washing machine (though she assured me she loved the woman dearly). Laura also noted with interest my undergraduate training at McGill University and introduced me to her son, a medical student with an interest in perhaps studying there himself.

This in-depth look at the "other" side of the inequities of banana production was revealing, while also enabled by the (unintended) appearance of a shared political orientation. This appearance persisted when I returned to Machala and was invited by Laura to a "poker keno" night with her and other banana farm owners. One of the other banana farm owners in attendance tried out his English with me, a product of his time working in New Jersey, and introduced me to the tradition of drinking coffee with *humitas*, a kind of sweet corn tamale. The filter used to make the coffee, he asserted with a grin, was traditionally made from a woman's stocking. The camaraderie among the plantation owners soon extended to a frank discussion of their difficulties getting good workers and resulting need to employ illegal worker blacklists of the kind made notorious by the 2002 Human Rights Watch report and other exposés.

There was a sense of protectiveness in Laura's efforts to show me around Machala, along with admonishments that I should not "get the wrong idea" about issues such as pesticide exposure and worker rights on banana farms. She once warned me not to eat at Chinese restaurants in Ecuador (termed *chifas*) as, she explained, "Chinese people are dirty" (*los chinos son sucios*). She also applied the same description to people in Machala, or perhaps *la costa* more generally: *la gente aquí es sucia*. This latter conversation moved quickly to the need for a coup like the 1973 one in Chile, to eliminate President Correa and replace him with "a Pinochet." Such experiences with Laura vividly demonstrated how individualizing explanations for pesticide risk—overlapping with paternalistic attitudes towards Indigenous peoples—could cohere with racist and extreme-right-wing political views. They were enabled in part by my somewhat stunned take on the uncomfortable social situations I was a part of (as well as the effort it took me to follow conversations in Spanish), which seemingly allowed people to interpret my lack of reaction as agreement. They were also enabled by the fact that I was socially connected to these people. I had accepted their hospitality, after being introduced through a friend connected to Laura's family. I was the kind of person—a *gringo*—that their social circle sometimes formed personal and professional relationships with.

While not always unearthing such vivid and disturbing narratives, my time in *la costa* was shaped by social networks in which I featured as a *gringo*. The organic banana producer co-operative and Ecuadorian university professors who helped connect me to potential interviewees had been collaborating with researchers and civil society organizations in the global North for decades. I was an invited guest at the co-operative's annual meeting, and my name appeared along with my nationality in a local newspaper article about the event (I noticed that other foreigners were often profiled in this way in the media). While such interactions mixed friendship and shared project goals with attention to my institutional and national positionality, other interactions more directly invoked the currency of *gringo* status. The affluent owner of a downtown Machala eatery, for example, befriended me and helped me to find participants for my interviews, while also asking me for advice on sending her children to learn English in Canada.

As when I was asked to invest in a plan to make sweets or juice from bananas, my *gringo* status often attributed to me powers and privileges I did not actually have. My investment capital was limited, as was my ability to shape the actions of the Canadian government. Other frustrations or apparent misunderstandings turned out to reveal kernels of truth, however, suggesting that my reception as a *gringo* (or *gringuito*, more affectionately)

was more than just a source of memorable stories and impractical requests. It also evoked the ongoing extraction of wealth from Latin America by Northern interests, with Canada-Ecuador relations turning out to be a disturbingly prominent example.

In particular, I learned that many of Ecuador's most controversial mines were Canadian ones, reflecting my country's identity as the "legal haven of choice for the world's mining industries," as the revealingly titled *Imperial Canada Inc.* puts it.[3] The Toronto Stock Exchange (TSX) and TSX Venture Exchange are "the world's primary listing venues for mining and mineral exploration companies, with more than 1,200 issuers, accounting for almost 50% of global listings in 2018."[4] Canada's companies and stock exchanges play leading roles in both precious metals mining and high-risk exploration by "junior" companies, thereby facilitating mining by "senior" companies, Canadian or otherwise.[5] A growing body of critical literature has documented how Canada's "imperialist" foreign policy has tended to push governments—prominently including Ecuador's—to grant Canadian companies unfettered access to mineral and metal resources around the world while refusing to sanction those same companies for the environmental and human rights abuses they frequently perpetrate.[6]

As explored in more detail in Chapter 24, many of the companies most active and notorious in Ecuador and elsewhere in Latin America are also donors to the very academic institutions that have enabled my research on the health effects of pesticides in banana production.[7] Following the logic of exploitation in banana production through the Ecuadorian government to the interests driving and profiting from its development model led back ... to me. When Ecuadorians attributed more *gringo* power and influence to me than I felt I possessed, they were reflecting a deeply problematic set of ongoing relationships between my country and theirs, against the backdrop of ongoing Northern extraction of Latin American wealth.

I therefore began looking even more skeptically at the premise that I was doing something straightforwardly helpful in my time in Ecuador. The degree to which Canada's mining industry—a vehicle for both transnational and Canadian capital accumulation[8]—was generating controversy in relation to supposedly progressive Ecuador in the twenty-first century added further weight to my growing sense that focusing on toxic chemicals in the production of a single tropical fruit might be less than helpful. Subsequent developments in the situation facing banana workers would further emphasize the need to challenge the overall development model generating such forms of toxicity.

CHAPTER 17
SAME JOKE, DIFFERENT CLOWN

Despite the twenty-first-century socialist ambitions that characterized Rafael Correa's early years as president, the extraction of wealth from (specific) Ecuadorian territories and bodies continued under his "post-neoliberal" administration. As a result, Correa's gradual estrangement from the social movements that had brought him to power was especially demoralizing. For banana workers and farmers fighting for their rights, Correa's second mandate would feel disturbingly familiar. Continuities in terms of precarious labour and promotion of pesticide-intensive agroindustry characterized the terrain on which environmental justice battles would be fought.

Jorge Acosta is the former military and then pesticide-fumigation pilot who led the pilots' 2007 pesticide-related complaint to Ecuador's Defensoría del Pueblo.[1] After the 2009 workshop that first brought me to Ecuador, he had volunteered to show me another side of banana production in the country, beyond the small- and medium-sized farms we had been shown during the workshop by our hosts from the organic fairtrade small-producer co-op UROCAL. We travelled from El Oro to Guayas and then Los Ríos, where Jorge took me to a school for children with disabilities in the midst of banana plantations. I met the children and their teachers, who explained to me that the kids' parents had worked on pesticide-intensive banana farms and been frequently bathed in fungicides outside their homes by exhausted or careless pilots.

Next Jorge took me to meet a group of banana workers who told stories of dangerous working conditions, low pay, lack of job security, and pervasive intimidation that kept them from speaking up for fear of being fired and put on ubiquitous blacklists. Jorge took advantage of the gathering my visit had occasioned to make a call for the workers to organize. Despite my imperfect Spanish, I caught his analogy: when buffaloes cross the river in groups, they stay safe; when they cross one at a time, crocodiles pick them off easily. The unfair circumstances facing these banana workers belied the promise of the Citizen's Revolution, as Correa had been in power for two years at the time after campaigning on promises to eliminate just such labour rights abuses. This continuation of precarious banana labour in spite of supposedly progressive measures, such as the elimination of the practice of farm owners contracting *capitanes* to provide workers, would be memorably expressed by a worker interviewed in a later ASTAC-supported study: *it's like hearing the same joke, but with a different clown*.[2]

After Ecuador's turbulent neoliberal decades (not to mention the exploitative centuries that preceded them), the progressive policies and inspiring rhetoric of Correa's initial years in government had fuelled hope among many Ecuadorians and left-leaning international observers. Important new social programs in this period included income supports, spending on education and public health care, credit programs for affordable housing, and road construction and other job-creating infrastructure projects. These programs led to a major reduction in poverty in the country, from 46 to 30 percent between 2007 and late 2014.[3] The Gini coefficient expressing inequality in incomes of households also declined in this period from 0.547 to 0.476, although this figure excludes sources of income such as investment and likely overestimates the decrease in inequality.[4]

More ominously, such social spending was largely enabled by windfall profits due to high oil prices from 2010 to 2012, with poverty actually slightly increasing afterwards as oil prices fell.[5] Inequalities in land concentration also persisted, despite Alianza País promises to the contrary.[6] Correa established a national land plan (*Plan Tierras*) in 2010, providing land titles to some Indigenous groups and selling to peasant organizations some lands confiscated from banking groups implicated in the 2000 financial crisis. Larrea and Greene note that the amount of land redistributed in this highly publicized plan "came to a mere 17,807.4 ha for the entire country."[7] They explain that Ecuador's land reforms in 1964 and 1973 were spurred by major peasant mobilizations, while the conservative government of Rodrigo Borja had been forced by the 1990 *levantamiento indígena* to implement more substantial land reform than that of the "socialist" Correa. Weakened peasant and Indigenous organizations of the twenty-first century were unable to force Alianza País to back up its rhetorical support for peasants and the environment. The result was a land law that "relies on markets for redistribution and betrays a narrow technocratic approach to agrarian issues, an approach that favours large-scale export interests and agroindustrial enterprises."[8]

Indeed, political ecologist Galarza Suarez observes that the agricultural development policies of the *revolución ciudadana* transformed rural territories of the coast by linking them even more thoroughly into globalized commodity chains such as that of bananas.[9] Such agricultural reforms included technical support for small- and medium-sized banana producers, accompanied by Green Revolution–inspired rhetoric emphasizing the inefficiencies of peasant farmers. As Correa put it in 2011, small properties in the countryside were in conflict with "productive efficiency and poverty reduction."[10] With characteristic pithiness, he concluded that "to redistribute a large property into many small properties is to redistribute poverty."[11] And so Alianza País's productivity-enhancing supports served to incorporate small- and medium-sized producers into "a globalized and highly competitive chain of production . . . [and] reproduce their vulnerability and subordination within this oligopolistic market."[12]

Correa and his Alianza País successor, Lenín Moreno, largely supported the interests of large agricultural capitalists and promoted a technology-intensive form of agriculture requiring significant capital (and pesticide use) and oriented towards overseas markets.[13] The pairing of a petroleum-centred economy with redistributive and progressive policies in the Correa years was also a precarious one in light of the inevitable busts that accompany resource booms. Its longer-term benefits were limited by the fact that poverty reduction was essentially accomplished in the short-term without touching the wealth of the country's powerful economic elites.[14] Similarly problematic were the inherent contradictions between intensified production of primary export commodities and the environmental and social protections espoused by the diverse social movements that had initially brought Alianza País to power. The government nevertheless repeatedly portrayed petroleum extraction, mega-mining, and large-scale agribusiness as the path to societal health and well-being via increased state budgets, essentially treating areas of the country where such activities were to occur as "sacrifice zones" whose human and more-than-human communities were unfortunate casualties of national development.[15]

These tensions eventually came to a head and fractures emerged between Alianza País and some of the most prominent groups that had helped elect it. Such critics increasingly invoked the concept of *extractivismo* (extractivism) to describe Correa's combination of primary commodity exports with social spending.[16] They also pointed out that environmentally destructive resource extraction projects and plantation monocultures were inconsistent with the rights given to nature in the constitution, as well as the constitutional right of Ecuadorians to live in a healthy environment.[17] Additional opposition emerged from Indigenous and other rural communities whose livelihoods and cultures were threatened by resource extraction on their territories. Correa responded with police action, incarcerations, and de-registration of non-governmental organizations, tools that criminalized and repressed such opposition to *extractivismo*. Belying the constitution's proclamation of Ecuador as a "plurinational" state, moreover, the Correa government often used racist arguments and language to dismiss Indigenous and environmentalist critics as "childish" obstacles to national progress.[18]

For banana farmers and workers, Alianza País's extractivist policies largely reinforced plantation agriculture's commodification and exploitation of labour and the environment. The labour rights protections instituted in the constitution and Mandate 8 were progressively weakened as Correa's first term ended and his second progressed.[19] The elimination of labour subcontracting was compromised through measures ostensibly meant to reduce burdens on large banana farm owners; these generally weakened banana workers' ability to unionize and demand adequate pay and safe working conditions.[20] Such agricultural and labour policies favouring large agroindustry reflected both an ideological commitment to "modern" agriculture consistent with Green Revolution narratives and the significant influence of banana sector elites on the Ecuadorian government.[21]

The impacts of agricultural extractivism on banana workers and their toxic working environments were repeatedly documented by researchers and civil society organizations in this period, frequently partnering with ASTAC.[22] Multiple studies published between 2016 and 2020 revealed continuing labour rights abuses in the country's ongoing "union vacuum," especially precarious, low-paid, and unsafe work on banana farms.[23] Such conditions were particularly evident in Los Ríos, which had emerged by this point as the leading banana producer in Ecuador thanks to its numerous large-scale plantations.[24] A 2016 study in three regions of the province found "the most archaic forms of exploitation of workers," consisting of various forms of precarious work, low salaries, long and difficult work days, and dangerous working conditions.[25]

Of the forty-four workers interviewed, 50 percent reported working without contracts or health insurance, while 23.3 percent reported having either a verbal contract or a hastily signed contract whose terms they did not know, and of which they did not have a copy (as was required by law). The workers told familiar stories of precarity and exploitation: making less than the national minimum wage (47 percent of interviewed workers); ongoing operations of labour subcontractors or *capitanes*, explicitly outlawed by Mandate 8; ongoing exposure to pesticides and other agrochemicals with virtually no PPE, including while caught in the plantation during overhead fumigations; stress-related and musculoskeletal injuries stemming from intense and long workdays; and widespread sexual harassment of women, along with dismissal if they became pregnant.[26]

Mixed but also disturbing findings emerged in a 2016 study by Oxfam Germany following earlier reports in 2008 and 2011.[27] The report found that between 65 and 95 percent (depending on the plantation) of interviewed banana workers were affiliated to Ecuador's social security system, representing a major improvement on the situation found in the 2011 report but compromised by the classification of some workers as part-time, despite working over forty hours per week. A worker in such a position "would have to pay into the pension fund for 60 years in order to be eligible for payments."[28] The report also observed steady increases in the Ecuadorian minimum wage, to the point where—on paper—banana workers were supposed to receive $427 per month. In spite of such increases, the minimum wage was still not enough to cover the government-estimated costs of a "basic family shopping basket," or $675 per month. Overall, the report concluded that the conditions on Ecuadorian plantations had "hardly improved since 2008 or 2011."²⁹ Interviews with 165 workers on twenty different farms found no independent employee organizations; pervasive fear of dismissal or reprisals—including being placed on worker blacklists—that scared workers away from union activity; frequent lack of written contracts allowing workers to know if they were receiving what they were supposed to be paid (between 27 and 47 percent of workers, depending on the plantation); women being required to submit to pregnancy tests before hiring, being paid less than men (33 percent less on some plantations), and being fired without compensation or insurance coverage in the event of pregnancy; and use of highly toxic pesticides banned in the EU, with frequent exposures from fumigations with workers in the field or non-observance of the required re-entry period (again, varying from farm to farm). The study also found that banana producers were often paid less than the Ecuadorian minimum price of $6.16 for a case of bananas, suggesting one reason for cutting of corners on farms.³⁰

While Los Ríos epitomizes the plight of precarious workers on large banana plantations, comparable inequities exist in Ecuador's other two major banana-producing provinces. In another recent study, banana workers in the parish of Tenguel in Guayas reported labour rights abuses such as low pay and either non-existent or belated affiliation with the social security system; unpaid overtime or extra tasks; labour subcontracting, despite its illegal nature after 2008; failure to observe basic health and safety standards; and both summary dismissals and the assignment of difficult or unpleasant work tasks as punishment for complaints or labour organizing in response to such abuses.³¹ Experiences of precarity in this period were also particularly hard on women, with household or family work of social reproduction both falling on women's shoulders and becoming more intense due to the over-exploitation of male partners or relatives on banana farms. Health hazards consistent with such abuses included mosquito bites in a region where dengue and other vector-borne diseases are real risks; snakebites; noise, intense solar radiation, rain, and humidity; cuts from machetes and the sharp knives used to cut bananas off bunches, as well as the risk of falls from ladders used to help harvest bananas; fast-paced and strenuous work routines leading to both psycho-social and musculoskeletal risks; and, of course, regular exposure to the toxic pesticides that are ubiquitous in conventional banana production.

Galarza Suarez's ethnographic work in El Oro documented similar patterns of exploitation, despite the province's greater proportion of small- and medium-sized producers.[32] This study published in 2019 focused on underemployed members of the banana workforce, who tended to live in urban settings and congregate every morning in a park or other central public location in hope of getting work. Labour subcontractors or *capitanes*, who were supposed to be illegal after 2008, nevertheless operated in these settings, obtaining workers each morning to satisfy requests made the previous evening by their client farms. Those workers would then be loaded into the backs of trucks and transported to the farm "like animals," as one banana worker put it. Several types of labour rights abuses reported in Guayas and Los Ríos were also uncovered in this study done in El Oro, such as when banana workers are told they are affiliated with social security (with deductions taken from their paycheques), as is required by law, only to find that such coverage is non-existent or "ghost-like" (*seguro fantasma*) when they try to access medical treatment. Many workers with coverage also reported declining to use it for fear of being replaced because they were not allowed to take time off work.

A more quantitative analysis facilitated by ASTAC and UROCAL was first published in 2016 by Austrian physicians and epidemiologists focusing on all three provinces as part of the European "Make Fruit Fair" solidarity campaign. The study compared the health of organic banana farmers with pesticide-exposed conventional banana workers.[33] One part of this study found the pesticide-exposed workers to have higher levels of genotoxicity or DNA damage, a precursor or indicator of cancer risk. A second found the pesticide-exposed workers to have higher levels of self-reported symptoms consistent with the known impacts of the pesticides being used (although many workers did not know which pesticides they were working with).[34] Another quantitative study by two researchers from Guayaquil-area universities found low acetylcholinesterase levels and neuropsychological impairment in a sample of banana workers, consistent with chronic overexposure to organophosphate pesticides.[35]

Galarza Suarez's participants also confirmed that banana farm owners and labour contractors would evade the (increasingly watered-down) social protections instituted by the Correa government in its first term by forcing workers to sign documents claiming receipt of benefits or pay that they did not actually receive; via ongoing suppression of unions, including through blacklists and death threats targeting labour leaders; and through underreporting of actual employee numbers by farms in order to stay under the legally outlined minimum of thirty workers per enterprise required to form a union. Galarza Suarez suggests that such abuses were known to local authorities who turned a blind eye because of a revolving door and pervasive family and social connections between local governments and the banana industry in El Oro (a charge I also heard frequently in my own interviews in the province). They were also enabled by the Correa government's criminalization of dissent through legislation such as the Organic Integral Criminal Code (COIP from *Código Orgánico Integral Penal*), through which marches, protests, and strikes could be prosecuted as forms of sabotage or terrorism, thereby discouraging organizing by banana workers to protect their rights.[36]

Alianza País's early policies and rhetoric about protecting workers, nature, and "food sovereignty" ultimately gave way in the face of imperatives to maximize the extraction of value from banana-producing territories and bodies. But as I began to learn about extractivism under the Correa government, he left office in 2017. What came next would continue some of the worst tendencies of his development model but abandon much of the anti-imperialist, "post-neoliberal" impetus behind it.

CHAPTER 18
PLAGAS

When I first got to Ecuador, I thought the proper translation of "pesticide" was the dramatic-sounding *plaguicida*. I found that I often had to explain myself, as many banana farmers and workers were more familiar with terms such as *producto* (product), *químico* (chemical), or simply *veneno* (poison). Neither did I hear much reference to the root of *plaguicida*: *plaga* (plague or blight). People would refer to black sigatoka as *el hongo* (the fungus), or to insect pests as *bichos*. Two decades into the twenty-first century, however, Ecuador would be visited by three infectious agents whose world-changing potential—separately and in their intimate interconnections—merits the Biblical term *plagas*. They brought the hopes of twenty-first-century socialism to a definitive end, while extending the toxic exploitation of banana farmers and workers it had often failed to address and casting a shadow over the future of the banana industry.

The first *plaga*, neoliberalism, was not a literal disease, although it has been compared to one by numerous commentators.¹ It was also not new to Ecuador, but rather resurgent. Rafael Correa's "post-neoliberal" development model had attempted to carry out redistributive measures and poverty alleviation through state action, albeit in ways that were financed by windfall resource rents and shored up by criminalization and racist dismissals of opposition to *extractivismo*. Correa's former vice-president Lenín Moreno was elected in 2017 and continued to prioritize resource extraction and agribusiness but dropped much of twenty-first-century socialism's overtures towards redistribution of wealth. He also brought corruption charges against Correa and many of his officials and allies.[2] With respect to the banana industry, he introduced measures to promote "flexible" employment, extending the weakening of protection for workers and small farmers that had occurred after Correa's initial promising policy measures.[3]

A 2018 follow-up to the 2016 Oxfam Germany report documented additional threats to labour rights created by such moves to promote flexible labour. The 2018 report drew on further investigative work by ASTAC such as interviews with thirty workers on plantations that either supplied, or had supplied, bananas to the German supermarket chain Lidl.[4] The update also affirmed the 2016 report's finding that none of the plantations on which interviewees were working would allow formation of a trade union, as illustrated by the firing of at least ten union members at one plantation supplying Lidl. A separate study of female workers in Los Ríos, also facilitated by ASTAC, explored how "banana production is a laboratory in which it is possible to see explicitly the intrinsic relationship between peripheral dependent capitalism and patriarchy."[5] This later study characterizes sexual assault and other violations of female banana workers' rights as part of the process through which agricultural capitalists exert control over both rural territories and the bodies of the workers within them, culminating in especially extractive or exploitative use of women's bodies.

Mechanisms such as contract-based banana production and control over agricultural input industries help accomplish this control over both rural spaces and workers' bodies, as highly indebted small farmers are forced to sell their properties and become incorporated into banana labour markets as workers, while spaces of subsistence farming and independence for women on small farms are eliminated. As reported in the study, ASTAC— which includes pay equity between men and women as a central part of its demands—estimated 15 to 20 percent of work on Ecuadorian banana farms is done by women, who tend to earn less because the tasks to which they are assigned are deemed to be easier. Women also reported being assigned tasks at the discretion of managers, with less-unpleasant roles reserved for women who would put up with those managers' unwanted advances or other forms of sexual harassment.

While bearing such greater burdens, women were found to be even less inclined than men to organize or complain in response to labour rights violations because they are often threatened with sanctions not just to them but also to their family members or partners (they also generally have less free time to participate in labour organizing due to their greater household burden of work). Women's preoccupation with providing for their families also served as a deterrent to speaking up in response to sexual harassment or other violations. An additional burden placed on women by banana work is through the vehicle of long workdays for male workers, forcing their wives or other female relatives to carry out greater shares of household or care work.[6] In this way the extraction of wealth from banana-producing lands and peoples emerged as particularly severe in relation to women's bodies.

In 2019, about a decade after Correa had proclaimed an end to the "long, sad neoliberal night" and eliminated the country's dependence on the IMF, Moreno's administration returned to the fund's table in hope of obtaining loan support. After promising to implement a range of austerity measures, Ecuador was approved for an additional $4.2 billion loan. Conditions included reductions in public sector spending and promotion of intensified petroleum extraction, mining, and agroindustry, along with scrapping the country's long-standing and popular fuel subsidy.[7] The scrapping of the subsidy served to trigger a broader uprising—*el paro*—that shut down the country in late September and early October of 2019. Indigenous groups backed by the Confederation of Indigenous Nationalities of Ecuador (CONAIE from *Confederación de Nacionalidades Indígenas del Ecuador*) played leading roles, marching to Quito and other urban centres and occupying public spaces and government buildings. Unions in the coastal region and elsewhere joined in the uprising, as did various environmental and popular sectors in urban settings. Indigenous nationalities in the Amazon region occupied oil extraction facilities and built blockades limiting access to their territories. After the government imposed a curfew in urban areas, middle-class residents took to their balconies to express support for the demonstrators, using pots and pans as noisemakers in a gesture that was termed *el cacerolazo* (based on the word *cacerol*, a casserole).

The government, in turn, reacted with a combination of heavy-handed police and military violence and portrayals of *el paro* as senseless, random violence lacking a coherent political message (Moreno also claimed publicly that his former mentor Correa was pulling the strings from abroad).[8] *El paro* eventually ended, although investigations and accusations would continue regarding alleged abuses perpetrated on all sides. One legacy of the stoppage was a temporary backing away from the IMF program. This reprieve from the ravages of neoliberalism was short-lived, however, as Ecuador—and the rest of the world—would be visited in early 2020 by another *plaga*: COVID-19.

The large numbers of Ecuadorian migrants working in Europe (especially Spain) and the United States meant that the virus had numerous opportunities to arrive as industrialized countries began to lock down their economies in response to the pandemic and migrants returned home. In addition to this transnational flow, which reflected the fact that neoliberal reforms of the '80s and '90s had pushed millions of Ecuadorians abroad to survive, more recent austerity measures made the country particularly ill-prepared to fight the pandemic.[9] Deep cuts to health spending in 2019 had weakened the country's health system, and the health minister resigned early in the pandemic because, as he put it, there were simply no resources available to meet this major new threat. The highly publicized piling up of bodies in the streets of Guayaquil created apocalyptic scenes that compounded the sense of crisis.[10]

Despite massive government supports for pandemic response in countries around the world and IMF rhetoric stating that public spending was required to fight COVID-19, Ecuador appeared to be reluctant to diverge from its mandated austerity program. While not spending public funds on a pandemic response, the country did faithfully meet its obligations to make payments to international creditors, showing the government to be more responsive to the money-making ambitions of wealthy foreigners than to the life-or-death struggles of its own population.[11] Ecuador thus became one of the South American countries hit hardest by COVID-19, with extremely high although severely under-reported per capita infection and death rates.[12]

Despite this dire situation, the country deemed export-based agriculture to be an essential service and banana workers (among others) were required to continue working in conditions that were anything but protective against the virus.[13] Circumstances that had made people vulnerable to pesticide exposures and other health hazards before the pandemic were also highly conducive to COVID-19 transmission and severity. For example, workers living in peri-urban slums with precarious employment status could not often stay home to self-isolate. Precarious employment also meant that banana workers would have to work through illnesses and often had multiple employers, increasing their chances of acquiring or spreading the disease. The practice of hiring workers in the pre-dawn hours in urban centres and transporting them to farms in the backs of trucks similarly eliminated the possibility of effective social distancing. And populations who already lacked PPE for pesticides on farms often did not get it for COVID-19. A report by Acción Ecológica pointed out that the history of pesticide exposure among banana workers meant that their respiratory systems were particularly vulnerable to COVID-19. As one worker wryly observed, they had been fumigated for so many years that the government and banana companies apparently viewed them as COVID-proof due to the pesticides they had been "treated" with.[14]

The Ecuadorian government took advantage of the pandemic and the "shocked" population it created to push through many of the unpopular neoliberal reforms that *el paro* of 2019 had so emphatically rejected.[15] These included measures to further reduce public sector spending, "flexibilize" labour, and promote extractivist development activities. Then, in February of 2021, Ecuadorians voted in a national election. Moreno and Alianza País had been effectively eliminated as a political option. The first round of the election saw a new Correa protege, economist Andrés Arauz, take the most votes. A conservative candidate named Guillermo Lasso and the former governor of Azuay province Yaku Pérez—running for the Indigenous Pachakutik party—appeared to have both garnered approximately 20 percent of the national vote. Pérez's unprecedented strong showing sparked both intense enthusiasm and intense criticism from both the right and the left.[16] Lasso nevertheless emerged as the second-place candidate and then won the runoff election in April. Fifteen years after the start of the *revolución ciudadana*, an openly neoliberal political vision reigned once again in Ecuador.

The challenges to health and well-being accompanying this transition were compounded by the economic impacts of the COVID-19 pandemic, as deepening poverty and unemployment in Ecuador contributed to a major increase in crime in the country from 2021 to 2023. Colombia's peace process—ending a conflict whose history prominently included the 1928 banana worker massacre and its political legacies—simultaneously disrupted routes for the traffic of cocaine to Mexico and ultimately Northern drug users. Mexican cartels soon took advantage of impoverished Ecuadorians and the country's weak law enforcement capacity to begin transporting drugs through the northern province of Esmeraldas. The accompanying violent crime vaulted Ecuador into third place in Latin America for its murder rate (26.6 per 100,000 residents in 2022, a 245 percent increase from 2020), behind only Honduras and Venezuela.[17] Then, in August of 2023, as Ecuadorians prepared to vote in national elections to replace Lasso, presidential candidate and anti-corruption campaigner Fernando Villavicencio was assassinated at a campaign rally. The August 20 election narrowed the field to a left-wing candidate running on an anti-Correista platform, and the centre-right Daniel Noboa, son of banana tycoon and failed presidential candidate Álvaro Noboa.[18] Noboa's victory in the October runoff election made him Ecuador's youngest-ever president, at age thirty-six, and prompted left-wing sources to announce the advent of the Banana Republic of Ecuador (*república bananera del Ecuador*).[19]

The *plaga* of neoliberalism had worsened Ecuador's experience of COVID-19, which in turn enabled further neoliberal reforms to be forced onto the beleaguered population. Beyond this commonality, the emergence of viral pathogens has been compellingly linked to the global dominance of monocultural agroindustry and the neoliberal economic reforms that typically promote it (although this pathway does not apply straightforwardly to COVID-19).[20] Such common origins were shared by a third *plaga* that reached South America in the same time period, with similarly ominous implications for the future of peoples dependent on banana production.

Over half a century after Gros Michel banana production had been ended by the globalized fungal threat of Panama disease, a new variant of the fungus—*Fusarium oxysporum* f.sp. *cubense* § *Tropical Race 4* (TR4)—emerged to threaten the viability of the Cavendish-based industry. TR4 had been spreading throughout Asia, Oceania, and Africa over a period of decades, with bananas' monocultural export-based production model, deregulated global markets, and neoliberal finger-pointing at the practices of individual farmers doing little to slow it down.²¹ In early 2019, Colombian farmers sent pictures of their distressed banana plants to a phytopathology expert, leading to quick laboratory confirmation that Panama disease's new incarnation had indeed reached the Americas.²² The new variant is about as devastating to Cavendish plantations as the original Panama disease was to Gros Michel, leading to numerous news stories about the imminent "extinction" of bananas.²³

TR4 has yet to be observed in Ecuador, although it was detected in northern Peru in early 2021 and Venezuela in 2023; phytopathologists and the industry as a whole are fairly certain it's only a matter of time before the devastating disease reaches the country.²⁴ Chemical solutions are among those being most aggressively pursued, despite their ineffectiveness, and producers have lobbied for permission to use the banned ozone-depleting chemical methyl bromide in the hopes it might fend off the coming disaster.²⁵ At the time of writing, banana production's precarious twenty-first century is entering a period of transition whose ultimate outcome is very much up in the air, with major risk of continuing or worsening the toxic injustices experienced by workers, farmers, and the planet.

CHAPTER 19
THE BANANTHROPOCENE

By exploring banana production's past through more and better stories than the dominant ones that motivate conventional responses to such injustices, this book has sought to arrive at *better* responses. But the calm pursuit of better stories for better solutions came to seem increasingly rushed and beset by anxieties as the twenty-first century neared the crisis-ridden end of its first quarter. That period in the history of the world's leading exporter of bananas was supposed to be the end of the long, sad neoliberal night and a victory for *Pachamama* over ecologically damaging imperialism. Then came streets full of protesters in the 2018 *paro*, sparked by the scrapping of a petroleum subsidy and an IMF-imposed plan to double down on neoliberal extractivism. The 2020 pandemic saw streets full of bodies (dead, not protesting) as COVID-19 descended on Guayaquil, the neoliberalized centre of power of Ecuadorian banana production, foreshadowing what are projected to be numerous such zoonotic pandemics generated by the agro-industrial food system that bananas exemplify. More bodies in the streets followed in 2022 and 2023, these ones murdered and gruesomely displayed by *narcotraficantes*. And in the ecological backdrop to such human dramas, the monoculture-loving TR4 fungus reached the Americas in 2019, threatening banana production's worlds and ways of life (however precarious and unfair they might be).

Such apocalyptic omens are linked to global flows of bananas, workers, money, ideas, drugs, viruses, fungi, and toxic chemicals. They therefore serve as vivid reminders that thinking about justice in relation to health, environment, and the future requires accounting for global interconnections. Indeed, few serious conversations about environmental or social justice now occur without consideration of anthropogenic climate change. What, then, does the uncertain future of the planet mean for the pursuit of justice in relation to bananas and pesticides?

A place that speaks vividly to such questions is found at the end of yet another bus trip down the Andes, though not in the westward direction that leads to Machala. The roads eastwards, linking *la sierra* to Ecuador's Amazon region, are similarly spectacular, winding, and nerve-wracking. One notable difference on the route from Quito to the Amazonian city of Lago Agrio[1] is the presence of a black oil pipeline running next to the highway, occasionally diverted by topography but quickly returning to parallel the road. It also goes underground at times, a petroleum thread sewing together a patchwork quilt of farms and other rural land uses. When I first travelled the route in late 2018, I was intrigued to see graffiti painted on the pipeline with messages such as CHEVRON TOXICO and 30,000 AFECTADOS (30,000 people affected). I knew this referred to the interminable legal battle waged by Amazonian peasants and Indigenous peoples against Chevron over Texaco's decades of polluting oil extraction in the region (Texaco merged with Chevron in 2001 and took on its name).[2] I took a series of blurry pipeline photos through the bus window before eventually getting a clear one on my return journey when the bus I was on broke down.

As we spent hours by the side of the road waiting for another, I also saw a vaguely familiar distinguished-looking man among the passengers gathered by the roadside during the delay. It was only later when I ran into him at a PhD defence in Quito that I placed him as Adolfo Maldonado, the Quito-based Basque physician with the NGO Acción Ecológica who had led the 2007 pesticide epidemiology study in the banana-producing community of Las Ramas, Guayas.[3] Adolfo had been in Lago Agrio in connection with another Acción Ecológica initiative, the *Clínica Ambiental* (environmental clinic).[4] On another trip to Ecuador the following year, I would attend the graduation ceremony for a Clínica Ambiental course at Amisacho, a reforested cacao farm on the outskirts of Lago Agrio. Both the event and the setting in which it took place evoke many of the contradictions of life in the beautiful, badly contaminated Amazon region

Figure 19.01: Anti-Chevron pipeline graffiti on the highway to *el oriente*

of Ecuador (known as *el oriente*—"the east"). Despite being on the other side of the Andes from the banana-producing coast, they also bring the troubled history and uncertain future of banana production—and of the planet—into sharp relief.

Amisacho is a complex whose entrance adjacent to an abandoned oil well—one of many found throughout the region—gives little indication of the beauty within. The site is breathtakingly alive with abundant vegetation and wildlife, such as squirrel monkeys, dusky titis (known as *pequeños aulladores*, or little howlers), and endangered mustachioed tamarins, known locally as *bebe leche* (drinks milk) for the white around their mouths. Even with its history of cacao production, the contrast between Amisacho and banana plantations in *la costa* is striking. While both are very green, the unruly abundance of an Amazonian forest ecosystem is worlds away from a herbicide-treated banana plantation with its lack of undergrowth and straight irrigation channels. Capturing this disconnect was the contempt of a small banana farmer I had interviewed at Chiquita's use of Rainforest Alliance certification standards on their farms: "Go look at a Chiquita plantation and see if you can find a tree where a bird could land. It's just bananas. You don't see an alliance with the forest. You don't even see a tree."

At Amisacho, in contrast, birds, frogs, dusky titis, and other members of the Amazon's amazing more-than-human community provide a constant backing chorus, accompanied by quieter species such as snakes, spiders, and incredibly diverse insects (a caiman has also been seen in the stream running through the site). It is a place where I have spent time in Ecuador when not on the banana-producing coast, and some of this book was conceived and written there while working in the open-air kitchen and pausing to watch troops of monkeys passing through the forest canopy overhead. Two non-governmental organizations work out of the complex in support of, and collaboration with, the Indigenous nationalities—Cofán, Siekopai, Kichwa, Huaorani, and Siona—affected by decades of oil extraction in the northern *oriente*.

Also on-site is an innovative oyster-mushroom-growing operation, based on principles of permaculture and integrated into a growing network of farms known as the *Ruta Amazónica de la Esperanza* (Amazonian Route of Hope) and allied with the Clínica Ambiental.[5] Given the ecological devastation triggering such initiatives, the oyster mushrooms of Amisacho (at least for many social scientists) might bring to mind the matsutake "mushroom at the end of the world" used by anthropologist Anna Tsing to explore "possibilities for life in the capitalist ruins."[6] The premise of the Clínica Ambiental and the farms on the Ruta is that healing the land—and human relationships to it—through agro-ecological farming or permaculture is a way to heal the region's people after over half a century of petroleum-related pollution.[7]

Such objectives were the focus of the graduation ceremony I found myself at in late 2019, where the attendees were mostly *mestizo* residents of the Amazon region, or *colonos* (settlers). After the discovery of oil in *el oriente* in 1967, Ecuador's second round of agrarian reforms had seen the military dictatorship that redistributed some lands in *la costa* also encourage poor, landless *mestizo* and Afro-Ecuadorians to settle and farm supposedly empty lands in the Amazon region (which were Indigenous lands and not empty at all).[8] These common roots came to mind when I met *colonos* in *el oriente* who had left *la sierra* at approximately the same time as those who ended up on *la costa* working on banana farms, and for many of the same reasons: land concentration, poverty, and events such as the drought that affected the province of Loja in the 1970s. In both places, moreover, such migrants had been encouraged by Ecuador's agricultural and overall development trajectories to engage in increasingly technology- and pesticide-intensive agriculture.

During the 2019 event, I listened as Adolfo portrayed pesticide-intensive agriculture as a foreign imposition that positioned Ecuadorians as losers (*pendejos*). He went on to detail the extraordinary biodiversity and productivity of Amazonian ecosystems just prior to the 1492 arrival of Columbus, after millennia of careful tending by the region's Indigenous inhabitants. He compared the abundance of such ecosystems to the relatively low species diversity of North American landscapes, with a crowd-pleasing rude gesture directed, presumably northwards, at *los gringos* (I laughed at this, and the crowd laughed at my reaction).

It was strange to hear a European speaking to *mestizo* Ecuadorians (and one Canadian) on the benefits of Indigenous ways of managing ecosystems and the dangers of Euro-American pesticide-intensive agriculture. That strangeness triggered reflections on what Amisacho and *la costa* were linked by—beyond two Euro-descended health researchers who had occupied themselves with pesticides in banana production. One linkage clearly involved dynamics of *mestizaje* and within-Ecuador narratives of the inferiority and poor agricultural practices of those lacking *cultura*—a category that *colono* migrants to *el oriente* would generally fall into. Such racist narratives and the Green Revolution imaginaries within which they neatly fit thus underpinned both the chemical contamination of monocultural banana plantations in *la costa* and the simultaneous promotion of pesticide-intensive agriculture among *colono* farmers driven to *el oriente* by inequitable and elite-shaped processes of land reform.[9]

Additional commonalities were suggested by the petroleum that had shaped the fates of both regions. It was revenues from Amazonian oil extraction that had enabled Ecuador's second military government to subsidize fuel prices for banana exports in the 1970s, thereby enhancing their competitiveness internationally.[10] Similarly, that dictatorship had also invested in a fleet of boats for transporting bananas and leased it to Noboa, even when it ran at a loss (it was eventually privatized during Ecuador's neoliberalization and purchased, also by Noboa). Petroleum revenues had thereby helped to ensure the continued global pre-eminence of Ecuador's banana industry, and simultaneously empowered the company that came to dominate both that industry and its Ecuadorian workers and small farmers. Meanwhile, the advent of Cavendish banana production had seen banana plantations become increasingly reliant on petrochemically derived plastics, fumigation planes, and other forms of mechanization.[11] Ominously, inside the insecticide-impregnated plastic bags used to protect growing banana bunches can be found a micro-scale "greenhouse effect" as the bags trap heat from the sun while keeping out insects and other threats to perfect peels. Petroleum-derived plastics and pesticides feature in countless miniature versions of the climate change that Amazonian oil extraction and broader petroleum-intensive development have fuelled globally.

Synthetic pesticides central to both Green Revolution agriculture and carbon-intensive development more broadly are among the most insidious petroleum components of Cavendish banana production. In the second half of the twentieth century, enormous quantities of petrochemicals were refined in corporate laboratories into the poisons (pesticides) that have come to pervade the airways, waterways, and bodies of both the banana-producing coast and *el oriente*.[12] In addition to such synthesized petrochemicals were the less refined waste products of petroleum drilling in the Amazon, which Texaco disposed of in environmentally disastrous ways. In a classic example of environmental racism, those disposal methods failed to meet the industry standards they employed in their North American operations at the time.[13] This fact, along with scientific evidence such as epidemiology studies suggesting massive health effects of the contamination,[14] led an Ecuadorian judge in 2011 to award approximately $9 billion in damages to plaintiffs in the class action lawsuit aimed at holding Chevron accountable. In another eerie link to the history of banana production, a cutthroat legal manoeuvre known as the "kill step," pioneered by Dole's lawyers in the DBCP lawsuits discussed in Part 2 of this book, was later used by the same firm, this time engaged by Chevron, to make the judgment largely unenforceable (these two lawsuits are discussed again in Chapter 21).[15]

With this troubling and surprisingly banana-linked history as backdrop, the scenes of petroleum-related devastation that can routinely be found throughout *el oriente*, such as open pools of petrochemical waste with decades of vegetation growing overtop, start to inspire apocalyptic imaginings. Similarly, the furnace-like heat radiated by gas flares from ongoing oil extraction furthers the vivid sensory experience of visitors on "Toxic Tours," who can also see the extraordinary insect diversity of the area reduced to blackened corpses on the hardened surrounding ground. Such dystopian scenes and their linkages to global climate change evoke the *Anthropocene*, a term developed by physical scientists to express the magnitude of human influence on the planet. Based especially on the meteoric rise of atmospheric carbon dioxide over the twentieth century, the Anthropocene concept posits an end to the Holocene, the geological period that began with the end of the last Ice Age, and the beginning of an era in which humans are the dominant geological force.[16]

The history of banana production initially fits well with this conceit, in light of the industry's inseparability from fossil-fuel-intensive models of development.[17] The massive deforestation carried out to enable banana production represents an enormous loss of carbon-fixing tropical forest. Bananas also only became a commercially viable commodity when fossil-fuel-powered refrigerated ships turned the fruit into a reliable product to be marketed in North America's growing system of supermarkets—themselves tied to the establishment of food systems dependent on petroleum. Reliable rail networks, powered by fossil fuels, were another key to the banana's voyage into North American stomachs, both trips that brought bananas to Central American ports and those that allowed people in inland North American cities reliable access to tropical produce. Consumers learned to like fresh, cheap bananas at the same time as they became dependent on supermarket-purchased food and the agroindustries that could best supply it.[18]

Banana production is also tied up with the climate in the sense of being shaped by it. More-than-human atmospheric actors have been at the heart of the history of bananas since the nineteenth century. The constant threat of hurricanes in Central America helped drive the establishment of UFC in 1899, as well as its move to prioritize Ecuadorian bananas in 1960.[19] The strong El Niño–Southern Oscillation (ENSO) of 1982–83 saw increased cyclone activity in the Pacific and torrential rains and flooding damaging Ecuadorian banana farms. Banana exports from the country dropped from 1.2613 million metric tons in 1982 to 910,000 metric tons in 1983 and 906,300 in 1984, reflecting the multi-year process of replanting devastated plantations and bringing them to a state where exports could resume.[20] The ENSO event of 1997–98 also led to higher-than-normal temperatures, heavy rains, and flooding on the country's Pacific coast in early

1998, which a United Nations Environment Programme report blames for increased growth of fungal and other banana pests, followed by both increased pesticide use and the development of fungicide resistance by sigatoka fungi.[21] More recently, organic and fairtrade farmers in El Oro have reported threats to productivity due to heavy rains, especially in the rainy period leading up to the month of March, with high humidity fuelling sigatoka infestation and increased damage from the *mancha roja* (red stain) disease caused by insects (thrips) requiring increased agrochemical use.[22] They have also reported reduced rainfall from July to December, worsening water scarcity for the water-intensive process of growing and packing bananas in that annual dry season.

Not surprisingly, the future of a fruit embedded in the world's petroleum-fuelled past and present is not at all certain. Beyond Anthropocene worries are concerns that emerge when that concept's underlying assumptions are problematized. Indigenous scholars, for example, have pointed out that the world-ending devastation threatened by global environmental change is nothing new to their communities, whose worlds came to a kind of end after 1492 with the violent colonization of the Americas—a process that was central to the advent of fossil-fuel-intensive industrialization and capitalist development.[23] The "Capitalocene," for historian Jason Moore, is a better descriptor for the present, which in his estimation began around the fourteenth century with the entrenchment of European capitalism and the beginnings of its insatiable global spread.[24] In this analysis, contemporary greenhouse gas concentrations represent one symptom of the crisis rather than its central manifestation. Another critical alternative, the "Plantationocene," traces today's crises to a centuries-long extension of the logic of the plantation, which brings together alienated, interchangeable labour, more-than-humans, and land into a scalable formation that has enabled profit-making and empire-building from the sugar plantations of sixteenth-century Brazil to the twenty-first-century factories—and also, still, plantations—blamed for today's ecological crises.[25]

The comparable concepts of the Capitalocene and Plantationocene improve on the Anthropocene in making sense of today's crises in the banana-producing world and its Ecuadorian capital. Plantationocene conversations are especially relevant to banana production in the Americas.[26]

For example, the modern plantation and its reliance on coerced, racialized labour was trialled in the Middle East during the Crusades and then refined with coerced African labour in the New World through the transatlantic slave trade.[27] That plantation model—and the underemployed descendants of those Africans—would then be profitably employed and exploited by UFC and its competitors in a banana industry that both required and furthered the increasing carbonization of the atmosphere. The 2017 United Nations acknowledgement that "contemporary forms of slavery" continue to exist in Ecuador's banana industry attests to the ongoing relevance of the coerced labour characteristic of the Plantationocene. The scalable nature of the plantation is similarly evident in the interchangeability of bananas from Ecuador, Central America, and elsewhere in the tropics, which has enabled UFC and its successors and competitors to sidestep local resistance posed by place-based labour movements or ecological revolts.

UFC's use of migrant Jamaican labourers depended on their ancestors having been made into alienated, interchangeable labour via the transatlantic slave trade, but also on knowledge about how to grow bananas that originated on the margins of sugar and other plantations prior to emancipation.[28] The extra-capitalist agro-biodiversity found on such slave "plots" has been used to argue that Plantationocene discussions need to be more attentive to Black ecologies;[29] meanwhile, the fact that such plots enabled (white) wealth generation via plantation agriculture by sustaining the enslaved Africans working it might be termed *salvage accumulation* by Plantationocene scholar Anna Tsing,[30] as might UFC's reliance on the agro-ecological knowledge of their Jamaican labourers in the early twentieth-century establishment of banana plantations in Central America, and fungal-control efforts on them.[31]

Banana history also vividly displays the dominant ways of knowing associated with the Capitalocene, in creating involuntary commodities that can engender capital accumulation.[32] According to Moore, such creation of commodities occurs through capitalist record-keeping and interpretive practices. Those practices, comprising sciences, accounting practices, and discursive formations such as racism, patriarchy, and the rigid separation of humans from nature, enabled and were refined by capitalist expansion. They transformed people of colour, women, and the natural world—in short, everyone and everything except affluent, educated Euro-descended white men—into commodities to be profitably controlled and exploited.

As discussed in Part 1, for example, early twentieth-century narratives associated with UFC portrayed Central and South American countries as "virgin" lands populated by "tropical" peoples, just waiting to be made more productive by Northern men of science and business. Jumping forward almost a century, agricultural input billboards from twenty-first-century Ecuador feature banana fields as battlegrounds or sexy ladies, both of which welcome or even demand intervention and control (the Banana Queen candidates are also in this objectifying mix).

In the late twentieth century, similarly, toxicology-derived and corporate-origin narratives blamed Latin American workers for their own pesticide-related health impacts, compounded by stereotypes holding "tropical" peoples to be more careless and ignorant than temperate ones. Then, in the twenty-first century, urban Ecuadorians mobilized comparable individualizing generalizations to fit their poor, rural compatriots (implicitly racialized and lacking in *cultura*) into profitable banana-growing operations as slightly flawed factors of production, rather than as human beings living amidst toxic chemicals and toxic economic processes. Not surprisingly, then, banana production vividly illustrates the major tendencies that have culminated in today's global ecological and social crises.

Deciding what global transformations—such as anthropogenic climate change, ubiquitous chemical contamination, and the threat of pandemic diseases (of plants and people)—mean for efforts to confront banana-related toxicity depends, once again, on the stories you tell about them. An Anthropocene framing in which today's ecological crises stem from petroleum-intensive development in the twentieth century, or even as far back as the Industrial Revolution, can easily naturalize the inequitable global economic order that originated well before even the nineteenth century. This move often accomplishes an opportunistic reframing of neocolonial inequities as unexplained "vulnerability" that can be fixed through research across disciplines to inform incremental policy change within existing politico-economic structures.[33] Such stories, in which an urgent existential threat to civilization puts us all "in the same boat," also tend to motivate technocratic incremental solutions that attempt to address the threat through a narrow focus on greenhouse gases and not the social processes that generate them.[34] Strategies to climate-proof monocultural banana production without addressing its Plantationocene commodification of people and nature are one such incremental approach; another is efforts to respond to the fungal menace of TR4 by using biotechnology to develop disease-resistant (though not exploitation-resistant) varieties that could presumably slide neatly into the inequitable world of banana production.[35] Still other status-quo-preserving "solutions" seek to mitigate climate change via the intensification of extractivist activities such as lithium mining for renewable technologies, or through market-based mitigation strategies in which windmills or other carbon offsets often serve to displace Indigenous and other marginalized communities (a phenomenon termed CO2lonialism).[36]

In the face of such challenges, historian John Soluri's illuminating account of transnationally linked ecological and cultural changes around bananas arrives at recommendations for going "beyond banana cultures." By this he means focusing beyond the monocultures that have dominated both the Americas and the attention of historians studying them. As he puts it, "By revealing histories that often lie hidden in the shadows of plantation-driven export economies, historians and others can help to imagine realizable agrarian futures beyond monocultures that are capable of nurturing and sustaining biocultural diversity."[37] Insight into what a focus beyond toxic monocultures can yield is found in one recent anthropological account of relationships to pesticides among smallholder farmers in Mozambique and Burkina Faso, which urges scholars to "not only treat toxicity in the negative sense of destruction and precarity, but explore the puzzles of desire, aspiration, and expectations of modernity, and how to proceed from those messy realities and contradictions."[38]

Such messiness and conflicting desires and aspirations were certainly evident in my own interviews with farmers and workers in *la costa*, involving fraught labour relations, interactions with nature and toxic chemicals, and subjective responses to inequity and narratives explaining it. Late in interviews I would ask those farmers and workers if they could imagine a future in which they or the Ecuadorian coastal region did not produce bananas for export. With recurrent banana price crises, exploitative power relations in the industry, fungal diseases, the decreasing usefulness of pesticides in addressing them, and the health and environmental costs of all of those things, I asked if it would not make sense to switch to another livelihood or economic development strategy. While not disputing my logic, few people I spoke to in 2011 or the years immediately after could even imagine such a transition for the banana capital of the world. Whether or not such an adherence to bananas has survived the turbulence of recent years and will survive the increasing precarity that global environmental change and its accelerating capitalist underpinnings will bring in the coming decades remains to be seen. Against the backdrop of such uncertainty, the final section of the book explores possible better banana futures and the main strategies that have been proposed for achieving them.

PART 4:
GREEN FUTURES

Underneath the plantations the earth breathed the overwhelming humidity of the coast and from this breathing fed water to a vegetable world that passed from seed to flower in an instant. A lacustrine vegetation of trees that formed huge and extensive green scars stretched out towards the infinitude of the sea. Rows and rows of banana plantations. On all sides. Everywhere, until dying out at the horizon. Thousands of plants that seemed to multiply in a series of mirrors. So similar and symmetrically planted that they seemed the same plants, at the same distance, of the same height, virtually the same colour, flowering both transiently and eternally, identically. The burnished trunks, with a metallic polish and branches forming arcs of fans, obscuring sight in a vegetable light, cells of green futures.

—MIGUEL ÁNGEL ASTURIAS, *Viento Fuerte*
(my translation)

CHAPTER 20
STORIES

Without warning, my mother pointed with her finger.
"Look," she said. "That's where the world ended."
I followed the direction of her index finger and saw the station: a building of peeling wood, sloping tin roofs, and running balconies, and in front of it an arid little square that could not hold more than two hundred people. It was there, my mother told me that day, where in 1928 the army had killed an undetermined number of banana workers. I knew the event as if I had lived it, having heard it recounted and repeated a thousand times by my grandfather from the time I had a memory: the soldier reading the decree by which the striking laborers were declared a gang of lawbreakers; the three thousand men, women, and children motionless under the savage sun after the officer gave them five minutes to evacuate the square; the order to fire, the clattering machine guns spitting in white-hot bursts, the crowd trapped by panic while it was cut down, little by little, by the methodical, insatiable scissors of the shrapnel.

—GABRIEL GARCÍA MÁRQUEZ, *Living to Tell the Tale*
(*Vivir para contarla*)

What does the toxic past and present of banana production imply for the future? Doing something helpful in relation to the health impacts of pesticides in Ecuador was the goal that launched me, and this book, into a targeted exploration of the history of the banana-producing Americas of the last almost century and a half. This final part of the book examines prospects for improving the disturbing situation facing farmers and workers in the banana capital of the world. Moreover, the pivotal role Ecuador plays in the globalized banana industry means that pursuing such improvements will inevitably imply changes at larger geographic scales.

As historian Ludmila Jordanova points out, versions of the past help legitimize specific visions for the future.[1] Sociologists also explain that how you frame a problem strongly determines the solutions that are deemed preferable, or even imaginable.[2] Before jumping to solutions, then, it's worth looking once again at some of the more powerful competing stories about bananas, as these continue to be drawn on to justify specific proposed banana futures by companies, governments, physicians, scientists, farmers, workers, and consumers, among others.

Of the countless disturbing episodes associated with UFC's role in the banana-producing Americas, the 1928 banana worker massacre by Colombia's military, acting on behalf of UFC, is among the most storied.[3] The massacre has been raised to near mythical status through its fictional depiction in the beloved novel *One Hundred Years of Solitude*, by Nobel laureate Gabriel García Márquez. The story also shows how UFC (now Chiquita) has carefully constructed its image in ways that systematically erase the massive bloodshed and exploitation that this book has detailed.[4] For example, an all-night effort by soldiers removed hundreds or even thousands of bodies from the Ciénaga train station and therefore created a less outrageous morning-after picture—one in which judicious and legally sanctioned (even legally required) use of force had successfully defused a dangerous and lawless powder keg. UFC's strict control of information about the strike helped them stick to a story in which—as the *New York Times* reported on December 6, 1928—"the uprising of 12,000 laborers endanger[ed] the lives and property of Americans."[5]

Historian Kevin Coleman revealingly compares the photos the company donated to Harvard University, where they can still be viewed in the UFC archives, with those it kept secret.[6] The pictures UFC donated to Harvard show company buildings destroyed by workers in the aftermath of the massacre, consistent with a story in which the strike was the work of the communist menace (foreshadowing the Cold War story that would justify the 1954 coup in Guatemala), mixed with random destructiveness. A different story is told by one of the hidden photos that was sent to the Bocas division as union-fighting guidance for UFC managers, and stored in a box and forgotten until anthropologist Philippe Bourgois stumbled across it while doing fieldwork in the 1980s. This image shows the four leaders of the strike looking dapper and earnest while posing in formal outfits for a photo, which the company later annotated to enable sharing of information on such dangerous elements. In the strike leaders' own accounts, and in stories reporting a significantly higher death toll than "official" figures, the workers merely wanted an enormously profitable foreign company that was breaking Colombia's laws to provide them with reasonable protections. The excessive violence, in both the strike leaders' and subsequent historians' accounts, was perpetrated by the Colombian state with the full support of the United States.

What is at stake in this struggle over stories is nothing less than the legitimacy of UFC's operations in Colombia, and of a broader imperialist vision in which US interventions brought progress and prosperity to Latin America. On Chiquita's website, for example, the tab entitled "The Chiquita Story" recounts events from the company's history, stretching back to before the founding of UFC when Captain Lorenzo Dow Baker sailed northwards from Jamaica with a ship full of bananas in 1870.[7] Subsequent events in the highly selective history include the 1899 founding of UFC, the 1907 coining of the term *Great White Fleet*, the 1944 introduction of Miss Chiquita and the Chiquita Banana jingle to the world, several additional marketing campaign highlights, the 1990 name change of the company into Chiquita Brands International, and the 2000 beginning of "Chiquita brand sustainability efforts"—but no mention of controversies they might be responding to. In fact, the turbulent history recounted in this book is entirely absent from "The Chiquita Story" presented on the company's website.

When Chiquita portrays the history of UFC without making reference to the company's status as the primary symbol of twentieth-century US imperialism in the Americas, they are telling a story in which something resembling justice or "sustainability" can be achieved through purchasing bananas grown in more responsible ways and marketed by Chiquita. In such accounts, the massive, largely northward, transfer of wealth that UFC accomplished (backstopped by US military interference in the Americas) is not "on the table" as something that should be redressed. Given the contrast between the Chiquita story and the story recounted in this book (and countless other critical histories of banana production), using *Despicable Me*'s Minions to market bananas emerges as a particularly brazen way to make Chiquita's existence and trajectory seem fun and family-friendly, rather than bloody, devious, and exploitative. The implication of such stories told on banana stickers is that the children's joy (and parental relief) brought by many animated films can be obtained by eating Chiquita bananas. Such a bold move by one of history's most notorious corporations invites a closer look at the story that beloved characters found on banana stickers can tell when accompanied by historical context such as that provided in this book.

Minions love bananas: "buh-na-na" is one of the only distinguishable words in their pidgin language, while the plot of *Minions* relies on bananas for multiple plot twists,[8] and one Minion can even be spotted in *Despicable Me 2* singing the Chiquita banana song while wearing a fruit-bowl hat.[9] Minions in the *Despicable Me* films are generally yellow, except in the second installment in the trilogy when the problematically stereotypical Mexican supervillain El Macho uses a serum to make them indestructible, ravenous, and purple.[10] They do El Macho's evil bidding when so transformed, instead of their normal duties supporting the initially "despicable" but eventually lovable Gru. The spectre of a cheerful, goofy, banana-obsessed, "of colour" (yellow or purple) workforce doing the bidding of a supposedly-evil-but-actually-lovable employer appears almost too good to be true as a marketing tie-in for today's incarnation of UFC. The Minions' vaguely tropical pidgin language with numerous Spanish elements rounds out an uncanny recapitulation of many of the stereotypes and tropes used to justify UFC/Chiquita's exploitation of Afro-Caribbean, *mestizo*, and Indigenous workers in Latin America. As the history recounted in Part 1 of this book suggests, however, such stereotypes fall apart when subjected to actual historical scrutiny into their exploitative (e.g., racial capitalist) dimensions.

Before the Minions are turned purple and monstrous in the second *Despicable Me* movie, they are rendered unemployed in the first instalment of the series. The bank refuses their ostensibly evil and vaguely Eastern Bloc–origin boss Gru's request for a loan to finance his plan to steal the moon with the aid of a shrink ray, after Gru's adopted daughters embarrass him in a video call with the bank manager. After dejectedly telling the Minions they should seek other employment, Gru's spirits—and finances—are restored when his daughter Agnes volunteers the contents of her piggy bank. The Minions follow suit in pooling their money to crowdfund the lunar theft. In a heartwarming feat of character development, Gru eventually returns the moon to the sky after duelling with rival supervillain Vector (who turns out to be the bank manager's son), then returns in time to catch his daughters' dance recital.

In this case it is the role of financiers in relation to evil projects that chillingly reflects the history of Chiquita's predecessor UFC, accompanied by the Cold War politics evoked by Gru's clear origins as a caricature of Soviet spies in popular culture.[11] As discussed in Chapter 4, the investor power that ultimately helps Gru to become a better person functioned differently in relation to mid-century Guatemala. In reality, powerful financiers steered the banana industry towards a precarious contract-based production model in the aftermath of a corporate- and CIA-backed coup justified by fears of communism and embodying murderous systemic racism at a genocidal scale. Once again, this feels like a more important story for Minions to be telling than one about how fun it is to eat Chiquita bananas.

As the "DBCP Facts" page on their website suggests, Dole's efforts to present the story of DBCP in a way that absolves it of responsibility (and puts the blame on workers) are similarly sophisticated and brazen. Beyond employing the "kill step" and numerous other legal tricks to avoid responsibility for its willful decision to expose thousands of banana workers to the sterilization- and cancer-causing nematicide, for example, the company launched legal action against Swedish filmmaker Fredrik Gertten in 2009 to suppress his documentary *Bananas!*, which told the story of DBCP and related ongoing lawsuits.[12]

When viewed in light of the toxic journeys of the neoliberal late twentieth century in Latin America, the Disney characters used by Dole to market bananas also start to tell a different story. In the 1997 film *A Bug's Life*, whose characters adorned stickers on Dole bananas in 2020, a colony of ants is initially oppressed by grasshoppers who demand annual tribute in the form of food before the ants mobilize to fight them with the help of a diverse team of circus insects.[13] The real-world story of plant pests on banana plantations in the Cavendish period features an eerily parallel drama involving different types of "bugs" (e.g., insects, fungi, and nematodes) jockeying for food and freedom to survive. In the real world, it was vast quantities of toxic chemicals that steered the plot, not the pluckiness of lovable misfits. As with the contrast between Minions and UFC's racist manipulation of its diverse workforce, the on-plantation drama playing out where bananas are grown is much more grown-up than the animated movie used to market them—involving chemical weapons, devastated agricultural battlegrounds, and numerous casualties, both human and more-than-human.

A similar disjuncture emerges when the Disney film *Coco* is read against the backdrop of banana history, as Dole's use of the film's hero Miguel on banana stickers invites one to do. In the film, Miguel accidentally crosses over into the afterlife on the Mexican *Día de Muertos*.[14] He encounters several of his ancestors and other spirits whose skeletal appearance initially frightens him and whose tendency to misplace heads and other body parts creates humour. Those lost body parts became less funny to me, however, when Miguel started appearing on bananas from a company that exposed workers to a toxic chemical linked to sterilization, death, cancers, and—by extension—severed limbs and appendages.[15] The film also features a heartwarming struggle to preserve intergenerational linkages in Miguel's family through the Mexican tradition of maintaining photographic shrines (*ofrendas*) with offerings that keep ancestors' spirits alive and enable them to cross over to the realm of the living one night a year. For me, Miguel's efforts to preserve the memory of his grandmother Coco and great-grandfather Hector now evoke intergenerational ties that should have existed but never did—involving the *children never born* to banana workers exposed to DBCP.

While I enjoyed watching Minions and Disney films as "research" for this book, celebratory assessments of banana history were lurking closer to my public health scholarly home. For example, Cuyamel Fruit Company founder and later UFC head Samuel Zemurray underwrote the founding of the Tulane University School of Hygiene and Tropical Medicine in 1912.[16] His donation came one year after Zemurray had engineered a coup in Honduras (the prototypical banana republic), and four decades before he would do the same in Guatemala. A 2012 global health journal article nevertheless celebrates a century of the school's operations and applauds the persistence of its founding vision into the contemporary global health era, displaying a remarkable lack of attention to the immense loss of life and imperialist exploitation enabled by UFC and Zemurray:

> With a global approach to public health grounded in the field and a strong emphasis on laboratory-based research, the Tulane School of Public Health and Tropical Medicine of today is, in fact, very close to what [the school's founding dean] envisioned in 1912. A recent *Lancet* paper labeled the Tulane School of Hygiene and Tropical Medicine an early experience in the process of the creation of schools of public health . . . It is without a doubt the foundation on which the Tulane School of Public Health and Tropical Medicine is built.[17]

So it appears that some prominent public health scientists have swallowed the imperialist version of history that finds its most "animated" expression on Chiquita's and Dole's kid-friendly banana stickers (though the solidarity efforts of epidemiologists documented in this book attest to the fact that this is not a universal trend). I can state from personal experiences of doing global health research and interacting with others in the field that such celebratory stories are seductive and emotionally rewarding. They are, in some ways, the Disney movies of global public health, and they similarly perpetuate narratives that reinforce the very inequities we claim we are trying to address with our work.

Carefully comparing the history recounted in this book to the compelling stories used to market various banana futures by corporations, health scientists, and other interested actors therefore suggests a couple of important points regarding what should be done about problems facing pesticide-exposed farmers and workers. One is that the poverty of banana-producing countries can never be taken as natural or accidental. Imperialist strategies have managed to extract enormous wealth from tropical territories and bodies through banana production, although never without facing serious resistance that necessitated constant adjustments and changes of plan. These unfair but unpredictable dynamics provide both an imperative to act and grounds for hope when the abuses wreaked by corporate power and its neocolonial structural backing seem overwhelming.

The second point suggested by the use of Minions and Disney/Pixar characters by Chiquita and Dole (and global health celebrations of banana-linked schools of tropical medicine) gets at this need for hope and other important human emotions. Solutions to problems of social and environmental justice will not be located and enacted solely on the strength of sound scientific or even social scientific analysis. Whether it is *One Hundred Years of Solitude* or epidemiology articles, *A Bug's Life* or *Despicable Me*, banana histories and futures are tied up with stories people relate to on an emotional level. We consume stories because they are fun or sad or otherwise moving, and they help us make sense of both history and our own experiences. Such emotional responses are also—political ecology of health explains—key to how people experience social and environmental structures that shape bodies and health outcomes. They are similarly central to how ideologies are embodied and perpetuated.[18] It therefore seems likely that solutions to the toxicity of banana production will have to be not just intellectually solid but also affectively aware. They will have to help satisfy people's emotional needs.

With those story-related lessons in mind, this part of the book proceeds through the main types of action or solutions I have encountered while looking for ways to improve the health of pesticide-exposed banana workers. These types of action include two interrelated uses of "evidence" about pesticide-related health impacts; market-based approaches to solving social and environmental challenges; nuanced social scientific "noticing" of how people experience toxicity; and finally, multiple kinds of "plotting" to make the world a better place through food, societal transformation, and—yet again—stories.

CHAPTER 21
EVIDENCE I:
REGULATING AND LITIGATING TOXICS

The term *evidence* has been cautiously used throughout this book to refer to public health science generated in methodologically rigorous ways, consistent with traditions of evidence-based medicine and evidence-based public health. The story told in this book features numerous public health scientists attempting to generate such forms of health science evidence and use them to alter regulatory structures, while legal struggles such as those of DBCP-affected banana workers have seen science and personal testimonies regarding health impacts become literal legal forms of evidence. State structures such as regulatory bodies and the courts are among the most central mechanisms by which societies purport to protect people and environments from toxic chemicals such as pesticides. This chapter examines how these mechanisms have succeeded or failed in protecting banana workers, farmers, and environments, and how they are likely to work in the future.

Among the Disney/Pixar characters enlisted to grace Dole bananas is the medieval Scottish princess Merida, heroine of *Brave*.[1] Merida sports unruly long red hair and excels in archery, but not at humouring the suitors her parents expect her to choose from to cement their political alliance with neighbouring clans. After she argues bitterly with her mother and rides off into the forest in a huff, Merida comes across a witch's cottage. The witch attempts to sell her handicrafts, having given up troublesome spell-peddling to become a more conventional small businesswoman, albeit one with a magical cauldron/answering machine. In the face of the economic opportunity presented by Merida's offer to buy the entire cottage's stock of handicrafts, however, the witch is persuaded to sell the princess a potion that will "change [her] fate." This meddling with magic has predictably disruptive impacts that drive the plot until Merida reconciles with her parents and the conflict resolves in a family-friendly way.

The confluence of bananas and entrepreneurial witches opens an unexpected but revealing window on the potential for health evidence to address environmental injustice in banana production. Biomedical sciences and professions have historically developed in opposition to—and often in violent suppression of—ways of knowing such as ones typically associated with witches, in a process that was integral to the development of capitalism.[2] Collard and Dempsey have drawn on Silvia Federici's *Caliban and the Witch* to illustrate how misogynistic European witch hunts used patriarchal violence to express and accomplish *difference-making* of a kind that has been integral to capitalism and is currently culminating in the global crises of the Anthropocene/Capitalocene/Plantationocene.[3] By violently disqualifying the healing and other "magical" practices of witches, European nations helped entrench an opposition between women's "lore" and male Christian reason and science. Such oppositions also illustrate the logic of other forms of difference-making—such as racism's hierarchies—that are similarly central to capitalist accumulation based on extracting value from such "lesser" bodies.[4]

And so biomedical evidence has always been produced through often violent processes of difference-making and tied up with the logics and institutions of capitalist accumulation. For example, marginalization of competing non-allopathic and Indigenous healing traditions was central to the violent establishment of colonial control over the territory that would become Canada.[5] Importantly, hierarchical differentiation between Western biomedical science and the so-called folklore, superstition, or quackery of competing healing traditions took place well before Western biomedicine had experimented on enough poor, marginalized bodies to become more helpful than harmful. The tendency to disqualify "non-scientific" knowledge on health and illness nevertheless proceeded apace, in ways that would later contribute to massive pesticide-related health impacts in banana production, and foil attempts to obtain legal redress for those impacts.

In particular, regulatory structures for pesticides and health sciences that inform them have always represented a poisonous game of catch-up whose playing field is systematically tilted by the industry-moulded regulatory systems of modern democracies and the occupational and environmental health sciences they draw on. After being developed by transnational chemical companies based in Northern countries, pesticides are generally approved for use in those jurisdictions on the basis of animal toxicology studies conducted by the company introducing the chemicals or their contracted consultants. The roots of toxicology include the application of laboratory techniques from pharmacology—especially animal experimentation—to new industrial chemicals, notably including pesticides or the chemical weapons that often developed into them.[6] The Toxicity Lab (or Tox Lab) at the University of Chicago was founded by the US National Defense Research Committee in 1941 to evaluate the toxicity of potential chemical weapons and then transitioned to less overtly military toxicology work after World War II ended. The influential Tox Lab, whose graduates would found toxicology programs at universities across the United States, was a key site for the discipline's professionalization, in which it became increasingly specialized (and also male) and thus distinguished itself from fields such as nursing. Its zoology pens also reflected the role of thousands of more-than-human experimental subjects whose deaths enabled this scientific success: "monkeys, dogs, rabbits, rats, and mice, not to mention cockroaches and silkworms, which were all subject to various forms of toxicity by air (inhalation), by eating (ingestion), and through the skin."[7]

While practices vary slightly across nations, the general preoccupation of regulators processing toxicology data generated with such organisms has been to approve chemicals as quickly as possible, while checking off the box of nominally protecting human and environmental health using profoundly narrow and tendentious risk assessment processes that systematically underestimate dangers to health.[8] The development and adoption of that risk assessment model, moreover, has been thoroughly tied up with chemical industry influence on policy-makers, especially in the United States and then abroad through that country's influence on regulatory systems in Europe and around the world.[9] Reflecting such influences, modern risk assessments typically employ the scientifically indefensible assumption that chemicals are safe below a certain threshold of exposure,[10] within syntheses of existing science that often rely heavily on one or two large, industry-funded toxicology trials conducted using standardized protocols (such large standardized trials tend to miss many impacts of importance to health, such as endocrine disruption endpoints).[11]

Studies used by regulators have also tended to evaluate a single chemical at a time, thereby neglecting the combined effects of multiple simultaneous chemical exposures and their cumulative effects in the face of social factors that enhance vulnerability, such as poverty; food insecurity; malnutrition; living in violent, stressful environments; and even intergenerational trauma stemming from colonization and systemic racism.[12] The result, as a large body of environmental health scholarship shows, is a tendency to deem chemicals safe by underestimating the effects they will have on people and the environment in real-world (i.e., not laboratory) situations.[13] As the composition of the banana workforce amply illustrates, such real-world situations consistently place marginalized (especially racialized and low-income) people in harm's way. It is only after decades of non-consensual experimentation on such populations, enabling the accumulation of evidence of those harms, that regulators sometimes re-evaluate chemicals and control them—and even this step is often hampered by a lack of studies or regulators' tendency to dismiss or ignore many of them (many epidemiology or smaller academic toxicology studies suffer this fate).[14] Finally, even such protections are limited in scope to those within the jurisdiction in question, as exports of hazardous pesticides to other countries (banana-producing ones, for example) are typically unimpeded by domestic protection measures.

Beyond such flaws in regulatory processes, the use of toxicology results by the professional and scientific fields tasked with protecting the health of workers has also been problematic. Industrial hygiene, the precursor of today's occupational and environmental health sciences, evolved in the context of capital-labour conflicts that boiled over in countless industrial sites across the United States in the first half of the twentieth century. These conflicts resulted in legislative developments in workers' compensation that began to hold employers at least partially responsible for health and safety damages suffered by their workers.[15] The resulting need for scientifically defensible information that could help to adjudicate damage claims in relation to industrial chemicals led industrial hygienists to gravitate towards toxicological methods and reasoning. They also tended to gravitate away from more social scientific methods involving contact with workers whose political demands and grievances would have jeopardized hygienists' relationships with the employers of those workers—and therefore put into question their access to the bodies and data sources required to further their scientific and professional practice. In this way workers' lived experiences were relegated to the same "non-scientific" domain that had been used to disqualify the knowledge of witches centuries earlier.

Focusing on exposures that could be studied in a toxicology lab allowed early industrial hygienists—generally physicians, and mostly men—to claim an "objective" position that was supposed to be independent of both worker alliances and the influence of management (even though hygienists were often employed or funded by industry). Historian Christopher Sellers points out that this vision of objectivity nevertheless tended to support management's or industry's interests over those of workers. For example, avoiding workers and their messy political struggles allowed hygienists—many of whom were also practising toxicologists—to persistently blame those workers for their own work-related health issues, focusing on ignorance or carelessness instead of unsafe working conditions created by management's decisions.[16]

The focus on laboratory methods in toxicology and industrial hygiene led to a somewhat predictable class-based, disciplinary interpretation of the real-world health effects of pesticides as due to workers' poor choices or inherent deficiencies. This (scientifically unsound) belief, which travelled south with DBCP and other pesticides, also smoothly incorporated racist ideas about racialized peoples it encountered. For example, historian Linda Nash documents how health professionals in California in the 1960s helped make sense of Mexican migrant workers' massive exposure to toxic pesticides by blaming it on their alleged cultural propensity for carelessness and poor hygiene.[17]

A related tendency to blame Latin American workers for their own pesticide exposures in circumstances where safe use is impossible has been documented repeatedly across a range of settings over the past several decades.[18] Beyond its obviously self-serving function for agricultural capitalists, blaming workers in this way also reflects persistent and problematic tendencies in toxicology and related environmental and occupational health sciences to ignore the political-economic and ecological complexities that make safe-use prescriptions derived from controlled laboratory studies on animals wildly inappropriate in the real world.[19] Therefore, when pesticides reached Latin America in the 1960s and beyond, their systematically inequitable impacts were interpreted through a problematic and often racist lens of individual responsibility. The scientific inaccuracy of such a lens is illustrated by the fact that the conditions in which pesticides were used in Latin America from the 1960s through the end of the century—especially pervasive poverty and various other constraints on the agency of farmers and labourers—were a far cry from the controlled laboratory conditions in which toxicological tests on pesticides were conducted and then used to create safety labels and other instructions for how to "safely" use pesticides. Nevertheless, the ideology that blames workers for their own pesticide exposures has proved remarkably durable. Chemical companies, development agencies, agricultural extension agents, banana companies and other agricultural capitalists, and even health professionals have been able to duck responsibility for the predictably enormous toxic exposures that have occurred by blaming these on the workers and farmers experiencing them.

Reasons for the persistence of such individualizing narratives include the global pesticide industry's promotion of educational-behavioural approaches to pesticide safety in the form of several "Global Safe Use Pilot Projects" in the 1990s.[20] These projects were part of a broader trend in which marginalized agricultural populations in Central America were subjected to safe-use messaging in contexts characterized by profound inequities. For example, Guatemala was one of the Global Safe Use Pilot Project countries, thirty-seven years after the 1954 coup ushered in decades of genocidal dictatorship.[21] US interventions to "fight communism" and install neoliberal economic practices in the region meant that such agriculturally dependent societies with both repressive governments and pesticide-intensive development programs were common in the region. Safe-use pesticide campaigns in such contexts essentially saw health and development agents counsel workers, not to challenge their repressive governments, but rather to put on their PPE.

Given such toxic histories, the prospects for even good-faith modern regulatory and occupational health efforts based on toxicology studies to protect banana workers and farmers in the future appear cloudy. The story of the sterility-causing nematicide and Dole's denial of any responsibility, featured in "DBCP Facts" on their website, extends such doubts to the courts and other legal mechanisms used by workers to seek redress for the shortcomings of such regulatory structures. DBCP was introduced into markets, ecosystems, and bodies when (problematic) chemicals regulation was in its infancy, as documented in Susanna Rankin Bohme's disturbing transnational history of the chemical.[22] Dow Chemical Company and its competitor, Shell Chemical Company, collaborated in bringing the nematicide to market under the trade names of Fumazone (Dow's brand) and Nemagon (Shell's). Shell got Nemagon on the market first in 1955, before the two companies and collaborating university researchers had completed toxicological testing on the chemical.

Dow's and Shell's internal toxicology studies in the late 1950s began to reveal worrisome findings such as testicular atrophy, growth retardation, and fatty livers in rats given DBCP. Dow toxicologists nevertheless signed off on Fumazone and got it on the market in 1957. Warning labels on the two brand names of DBCP did not reflect the troubling findings. Ongoing toxicology experiments at the two companies continued to reveal testicular damage and reduced—or eliminated—sperm production in exposed animals, but the companies held these results back from US regulators (while conferring with each other). When the companies' toxicologists published a peer-reviewed article in 1961 showing the damages done to experimental animals (monkeys, rats, guinea pigs, and rabbits) by DBCP and arguing for stricter controls on its use, company officials downplayed the dangers and argued that these results did not imply risk to humans (contrary to the central premise of toxicology testing on animals). After lobbying to relax permitted DBCP residue levels in imported bananas, both Fumazone and Nemagon were registered by the US Food and Drug Administration in 1964.

With nematodes posing increasing problems on banana farms, Standard Fruit (Dole) began using Nemagon in Honduras around the end of 1967, and quickly observed yield increases. UFC—which would soon be known as United Brands after a 1970 merger—also brought DBCP into widespread use, as did Del Monte, which acquired it under the brand name Nemabrom from an Israeli chemical company, the Dead Sea Bromine Company. These companies used the chemical on their own plantations and either strongly urged or even required it on farms of associated producers from whom they purchased bananas under contract.

Labels on DBCP containers reaching Latin America urged limited skin or other contact and use of personal protective equipment but did not contain any instructions reflecting the testicular damage observed by Shell and Dow toxicologists over a decade earlier. Putting aside this glaring oversight, even the more routine label instructions urging limited contact with the pesticide were unrealistic—verging on fantastical—in light of the actual conditions in which DBCP was used on banana plantations. Since toxicological studies (or at least the version of them that was reflected in labels) theoretically helped to identify conditions in which "safe use" of DBCP was possible, banana company officials and managers asserted again and again that workers' exposure was their own fault, either through their carelessness or their stubborn refusal to wear PPE.[23]

Use of the chemical in wilful ignorance of its clear dangers would continue until 1977, when workers in a California DBCP plant were found to be sterile, showing that the testicular abnormalities observed in animal studies in the 1950s (predictably) foreshadowed major reproductive impacts in humans.[24] Production of DBCP in the United States was quickly halted, and California suspended all use of the chemical in the state. United Brands promptly stopped using DBCP on its banana farms, in favour of two organophosphate nematicides (Mocap and Nemacur), but—rather than safely dispose of their stockpiles—moved to sell their remaining DBCP. Castle & Cooke (Standard Fruit's parent company), in contrast, resolved to continue using DBCP, and even indicated that they would hold Dow in breach of contract if that company refused to provide the chemical to them.

As Bohme documents in infuriating detail, subsequent regulatory and corporate decisions about DBCP throughout the Americas repeatedly devalued certain human lives, following racist patterns. When Dow resumed sales of DBCP to Dole, they did so with stipulations for protective measures (albeit clearly inadequate ones) such as the use of PPE and scheduling fumigations at night when workers were not in the field. Dole's internal documents show instructions to managers indicating that the protective measures were impractical and could essentially be ignored. Additional devaluation of specific lives occurred when US agencies began setting new regulatory standards in response to studies documenting the sterilization of chemical plant workers. The agency in charge of standards for exposure of most workers—the Occupational Safety and Health Administration, or OSHA—set a maximum allowed workplace concentration in March of 1978 of one part DBCP per billion, the most stringent standard it had available to it. However, farm workers (a group that was largely composed of Mexican and other migrant labourers) were not covered by OSHA and therefore continued to be exposed to much higher concentrations. Mexican lives were doubly devalued by OSHA's ruling as the American chemical company AMVAC sought to fill the market niche caused by the standard's effective elimination of American DBCP manufacturing by beginning production in Mexico, where chemical plant workers were then predictably found to have been sterilized by late 1978.

Comparable devaluation of specific bodies and lives in relation to DBCP occurred in banana-producing regions. Costa Rican physicians and health officials had begun noticing sterility among banana workers in late 1977. These cases were linked to DBCP and used as a basis to ban imports of the chemical in 1979 and request that Dole stop using it. Dole fought hard to continue using DBCP and succeeded in keeping the country from de-registering the pesticide until 1988, but the ban on imports was quietly maintained. The low-profile nature of Costa Rican interactions with Dole on the issue helped DBCP and its reproductive impacts fly under the radar with workers and other governments in the region, allowing Dole to make use of its Costa Rican DBCP stores (over 180,000 litres worth) by simply shipping them to use in its plantations in La Ceiba, Honduras (the company also purchased more DBCP from AMVAC in 1979 to continue using in Honduras, Nicaragua, Ecuador, and the Philippines). Ultimately, US DBCP regulations preferentially protected (predominantly white) American chemical plant workers over (predominantly Latino) agricultural workers, then protected American banana consumers but not Latin American banana workers. When Costa Rica began to regulate DBCP, it did so in a way that left workers in other, even poorer, countries unprotected. US corporations eagerly exploited and also shaped these differential protection regimes, with workers' lives counting for as much, or as little, as other factors of production that were moved around in response to ecological, labour relations, or regulatory challenges.

The debacle of DBCP would be among the factors motivating US president Jimmy Carter to issue an executive order in 1981 limiting exports of pesticides that had been banned within the United States. However, within a month of taking office that same year, President Ronald Reagan—who would also preside over the US's bloody military interventions in Central America—rescinded the order and cleared the way for dangerous pesticides to reach Latin America in huge quantities throughout the 1980s and beyond.[25] Eliminating supposedly unnecessary regulations that limit economic activity was a hallmark of Reagan's neoliberal presidency, and accompanied his violent imposition of similar economic climates abroad.

Against this political and scientific backdrop, the legal struggles of DBCP-affected workers are both inspiring and illustrative of the limitations of litigation as a strategy for achieving environmental justice.[26] Costa Rican and Nicaraguan workers were the early originators of such attempts to pursue justice in the United States, where the companies involved were headquartered. Dow, Shell, and Standard Fruit/Dole (and its subsidiaries), in response, employed a variety of strategies to move court proceedings to a venue outside the US where they were less likely to cost them money. The legal principle of *forum non conveniens* was frequently used to deem a particular state's or country's court system "not convenient," allowing the lawsuit to be kicked out of court with the expectation that it would be pursued elsewhere. Judges often went along with the argument that, while DBCP was made and used by American companies in a way that funnelled profits to the US, the issue of holding those companies accountable for any resulting harms was essentially a Central American one.

When plaintiffs succeeded in getting specific state courts in the US to refuse such manoeuvres, the defendant companies employed additional tactics. These included using various tricks to have trials moved from state to federal court after a Texas ruling held that *forum non conveniens* could not be applied. For example, the Dead Sea Bromine Company was partially owned by the Israeli government and had manufactured DBCP; its status as a state enterprise meant that including it among the defendants allowed them to shift the case to federal court, where they could argue for it to be kicked out of the US (although this strategy was ultimately defeated when it was ruled that the company was not state-owned enough to qualify as a foreign government).

When the cases reached federal court, they were consolidated and presided over by a Reagan appointee named Simeon Timothy "Sim" Lake III. As Bohme explains, Lake and other judges who supported companies' calls to apply *forum non conveniens* furthered a vision of globalization in which US corporations could freely travel across national boundaries, but the people affected by their actions abroad could not. Defendants and their judicial allies (such as Judge Lake) also enabled the use of delay, divide, and conquer strategies. When Central American judicial systems rejected Judge Lake's decision that *forum non conveniens* could be applied and plaintiffs re-filed their suit in the US, Judge Lake delayed a decision on resuming the case there, thereby allowing the companies to pursue additional settlements with individual plaintiffs. Companies had been approaching actual or potential plaintiffs with settlement offers that precluded pursuing legal action.[27]

In response to the recurring threat of *forum non conveniens* and corporate machinations designed to exploit it, Nicaragua banana workers would engage in highly visible forms of protest and put pressure—often successfully—on the Nicaraguan state.[28] These DBCP-affected workers (*los afectados*) used a variety of techniques such as long-distance marches, showcasing by banana workers of bodies scarred and disfigured by pesticides and gruelling working conditions, encampments in front of the national legislature, and even threats to march naked or bury themselves alive. By employing such tactics, *los afectados* were able to gain concessions from the Nicaraguan state such as legislation designed to discourage the use of *forum non conveniens* by requiring banana and chemical companies that were seeking to transfer lawsuits to Nicaragua to pay a deposit of $100,000 per plaintiff to cover any eventual damages assessed. Companies nevertheless ignored the new rules with impunity—as they did subsequent decisions by Nicaraguan judges holding them liable for millions of dollars in damages for sterilizing banana workers. When a Nicaraguan judge attempted to enforce these rulings by seizing Shell's trademark as intellectual property, Shell responded by launching proceedings against Nicaragua under an international trade agreement's state-investor dispute resolution mechanism. The cash-strapped and tiny Nicaraguan state, facing a transnational corporation with many times its financial resources, backed down.

Yet another hardball tactic used by the companies was the "kill step," involving assembling cases alleging fraud by plaintiffs and their lawyers.

This strategy was effective and resulted in decisions against the company becoming essentially unenforceable. It was also buttressed by a judge's racist depictions of Nicaragua as corruption-riddled, which could conceivably complicate any future Nicaraguan efforts to seek justice in a US court—in relation to *any* topic—without being dismissed as unreliable or fraudulent.[29] The lived experiences of DBCP-affected workers were thus deemed to be unreliable and even deceitful, consistent with the (convenient) dismissal of other "non-scientific" or non-authoritative forms of knowledge by health sciences and state structures going back at least as far as the European witch hunts.

The legal-scientific story of the DBCP lawsuit, along with the Chevron lawsuit discussed in Chapter 19, ranks among the most sustained efforts ever mounted for transnational environmental justice in relation to "tropical" countries. The limited results obtained by these efforts raise substantial doubts regarding "evidence" (health science or legal) as a tool for achieving such goals. As many community and Indigenous organizations have come to realize, channelling environmental justice struggles through the state and its legal and public health institutions tends to result in labour-intensive Sisyphean battles, while also reifying or legitimizing state structures that are themselves at the root of the injustices in question.[30] Such lawsuits, in which epidemiology and toxicology results are frequently contested as legal evidence,[31] help to clarify the uses and limitations of such data-driven manoeuvring within state structures. The numerous class action lawsuits that have attempted to hold Dole and other fruit and chemical corporations responsible for exposing banana workers to a chemical that was known to cause sterilization targeted companies and chemicals that had (profitably) crossed national borders, but legal accountability for their actions was unable to do the same.[32] Links from DBCP to human health outcomes were not generally in dispute, but a variety of arguments and legal tricks were employed to argue that, as Dole's website claims, "there is no credible scientific evidence that Dole's use of DBCP on banana farms caused any of the injuries claimed in any of the DBCP lawsuits, including sterility."[33]

Coupled with the corporate-shaped structures of regulatory toxicology and toxics regulation, such insights suggest a need to go beyond such existing and supposedly straightforward uses of "evidence" in fights for environmental justice. Still, legal battles such as those waged by DBCP-affected banana workers caused states and banana and chemical corporations to undertake major changes to their practices and policies.[34] Those same battles also helped to build coalitions among workers, farmers, lawyers, and various NGOs, contributing to significant learning that could be applied in future environmental justice battles (even ones that eschew or deprioritize lawsuits and other unproductive engagements with state structures).[35] Even the discipline of toxicology, which does not come out looking good in this chapter, contains seeds of hope in the form of attempts to better recognize its scientific limits and do a better job at understanding the combined effects of toxic chemicals and societal inequities such as systemic racism. And while toxicology is thoroughly tied up with state and corporate interests and career paths, many scientists embedded in those problematic structures still work hard to protect people and ecosystems from toxic chemicals.[36] Even more promising is the small minority of toxicologists carrying out solidarity-focused partnerships with communities and civil society organizations fighting for environmental justice.[37] Comparable glimmers of hope are explored in the next chapter with respect to epidemiologic evidence and the epidemiologists who generate and apply it.

CHAPTER 22
EVIDENCE II:
EPIDEMIOLOGY AND "DEVELOPING COUNTRIES"

> *One fact of life which cannot be avoided by the giant importers of the world's bananas is that the fruit grows best in tropical lands, and tropical nations—for reasons which can be debated endlessly—are usually very poor.*
>
> —THOMAS L. KARNES, *Tropical Enterprise*[1]

Complementing toxicology-informed regulatory and legal efforts for environmental justice are efforts based on evidence-based public health. The recent history of banana production shows that such efforts to apply the science of epidemiology to the pursuit of better policies and therefore health outcomes demonstrate promise but face substantial epistemological and political limitations.

Epidemiology formed the backbone of my coursework in UBC's School of Population and Public Health, which was also the home department of my friend and fellow Machala-focused doctoral researcher Kendra. We had bonded over the stresses of demanding courses in epidemiology and biostatistics, and over the challenges of pursuing the evidence-based goals our training environment suggested we should achieve in our work in coastal Ecuador. Epidemiologic evidence is arranged hierarchically, with certain study designs considered credible and authoritative—especially randomized controlled trials—and other types given less weight. While this system has its uses, its many negative implications include requiring that the legitimate grievances of marginalized groups in society around things like toxic exposures jump through often impossibly high or complicated hoops in order to "count" in public policy-making or legal decisions.[2]

The epistemological ranking of evidence-based public health extends the logic of witch hunts, discussed in the previous chapter, in which women's knowledge was disqualified by male Christian authorities helping to entrench capitalist social relations in Europe.[3] Additional linkages between health sciences, the supernatural, and the origins of capitalism are evoked by a trip I made to Ecuador in 2010, shortly after I completed my epidemiology-focused PhD comprehensive exam. I joined Kendra in Machala in July, as we both sought to apply public health evidence in solidarity with communities facing epistemological barriers to environmental justice (Kendra was doing her own PhD fieldwork on community-based dengue control with El Oro's vector-borne-disease control program). Possibly reflecting the accumulated stress of our doctoral coursework and life in a gritty banana town, we ended up venturing one night to *El Shopping* to watch a late-stage installment in the *Twilight* series of vampire films. We found ourselves laughing uncontrollably at especially melodramatic scenes and the seeming inability of Jacob, the heartthrob werewolf, to find a shirt. We then purchased the other films in the series at one of the many open-air bootleg DVD stalls in downtown Machala, where recent blockbusters and lurid horror films constantly play to passersby on TVs on the sidewalk (also how I first learned of the existence of the lurid *Zombeavers*). Watching the rest of *Twilight* therefore cost Kendra and I about four dollars and several hours of our lives.

A story involving vampires, zombies, stressed-out graduate students, public health, and communities can illuminate the history and possible futures of epidemiologic evidence as a strategy for pursuing environmental justice for banana farmers and workers (and others). Political economist David McNally has explored the relationship between vampire and zombie stories and the entrenchment or intensification of capitalist social relations.[4] Before Vlad the Impaler was immortalized by Bram Stoker in *Dracula*, for example, he was a wealthy agricultural capitalist who used enslaved Roma labourers in ways that bled them dry, even if he was not literally sucking their blood. McNally explains that the inherently monstrous nature of capitalism requires the violent consumption of human bodies, with capitalist ideology preventing the conscious recognition of such brutality.⁵ Stories of bloodsucking and flesh-eating monsters thus represent a kind of displaced psychological reaction to the broken bodies created by industrial worksites and the disciplining functions of capitalist states. That is, such stories are the unconscious or nightmarish expression of the horrors we are ideologically kept from attributing to their real causes.

McNally explains that theft, in a Europe undergoing transitions from more collectivist or communal social relations to predominantly capitalist ones in the seventeenth and eighteenth centuries, was often dealt with in highly visible and bloody ways, notably including public (human) dissections that horrifically punished such crimes against private property. Such dissections represented an alliance of the nascent modern medical profession with capitalist elites, enrolling healers in disciplining society's resistance to the brutal imposition of private property rules and symbolically linking grisly eviscerations and dismemberments to the exercise of class power. The vampiric or cannibalistic aspects of biomedicine's disciplining function are further suggested by Michel Foucault's documentation of how the evolution of medical perception has occurred in symbiosis with the establishment of Western liberal democratic states, in which the workings of capitalist labour markets generated both wealth and widespread poverty.⁶ Physicians historically used the resulting broken and ill bodies of the poor as raw material on which to experiment (sometimes in the horrifically public manner documented by McNally), thereby building biomedical science's advancement on dead and mutilated bodies.

This disturbing history helps to make sense of some puzzling aspects of contemporary science about pesticides and the health of banana workers and other Latin American workers or peasants. In the centuries after horrific public dissections fell out of fashion as a combined punishment/research tool, the medical profession's relationship to the poor became less lurid but nevertheless solidly in favour of the maintenance of capitalism. As Foucault documents, physicians took on a role that palliated some of the worst effects of poverty through charitable acts, helping maintain reasonably productive workforces and preserving social order in the face of disparities that threatened more revolutionary changes. Simultaneously, biomedical ways of knowing zeroed in on individual behavioural or physiological traits and technological interventions in relation to disease. They also shied away from the structural workings of the capitalist political economy that generated not only the privilege that enabled the practice of medicine, but also an enormous proportion of the illnesses that provided the field with a steady stream of broken and ill poor bodies to experiment on.[7] In this way medicine, and the health science research that supported it, came to systematically ignore the power relations of capitalism.[8]

Research informed by such ways of knowing uses the bodies of the poor as fodder for the advancement of science, while systematically avoiding and therefore helping to naturalize the inequitable politico-economic structures that generate such beleaguered bodies as well as biomedical professionals and scientists. How this can play out in relation to the health effects of pesticides in Latin America is especially evident in a 2001 review paper of "pesticide use in developing countries" by a toxicologist at a Canadian university. This article asserts that "pesticides have consistently demonstrated their worth by increasing global agricultural productivity ... in tropical regions seeking to enter the global economy," but later points out that "the largest proportion of human acute toxicity data related to pesticide intoxications comes from developing nations."[9] This well-cited article parrots a Green Revolution narrative in which "developing countries" benefit from pesticide-intensive agricultural development, with the resulting massive pesticide exposures representing an unfortunate but scientifically study-able side effect.

The article also illustrates how such stories almost inevitably conclude with technical or behavioural interventions leaving the root causes of poverty in the global South (and pesticide exposures) intact, holding that "the long-term solution to pesticide problems is education."[10] The commercial usefulness of such stories about the "benefits" of pesticide-intensive development is further illustrated by an international pesticide risk perception study funded by Syngenta, which has consistently worked to promote ineffectual and reactionary safe-use approaches to pesticides. Not surprisingly, workers are assigned responsibility for the problem by a research question asking "whether it will be possible to change farmers' attitudes to improve the way they use pesticides."[11]

In contrast, the epidemiologists discussed in Chapter 11 who partnered with banana workers and other pesticide-exposed Latin Americans in the late twentieth century were breaking with disciplinary conventions that tend to keep health professionals and scientists out of political struggles. Stories of solidarity between Northern and Latin American researchers and communities confronting the toxicity of banana and other agroindustries are often inspiring. They are a big part of why I focused my own research on pesticide problems in Latin America. However, in looking closely at the body of health science scholarship that issued from such collaborations, I found disturbing (undoubtedly unintended) continuities with biomedicine's symbiotic relationship to capitalism.

For example, such articles were often published in English-language journals and were also often framed as addressing the problem of pesticide impacts "in developing countries."[12] Articles generally open by asserting that pesticides are a major problem in such countries and then zero in—as scientific articles typically must—on the specific study the article was written to report on. An important study of cancer in banana plantation workers in Costa Rica, for example, asserts early on that "particularly high exposures to pesticides occur in developing countries" and then narrows in by stating that "working conditions in Costa Rica are insufficiently controlled," putting that country forth as a scientifically interesting example of a developing country.[13]

In this and most other such epidemiologic studies of pesticides in Latin America, tellingly, the region appears as impoverished or "underdeveloped," with primitive working conditions that lead to dangerous pesticide exposures.[14] This portrayal is miles ahead of studies that blame workers' exposures on their own supposed ignorance or carelessness, but nevertheless displays continuities with the imaginative geographies used to justify UFC's "civilizing mission" in early twentieth-century Latin America, which portrayed the region as untamed, backwards, and in need of Northern scientific improvement.

Modern portrayals such as those in pesticide epidemiology articles, while not advancing the blatantly racist arguments of UFC's cheerleaders, still neglect to explain why the poverty and unsafe working conditions leading to massive pesticide exposures persist. That is, the turbulent history recounted in the first two parts of this book is largely absent from the backgrounds of "developing" banana-producing countries as they appear in epidemiology articles, despite the fact that their authors often demonstrate in their non-epidemiologic writing and careers that they are well aware of factors such as pesticide and fruit company malfeasance, or the violence of US imperialism. When it comes time to explain pesticide exposures, the story recounted at length in this book often gets replaced by three words: "in developing countries."

So what's wrong with epidemiologists justifying their work as solving the problems of the developing world and writing journal articles that omit or gloss over the horrific histories (and present-day political and economic injustices) that create the situations they are studying? In general, the need for coherence in a scientific article means that academic contributions made by particular studies must appear to solve the problem outlined by how the article was framed, and also to cohere with particular outcomes or solutions. So if evidence-based public health interventions must be based on well-designed epidemiology studies, and those studies tend to be published in coherent articles that assume poverty as an inherent characteristic of Latin America, then the evidence-based interventions in question will be ones that seem appropriate for fixing pesticide exposures in a mysteriously or constitutionally poor part of the world. Since such articles don't take the real historical roots of Latin American poverty into account in how they are framed, fixing those root causes is just not on the evidence-based table.

After presenting pesticide exposures as emerging from the "developing" nature of the countries in question, epidemiologic studies of pesticides and health in Latin America generally conclude with recommendations for things like pesticide poisoning registries, education of workers, and provision of PPE—all routine and sensible public health measures, but none of them touching the politico-economic injustices that this book has gone into with respect to one particularly central Latin American agricultural industry. And so pesticide epidemiologists working in banana-producing Latin American countries appear to have reproduced the "discourse of development," to use the term coined by Colombian anthropologist Arturo Escobar.[15] In the linked stories and practices making up this discourse, developing countries appear as mysteriously or inherently impoverished and in need of rescue by countries of the global North and their technical expertise. Numerous "solutions" ensue that never get at the root causes of underdevelopment—namely colonial exploitation and its continuation in the late twentieth century via mechanisms such as forced neoliberalization.

This tendency to reproduce the discourse of development appears to be incentivized by the genres and conventions of public health sciences. That is, you can neatly and quickly demonstrate the importance of a particular pesticide epidemiology study by framing it as solving the problems of (mysteriously or inexplicably poor) developing countries. In contrast, if you talk about things like US imperialism or the callous actions of transnational corporations, you start to seem like you're not objective. Indeed, IRET scientists working with Foro Emaús and other banana-related social movement actors are said to have guarded their autonomy as scientists in such collaborations in order to avoid "a loss of the scientific value."[16] Even if those scientists did try to fit in more historical and politico-economic context, they would have also bumped up against the word limits and editorial guidance of the restrictive epidemiology journal article genre, often limited to 2,500 or even 2,000 words. Because epidemiologists know that they're going to have to publish their studies in such restrictive genres, they generally start to plan them in a way that most efficiently fits, purging supposedly extraneous political factors from epidemiology studies (whose statistical models generally tolerate them poorly anyway).[17]

The realization that such depoliticized framings of pesticide-related environmental injustice could facilitate scientific "progress" (and career advancement) troubled my attempt to learn from and work with pesticide epidemiology about Latin America published in international scientific journals. Dismissing the efforts of pesticide epidemiologists in banana-producing Latin American countries, however, was not an option. It's not terribly helpful to call them vampires, or fair to imply that they took a callous view towards the suffering of poor people exposed to pesticides. Despite some troubling features of their peer-reviewed articles and the biomedical disciplinary conventions that shaped them, for example, pesticide epidemiologists such as Catharina Wesseling and the socially engaged scientists at IRET showed themselves to be thoroughly and often inspiringly committed to protecting the well-being of banana workers, and other pesticide-exposed Latin American populations, by frequently working in solidarity with grassroots organizations.

In fact, the work of some such pesticide epidemiologists evolved from an initial faith in the standard public health narrative of epidemiologic evidence helping to "fix" developing countries to more meaningfully recognize politico-economic power relations and the lived experiences of banana workers.[18] In Wesseling and her colleagues' own words, "Despite this substantial body of literature and research generated in the Region, the public health establishment has failed to bring about a noticeable impact on the decision making process that regulates the importation, manufacture, and use of pesticides in Central American countries... No major governmental action towards reduction of pesticide use or towards banning of specific products was undertaken in Central America during the 1990s."[19]

The thoughtful and reflective later scholarship of such pesticide epidemiologists working in Latin America was one of the main sources of my disquiet with the simplistic evidence-based approaches my doctoral training environment prioritized. It started me on the path to understanding not only the limitations of pursuing environmental justice for banana farmers and workers through biomedicine's institutional structures, but also the important lessons that had been generated in the valiant attempt to do so.

As discussed in earlier chapters, some of those lessons relate to the scientific challenges of unequivocally documenting the health effects of pesticides found in complex chemical mixtures affecting hard-to-study populations with numerous competing health challenges (*confounders*). One response to difficulties in generating evidence that could compel policy change to protect people from pesticides is to call for more funding and research to overcome such methodological challenges. However, the efforts of health scientists documented in this book suggest that insufficient research funding or methodological rigour is not the problem. As discussed in Part 2, Catharina Wesseling's decades of sustained effort to carry out good epidemiology while simultaneously supporting the social struggles of Foro Emaús in Costa Rica tested the usefulness of evidence-based policy-making ambitions in banana-producing countries and found it to be woefully lacking. Parallel efforts to influence pesticide policy in Ecuador through a decades-long research program involving epidemiology studies with potato farmers similarly led to recognition of the dominant influence of the Ecuadorian and transnational pesticide industries on policy-makers.[20]

More recently, however, Austrian researchers imply that their epidemiology work, in combination with lobbying by UROCAL and ASTAC, has helped bring about added protection for Ecuadorian banana workers:

"Our report was delivered to the UROCAL consortium and used to lobby for legal restrictions of pesticide use in Ecuador after which paraquat was restricted in Ecuador in 2018."[21] Beyond raising the question of whether or not the report was a decisive factor in the decision to ban the highly toxic herbicide, this development illustrates another limitation of relying on biomedical science to resolve toxic inequities. A 2001 review article lead-authored by Wesseling on hazardous pesticide use in Central America observed that "despite the abundance of hard data on exposures to and effects of methamidophos [a highly toxic organophosphate insecticide] and paraquat, these pesticides remain among the most imported pesticides in a majority or all of the Central American countries."[22] As also outlined in a paraquat-focused review article Wesseling and her colleagues published simultaneously, the continuing use of the herbicide in 2001 represented a gross neglect and misinterpretation of existing evidence, influenced by factors such as industry-funded studies that tended to minimize the herbicide's dangers.[23]

The fact that Ecuador would not ban the chemical for almost another two decades points to a more serious problem than just a shortage of epidemiologic evidence or lobbying. As the previous chapter explains, it points to fundamental flaws in modern systems of risk assessment, the processes through which science is produced to inform them, and the subsequent movement of toxic chemicals and chemicals regulations across national borders. Ecuador's 2018 banning of paraquat is emblematic of the tendency for pesticides to be recklessly introduced into global North countries, disproportionately applied to the bodies of racialized and other marginalized populations at home but especially abroad, controlled in a belated way by Northern regulators, and then—sometimes—controlled in an even more grossly belated way by governments in Southern countries.

Such realities suggest that focusing scientific attention on ascertaining the effects of individual pesticides and then using the resulting evidence to argue for bans on such chemicals is a noble but losing battle. That is, regulatory structures and scientific standards of proof mean that industry is generally able to introduce new pesticides and other chemicals into societies at a rate many times (and sometimes many hundreds of times) faster than researchers and regulators can laboriously assess and then control their real-world impacts—a bind that worsens in relation to controlling the overseas impacts of pesticide exports.[24]

In addition, the economic inequities that tend to be found behind patterns of pesticide exposure are themselves linked by a large body of social determinants of health evidence to huge, negative health implications.[25] This reality was demonstrated by the banana farmer I spoke with in 2011 who acknowledged the health effects of pesticides but, when questioned about them, was more interested in discussing the economic challenges facing small producers in that year's banana price crisis. Evidence-based social policies targeting income, housing, health services, and education are sensible public health responses to such inequities, but such interventions and the redistribution of wealth they entail are typically contrary to the neoliberal policy priorities of states around the world.[26] Efforts by Ecuador's twenty-first-century socialist government to protect workers and the rural poor are a kind of exception to this rule that ultimately appears to prove it. For one, the policies appear not to have been respected or adequately enforced by the government of Rafael Correa and were financed through a combination of loans from Venezuela and China, high petroleum prices, and extractivist development backstopped by sometimes racist authoritarianism. Then the end of the oil boom ushered in a rolling-back of such protections under the IMF-influenced government of Lenín Moreno, worsened when the COVID-19 pandemic allowed for shock-doctrine tactics to further erode social and environmental protections.

The twenty-first-century Ecuadorian example thus provides a reminder that pursuing evidence-based policies in particular jurisdictions is hugely limited by international politico-economic forces, with their colonial roots and present-day neoliberal colouration. Indeed, (many) states and unions have attempted to protect banana workers for over a century, up to and including important labour solidarity initiatives linking Ecuadorian workers to global North organizations in the twenty-first century. Time after time, however, such efforts have achieved important victories only to be sidestepped by an industry whose enormous power and backing from the structures of the global economy makes it mobile and networked in ways that individual local unions and Latin American governments are not.[27] The banana industry's ability to sidestep obstacles to its profitability has also remained largely intact through transnational lawsuits challenging its lack of accountability through the use of various forms of legal evidence, as documented in the previous chapter. While the "kill step" pioneered by the companies' law firm in the DBCP lawsuits was ultimately key to helping the companies evade accountability for their actions, epidemiology's disciplinary conventions also often function as obstacles to marginalized communities seeking legal redress for environmental injustice.

In particular, norms of "objectivity" tend to associate methodological rigour with studies (including many corporate-funded ones) that eschew advocacy on behalf of marginalized populations because it is supposedly "biased."[28] I was reminded of this tendency as I watched recordings of testimony by one of Dole's expert witnesses in the *Tellez v. Dole* DBCP lawsuit, a physician-epidemiologist named Marc Schenker.[29] Schenker had previously led a Syngenta-funded study of the health effects of paraquat among Costa Rican banana, coffee, and oil palm workers that was published in a very tidy epidemiology article making no mention of public controversies that had motivated the study, and no recommendations beyond further research. In his later work for Dole, Schenker analyzed the individual medical records of twelve Nicaraguan plaintiffs who claimed to be sterilized by DBCP, and also reviewed the epidemiology literature on the chemical's health impacts.

I watched as Schenker began response after response with a pensive "Well . . ." that indicated he objected to the framing of the plaintiffs' lawyer's question and was about to provide a different sort of answer than the one being sought. He would then resolutely dismiss studies or aspects of any study suggesting that DBCP might have negative impacts on agricultural fieldworkers, on top of its more well-established role in sterilizing chemical plant workers exposed to high concentrations of the nematicide (the existence of a threshold below which toxic chemicals are supposed to cause no adverse effects is a scientifically questionable but commercially useful assumption[30]). It was a helpful review of my epidemiology training and occupational health teaching experience to watch Schenker's strategies for deflating the plaintiffs' lawyer's claim that the workers were exposed to greater concentrations of the chemical than Dole had asserted, and with real negative impacts on their fertility. Watching his testimony took about as much time as Kendra and I had spent on the *Twilight* series and certainly disturbed me more than had that melodramatic vampire saga. This courtroom drama used biomedical reasoning to weave the intimate details of the workers' lives and bodies—relationships, drinking habits, work schedules, and testicle size, for example—into an argument exculpating the multinational corporations that had knowingly exposed those workers to a sterility-causing chemical.

Comparable dynamics pitting marginalized communities against epidemiology's disciplinary conventions emerged a few years later in the legal battle against Chevron over its decades of contamination of the Ecuadorian Amazon. When "engaged" (i.e., justice-oriented) epidemiologists carried out a cross-sectional study on petroleum-health relationships in the Ecuadorian Amazon and sought to use the results to argue for environmental remediation and public health efforts, they were rebuked in the pages of an epidemiology journal for carrying out "epidemiology on the side of the angels" and getting carried away with public health recommendations based on relatively weak evidence.[31] Almost simultaneously, Chevron commissioned several prominent epidemiologists to critique the engaged epidemiologists' studies and then published the critiques in full-page ads in Ecuadorian newspapers. A resulting exchange in the pages of an academic journal saw one of Chevron's consultants, whose well-known epidemiology textbook was a component of my own doctoral coursework, claim that carrying out scientific activities for a major corporation embroiled in an environmental justice lawsuit was a neutral, defensible scientific activity. Defending such forms of objectivity, Kenneth Rothman explained, merely amounted to "elevating the level of scientific discourse." Of course, Chevron lost the lawsuit in Ecuador but appears unlikely to ever pay damages due to a successful portrayal of the plaintiffs and their lawyers as fraudulent.

Understanding health science as part of the vast system of interpretive resources co-dependent with capitalism helps make sense of the patterns and problems of pesticide-health science, from toxicology's reduction of the world into laboratory-sized chunks to be studied "objectively"; to victim-blaming narratives that accomplish profitable difference-making between pesticide-exposed (lacking in *cultura*) farmers and workers on the one hand, and scientists and other educated folks on the other; to journal article genres in epidemiology that preferentially select for truncated and depoliticizing versions of the world (and its "developing countries") to frame research.

Seeing health sciences in this way has been argued to motivate a focus on non-heroic everyday acts of care and resistance among people experiencing pervasive toxicity.[32] This conclusion is based on a lot of very good feminist scholarship about the dangers of "heroic" capitalist or even socialist visions for taking over the world and its state structures, while women and communities are getting on with the work or "arts" of living (now "on a damaged planet," to quote Anna Tsing).[33] I wholeheartedly endorse this valuation of everyday lived experience and acts of care, but find myself a bit less comfortable with totally forgetting about the "heroic," a category that definitely applies to the dream of evidence-based medicine.

My lived experience—some of which comes across in this book—teaches that the efforts of epidemiologists and others (even many toxicologists) to pursue equitable and non-world-destroying futures using the flawed tools of evidence-based public health and other biomedical sciences could provide seeds for helping to more effectively transform such hegemonic "heroic" discourses (which are so pervasive that we're all tied up with them to one degree or another). The Ecuadorian organization ASTAC and comparable banana worker organizations in Central America also collaborate with epidemiologists as part of their overall strategy, meaning that social scientific analyses of evidence-based public health should ideally be constructively critical ones that support the aspirations of social movements. Those grassroots strategies have also increasingly involved attempts to leverage consumer pressure to improve working and environmental conditions, as discussed in the next chapter. (This is also the point at which I can no longer avoid the question of what sort of bananas people should be buying.)

CHAPTER 23
SHOPPING

> *The commodity economy has been here on Turtle Island for four hundred years, eating up the white strawberries and everything else. But people have grown weary of the sour taste in their mouths. A great longing is on us, to live again in a world made of gifts. I can scent it coming, like the fragrance of ripening strawberries rising on the breeze.*
>
> —ROBIN WALL KIMMERER, *Braiding Sweetgrass*

I don't fucking care what kind of bananas you buy.

That was the original working title of this chapter. The seeds of that outburst were planted when I was derailed from my early conversational monologues on the revolutionary implications of banana history by questions such as "Should I only be buying organic bananas?" They then germinated post-PhD as I taught multiple cohorts of Master of Public Health students, many of whom would respond to political ecology and banana-related lecture examples with ideas about making different purchasing choices. Despite my ongoing efforts to show them how inequities such as pesticide exposure in banana production are not primarily caused by shopping decisions and won't be fixed by them, disturbing facts about environmental injustice seem to inevitably lead many people to think about voting with their wallets. Finally, the last stage in the life cycle of that working title accompanied my short stint working for a Canadian environmental NGO in which I was responsible for running problematic campaigns to get corporations to voluntarily retire toxic chemicals from their supply chains.[1]

It might have been the exhausted state I found myself in after quitting that last job (after years of precarious sessional teaching) that caused me to back off from swearing at readers right in the table of contents. I worried as well about being unnecessarily harsh towards people who genuinely want to make the world a better place and genuinely need to buy groceries. Insulting readers with such aspirations would also ignore perceptive scholarship on the rootedness of "conscious consumption" ambitions in important human desires, and on how the burden of care work in conscious consumption disproportionately falls on women in the absence of adequate state regulation of toxic chemicals.[2] Equally importantly, outright dismissal of conscious consumption would fail to do justice to the tireless work that social movements have done to protect workers, farmers, and environmental rights through market-based approaches such as organic and fairtrade labels and consumer activism. Early fairtrade activism occurred in solidarity with Third World revolutionary movements during the Cold War, while important social and environmental protections have been won through Ecuadorian small farmer and worker alliances with banana consumers.[3]

Such mixed feelings on addressing environmental and social injustice through voluntary actions of corporations and consumers (market-based mechanisms), and the normalized state of such approaches, has evoked scholarship on neoliberalism's seepage into hearts and minds globally. As geographer Julie Guthman puts it, market-based mechanisms such as organic and fairtrade labels are thoroughly neoliberal in that they

> are governed by a complex array of state/private/NGO/multilateral bodies that subscribe to notions of audit/transparency as "action at a distance"... they extend property rights to practices where none previously existed; they entail forms of enclosure in ways that produce scarcity; they attach economic values to ethical behaviors; and, finally, they "devolve" regulatory responsibility to consumers. In other words, not only do these labels concede the market as the locus of regulation, in keeping with neoliberalism's fetish of market mechanisms, they employ tools designed to create markets.[4]

The advocacy of such approaches by many smart and well-intentioned people helps explain the profanity I used to open the chapter. Anarchist geographer Simon Springer's article "Fuck Neoliberalism" caps the author's trajectory of carrying out nuanced analyses of processes of neoliberalization and ultimately losing patience. In his words, "neoliberalism is a particularly foul idea that comes with a whole host of vulgar outcomes and crass assumptions. In response, it deserves to be met with equally offensive language and action."[5] But while I echo this appropriately shocking stance, I still want to respond to the entanglements of good intentions and good people with the "offensive" ideas of neoliberal capitalism (and I do not exempt myself from such entanglements). In response to questions about what sort of bananas to buy, this chapter therefore briefly—and I hope compassionately—contextualizes some key market-based responses to environmental injustice in light of the history recounted in this book.

A 2002 article by John Soluri sought to "lend agency to the consuming masses" by showing how US consumers' adherence to the shape and flavour of Gros Michel bananas drove massive environmental change in banana-producing countries such as Honduras, especially through UFC's slash-and-burn agricultural approach to managing Panama disease by simply cutting tropical rainforest to start new, uninfected plantations.[6] In its interaction with the exploitative labour control practices and political machinations that helped banana transnationals dodge plant diseases,[7] such consumer influence shows that banana-buying practices have certainly never been irrelevant to the social and ecological destructiveness of the banana industry. Of course, consumers' adherence to Gros Michel was itself a product of UFC's immense public relations efforts to install that specific variety in the hearts and "healthy" diets of North Americans.[8] Consumer preferences are therefore not a decisive and apolitical variable in the histories and possibly emancipatory futures of bananas.

In the Cavendish era, studies of market-based attempts to improve the social and environmental performance of banana production largely begin with changes to banana production in the 1990s, amidst broader neoliberalization trends towards voluntary rather than state-mandated pursuit of social and environmental goals.[9] Specific impetus in the banana sector came from controversies experienced by the large transnationals over labour rights and environmental destruction in places such as Costa Rica and Honduras, as well as the debacle of all three transnationals' payments to paramilitaries in Colombia.[10] In response, Chiquita continued its tradition of aggressively and creatively managing public opinion by partnering with the conservation NGO Rainforest Alliance to develop an environmental certification system for their bananas.[11] Del Monte and Dole chose not to participate in the Rainforest Alliance program and adopted more generic ISO (International Organization for Standardization) standards, with Dole's decision reflecting a corporate culture oriented around internal scientific research and imperviousness to environmentalist pressure.[12] The Rainforest Alliance label nevertheless remains in use today with some attention to labour rights complementing its original sustainability focus, and also serves as the basis for some European supermarkets' own banana labels.[13]

The fact that supermarkets have both relied on the Rainforest Alliance certification and developed their own labels illustrates a major transformation of banana markets in the 1990s and beyond. Global North and transnational supermarket chains have increased their ability to purchase bananas directly from producers, in many ways shifting the balance of power in the industry away from the transnational banana companies Dole, Chiquita, and Del Monte.[14] Along with this increased buying power has come greater involvement in shaping production practices in the form of good agricultural practices (GAP) standards such as EurepGAP and its later incarnation, GlobalGAP. These standards, which apply to bananas purchased directly from producers but also via traditional exporters such as Dole and Chiquita, include some measure that would protect workers and the environment, along with a central focus on producing visually perfect, marketable produce.

The impacts of banana certification systems have been mixed. Sociologist Kees Jansen raised questions of accountability and comprehensiveness in regard to Chiquita's and Dole's labelling initiatives in the late 1990s, and observed that major decisions regarding pesticide use with implications for worker and environmental contamination were made for reasons other than certification requirements.[15] Even if certified farms do indeed marginally improve pesticide safety for workers, as Jansen's analysis suggests, the non-certified producers from whom bananas are sourced through contract or spot purchases by fruit and supermarket transnationals often fail to meet such performance measures.[16] In addition, as my interviewees often reminded me, a narrow focus on pesticides obscures more insidious and consequential socio-economic changes brought about by such power-laden transformations. For example, GAP standards can be met primarily by large farms with the capital to make the necessary investments, which are often for sensible measures like on-farm bathrooms for workers and more careful pesticide management practices.[17] Such investments are most possible for large farms that are already doing well, and whose existing capital allows them to claim greater market share in the future by qualifying for contracts requiring GAP.

People in El Oro told me how this was playing out during my fieldwork, as many small farmers were facing the requirement to obtain GlobalGAP status at that time but were not sure they could afford the required changes. Since these small farmers were already marginal and on the verge of losing their farms, it appeared likely that GlobalGAP was contributing to ongoing re-concentration of land in *la costa*, in which small farmers would sell their land to larger agro-industrial interests.[18] Such farmers would then often join the masses of landless labourers living in unhealthy neighbourhoods of *la costa* and competing for precarious and poorly paid work on larger farms.[19] And so, while certification systems imposed by large transnational fruit and supermarket corporations may have some arguably positive social and environmental impacts on specific farms, they also entrench corporate control over banana production and deepen its associated societal inequities.[20]

Certified organic bananas also come with problematic implications for social equity. For example, organic farmers who had successfully made the transition to certified organic banana production told me this involved about three years of hard work while operating at a loss. During this period, yields were low and the fruit produced did not yet qualify for the higher prices organic bananas command. Since small farmers are often only a few steps away from losing their farms, making this transition is typically not economically viable without external support such as from European development NGOs. As a result, only a limited number of small farmers within the universe of banana producers are able to make the transition to organic production. Large transnationals like Dole and Chiquita, in contrast, can easily afford to convert some of their farms to organic production—or buy under contract from certified farms—to take advantage of demand.

This situation appears to mirror the GlobalGAP phenomenon, in which a certification requirement is generally more accessible to larger and better-capitalized farmers. Smaller ones, or at least those not benefiting from external support such as NGO funding, will miss out and end up competing—and foundering—in the rough seas of conventional banana markets. The organic market niches that enabled the small farmers of UROCAL to survive in the cutthroat international banana market are also under constant threat from much larger and more powerful players, whether through transnationals' own certified organic bananas or through alternatives like Rainforest Alliance that appear to promise comparable environmental performance benefits.[21] Finally, organic production only protects people who own farms, and contributes little to wealth redistribution or broader environmental protection off those farms (beyond reducing pesticide drift or runoff into downstream ecosystems).[22]

In addition to organic certification, however, many producers in Ecuador and elsewhere have been protected by fairtrade certification, which some point to as the most promising way to alleviate the social and environmental impacts of banana production.[23] As I've mentioned, fairtrade banana production can keep small producers afloat when they're just barely surviving. It can also provide some protection for workers, although reports have documented problems with some fairtrade banana farmers' treatment of their workers.[24] But if fairtrade can keep a small proportion of farmers afloat, it's worth asking what it does for the vast majority of vulnerable farmers and workers who are not protected by such progressive North-South linkages. It's hard to see a plausible mechanism by which certifying a small proportion of small farms will transform an entire industry.[25] Geographer Sandy Brown's study of the Ecuadorian fairtrade co-operative AsoGuabo found that the market access benefits of fairtrade production accrued primarily to larger, better-capitalized conventional farms, which were also better able to meet the certification's audit requirements.[26] Smaller farms such as agroforestry operations on marginal land—the classic fairtrade beneficiary in marketing materials—faced pressures to increase production that compromised agro-ecological practices or even led to suspension from the co-op.

Moreover, fairtrade-certified farms not large enough to qualify for fairtrade's large-farm labour standards still made exploitative use of precarious labour in much the same way as non-fairtrade plantations in Ecuador do. Brown attributes such contradictions to fairtrade's identity as an attempt to compete within existing market structures, where "the imperatives of growth and accumulation inherent in capitalist commodity production... shape outcomes for banana farmers, workers, and environments."[27] With respect to the wealth redistribution or development benefits of fairtrade and its requirement that a good chunk of the fairtrade premium go to community development projects, similarly, anthropologist Mark Moberg points out that the allocation and benefits of such projects tends to be filtered through existing (often inequitable) social structures. Wealthier, better-educated individuals tend to be over-represented in both fairtrade co-operative leadership positions and professional positions in the communities where fairtrade development projects will be carried out. In Dominica—a country more economically dependent on banana production than any other—such class structures have also led to unfairness in how fairtrade's benefits are allocated.[28]

Moberg also vividly shows how neoliberalization processes, such as the striking down of preferential European market access for bananas from former colonies and IMF-imposed austerity programs, have left Dominica so bereft of public services that such problematic fairtrade mechanisms represent one of the only forms of development still possible. Moberg's juxtaposition of neoliberal and neocolonial macroeconomic transformations with inequitable local market-based "development" illustrates the sobering fact that fairtrade banana production still involves a powerful Northern group (in this case, progressive banana buyers) dictating conditions for Southern farmers. Similarly, two former student leaders in the North American fairtrade movement conclude that the movement's activities and motivation betray neocolonial ideals of whiteness surrounding Northerners' supposed right and responsibility to help.[29]

The idea that a privileged outsider's gaze (either Northern or a deputized metropolitan Southern certification agent) can and should ensure adherence to social and environmental performance standards presupposes the superiority of that outsider's knowledge. It also takes for granted the existence of a globalized surveillance infrastructure to dictate how banana producers or other farmers in the global South should conduct their business. While this book attests to the fact that such business is often conducted in unfair or environmentally destructive ways, the idea that people in banana-consuming countries have the knowledge and the right to fix that situation betrays disturbingly neocolonial assumptions. Another sobering feature of fairtrade and other forms of market-based solidarity is that they leave the power structures of the banana supply chain in place and attempt to make them a little bit fairer.[30] Attempting to apply specific technologies—and market-based certification systems are a kind of technology—to solve problems in "developing" countries without addressing the reasons why those countries are in such a state is a hallmark of the discourse of development,[31] as this book's discussion of Green Revolution narratives has shown.

Indeed, both the European Make Fruit Fair banana advocacy campaign and its British member organization, Banana Link, have explicitly tied their work to specific Sustainable Development Goals (SDGs) adopted by the United Nations, which represent the international community's latest attempt to purportedly bring about a fairer and more environmentally responsible future. The SDGs operationalize the quest for sustainable development, or economic growth that does not compromise the ability of the planet to support future generations. Like earlier forms of the discourse of development, they take the poverty of the global South as an unexplained given and then try to palliate its impacts while leaving the root causes that create(d) it in place. They are also thoroughly infused with the neoliberal faith that markets can fix societal challenges, if capitalism's destructive tendencies can be reined in through voluntary corporate social responsibility efforts.[32]

Despite the critical literature reviewed above, I don't want to dismiss market-based mechanisms as useless. Market-based approaches have provided lifesaving protection for some marginalized groups as part of a broader range of strategies. My own interviews also showed fairtrade and organic certification protecting the livelihoods of small producers "suffering" in globalized banana markets, with impacts that went beyond the economic to the emotional. The fraught relationship of many such small producers to landless workers and their supposed lack of *cultura*, however, attests to the unfair power relations underpinning labour-rights abuses in even small-scale banana production. Relationships of market-based mechanisms to such impacts of broader capitalist structures are illustrated by a quote from food sovereignty researcher Chris Hergesheimer's interview with the late Joaquín Vasquez, president of the organic co-operative UROCAL:

> We establish that we need to improve the living conditions of producers, any variable is important to meet this goal. If exporting products [is the means] because we are

an exclusively exporting area, *agroexportadora*, we cannot topple the cocoa or banana to dedicate ourselves to produce only products of basic consumption. Because we would be left to intervene in something that is [im]practical for the culture of the region. *We cannot go against history.* We are part of the story and therefore we must rather improve this situation.[33]

The history of UROCAL and its efforts for agro-ecological peasant agriculture (discussed in more detail in the following chapter) illustrate such a pragmatic accommodation to global market structures. They also evoke Guthman's observation that resistances to neoliberal globalization may be found in the unruliness and context-dependence of certification systems' rollout within "actually existing neoliberalisms."[34] She suggests that participating in fairtrade and other market-based approaches to social and environmental justice in food systems can help to incubate more radical oppositional visions, even if the overall logic of such certification systems is irredeemably neoliberal and even neocolonial.

When I looked for such a radical vision incubating in the most well-developed market-based attempts to address environmental injustice in banana production, I did find what seemed like promising seeds. Under the broader Make Fruit Fair umbrella, for example, the 2016 Oxfam Germany report discussed in Chapter 17 seeks to trouble the "clean conscience" supposedly provided to German fruit consumers by banana labels.[35] Several recommendations made in the report are summarized under the heading "What is to be done?," echoing the famous book of that title in which Russian revolutionary V.I. Lenin outlines his thinking on communist strategy.[36] But while nineteenth-century Germans such as Karl Marx were among the inspirations of Lenin's anti-capitalist analysis, Oxfam Germany's twenty-first-century recommendations involve a mixture of government, corporate, and consumer action within the existing structures of global capitalism.

More recently, the broader disruptions provided by COVID-19, TR4, and climate change motivated another intriguing comment in a 2021 summary of Banana Link's experiences supporting banana farmers and workers: "the emergence—in the framework of increasingly tangible climatic deregulation and a global zoonosis-induced pandemic—of a questioning of the very modes of production, such as disease-prone industrial monoculture in the case of bananas, opens the field for even more interesting innovations and value system changes."³⁷ Thus while small banana farmers generally cannot "go against history" on their own, history itself appears to be opening space for transformation, albeit with no guarantee that such transformation will be emancipatory. "Interesting innovations and value system changes" could easily amount to incremental measures that look good on SDG-oriented reports to NGO funders, rather than the more revolutionary implications of a "questioning of the very modes of production." The stickiness of neoliberal models of change, within the emotionally complex edifice of capitalist ideology,³⁸ therefore suggests that something more inspiring than social scientific arguments (even supplemented with profanity) is necessary to shake our faith in markets as a vehicle for justice.

Early on in the inspiring *Braiding Sweetgrass*, botanist and enrolled member of the Citizen Potawatomi Nation Robin Wall Kimmerer introduces the idea of the "gift economy" by contrasting the wild strawberries she grew up eating with the commodity strawberries she picked while working for a local farmer. Kimmerer, like Joaquín Vasquez, recognizes the profoundly entrenched nature of capitalist food production: "How, in our modern world, can we find our way to understand the earth as a gift again, to make our relations with the world sacred again? I know we cannot all become hunter-gatherers—the living world could not bear our weight—but even in a market economy, can we behave 'as if' the living world were a gift?"³⁹

The 2021 arrival of *Braiding Sweetgrass* (published in 2013) in my life provided me with inspiration in the form of Kimmerer's weaving together of scientific knowledge, Indigenous wisdom, and her own life experiences. While most of those experiences were based in North America, one involved a time Dr. Kimmerer was "lucky enough" to do research in the Andes. She recounts visits to a village market with vendors such as women wearing long skirts and bowler hats selling fresh fruits and vegetables and medicinal plants. At the stall of her favourite such vendor, Edita, she would buy produce and converse, despite knowing she was paying the "*gringa* prices."⁴⁰ The market would appear in her dreams long afterwards, but this time without the exchanges of money that occurred in real life. In this dreamworld gift economy, "gratitude was the only currency . . . the merchants were just intermediaries passing on gifts from the earth."⁴¹

I, too, have visited such Andean markets (the waking kind), most frequently in the Ecuadorian highland city of Cuenca, which lies four hours east of and over two kilometres above sea-level Machala. There, women in long skirts and bowler-like hats are also omnipresent. Other features of the market in Cuenca include stalls with numerous live fluffy guinea pigs, or *cuyes*, whose cuteness melts the hearts of North American visitors just before they realize that the animals are destined to be roasted on a spit and eaten. Another jarring experience at the Cuenca market was encountering a man with a variety of pesticide containers spread out on a blanket on the ground, including an ancient packet containing DDT.

Dr. Kimmerer's good-natured acknowledgement of the *gringa* prices she was paying (despite being an Indigenous *gringa*), for me, raises questions regarding the interactions between colonialism's economic legacies and contemporary economic models, whether neoliberal capitalist or gift (or other). The Andean region that allowed both Kimmerer (Potawatomi) and I (settler Canadian) to be *gringo* market patrons has generated inspirational challenges to capitalism through Indigenous ideals of *sumak kawsay* (*buen vivir*, or "good living," in Kichwa,) in the twenty-first century. It was also the setting for Michael Taussig's classic exploration of the violent imposition of capitalism on Colombian and Bolivian Afro-descended and Indigenous peoples.[42] Such violence through which people and territories of the Americas have been inducted into capitalist enterprises has in the nineteenth and twentieth centuries been enabled by US imperialism that was itself an extension of violent domestic campaigns against Indigenous peoples of Turtle Island (North America). Enemy combatants in Latin America were referred to as "Indians," their territory as "Indian country," and their loss of life considered to be almost a sport for American soldiers.[43] Meanwhile, the Canadian mining imperialism that enabled my research in Ecuador extended the violent expropriation of Indigenous territories in my own country.[44]

These violent histories and the present-day economic disparities they have created—and continue to create—are among the factors I can't forget when faced with the question of what bananas to buy, and more generally how people embedded in capitalist markets might try to do good things in our embeddedness. The vivid and unexpected confluences opened up by visits to Andean markets make the familiar strange, by re-presenting the horrifying violence hiding behind innocuous capitalist transactions.[45] Paying attention to the ways in which societies have been transformed away from gift economies or other more collectivist and reciprocal models—while being careful not to romanticize such non-capitalist economies—underscores just how brutal that transformation has been. Such brutality should give pause to anyone who thinks that minor tweaks or reforms to capitalism (such as certification labels and CSR initiatives) are an adequate response to banana-related injustices.

The history and other stories recounted in this book clearly show that the ongoing processes that have generated problematic conditions in today's banana industry are beyond unfair. Those processes—colonialism and imperialism, leading into today's neoliberal (and racial) capitalism—also largely explain the relative impoverishment of those countries known as "Southern," and the wealth of the banana-consuming North. Paying attention to them makes it clear that there is nothing inherently poor, backwards, or underdeveloped about the countries that export bananas, or about the regions within them that participate in such forms of primary commodity production. These regions of the world, and of the South, are poor because of theft and exploitation, and that theft is ongoing. Understanding banana production's past (and the broader history it illustrates) as a process of racist, patriarchal, ecocidal theft makes it pretty much impossible to imagine solving the problems of banana commodity chains by throwing more capitalism at them.

That is, if you realize how grotesquely unfair the history of banana production has been, it's a lot harder to propose grocery shopping decisions (even "conscious" ones) as a workable or plausible way to fix things. So long as the disparities that imperialism created (and continues to create) are in place, markets for fruits will always be so skewed that huge injustices will persist. Put differently, colonialism and its continuing manifestations are processes of theft that have occurred within an evolving legal context that solidifies and extends the rules of capitalism to every corner of the globe. Those processes of theft—what Karl Marx referred to as "primitive accumulation"[46]—have systematically enriched certain people and parts of the world, and impoverished others (there are always exceptions and local particularities in relation to such generalizations, but these are exceptions that tend to prove the rule). Such stealing was done either outside the law or within ridiculous and self-serving legal structures such as those making it permissible to own Africans and other people of colour, but the disparities it created are now protected by the rules of capitalism.

So while the United Fruit Company was able to operate outside the law—or manipulate laws and the Latin American governments making them—the profits they generated for their shareholders and a limited number of Latin American elites are legally protected (Standard Fruit's DBCP-enabled profits are another example). Now, when small banana producers attempt to compete in banana markets, they often lose because, well, markets work. You have to spend money to make money, and you have to have money (or credit) to spend money. This helps to explain why land and market share in bananas are reconcentrating in *la costa*, while protected niches such as organic and fairtrade production are under constant threat from vast multinational corporations.

Efforts by governments, social movements, and workers to push back against such injustices—in a complex dance with the more-than-human actors who also play major roles—can and do provide lifesaving protection from this tendency of capitalism towards monopoly and the complete "subsumption" of life to money-making interests. However, this protection is always temporary, uneven, and riddled with contradictions and unfairness. These realities suggest to me that there will be no fair and sustainable solution to problems such as unsafe working conditions and environmental contamination in banana production without changing the entire racist, neocolonial, and planet-destroying economic model in which those problems originate.

To the question of what sort of bananas should you be buying, then, a more thoughtful response than the one that opened this chapter might therefore involve something like the following: Buy organic or fairtrade bananas if you want, but don't stop there and don't fall into the neoliberal trap of feeling bad if you can't afford them. Individual shopping choices didn't cause the problem and they won't be the solution. But if buying certified bananas is the first step in a process of learning and developing better relationships to the people and places who currently grow bananas, then it could be an entry point to much more profound changes that would actually make a difference.

Those more meaningful changes are the subject of the remaining two chapters of the book.

CHAPTER 24
NOTICING

This book began with a quest for evidence-based policy and practice based on biomedical sciences, to address instances of environmental injustice such as pesticide toxicity in Ecuadorian banana production. The limitations of such evidence-based approaches (as detailed in Chapters 21 and 22) were among the factors pushing me to employ more social scientific approaches in my own research and attempts at praxis. Recent work on the "permanently polluted" nature of today's world and how researchers might focus on the non-heroic everyday actions of affected people similarly echoes such insights on the persistently ineffective and even oppressive responses of scientific and state structures to environmental injustice.[1]

This focus on the non-heroic is coherent with Anna Tsing's call for social scientific "noticing" of the everyday ways in which people and our more-than-human peers pursue "the possibility of life in capitalist ruins."[2] Tsing posits noticing as a key scholarly responsibility in the contemporary (Plantationocene) period and contrasts it to various impractical utopian schemes to fix those capitalist ruins. Tsing and comparable social scientists are among the most thoughtful guides I have been able to find when seeking to understand how people experience situations of toxicity such as the pesticide mist permeating Ecuador's banana regions. This chapter therefore explores what such social scientific noticing can accomplish, but also "notices" where it likely stops being helpful in relation to environmental justice struggles.

Around an hour before they arrive in Machala, buses from Guayaquil reach the former Hacienda Tenguel. The highway passes to the east of the town of Tenguel itself, which still features remarkably durable wooden buildings that were part of UFC's infrastructure in mid-century. Banana plantations dominate the roadsides and products used in them dominate roadside advertising. These billboards then give way near the city of Camilo Ponce Enríquez (La Ponce) to ones advertising supplies for small- and medium-scale gold mining, which occurs where the hacienda once reached into the Andean foothills to the east. On one bus trip, the TVs of the bus I was on were playing a Korean horror movie involving ghosts, when a small boy in his school uniform got on the bus in La Ponce and sat next to me. I described the film as a *película de terror* (horror movie) when he asked me about it. He then made me laugh by asking if it was a *película de Chooky*, referencing the murderous possessed doll (Chucky) from the recently relaunched *Child's Play* franchise.

In the Andean foothills to the east of the highway are found communities that can be traced back to the invasion of the hacienda by its laid-off workers in and around 1962. Many of the small-scale banana and cacao farmers living in such communities are descendants of those workers (themselves often migrants from *la sierra*) and also, now, members of small-scale farmer co-operatives.[3] One prominent such organization is UROCAL, the organic and fairtrade co-op I relied on most heavily during my fieldwork. In the decades following the occupation of Hacienda Tenguel, and subsequent military takeover of both the country and the plantation, UROCAL's members undertook well-documented efforts to gain formal title to their lands.[4] Those efforts were assisted by a priest named Father Hernán Rodas and Basque social justice volunteers, as were community development programs for drinking water provision, health, education, and acquisition of credit that would enable survival in agricultural markets. Initially the agricultural markets in question were largely those involving cacao for export, but UROCAL and its component organizations branched out into banana production in the 1990s in response to a collapse of cacao prices and the opening of market niches for fairtrade and organic bananas. With the help of European banana importers and NGOs, UROCAL became a leading producer of such "progressive" bananas, going beyond the formal requirements of organic certifiers to implement a model of agro-ecological, often agroforestry, banana production. I also learned during my fieldwork that fairtrade co-operatives such as the Association of Small-Scale Producers of El Guabo (AsoGuabo) and Regional Association of Small-Scale Banana Producers of Cerro Azul had once been part of UROCAL.

UROCAL's staff, farmers, and former president Joaquín Vasquez provided substantial help to me as I planned and conducted my fieldwork, and I spent considerable time in the co-operative's Machala office. Indeed, UROCAL has been an active facilitator of research for decades. Steve Striffler's illuminating historical ethnography of the occupation of Hacienda Tenguel and its legacies was facilitated by UROCAL.[5] So was an Ecuadorian political ecology analysis carried out by Quito-based researcher and former national minister of the environment Edgar Isch, and perceptive doctoral research by Spanish historian Germán Carrillo García.[6] More recently, a pesticide epidemiology study carried out by an Austria-based team, discussed in Chapter 17, was facilitated by UROCAL and ASTAC.[7] The organization has thus helped allies from various parts of Ecuador and the banana-consuming world generate research that helps to bring the plight of banana workers and the benefits of agro-ecological banana production into the sphere of public discourse.

In general, researchers collaborating with UROCAL appear to have avoided what Patrica Polo, whose own research has focused on banana workers in the vicinity of Tenguel, calls "academic extractivism" (*extractivismo academico*), in which knowledge accumulates "without bringing about even minimal changes in the study population."[8] The descendants of the workers of Hacienda Tenguel, however, would still have to deal with more conventional *extractivismo* in the Correa years and beyond. In addition to his agricultural development policies promoting large-scale agro-industrial production, Correa put limits on the number of terms a co-operative president could serve. Unable to continue pursuing his vision for agro-ecological peasant banana and cacao production within UROCAL, Joaquín Vasquez left the organization to found a banana exporting business that would enable him to pursue such objectives. As he explained to me in the new business's office in Machala in 2019, he felt the new leadership of UROCAL had made promotion of peasant agro-ecological farming secondary to maximizing monocultural production and exports.

That meeting turned out to be the last time I would see Joaquín before he passed away of COVID-19 in 2021. He showed me a WhatsApp video of protesters in the higher-altitude end of the former hacienda, engaged in a protest march to protect the area's rivers from the contamination caused by mining in the Andean foothills. I was later told by a member of the environmental committee of the town of Shumiral—a community founded by former UFC workers and their families—how torrential rains in the early 1980s had caused erosion that led to the discovery of gold in a local river. The Chico, Gala, Tenguel, and Siete Rivers descending the Andes and passing through the region have subsequently been heavily contaminated by the impacts of small- and medium-scale gold mining operations. As one small banana farmer explained, the contamination of surface waters is one more factor pushing small producers off their land, as they lack the capital to drill deep wells and their productivity has suffered due to the upstream contamination.⁹

In the early years of the Correa administration, residents of the area responded to the contamination by calling for a moratorium on mining in local watersheds, also obtaining support for water quality testing of the rivers, which revealed contamination with heavy metals.¹⁰ They were emboldened by the 2008 Mining Mandate, which temporarily halted large-scale mining throughout the country, returned the majority of existing mining concessions to the state, and outlined stricter requirements for obtaining permission to operate large-scale mines. Nevertheless, when the minister of mines and petroleum visited the region soon after, he first toured a small-scale mine with an overflowing tailings pond, then a larger mine whose "million dollar investments," he gushed, had created a facility "in perfect order with everything in its right place."¹¹

The tendentious itinerary of the minister of mines and petroleum highlights the extractivist orientation of the Correa government, while the numerous foreign and metropolitan Ecuadorian research efforts facilitated by the descendants of laid-off Hacienda Tenguel workers (i.e., in the organization UROCAL) joined with it in a disturbing story as I progressively came to better understand the chemical and social toxicity of the Ecuadorian coastal region. I began uncovering more of this story as I defended my dissertation in 2014 and moved on to postdoctoral work at the University of Toronto, initially supported by a small fellowship originating with Canada's International Development Research Centre (IDRC). I began to publish findings from my research in academic journals, applying and refining the application of public health science, human geography, and medical anthropology under the broad framework of political ecology of health (PEH, described in this book's Introduction). The data to which I applied this framework steadily yielded fascinating insights, which I have attempted to recount in this book.

Consistent with PEH's attention to history as a shaper of present-day environmental conditions and their human impacts in specific places,[12] the precarity and pesticide exposures of banana workers in twenty-first-century Ecuador turned out to be rooted in the unfair hemispheric twentieth-century history of banana production, as recounted in Parts 1 and 2 of the book. Political ecology's long-standing critique of "apolitical ecologies" that blame environmental degradation on the ignorance and poor choices of marginalized peoples[13] affirmed my own attribution of pesticide contamination to the workings of powerful interests such as transnational fruit and pesticide companies, Ecuadorian elites, and governmental organizations at multiple scales. My findings on the historically fraught use of the concept of *cultura* by relatively privileged individuals in the banana sector to explain away the toxic poverty and illnesses of poor rural *costeños* also resonated with PEH's guidance on the importance of conflicting discursive interpretations of environmental change and health.[14] The field's lens on affect and "entanglement" was particularly incisive regarding the emotional, embodied, and relational ways in which people in *la costa* experienced relationships to each other, to the more-than-human landscape, to global politico-economic power dynamics, and to both subversive and oppressive narratives about how all those things interact.[15]

Finally, a substantial portion of my work resonated with PEH's focus on the social production of science regarding environmental change and its health impacts.[16] In particular, I've been informed by scholarship showing how the ability of people in the global North to carry out research in the global South has for centuries been enabled by colonialism and the global disparities it continues to widen. The history of banana production recounted in this book echoes such studies showing how countless scientific advances have been enabled by and, in turn, contributed to Euro-American appropriation of foreign lands and resources.[17] For example, banana phytopathology developed in ways that relied on European and American control over tropical countries around the globe. Pesticide epidemiology and toxicology advanced through the (un)natural experiment perpetrated on Latin Americans exposed to pesticides by imperialism, corporate indifference, Green Revolution fairy tales, and racism. Similarly, the genres and biomedical scientific conventions of pesticide epidemiology have channelled thinking and action in discourse-of-development directions that take the poverty of banana-producing Latin America as inherent or inevitable.[18]

In ways that evoke literature on "internal colonialism,"[19] moreover, twenty-first-century research on pesticides and health in Ecuador's coastal region has been enabled by regional inequities that funnel banana-generated wealth to Machala, to Guayaquil, to Quito, and—especially—abroad. Such wealth helped build the health system and university infrastructures in both Northern and Southern metropolitan centres enabling researchers to occupy themselves with the health of banana workers.[20] Stereotypes of rural *costeños* (so-called *monos* or *montubios*) as inherently violent, promiscuous, hard-drinking, and disease-ridden sometimes seep into the narratives perpetuated by many such Southern metropolitan researchers, while others point their gaze firmly upstream at the "social determination" of health by social structures.[21]

One logical career progression for me post-PhD would have been to leverage such publishable PEH insights and move smoothly into a stable academic career. Instead, however, I found myself overtaken by controversies over Canadian mining companies and their pervasive influence on seemingly all of the research institutions I was connected to. Somewhat like the descendants of the workers of Hacienda Tenguel as they sought to protect their livelihoods and local rivers from upstream contamination, I found myself in the years after my PhD trying to focus on agriculture but unable to get away from mining.

While I was using an IDRC fellowship to support my postdoctoral work, for example, the Canadian Conservative government of Prime Minister Stephen Harper was adding a vice-president from Barrick Gold, then the world's largest gold mining company and one of its most controversial, to that respected organization's board of governors.[22] When I arrived at the University of Toronto (U of T) to carry out that postdoctoral work, I similarly found myself confronted by evidence of that institution's enrolment in the mining sector's quest for legitimization. One conservative estimate reveals that mining companies contributed over half a billion dollars to Canada's twenty-one largest universities between 1995 and 2013, with U of

T the second-leading recipient (and likely in first place if donations to the affiliated University Health Network are counted).[23] The role of U of T in legitimizing the country's mining sector and the neoliberal foreign policy that promotes it has been most notably documented in relation to the controversial establishment and published foreign policy scholarship of the Munk School of Global Affairs and Public Policy, named after major donor and Pinochet-admirer Peter Munk.[24]

A more recent controversy involved University of British Columbia (UBC), the university I had just graduated from and the only Canadian university to receive more money from the mining industry than U of T. In 2013, UBC founded a research institute—the Canadian International Resources and Development Institute (CIRDI)—premised on promoting Canada's extractive sector overseas. A CIRDI donation to a global health organization I was carrying out contract work for soon sparked controversy and inquiry into the mining industry partners of that institute and its links to Canada's joint government-corporate quest to promote mining. CIRDI's vision turned out to have much in common with the discourse-of-development narratives that have guided pesticide-intensive banana production since at least the 1950s (that subtly innovate on more blatantly racist colonial narratives of the early twentieth century and earlier).[25] In such narratives, the violence of imperialism magically disappears and the inequities caused by it appear both natural and tractable in the face of Northern science and technology—whether in large-scale mines or pesticide-intensive banana plantations.[26]

The racism that has always accompanied and supported imperialist patterns of exploitation is also often reproduced in such narratives of progress and development. For example, Guatemala's racist elite (from many of the same families who conspired with the CIA to overthrow Árbenz in 1954 in support of United Fruit) typically describe Indigenous resistance to large-scale mines as inherently irrational or due to external meddling in the affairs of such impressionable primitive folks, for example by environmental NGOs.[27] This narrative echoes the ones found in official Canadian mining CSR documents, but not only there. Shortly after the 2019 *paro*, an Ecuadorian anthropologist I know provided an eerily similar description of Indigenous political action in his country as motivated by foreign meddlers and the corrupt Indigenous leaders they supposedly pay off, rather than by legitimate grievances stemming from colonial exploitation.

While I was attempting to publish and "be helpful" in relation to environmental injustice in banana production, I found my Canadian academic institutional training environments to be thoroughly entangled with the development model causing massive environmental injustice. That model has been promoted throughout the world via neoliberal reforms imposed by international financial institutions, which typically feature promotion of primary commodity production such as mining, petroleum extraction, and agro-industrial export production (the extension of such primary commodity production in so-called post-neoliberal Ecuador shows that *extractivismo* maintains key continuities with neoliberalism).[28] As previously mentioned, it is also typically promoted via bilateral mechanisms such as country-to-country trade agreements, diplomatic services, and other more personalized or intimate connections. Such country-to-country connections hit particularly close to home for me, for example when the enrolment of the IDRC in Canada's mining CSR campaigns brought into sharp relief several IDRC-funded Ecuadorian projects led by researchers such as my doctoral and postdoctoral supervisors and their collaborators.[29] CIRDI's "strategic partners" also included an Ecuadorian government research institute, attesting to the Correa government's support for its model of development. The prestigious Centre for Addictions and Mental Health, connected to my postdoctoral training environment at the University of Toronto, has repeatedly accepted donations from IAMGOLD, one of the Canadian companies behind the controversial Loma Larga mine in Ecuador, just off the highway between Machala and Cuenca.[30]

These connections show how the conditions of possibility for my research on bananas, pesticides, and health in Ecuador ultimately rested on the imperialist extraction of wealth from that country and others in Latin America and around the world (and, of course, Canadian settler colonialism at home).[31] Those conditions also featured increasingly neoliberalized universities—of which U of T and UBC are prime examples—that had been made to run in business-like ways that prioritized the promotion of private sector interests, and incentivized rapid-fire academic work that tended to reproduce oppressive narratives such as the discourse of development.[32] The specifics of my research connections to Ecuador and such broader relationships between global North researchers and the postcolonial world strongly call into question the premise that people like me are actually improving the world through our collection, analysis, and publication of data on the lives of "tropical" peoples and places. Whether or not we are solving specific problems like how to keep pesticides off banana workers, we are also often reproducing, reinforcing, naturalizing, or just failing to challenge the broader economic patterns of exploitation that create the very specific health, social, or environmental problems we organize our supposed helpfulness around.

Political ecology and the critical social scientific insights it uses to make sense of environmental change and its human dimensions helped me to arrive at the story told in this book, not to mention the published articles that preceded it. Such perceptive social scientific approaches therefore led me to my disturbing conclusion that the complicity or entanglement of academic and public health institutions with the structures creating environmental injustice undermines (figuratively or sometimes literally) the good work we claim we are doing.[33] But at a certain point, following PEH's methodological and theoretical guidance led me to places where that guidance seemed to lose its direction, especially with respect to real-world praxis implications and the social location of researchers. It was still very interesting and said important things, but none of those important things seriously addressed the gravity of entanglements such as those connecting my Canadian academic training environments to the imposition of neoliberal and extractivist development models in places such as Ecuador.

Good social scientists are certainly not unaware of the need to be reflexive in relation to privileged social locations such as those enabling one to become a social scientist. Writing in a 2015 handbook of political ecology, UBC geographer Juanita Sundberg draws on the history of US imperialism in Latin America and her own role as an American researcher in Guatemala to describe how even researchers attuned to critical and postcolonial themes "are situated in, complicit with, and benefit from the very politico-economic systems that constitute our research subjects."[34] Writing in the same handbook, PEH scholars Neely and Nguse thoughtfully reflect on "the complexity of relationships—between us, between us and the people with whom we conduct our research, and between us and the institutions that govern higher education—and their importance for research methods in political ecology."[35] Such perceptive looks at links between people such as tenured social scientists in North America and Guatemalan Indigenous peoples or South African villagers reflect important feminist insights on situated knowledge and the need to avoid pretensions at objectivity based on some imagined position outside or above society.[36] Lived experiences, affect, and relationships are key features of the approaches such scholars advocate, and of PEH and related social scientific literature on living in a toxic world, where "acts of care such as feeding, watering, cleaning, or replanting damaged crops momentarily disrupt toxicity," but are primarily undertaken "less in a grand effort to politically transform or purify the world than in a more intimate attempt to make it habitable."[37]

As I have mentioned, such a focus on lived experience and the complexity of local specificities and entanglements was very helpful to me as I learned how people in Ecuador's "permanently polluted" banana zones emotionally and relationally experience pesticide toxicity. Valuing and supporting the priorities of the complex people inhabiting such toxic spaces is a perceptive recommendation of PEH scholarship. However, I have felt unease at what seems like an excessively premature abandonment of the "grand effort to politically transform or purify the world," especially in my postdoctoral years as I circled around the academic career trajectories within which such abandonments could be made theoretically novel and publishable. When PEH-informed anthropologist Alex Nading's fascinating review on "living in a toxic world" concludes that "the future for a toxic anthropology ... lies in slowing down and working through the mess ... [because it] isn't going anywhere,"[38] I can't help but think of the relationships between toxic exposures in Latin America and my own academic training environments, and the laborious and career-impeding action and research I ended up pursuing to understand and address such complicities (including my own).

Canada's mining-dominated foreign policy with respect to Latin America and the rest of the world is certainly imperialist and contributes to broad neoliberal politico-economic transformations that undermine social determinants of health for entire societies.[39] With its symbiotic relationship between scholarship and empire—and hugely imperialist past and present—a focus on the United States would undoubtedly uncover vastly *more* consequential implications that I have yet to see meaningfully challenged by even excellent health-environment scholars. Simply slowing down and working through the mess using sound ethnographic approaches while pursuing career success in the "academic capitalist" environment of North American universities therefore felt like it would yield many fascinating articles and books, but would leave the structures linking metropolitan countries and their scholars to global environmental injustices largely intact.

Saying that the toxic mess found in our permanently polluted world isn't going anywhere seemed to be an accurate depiction of biophysical reality and a nuanced position regarding questions of objectivity and social science methodology, but it also seemed to be something else. It came to seem increasingly like a refusal or inability to *really do something* about our varying entangled complicities with the structures that generate both researchers and the environmental injustices we claim to be helping address. This is not to say that PEH and other engaged, critical social science scholars don't do things in partnership with communities affected by toxic environmental injustices. Recent efforts to use community-based participatory research methods to avoid stigmatizing such communities and doing harm struck me as eminently sensible.[40] At no point, though, did I see such sophisticated health-environment scholars seriously propose anything that would urgently tackle the macroeconomic (i.e., capitalist) root causes of the kinds of issues they and I were attempting to address. As I put it in a 2019 article written with my supervisor and a member of my committee,

> As a caution with respect to the role of scientists and social scientists in addressing health legacies of colonialism, it is important to note that nothing in our decade-long focus on pesticide-related health impacts in Ecuador's banana industry has suggested "lack of research" as a significant cause of such impacts. Indeed, compelling analyses showing colonial and postcolonial structural inequities to drive social and environmental determinants of poor health are now decades old . . . Nevertheless, research continues in ways that are facilitated and bounded by such political economic structures.[41]

So while reading perceptive social science research had helped me immeasurably in learning about the injustices I was studying, all those perceptive researchers could seem to propose as a solution was social scientific "noticing," or doing more research—research that would move us along competitive career trajectories (some more successfully than others) in universities whose competitive academic capitalism fit comfortably within broader neoliberal racial capitalist structures. As critical geographers Castree and Sparke explain, "Universities have always cosily coexisted with the state, whether it has been absolutist, capitalist, welfarist or communist ... modern universities in the twentieth century have served far more to buttress military-capitalist complexes than to question their instrumentalization of knowledge."[42]

This observation points to what Antonio Gramsci referred to as the *esprit de corps* through which a society's intellectuals tend to view themselves as making the world a better place, while instead largely helping to legitimize inequitable structures of capitalist societies.[43] Once I started "noticing" such complicities, I found myself questioning the truism that "further research is necessary" and wondering what else could be done.

CHAPTER 25
PLOTTING

Do it for the plot.
—GEN Z slang

Strategies for achieving justice using biomedical evidence, conscious consumption, or nuanced social science analysis represent modifications to the existing social order. Now that the last few chapters have examined the strengths and limitations of such reforms, this chapter attempts to move past their limitations while not discarding the strengths. Its contents are the closest this book gets to take-home messages.

In 2010, a few months after my first trip to Ecuador and almost fifty-six years after the 1954 coup that removed Guatemalan president Jacobo Árbenz from power, I met up with my sister Marie Claire in Guatemala, where she was visiting the site of her recent Canadian International Development Agency internship. She had done the internship in part because our grandfather—who passed away in 1976, before either of us were born—had been the unlikely consul general of that country in Canada for part of the 1970s. Despite having no Guatemalan or even Latin American ancestry, our grandfather had become involved in the country in relation to his charitable work with the Catholic Sovereign Military Order of Malta.[1] Also known as the Knights of Malta, the order had responded to an appeal from the pope in the late 1960s to "assist orphans in Guatemala." Beginning in 1970, the Knights adopted the

Mater Orphanorum, "a home for orphans and abandoned children," and "entrusted" it to our grandfather.[2]

The Knights of Malta were founded as an actual crusading army during the Crusades, and used coerced Muslim labour to experiment with plantation agriculture in temporarily conquered parts of the Middle East, thereby helping along the introduction of sugar into European diets.[3] Similarly disturbing was the Guatemalan dictatorship (one of several that had ruled the country since the UFC-backed coup that removed Árbenz from power in 1954) on behalf of which our grandfather worked to process visa applications and carry out other diplomatic functions in Toronto.[4] Cancer killed our chain-smoking grandfather before he could see the most horrifying actions of the Guatemalan dictatorships (and their Canadian connections) in the late 1970s and 1980s. The 1978 massacre at Panzós, for example, quelled opposition to the Canadian mining company Inco's operations and represented what one historian terms "the terrible opening act of the Guatemala genocide."[5]

After this disturbing start to our family's involvement with Latin America, our high-school teacher parents worked with and learned from priests, nuns, and Catholic-teacher colleagues working in liberation theology traditions that rejected Catholicism's historical alliance with repressive governments and wealthy interests. Liberation theology adherents typically side with peasant, worker, and other left-wing political movements, often coming into conflict with the church's power structures.[6] They both support and are enabled by the faith of impoverished communities. Liberation theology is already prominent in this book: Bishop Coto of Costa Rica's Limón parish, who helped to found Foro Emaús and thereby enable its environmental justice activism and epidemiology collaborations, is one example of a liberation theology priest; Father Hernán Rodas, who helped Hacienda Tenguel's former workers gain legal title to their land on the Ecuadorian coast and helped found the co-operative UROCAL, is another.

Reflecting such liberation theology influences, Marie Claire and I had done "development exposure" trips that our father organized for students at the high school we attended, based on principles of solidarity and social justice (as opposed to paternalistic charity). It was on the trip I participated in, to Cuernavaca, Mexico, that I first remember hearing the words *neoliberalism, Pinochet,* and *Zapatista.* My sixteen-year-old understanding of these terms was somewhat hazy, although I think I understood that neoliberalism was bad, Pinochet and the United States were associated with it, and the Zapatistas were against it. It would be decades later—and only after spending years writing this book—before I would really begin to understand their profound influence on today's world and how it shapes prospects for addressing the health impacts of banana production.

To meet up with Marie Claire in 2010, I flew to Cancún in order to travel by overnight bus to San Cristóbal de las Casas, in Mexico's Chiapas state, and then on to Guatemala. My upcoming doctoral comprehensive exam meant that my luggage contained a copy of Szklo and Nieto's *Epidemiology: Beyond the Basics*. The ticket agent at the Cancún bus station informed me that there were at least two classes of bus and that I should take the more expensive and comfortable one. Not to be deterred, I boarded the second-class bus soon after and found a seat near the back, next to a small, elderly Mayan lady with a birdcage containing two kittens. I chatted with her and learned that they were a gift for a relative in her hometown. They were slightly cramped in the cage, which contained a bar through the centre for its intended bird inhabitants to perch on. They meowed frequently and, as the hours passed and darkness fell, more gutturally and alarmingly.

The woman repeatedly and ineffectively shushed the kittens and I tried to reassure her that they weren't bothering me. But whether for my benefit or for that of the other passengers, she redoubled her efforts, wrapping the cage in a bag and slapping the top. Sometime after midnight the kittens pooped, and the back of the bus smelled awful from that point on. It felt like no one on the bus was comfortable by this point, although I was the only one for whom the situation was unusual. Also, after midnight the bus was stopped briefly at a military checkpoint, with the soldiers who entered the bus inspiring even less enthusiasm among the passengers than the smell of kitten diarrhea. This reaction was not unreasonable, as such checkpoints in Mexico have been a frequent tool of collusion between the military and drug traffickers, and of what has been described as state terrorism. Four years later, for example, a comparable military checkpoint in the state of Guerrero would see forty-three students from the Ayotzinapa Rural Teachers' College—who had been under military surveillance for their leftist politics—kidnapped, turned over by authorities to a local cartel, and killed.[7]

At the end of the bus route were the mountain landscapes and colonial beauty of San Cristóbal, the focal point of the Zapatista uprising on January 1, 1994 (the day the North American Free Trade Agreement went into effect and endorsed Mexican democracy by inducting the country into the North American economic community). The uprising continued resistance to Chiapas's racist agrarian elites, on whose haciendas local Indigenous peoples—Tzeltal, Tzotzil, Chol, Zoque, Tojolabal, Mame, Kaqchikel, Lacandón, Mocho', Jacalteco, Chuj, and Kanjobal—had experienced brutal exploitation and abuses up to and including the 1970s and '80s.[8] You can now buy T-shirts featuring Che Guevara or *Radio Insurgente*, the revolutionary Zapatista radio station, in the markets in San Cristóbal. Small children walk around offering to sell you *una Marcos* (a doll made in the image of the masked, pipe-smoking Zapatista leader Subcommandante Insurgente Marcos—there is now one on a mantel in my parents' house).

The romanticized vision of the Zapatistas that draws many left-leaning tourists (me included) to purchase such goods is shaken somewhat by knowledge of the decades of ongoing paramilitary violence that have followed Marcos's initial apology to tourists in San Cristobal: "We're sorry for the inconvenience, but this is a revolution." Wealthy landowners supported by local police, the military, and governments both local and federal (especially of the nefarious PRI party) have armed and paid paramilitary groups to create a climate of terror and uncertainty among the Indigenous inhabitants of the state using killings, sexual violence, arson, displacement, and torture in a bid to disrupt social fabrics and restore those landowners' profitable use of Indigenous land. For example, the 1997 Acteal massacre saw paramilitaries kill forty-five Tzotzil community members who had declared neutrality in relation to the Zapatista's struggle.[9]

Meanwhile, Indigenous resistances and livelihoods have continued, affected by such "low intensity conflict" but also galvanized to defend communities, and the land and agricultural practices that support them.[10] For example, Tzeltal communities have employed a variety of livelihood strategies to pursue *buhts'an qu'inal* (Tzeltal community well-being), a state involving good and joyful relationships among people, the environment, health, food, and work (resonating as well with Andean visions of *sumak kawsay* or *buen vivir*).[11]

After disembarking in San Cristóbal I set out by bus across the border into Guatemala, eventually arriving at the similarly beautiful colonial city of Antigua with my persistent lower-back pain (a symptom of being a doctoral student) flaring up. That night I got violently sick with *Entamoeba histolytica*, or amoebas, which Marie Claire had already gotten and recovered from on the trip. During her previous internship she had been chronically sick with similar gastrointestinal parasites, as her project's focus on water treatment did not stop her from coming into frequent contact with unsafe drinking water in her home-stay accommodations. Amoebas are colloquially known as *animalitos* (little animals) and are a symptom of the grinding poverty Jacobo Árbenz had attempted to address in the early 1950s. Continuing such efforts was deemed less important by subsequent dictatorships—with their US and Israeli financing, training, and weapons—than scorched-earth military campaigns against Mayan communities and other supposed communists (the techniques of state-backed terror used to create fear and uncertainty in Guatemala would also serve to inform the organizers and funders of paramilitary violence in Chiapas after 1994).[12]

I started feeling better after getting on the right medication and carefully restarting on solid food. This was a process Marie Claire had gone through numerous times, a different kind of scorched-earth campaign that left her researching ways to rebuild the intestinal flora (i.e., a healthy internal ecology) that antibiotics and antiparasitics decimate. We next travelled by bus to the highland city of Quetzaltenango (also known as Xela) for a week of Spanish school. Xela happens to be the birthplace of Árbenz, whom my Spanish teacher Rony informed me remains the best leader Guatemala has ever had. After our week of class, we set out on a bus towards Mexico, from where we would fly back to Canada. We took a yellow school bus bearing a decal indicating that it had once taken children to school in the province of Québec. It also had a Kung Fu Panda sticker at the front, as well as another declaring that *He puesto los ojos en Jesús* (I've raised my eyes to Jesus). Despite this protection from both faith and a popular children's animated character (two elements with unexpected relevance to banana history), Marie Claire warned me to be careful with my belongings. She and her fellow interns had experienced and heard about numerous creative strategies for robbing foreigners on

Guatemalan buses, another legacy of the poverty the 1954 coup helped to preserve (and of the Northern wealth it simultaneously reinforced).

I was interested in the scenery and familiar with the controversy over the infamous Marlin Mine our route would take us past. The mine was owned by a Guatemalan subsidiary of the Canadian company Goldcorp, whose head office I frequently passed on my bus commute to UBC in Vancouver. But as I tried to talk to Marie Claire about it—in loud Spanish—she shushed me and whispered that tensions were so high over the mine that it wasn't really safe to mention it in public (the organization she had done her internship with also carried out human rights observing, attempting to use their foreign passports to protect Guatemalan Indigenous and peasant communities from extra-judicial or even legal violence carried out in the country's climate of impunity). Shortly after, as I looked out the window in a chastened mood, she sharply said, "Ben, watch your bag." I had left a cloth bag beside me on the seat, containing my copy of Szklo and Nieto and a camera. I put my hand nonchalantly down on the bag and the man who was leaning over the seat back and inching his hand towards it settled into his seat with equal nonchalance.

I didn't see many bananas on that mostly highland voyage in 2010. Still, my experiences there repeatedly came back to me as I wrote this book and especially this last chapter. The epidemiology textbook I lugged with me from Canada to Central America paralleled earlier voyages of Northern science and scientists to the same region to study the impacts of chemical-intensive agriculture in "developing" countries. The overconfidence with which I purchased Zapatista paraphernalia and loudly discussed sensitive local issues also uncomfortably signals the problematic Northern gaze and beliefs such health scientists often bring with them on their travels. Other elements that resonate with the history recounted in this book include the persistent poverty of Guatemala and its neighbours; repressive governments, brutal violence, and grassroots resistance to them; transnational corporations continuing to treat Latin America as a profitable source of bodies and raw materials to exploit; unexpected Northern complicities and solidarities; microscopic organisms with macroscopic impacts; disrupted ecologies and scorched-earth chemical responses to them; and, thanks to the massive animal experimentation of pesticide toxicology, an unsettling number of little animals in cages who have suffered far worse fates than the caged kittens on that bus to Chiapas.

It was the beleaguered, uncomfortable, and chastened physical and emotional state that journey left me in that would resonate most with the challenge of summing up this book's lessons for the pursuit of environmental and social justice. A standard plot in the Disney/Pixar movies that Dole uses to sell bananas features the protagonist behaving arrogantly or irresponsibly at the beginning, then embarking on a quest to resolve the ensuing conflict. An earlier version of this simplified hero's quest is found in Voltaire's satirical eighteenth-century classic *Candide*, whose eponymous hero is expelled from his home and travels the world through horrific circumstances that test his tutor Pangloss's nonsensical philosophical optimism.[13] The pair ends up living and working on a farm where Pangloss persists in describing their voyage as "a concatenation of all events in the best of possible worlds." Candide does at least appear to have learned something from his travels, though, as illustrated by his rejoinder: "'Excellently observed,' answered Candide; 'but let us cultivate our garden.'"[14]

Candide's hard-won wisdom came to mind as I neared the end of this book's turbulent voyage through the toxic world of bananas, with its own parade of horrors: the machine-gunning of striking Colombian banana workers; cynical manipulation by UFC of legacies of slavery and Indigenous dispossession to undermine worker solidarity in Central America; replacement by the CIA, UFC, and Guatemalan elites of the progressive and democratically elected Jacobo Árbenz with a genocidal dictatorship; the callous sterilization of thousands of banana workers by North American companies and their profitable poisons; the ending of innumerable more-than-human lives and worlds as biodiverse tropical forests and swamps were converted into monocultural plantations with depleted and contaminated soils; the heartbreaking image of pre-teens huddling under cardboard boxes and banana leaves to escape a toxic fungicidal rain; and Ecuador's dizzying journey from neoliberalism to twenty-first-century socialism and back again, culminating in the apocalyptic spectres of the TR4 fungus, COVID-19, and climate change.

When I looked for the Panglossian optimism driving this book's troubled journey, I initially thought of evidence-based health approaches and neoliberal ideology, given the questions raised in the book's Introduction about better public health interventions and banana purchases to make the world a better place. The assertion that more nuanced social scientific research (*noticing*) is adequate to grapple with today's Plantationocene toxic world is also a good candidate. Such musings crystallized for me over the 2020–23 period as I wrote this book and tended my own garden—a Three Sisters (corn, beans, and squash or pumpkin) plot that the COVID-19 pandemic provided me with the circumstances to attempt, somewhat like ones grown by Indigenous peoples in Guatemala, Chiapas, and even southeastern Canada.

Candide's beleaguered state after voyaging through the horrors of early capitalist Europe and its overseas expansion, impelled by Pangloss's misguidance, seemed to parallel my own state as I tended this garden (often unsuccessfully, thanks to persistent slugs and raccoons) and wrote up the journey recounted in this book. Further exhausting parallels emerged as I made a precarious living through sessional teaching with public health students who were generally seeking to make a difference in the world while steeped in evidence-based approaches and neoliberal faith in the power of conscious consumption (though they were usually good about questioning these assumptions in class). The linkages grew stronger as I took on and then fled from the challenge of working within the environmental NGO sector with its faith in market-based solutions and the tractability of Canada's policy structures to evidence-informed advocacy. Then as I recuperated from the strange "concatenation" of occupational and stress-related injuries that had forced the issue of my departure (including the lower back pain that had accompanied me through Chiapas to Guatemala, and indeed through the rest of my academic career), focusing on my embattled garden's flourishing seemed like a suitably wise rejoinder to the "excellently observed" common sense of evidence-based, neoliberal, and even academic social science reasoning.[15]

So what can tending our garden mean, and accomplish? Some of the most promising ideas I've encountered in researching and writing this book are evoked by the word *plotting*. First is the idea of a garden as a plot, suggested by literature on the Plantationocene, urging greater attention to the role of enslaved people's garden plots and the human and agro-biodiversity they preserved at the margins of the brutal exploitation of humans and nature on sugar and other plantations from the seventeenth to the nineteenth century.¹⁶ As mentioned previously, such life-sustaining diversity in the West Indies was also tied up with agro-ecological knowledge such as the banana-growing expertise that UFC's Jamaican migrant workers would bring to Central America in the early twentieth century.¹⁷ That UFC initially profited from such knowledge ("salvage accumulation"¹⁸) but then derided it as they developed centralized scientific but ineffective Panama disease control strategies underscores the importance of this kind of plotting for resisting and recovering from plantation agriculture's assault on human and more-than-human life.

Jumping forward a century, the agro-ecological farming model practised by descendants of the UFC workers who invaded Ecuador's Hacienda Tenguel illustrates the ongoing potential of small-scale peasant agricultural resistance to the dominance of plantation agriculture, notwithstanding contradictions such as the production of an export commodity for consumers in wealthier (banana-consuming) countries. Scholarship on food systems in relation to health suggests that efforts to achieve "food sovereignty" are among the more promising responses to the myriad health issues (such as pesticide exposures in banana production) generated by the current agro-industrial model.¹⁹ Definitions of food sovereignty vary but generally involve people's right to have control over their food, both in terms of how it is grown and how it is consumed (the latter being where the concept of "food security" mostly lives).²⁰ While the pursuit of food sovereignty in Ecuador reveals important complications involving regional, labour, and Indigenous politics, agro-ecological farming is often central to the heterogeneous movement.²¹ To the tired Green Revolution refrain that industrial agriculture is necessary to feed the world's expanding population, it is possible to respond with evidence on the unexpectedly high productivity of agro-ecological production systems in terms of overall nutritional value (though not in terms of maximizing production of a single crop for sale and export).²²

Foregrounding agroecology and local food as a response to the ravages of the industrial food system can quite easily lead to "foodie-ism" and a privileged introspection that leaves the sources of that privilege intact²³ (my Three Sisters gardens, for example, have been planted on stolen Indigenous land in the absence of meaningful relationships to local Haudenosaunee or Anishinaabe knowledge keepers or political struggles). In addition, "proving" agro-ecologically rooted food sovereignty to be a viable improvement on the agro-industrial model currently dominating global agriculture is beyond the scope of this book. Still, I hope that the story told here has planted seeds of doubt about many of the claims used to justify Green Revolution production—and possibly about the entire racist, patriarchal, and ecocidal global economy it is central to.

In fact, truly achieving food sovereignty implies such major changes to that global economy as to be frankly revolutionary,[24] leading to a second kind of plotting among the promising ways forward from the mess described in this book. There might now exist more than a little unease about trying to achieve justice by making capitalist markets and their corresponding nation-states work marginally better, whether through the application of evidence, social science, conscious consumption, or other reformist strategies. To make a huge but important claim, the sheer magnitude of theft and ecological destruction represented by the colonial and neocolonial violence essential to bananas means that there will be no effective or just solution without dismantling the societal structures built by that violence.

How to do that will require some planning, imagining, and even "plotting." The story in this book involves several relevant examples. The 1928 massacre of banana workers in Colombia, the 1954 coup in Guatemala, and the military occupation of Hacienda Tenguel were all justified using trumped-up fears of communist plots, although the real plot in Guatemala turned out to be a CIA-backed coup that ousted a democratically elected government. The Sandinista revolution in Nicaragua, in contrast, was an actual revolutionary movement.[25] While certainly not perfect, the Sandinistas' legacies would reverberate over the years in forms such as the sense of empowerment motivating Nicaraguan banana workers' subsequent advocacy and legal battles over DBCP, and the work of *sandalista* epidemiologists and their Central American colleagues, who represent the most concerted health science effort to counter imperialist (pesticide) toxicity in Latin America.[26] Learning from the lessons of such revolutionary results of plotting and solidarity (and the Zapatista uprising represents an even more recent example) can inform efforts at social change that go beyond reformist research and activism within existing state and market structures.

The situation we are in thus seems to require both plotting in the sense of food sovereignty and plotting in the related sense of seriously changing the world. Transforming the world is easier said than done, and there is considerable resistance or inertia because of the powerful belief that we already live in the best of all possible worlds. This book has shown several kinds of powerful stories shaping historical events and grocery shopping decisions, suggesting one last type of plotting. There might by now be (more) reason to question some of the easy answers or happy endings provided by simple stories such as the discourse of development, with its Green Revolution agriculture and narrow evidence-based responses to the resulting problems (or neoliberal ideology and its supposedly autonomous pesticide users and conscious consumers). Intellectually evaluating such stories is a helpful exercise, but unlikely to work on its own. We believe in problematic stories for very human reasons that involve our important relationships to friends, loved ones, nature, and social structures. Similarly, stories big enough to qualify as ideologies take root not just because they bring people financial or material rewards but also because they resonate with our emotional needs for belonging, community, and a sense of purpose.[27]

Our entanglements with stories also involve our bodies and their interactions with the more-than-human world, as vividly underscored for me by the role of my sore lower back, parasites, and kittens in my learning about violence in Chiapas and Guatemala (and about the entire violent history of banana production told in this book).[28] If beliefs take root through such complex and entangled mechanisms, I'm certainly not going to alter them simply by telling people they're wrong about things like bananas and tropical countries and capitalism and agroindustry—and that's even if I was sure I had the last word on the subject. Experiences such as the trip through Mexico and Central America with which I began this chapter illustrate the ongoing learning I have had to engage in just to get the story this far, as well as uncomfortable realizations about family entanglements with imperialism that—while vivid—are by no means unique among settler Canadians and other people who might find themselves buying bananas.

Humility about what the "real" story is, and should be, therefore seems necessary. Nevertheless, it appears increasingly clear that people's real human needs and the needs of the planet are currently being inadequately provided for by the dominant stories through which we come to know places such as the banana capital of the world and the foods that flow out of them. Promising alternative stories include feminist-inspired visions for everyday, grounded resistance to capitalist exploitation;[29] "compostist" visions based on symbiotically "making kin" with other humans and critters (although I now prefer the term *animalitos*);[30] anti-capitalist sustainability transitions in which decarbonization also involves political emancipation;[31] and decolonial Turtle Island Indigenous visions for the future.[32] With specific respect to the challenges facing farmers and workers in banana-producing countries, initiatives such as the labour rights organizations ASTAC and, at the international level, COLSIBA, complement the agro-ecological vision of small producers such as the farmers of UROCAL and other co-operatives in *la costa*. Challenges to the broader extractivist model within which bananas are central include visions such as *Kawsak Sacha* ("Living Forest," as named by the Amazonian Kichwa nationalities of Ecuador's Pastaza province), which "recognize nature as sentient and humans as inextricably connected to nature as alternatives to dominant political and economic models."[33]

Deciding on which specific promising story (or combination of stories) to get into is beyond what this book can accomplish. The discomfort of not knowing exactly how to proceed recalls the discomfort of my trip through Chiapas and Guatemala. Discomfort is an unavoidable element of confronting gulfs of privilege such as the ones separating me from the Mayan lady and her kittens on the bus, or from essentially all of the banana workers and small farmers I've written this book about.[34] And while I attempted to make this book emotionally rewarding to read by sharing many of the fascinating stories I've encountered in researching it, those stories are also disturbing. They implicate those of us living in the export banana-consuming world (a region that overlaps substantially with the global North), which is an uncomfortable realization. What to do with such discomfort is ultimately up to the people experiencing it. For my part I'll end with an invitation to unflinchingly explore, share, and live better stories that might lead to a better world, and better lives within it. There should be some good food involved.[35]

ACKNOWLEDGEMENTS

Acknowledgements sections are potentially interesting to the people being acknowledged, but also to certain types of readers like me, who look to them for greater insight into how knowledge is produced and stories are pieced together. This book took about fifteen years to research and write, with lots of productive detours that shaped the story and left me with numerous debts of gratitude. I try to address these in roughly chronological order. I apologize for the important people I have almost inevitably forgotten.

The book emerged from my doctoral studies at the University of British Columbia, under the politically insightful and intellectually rich supervision of Jerry Spiegel. He and Annalee Yassi provided a supportive academic home in the social justice–oriented Global Health Research Program and opened their home to me at crucial times. Their long-standing collaboration with Ecuadorian universities, researchers, and communities provided me with a wealth of possible research topics and ample support once I settled on bananas and pesticides. The process of arriving at that topic involved a challenging and rewarding group project with classmates Sara Elder and Dave Roth. Friendship and intellectual support came from fellow GHRP students Kendra Mitchell-Foster, Angeli Rawat, and Bjorn Stime. Kendra's support in both Ecuador and Canada was crucial to my fieldwork. Intellectual guidance for that fieldwork came from official PhD committee members, as well as other supportive UBC faculty. Leila Harris helped introduce me to political ecology and provided careful and insightful feedback on research proposals, dissertation chapters, and, eventually, co-authored journal articles. Patricia Spittal allowed me to first audit and then be a teaching assistant for her course on qualitative methods in public health, and the specific research techniques I used in Ecuador owe a lot to her. The late Alejandro Rojas helped to guide and inspire me with respect to participatory research in the early years of my PhD before having to step down from my committee for health reasons. His wife, Elena Orrego, graciously reviewed and corrected my account of how they met. Throughout my project, Jeannie Shoveller was an extremely helpful "unofficial committee member," generously sharing her time and helping me to juggle methods such as ethnography and discourse analysis while checking the boxes of the School of Population and Public Health (SPPH) doctoral program. Financial support for my doctoral studies came from an SPPH scholarship, UBC's Bridge Program, and a Canadian Institutes of Health Research (CIHR) doctoral research award. In addition, specific trips to Ecuador were supported by the Canadian Coalition for Global Health Research, the Antipode Foundation, and CIHR funding held by Jerry Spiegel.

While in Ecuador, I received major support from people in several academic and civil society organizations. UROCAL opened its doors, meetings, and members' farms to me, providing me with experience of small-scale banana production and connections with a large proportion of my research participants. The late Joaquín Vasquez led this support as UROCAL's president, and then again in his later role as founder of Emprocompt, where I also received substantial support from William Justavino. With UROCAL's help I met leadership and producers of the co-operatives AsoGuabo and Cerro Azul, who also helped me to connect with interviewees and just to generally understand the world of banana production in Ecuador. Jorge Acosta of ASTAC introduced me to the world of banana plantations in Guayas and Los Ríos, providing both incisive political analysis and connections to labour organizers. The staff of the Hotel Ejecutivo in Machala, where I rented an apartment during my fieldwork, were friendly faces during the lonely process of ethnographic fieldwork in the banana capital of the world (they also pushed my face into a birthday cake). Carmen Silverio of the Universidad Técnica de Machala (UTM) provided friendship, advice, and help translating and refining my interview guides. I would like to thank Rodrigo Murillo of UTM for anthropologic insights on the Ecuadorian coast, and Rosa Murillo for making sure I understood what people told me in my interviews there. Alberto Game and Clodoveo Astudillo of UTM also provided valuable guidance and leads as I was getting my project off the ground. Most importantly, dozens of banana farmers and workers I am not allowed to name contributed their time and knowledge as research participants.

My work in Machala and development of this book were also enabled by friends and colleagues in other parts of Ecuador. Patricia Polo has been my Ecuadorian banana research sibling, providing friendship, a place to stay in Quito, always-interesting conversations, feedback on large portions of this book, and the opportunity to work together on other rewarding projects. Juan Gaibor, Maria Jose Fierro, and their family provided a home away from home in Guaranda. Jena Webb, Lindsay Ofrias, and Lexie Gropper helped me to experience and fall under the spell of Ecuador's Amazon region. Erika Arteaga, Kléver Calle, and the *compañeros* of YASunidos-Guapondelig (Cuenca) have helped to educate me on anti-extractivist struggles in Ecuador, and their Canadian dimensions. Jaime Breilh, Maria Jose Breilh, and the committed *compañeros* in the Área de Salud of the Universidad Andina Simón Bolívar have been unfailingly supportive over the years.

In the years after my PhD, I was fortunate to work as a postdoctoral fellow and develop many of the ideas in this book under the supervision of Donald Cole, Anne-Emanuelle Birn, and Patricia O'Campo (with unofficial supervision from Blake Poland). Both Donald and Anne-Emanuelle provided invaluable detailed feedback on parts of this book, and on the journal articles that preceded it. Financial support for these fellowships came from the International Development Research Centre–funded EkoSanté initiative, the University of Toronto, and the Northern Health Authority of British Columbia. The period after my PhD also saw me drawn into the world of mining-related scholarship and activism, generating research results and stories that enriched this book. For various types of support in these efforts, including employment that helped "keep body and soul together," I would like to thank Margot Parkes, Craig Janes, and Katrina Plamondon.

The decision to turn my doctoral research and related stories into a book owes a lot to Sarah Elton, who first invited me to contribute to the University of Regina Press's Digestions series and provided valuable advice and feedback throughout the project. Lenore Newman provided helpful editorial guidance in her role as series editor. Karen Clark was a champion of the book at the press for years, providing encouragement and ongoing insightful writing advice. Two anonymous and very patient reviewers helped improve the book immeasurably, especially when one volunteered to review it a second time. Rachel Stapleton provided encouragement and valuable editorial guidance in getting the book to the finish line. Kelly Laycock's amazing attention to detail as a copy editor caught numerous errors (any that remain are my own responsibility).

Various friends and loved ones provided intellectual, emotional, and material support over a decade and a half. Tanya Chung Tiam Fook's care and support both in Ecuador and up to the present have helped me to understand the history and politics of the Americas, while staying healthy and relatively sane. Matt Feagan provided detailed feedback on a draft of the book and his intellectual footprints are all over its theoretical foundations. Leigh Eagles introduced me to Robin Wall Kimmerer's work at a crucial time. Brie McAloney kept me constantly supplied with banana memes and also read and insightfully commented on portions of the book. Bjorn Stime provided detailed comments on an entire draft of the book, while also animating the anti-extractivist advocacy that came to inform it. My partner, Marisol Campos Navarrete, carefully read the book in its entirety and has shared too much with me to be adequately described here. A short list includes profound knowledge of Latin America, political commitment, laughter, and our lives together. My aunts Anne, Anna, and Mary shared stories about my grandfather that helped to inform the book's final chapter. My sisters Marie Claire and Mackenzie, as well as my brother-in-law Damian and niece and nephews June, Aubrey, and Luke, talked about bananas with me and just generally supported me in numerous important ways over the years. My parents, John and Lenore, read (to each other) and commented on the book, simultaneously providing me with the love, support, intellectual curiosity, commitment to social justice, and unexpected connections to Latin America that made the book possible.

The book was researched and written while living and working on the traditional territories of several First Nations: Musqueam (Coast Salish, Vancouver); Mississauga Anishinaabeg (Peterborough/Nogojiwanong and Toronto); Huron-Wendat, Chippewa, and Haudenosaunee (Toronto); and Mi'kmaq (Charlottetown). It was also written with specific information and communication technologies, and a more general privileged standard of living, made available by the extraction of wealth from territories around the world over centuries.

GLOSSARY

ASTAC (*Asociación Sindical de Trabajadores Agrícolas y Campesinos*): Union Association of Agricultural and Peasant Workers, an Ecuadorian banana worker organization

Bonita: banana label of the Exportadora Bananera Noboa, Ecuador's leading exporter of bananas

Bordeaux mixture: a fungicide consisting of copper sulphate mixed with quicklime in water, used on sigatoka fungus from 1938 to 1962

Chiquita (Chiquita Brands International S.à.r.l.): present-day name of the former United Fruit Company, later United Brands and Chiquita Brands International Inc.; a major transnational corporation in the banana trade

COLSIBA (*Coordinadora Latinoamericana de Sindicatos Bananeros*): Latin American Organization of Banana Unions, an international banana worker and agro-industrial organization

la costa: the Ecuadorian Pacific coastal lowlands

DBCP **(dibromochloropropane):** a nematicide, meaning a pesticide used for killing soil worms known as nematodes

Del Monte (Del Monte Foods Inc.): a major transnational corporation in the banana trade

Dole (Dole plc): present-day name of the Standard Fruit & Steamship Company, later the Standard Fruit & Steamship Corporation, and (after being purchased by the Castle & Cooke Corporation) the Dole Food Company; a major transnational corporation in the banana trade

IRET (*Instituto Regional de Estudios en Sustancias Tóxicas*): Central American Institute for Studies on Toxic Substances

Noboa Group: Ecuadorian family controlling the Exportadora Bananera Noboa; family member Daniel Noboa was elected Ecuadorian president in 2023

el oriente: the Ecuadorian Amazon region to the east of the Andes

Panama disease: major fungal disease of bananas over the first half of the twentieth century, also known as fusarium wilt; scientific name *Fusarium oxysporum* f.sp. *cubense*.

la sierra: the Ecuadorian central highlands or Andean plateau

sigatoka: major fungal disease of bananas with multiple variants, including yellow sigatoka disease (*Mycospharella musicola*, also known as *Pseudocercospora musae*) and the more serious black sigatoka (*Mycosphaerella fijiensis*, also known as *Pseudocercospora fijiensis*)

SITRAP (*Sindicato de Trabajadores de Plantaciones Agrícolas*): Agricultural Plantation Workers' Union, a Costa Rican organization for plantation workers

Standard Fruit (Standard Fruit & Steamship Company, later Standard Fruit & Steamship Corporation): leading banana exporter over the twentieth century; today known as Dole

TR4: fungal disease of bananas threatening the industry in the twenty-first century, closely related to Panama disease; scientific name *Fusarium oxysporum* f.sp. *cubense* § *Tropical Race 4*

United Fruit Company (UFC): preeminent exporter of bananas over the first half of the twentieth century; today known as Chiquita

UPEB (*Unión de Países Exportadores de Banano*): Union of Banana Exporting Countries, an organization for Central and South American banana-exporting countries established in 1974

UROCAL (*Unión Regional de Organizaciones Campesinas del Litoral*): Regional Union of Peasant Organizations of the Coast, an Ecuadorian banana and cacao small-farmer organization

NOTES

PREFACE

1. A pseudonym. All names of research participants have been changed to preserve anonymity.
2. I have kept the exact name vague to avoid the possibility that specific research participants might be identifiable.
3. Seemingly derogatory terms in Latin American Spanish are often made into terms of endearment with the addition of diminutive endings (*-ito/a* or *-cito/a*). For example, many wives refer to their husbands as *gordito*, which translates roughly as "little fatty." Affectionate use of specifically racialized terms is discussed in Whitten, "Symbolic Inversion"; Roitman and Oviedo, "Mestizo Racism in Ecuador."
4. Spiegel, Breilh, and Yassi, "Why Language Matters."
5. Pier, *Tainted Harvest*. The term *precarious* refers to temporary, part-time, casual, and generally insecure forms of employment.
6. Pier.
7. Brisbois et al., "Ecosystem Approaches."

INTRODUCTION

1. Vitali and Marega, *Investigación*; Galarza Suárez, "Tierra, trabajo y tóxicos."
2. Hutter et al., "Health Symptoms Related to Pesticide Use"; Naranjo et al., *Cosechas bañadas en tóxicos*; Naranjo Márquez, *El veneno llega por el aire*.
3. Brulle and Pellow, "Environmental Justice."
4. Macaroff et al., "Estado del banano en Ecuador"; Naranjo et al., *Cosechas bañadas en tóxicos* ; Polo Almeida, "Determinación social"; Galarza Suárez, "Toxic Tropics"; Brisbois, Spiegel, and Harris, "Health, Environment and Colonial Legacies."
5. Weiler et al., "Food Sovereignty, Food Security and Health Equity"; Wallace, *Dead Epidemiologists*.
6. Soluri, *Banana Cultures*.
7. Harari et al., *Producción Bananera*; Breilh, Campaña, and Maldonado, "Informe peritaje"; Maldonado and Martínez, "Impacto de las fumigaciones aéreas"; Hutter

8   et al., "Health Symptoms Related to Pesticide"; Hutter et al., "Indicators of Genotoxicity."
8   Shattuck, "Risky Subjects"; London, "Neurobehavioural Methods, Effects and Prevention."
9   Moberg and Striffler, "Introduction."
10   Shattuck, "Risky Subjects"; Shattuck, "Generic, Growing, Green?"; Murray and Taylor, "Claim No Easy Victories"; Jansen, "The Unspeakable Ban"; Sherwood and Paredes, "Dynamics of Perpetuation"; Galt, "From *Homo economicus*."
11   Nading, "Living in a Toxic World," 218.
12   CSDH, *Closing the Gap in a Generation*, 1.
13   London, "Neurobehavioural Methods, Effects and Prevention."
14   I gravitated towards theories from human geography on the scalar reasoning people use to understand how individuals, communities, nation-states, and the globe relate to each other in the genesis and possible solutions of environmental injustices. See Harrison, "Abandoned Bodies"; Marston, Jones III, and Woodward, "Human Geography without Scale."
15   Douglas and Wildavsky, *Risk and Culture*; Tansey, "Risk as Politics, Culture as Power." For a cautionary note on drawing such links, see Kleinman and Kleinman, "Suffering and Its Professional Transformation."
16   Taussig, *The Devil and Commodity Fetishism*. Similarly, "conspiracy theories" among Venezuelan Indigenous peoples in the wake of the 1991 cholera epidemic foregrounded health-relevant structural factors that were systematically overlooked by the country's white supremacist medical and media establishments; see Briggs, "Theorizing Modernity Conspiratorially."
17   On the slipperiness of the concept of culture and of how it might "get into the body" and affect health, see Janes, "Commentary"; Trostle, *Epidemiology and Culture*; Mitchell, "There's No Such Thing as Culture."
18   Mayer, "The Political Ecology of Disease"; King, "Political Ecologies of Health"; Turshen, *The Political Ecology of Disease in Tanzania*. PEH is a subset of a broader field known as political ecology, which examines environmental degradation and change in relation to political economy, with a major focus on narratives, discourse, and human-environment relations. See Blaikie and Brookfield, *Land Degradation and Society*; Robbins, *Political Ecology*; Peet and Watts, *Liberation Ecologies*. While fitting more squarely in the "health" portion of political ecology, the story told in this book draws liberally from the broader field's perceptive analyses.
19   Sultana, "Emotional Political Ecology"; Shattuck, "Risky Subjects." See also Galt, "From *Homo economicus*."
20   Guthman and Mansfield, "The Implications of Environmental Epigenetics"; Neely, "Internal Ecologies."
21   Jackson and Neely, "Triangulating Health"; Nading, *Mosquito Trails*.
22   Moberg and Striffler, "Introduction," 12.
23   Fairtrade America, "Fairtrade Commits to a Better Future."
24   Soluri, *Banana Cultures*.
25   Chiquita, "The Chiquita Story." The full company name after many mergers and acquisitions is currently Chiquita Brands International S.à.r.l.
26   Coleman, *A Camera in the Garden of Eden*.

27 The term *banana republic* is in fact a kind of racist essentialization with a complex history. See Coleman.
28 Andreatta, "Bananas."
29 Soluri, *Banana Cultures*.
30 Chiquita, "Recipes."
31 Dole, "Recipes."
32 Bohme, *Toxic Injustice*.
33 Dole, "DBCP Facts."
34 Dole, "Dole Delivers Original Recipes."
35 Keifer et al., "Solving the Pesticide Problem"; Barraza et al., "Social Movements and Risk Perception"; Bohme, *Toxic Injustice*; Cole, Crissman, and Orozco, "Eco-Health Projects."
36 Pulido, "Geographies of Race and Ethnicity II"; Liboiron, Tironi, and Calvillo, "Toxic Politics."
37 Brown, "One Hundred Years of Labor Control."
38 Haraway, "Situated Knowledges."
39 Brisbois, "Epidemiology and 'Developing Countries.'"
40 I carried out ethnographic fieldwork in the country from 2011 to 2014, involving a total of approximately one year of naturalistic observation and interviews in *la costa* (fourteen "key informants" from a range of demographic categories participated, as well as thirty people involved in banana production who completed more in-depth "semi-structured interviews"). In addition, I visited the country three times after completing my PhD, and observations from those trips inform the book. For more details on the methodology I employed during my fieldwork, see Brisbois, "Bananas, Pesticides and Health in Southwestern Ecuador."
41 Deleuze and Guattari, *A Thousand Plateaus*.

1. EL PULPO

1 Neruda, *Canto General*, 179.
2 Chomsky, *West Indian Workers*.
3 Soluri, "Bananas Before Plantations."
4 Soluri.
5 Soluri, *Banana Cultures*.
6 Marquardt, "'Green Havoc'"; Martin, *Banana Cowboys*.
7 Soluri, *Banana Cultures*.
8 Clare, "El desarrollo del banano."
9 The literature generated by historians on UFC is enormous. Notable recent highlights in English include Soluri, *Banana Cultures*; Striffler, *In the Shadows*; Bucheli, *Bananas and Business*; Coleman, *A Camera in the Garden of Eden*; Colby, *The Business of Empire*; Marquardt, "'Green Havoc'"; Martin, *Banana Cowboys*. See also Elías Caro and Vidal Ortega, "The Worker's Massacre of 1928." While numerous Latin American scholars have also analyzed banana history, and several of them are cited in this part of the book, Colombian historians Jorge Enrique Elías Caro and Antonino Vidal Ortega attribute the less-developed Spanish-language focus to the company archives' home in the Harvard Business School, where they are less accessible to Latin American historians.

10. Soluri, "Accounting for Taste."
11. Soluri.
12. Soluri, *Banana Cultures*.
13. Grandin, *Empire's Workshop*.
14. Grandin, 3.
15. Cohen, *The Fish That Ate the Whale*. The term was coined by the short story writer O. Henry, who dodged embezzlement charges in the United States by living in Honduras.
16. The story of the larger-than-life Zemurray is told in the informative, albeit US-centric, account by Cohen.
17. Viales Hurtado, "Más allá del enclave."
18. Euraque, *Reinterpreting the Banana Republic*; LeGrand, "Living in Macondo."
19. Ellis, *Las transnacionales del banano*; Slutzky and Alonso, *Empresas transnacionales y agricultura*; Larrea, *El banano en el Ecuador*.
20. LeGrand, "Living in Macondo."
21. Coleman, "The Photos That We Don't Get to See"; Elías Caro, "La masacre obrera de 1928."
22. Quoted in Coleman, "The Photos That We Don't Get to See," 116.
23. Coleman.
24. Herrick, "Alcohol, Ideological Schisms and a Science," 20.
25. Karnes, *Tropical Enterprise*, 67–68.

2. RACE TO THE EQUATOR

1. Martin, *Banana Cowboys*.
2. Martínez, *A la costa*.
3. Martínez, 92.
4. Koeppel, *Banana*; Soluri, "Bananas Before Plantations"; Clare, "El desarrollo del banano."
5. Grandin, *Empire's Workshop*.
6. Pratt, *Imperial Eyes*.
7. Clare, "El desarrollo del banano."
8. Escobar, "Displacement, Development, and Modernity"; Roitman and Oviedo, "Mestizo Racism in Ecuador."
9. Bourgois, *Ethnicity at Work*.
10. Colby, *The Business of Empire*. Such debts owed by Latin American countries to European powers were a common mechanism of economic imperialism in the late nineteenth and early twentieth centuries, subsequently also employed by the United States after purchasing those debts and leveraging them to advance UFC and other commercial interests. See also Euraque, *Reinterpreting the Banana Republic*; Bucheli, "Multinational Corporations."
11. Colby, *The Business of Empire*, 67.
12. Larrea Maldonado, *Hacia una historia ecológica*.
13. Larrea Maldonado.
14. Acosta, *Breve historia económica*.
15. Whitten, "Symbolic Inversion"; Roitman and Oviedo, "Mestizo Racism in Ecuador"; Clark, "Racial Ideologies"; Ibarra, *Indios y cholos*. Ecuador's complex

racial hierarchies have generally put white Euro-descended peoples at the top, with Afro-descended and Indigenous peoples at the bottom and a complex interplay of racialized and class-based characteristics creating different levels within the mixed European-Indigenous *mestizo* population.
16 Chomsky, *West Indian Workers*.
17 Colby, *The Business of Empire*.
18 Bourgois, *Ethnicity at Work*.
19 Marquardt, "'Green Havoc'"
20 Colby, *The Business of Empire*. Centuries of slavery and white supremacy meant that Black workers were understood by white US managers to have a natural lowly place in commercial enterprises, largely as menial labourers.
21 Bourgois, *Ethnicity at Work*; Colby, *The Business of Empire*. While the material in this paragraph is largely drawn from Bourgois's ethnography, Colby makes the point that such "divide and conquer" labour relations strategies were increasingly common in the United States as successive waves of nineteenth- and twentieth-century immigrants allowed for specific ethnic groups to be assigned distinct roles following a racializing hierarchy, and played off of each other in the event of labour disputes.
22 Bourgois, *Ethnicity at Work*, 109.
23 Colby, "'Banana Growing and Negro Management.'"
24 Colby, *The Business of Empire*.
25 Said, *Culture and Imperialism*.
26 Heron, *Desire for Development*.
27 On portrayals of Latin America, see Pratt, *Imperial Eyes*; Brisbois, "Epidemiology and 'Developing Countries'"; and Raffles, *In Amazonia*. On the concept of imaginative geographies and their relationship to imperialism, see Said, *Orientalism*.
28 Soluri, "Accounting for Taste," 393; Harding, *Sciences from Below*. Sandra Harding explains that such celebratory stories have been found throughout Western portrayals of the interactions of science with "tropical" places and peoples.
29 Whitten, "Symbolic Inversion"; Roitman and Oviedo, "Mestizo Racism in Ecuador."
30 Roitman, "Hybridity, Mestizaje, and Montubios"; cf. de la Cuadra, *El montuvio ecuatoriano*. A very nice middle-class *serrana* woman I spoke with near Quito once informed me that such characteristics were both real and caused by the increased amounts of oxygen in the air at sea level. In her interpretation—which I am certain is not hers alone—the dense air at sea level permits impulsive behaviours that the more reserved peoples of *la sierra* would be prevented from enacting by the thin air, which imposes enough of a time between impulse and action for sober second thought to prevail. Another *serrano* I described my research to in the highland city of Cuenca informed me that I would have trouble getting straight answers about the situation prevailing on banana plantations. As he explained, *serranos* would lie to me, and *costeños* would lie to me even more. Another term in common usage to describe *costeños* is *mono* (the Spanish word for monkey), possibly reflecting racism towards the Afro-Ecuadorian peoples who dominate the population of the northern coastal province of Esmeraldas and are a significant presence in the central and southern coastal provinces. The story I have heard about the more specific origins of this term involves the king of Spain being presented with the gift of a monkey

from coastal Ecuador in the colonial era. The king's fright at the monkey allegedly led to jokes about *monos* from Guayaquil and their unruly nature. Consistent with the way in which terms such as *longo, cholo,* and *negro* can be used by *mestizos* to affectionately refer to their friends and loved ones—while subtly commenting on their unruly or lacking-in-*cultura* behaviours—*mono* can be used semi-affectionately. A fast-food outlet operating in Machala during my fieldwork was named *El Monito* (the diminutive form of *mono*), with a cartoon monkey in the logo.

31 Whitten, "Symbolic Inversion"; Neyra Ballestero, *Presencia de la etnia negra*.
32 Bourgois, *Ethnicity at Work*. In the Bocas division, the land West Indian workers could acquire had previously been violently taken away from the Bribri and other Indigenous groups, some of whom would also intermarry with West Indian migrants, making the story of race and banana production even more complicated.
33 Bourgois.
34 Colby, *The Business of Empire*; Chomsky, *West Indian Workers*. Aviva Chomsky describes several comparable incidents in Costa Rica in the early twentieth century.
35 Lofters and O'Campo, "Differences That Matter"; McClure et al., "Racial Capitalism."
36 Robinson, *Black Marxism*.
37 Pulido, "Geographies of Race and Ethnicity 11." Kish and Leroy, "Bonded Life." As Kish and Leroy document, the ways in which modern high finance grew out of insurance infrastructure designed to protect the investments of European slave traders provide one vivid example of racial capitalism.

3. BANANAS, ENVIRONMENTS, AND HISTORIES

1 For more detail on the concept of the "more-than-human" world, see Abram, *The Spell of the Sensuous*.
2 Clare, "El desarrollo del banano."
3 Asturias, *Viento Fuerte*, 9.
4 Grossman, *The Political Ecology of Bananas*.
5 Colby, *The Business of Empire*.
6 Anne-Emanuelle Birn, personal communication.
7 Soluri, *Banana Cultures*; Marquardt, "'Green Havoc.'"
8 Henriques et al., "Agrochemical Use."
9 Soluri, *Banana Cultures*; Marquardt, "'Green Havoc.'"
10 Marquardt, "'Green Havoc.'"
11 Soluri, "Accounting for Taste."
12 Marquardt, "'Green Havoc.'" One example of this ecological knowledge was the use of felled trees to provide nutrients to banana plants in newly cleared tropical soils.
13 Marquardt.
14 Clare, "El desarrollo del banano."
15 Clare.
16 Karnes, *Tropical Enterprise*.
17 Soluri, "Accounting for Taste."
18 Soluri, *Banana Cultures*.
19 Soluri, "Bananas, Biodiversity and the Paradox."

20 On the fragility of the distinction between "scientific" and "traditional" knowledge, see Watson-Verran and Turnbull, "Science and Other Indigenous Knowledge Systems."
21 Brisbois, Spiegel, and Harris, "Health, Environment and Colonial Legacies."
22 Marquardt, "'Green Havoc'"; Clare, "El desarrollo del banano."; Soluri, "Bananas, Biodiversity and the Paradox."
23 Ploetz, "Panama Disease, Part 1."
24 For more detail, see Brisbois, Spiegel, and Harris, "Health, Environment and Colonial Legacies."
25 Aliano, "Curing the Ills of Central America."
26 Aliano, 47.
27 Martin, *Banana Cowboys*.
28 Colby, *The Business of Empire*.
29 Buse et al., "Public Health Guide."
30 For critiques of apolitical approaches in fields such as One Health, Ecohealth, and Planetary Health, see Jones, Reid, and Macmillan, "Navigating Fundamental Tensions"; Wallace, *Dead Epidemiologists*; Brisbois et al., "Ecosystem Approaches."
31 Marquardt, "'Green Havoc.'" Other divisions closed due to Panama disease included Almirante, Panama, in 1926; the Truxillo division in Honduras in 1939; Nicaragua's entire export industry in 1942; and the Quepos division in Costa Rica in 1956.
32 Bourgois, *Ethnicity at Work*; Colby, "'Banana Growing and Negro Management.'"

4. BEYOND ITS CONTROL

1 Colby, "'Banana Growing and Negro Management.'"
2 Grandin, *The Last Colonial Massacre*.
3 Bucheli, "Multinational Corporations."
4 Cohen, *The Fish That Ate the Whale*.
5 Cohen. The title of Cohen's account refers to Zemurray's unexpected takeover of UFC from within.
6 Forster, "'The Macondo of Guatemala.'"
7 Schlesinger, Nuccio, and Schirmer, "Preserving Bitter Fruit."
8 Forster, "'The Macondo of Guatemala,'" 194–95.
9 Forster, 220. On Indigenous (Q'eqchi' Mayan) political resistance to such repression, see Grandin, *The Last Colonial Massacre*.
10 Marquardt, "'Green Havoc.'" Marquardt has described Panama disease and UFC's losing battle with it as an important neglected factor helping to explain the company's actions in fomenting the coup.
11 Forster, "'The Macondo of Guatemala'"; Grandin, *The Last Colonial Massacre*.
12 The balance of factors that motivated the United States to intervene in Guatemala—specific corporate interests as opposed to more general fear of communism—continues to be debated among historians. See Grandin.
13 Cohen, *The Fish That Ate the Whale*.
14 Soluri, *Banana Cultures*; Cohen, *The Fish That Ate the Whale*.
15 Bucheli, "Multinational Corporations"; Karnes, *Tropical Enterprise*.
16 Bucheli, *Bananas and Business*.
17 Quoted in Bucheli, "United Fruit Company," 89.

18 Moody's December 1956 stock survey, quoted in Bucheli, 91.
19 Sylva Charvet, "Los Productores de Banano."
20 Bucheli, "United Fruit Company."

5. THE VERY, VERY TROPICAL EQUATOR

1   Larrea Maldonado, *Hacia una historia ecológica*.
2   Larrea, *El banano en el Ecuador*. I draw extensively here on the excellent history of Ecuadorian banana production by Carlos Larrea and collaborators.
3   Larrea; Striffler, "Rebellion, Revolution, and Reversal."
4   Striffler, "Rebellion, Revolution, and Reversal"; Martínez Valle, "Trabajo flexible."
5   Striffler, *In the Shadows*.
6   Striffler.
7   Neyra Ballestero, *Presencia de la etnia negra*. One exception was the use of Afro-Ecuadorian workers as stevedores in port cities, where they worked to load bananas onto ships travelling north.
8   Striffler, *In the Shadows*.
9   Striffler.
10 Larrea, *El banano en el Ecuador*.
11 Sylva Charvet, "Los Productores de Banano," 120; see also Roberts, *Empresarios ecuatorianos del banano*.
12 Larrea, *El banano en el Ecuador*, 56.
13 Southgate and Roberts, *Globalized Fruit, Local Entrepreneurs*.
14 Moberg, "Review of *Globalized Fruit, Local Entrepreneurs*."
15 Striffler, *In the Shadows*.
16 Larrea, *El banano en el Ecuador*.

6. THE PARAKEET IN THE PLANTATION

1   Eschner, "The Story of the Real Canary."
2   Brisbois, Spiegel, and Harris, "Health, Environment and Colonial Legacies." Global scientific networks that catalogued the global diversity of sigatoka drew on observations of different varieties in Java, Hawaii, and Fiji, with eventual fungicide resistance developing in the French Antilles, Cameroon, and Belize. This distribution of banana phytopathological research uncannily mirrors the geography of colonial occupations, whether of Java by the Netherlands, the French Antilles by France, Hawaii by the United States, or Fiji, Cameroon, and Belize by Great Britain.
3   Marquardt, "Pesticides, Parakeets, and Unions," 7.
4   Soluri, "Accounting for Taste."
5   Marquardt, "Pesticides, Parakeets, and Unions," 7.
6   Marquardt.
7   Marquardt; Soluri, "Accounting for Taste."
8   Marquardt, "Pesticides, Parakeets, and Unions," 11.
9   Bourgois, *Ethnicity at Work*.
10 Marquardt, "Pesticides, Parakeets, and Unions."
11 On the concept of "internal ecologies," see Neely, "Internal Ecologies."
12 Marquardt, "Pesticides, Parakeets, and Unions."
13 Marquardt.

14   Bourgois, *Ethnicity at Work*.
15   Marquardt, "Pesticides, Parakeets, and Unions."

7. AN INSULT
1   Larrea, *El banano en el Ecuador*.
2   Larrea.
3   Sylva Charvet, "Los Productores de Banano," 134.
4   Sylva Charvet, 142.
5   Larrea, *El banano en el Ecuador*, 60–62.
6   Larrea, 69.
7   Cepeda-Bastidas, "Ces mains qui font le régime," 181.
8   Striffler, "Rebellion, Revolution, and Reversal."
9   Galarza Suárez, "Tierra, Trabajo y Tóxicos."
10   Carrillo García, *Desarrollo rural*; Galarza Suárez, "Tierra, Trabajo y Tóxicos."
11   Striffler, "Rebellion, Revolution, and Reversal."
12   Galarza Suárez, "Tierra, Trabajo y Tóxicos"; Striffler, "Rebellion, Revolution, and Reversal."
13   Larrea, *El banano en el Ecuador*.
14   Carrillo García, *Desarrollo rural*.
15   Striffler, *In the Shadows*. Striffler's ethnographic study of Hacienda Tenguel makes this point and poignantly traces its implications for the landless descendants of the UFC workers who gained land after the occupation.

8. CAVENDISH ECOLOGIES
1   Amaya Amador, *Prisión Verde*, 149.
2   Jansen, "Banana Wars," 108.
3   Cohen, *The Fish That Ate the Whale*.
4   Soluri, "Bananas, Biodiversity and the Paradox."
5   Jansen, "Banana Wars."
6   Neely, "Internal Ecologies."
7   Striffler, "Wedded to Work."
8   Henriques et al., "Agrochemical Use."
9   Thrupp, "The Political Ecology."
10   Bohme, *Toxic Injustice*.
11   Bohme.
12   Russell, *War and Nature*.
13   Thrupp, "The Political Ecology," 243.
14   Thrupp.
15   Thrupp, 133, 231.
16   Thrupp.
17   Thrupp.
18   Thrupp.
19   Thrupp.
20   Soluri, *Banana Cultures*.
21   Thrupp, "The Political Ecology."
22   Thrupp.

23 Thrupp, 121, 125.
24 Henriques et al., "Agrochemical Use."
25 Castillo, Ruepert, and Solis, "Pesticide Residues"; Castillo et al., "Water Quality"; Henriques et al., "Agrochemical Use"; Grant, Woudneh, and Ross, "Pesticides in Blood."
26 Wesseling et al., "Agricultural Pesticide Use"; Naranjo et al., *Cosechas bañadas en tóxicos*; Breilh, Campaña, and Maldonado, "Informe peritaje"; London, "Neurobehavioural Methods, Effects and Prevention."
27 Thrupp, "The Political Ecology," 147.
28 Bohme, *Toxic Injustice*.
29 Henriques et al., "Agrochemical Use."
30 Soluri, "Accounting for Taste."
31 Bohme, *Toxic Injustice*.
32 Bohme.
33 Hofmann et al., "Mortality"; Bohme, *Toxic Injustice*; Slutsky, Levin, and Levy, "Azoospermia and Oligospermia"; Sass, "Agricultural 'Killing Fields.'"

9. EMPIRE'S GUINEA PIGS

1 Shiva, *Monocultures of the Mind*.
2 Taylor, "Success for Whom?" A more complete explanation of the coup in Chile would involve factors such as the country's role in the global economy, its adoption of import substitution policies in the post-war period, and dissatisfaction of Chile's upper classes with Allende's redistributive policies and their own flagging economic prospects.
3 Klein, *The Shock Doctrine*; Machado Aráoz, "El auge de la minería transnacional."
4 Siebert, "U. de Chile lamenta."
5 Elena Orrego, personal communication. I am extremely grateful to Elena for reviewing my retelling of Alejandro's story.
6 Murray, *Cultivating Crisis*, 2.
7 On the historical development of, and sketchy scientific justification for, the Green Revolution, see Patel, "The Long Green Revolution."
8 Murray, *Cultivating Crisis*.
9 Kallet and Schlink, *100,000,000 Guinea Pigs*.
10 Larrea, *El banano en el Ecuador*; Ellis, *Las transnacionales del banano*.
11 Machado Aráoz, "El auge de la minería transnacional."
12 Klein, *The Shock Doctrine*.
13 Grandin, *Empire's Workshop*.
14 Taylor, "Success for Whom?"
15 Klein, *The Shock Doctrine*.
16 Rowe Davis, "On the Professionalization of Toxicology."
17 On the always locally contingent manifestations of "actually existing neoliberalism," see Brenner, Peck, and Theodore, "Variegated Neoliberalization"; Ferguson, "The Uses of Neoliberalism"; Bell and Green, "On the Perils."

10. EL FRUTO DEL NEOLIBERALISMO

1. Brenner, Peck, and Theodore, "Variegated Neoliberalization"; Ferguson, "The Uses of Neoliberalism."
2. Soluri, "Bananas Before Plantations." Overcoming the challenges to profitability posed by local social and environmental circumstances is precisely why, in many interpretations, the banana industry largely consolidated into UFC and a handful of competitors at the beginning of the twentieth century.
3. Hough, "A Race to the Bottom?"
4. Hough.
5. A detailed account of the EU and WTO banana-related trade dispute is provided in Wiley, *The Banana*.
6. Striffler, "El fruto del neoliberalismo."
7. Larrea, *El banano en el Ecuador*, 75.
8. Larrea, 60.
9. Larrea.
10. Larrea.
11. Larrea.
12. Larrea.
13. Larrea.
14. The importance of standardization to the overall trajectory of banana history is noted in Jansen, "Banana Wars."
15. Larrea, *El banano en el Ecuador*.
16. Larrea, 30.
17. Corkhill and Cubitt, *Ecuador*.
18. Breilh and Tilleria, *Aceleración global y despojo en Ecuador*.
19. Larrea Maldonado, *Pobreza, dolarización y crisis*, 23.
20. Breilh and Tilleria, *Aceleración global y despojo en Ecuador*, 64.
21. Larrea Maldonado, *Pobreza, dolarización y crisis*, 44.
22. Pan American Health Organization and UNICEF, cited in Breilh and Tilleria, *Aceleración global y despojo en Ecuador*, 65.
23. Comisión Económica para América Latina y el Caribe, cited in Larrea Maldonado, *Pobreza, dolarización y crisis*, 26.
24. Breilh and Tilleria, *Aceleración global y despojo en Ecuador*.
25. Breilh and Tilleria.
26. Corkhill and Cubitt, *Ecuador*.
27. Frundt, *Fair Bananas!*
28. Frundt; cf. Striffler, "El fruto del neoliberalismo."
29. Larrea Maldonado, *Pobreza, dolarización y crisis*.
30. Larrea, *El banano en el Ecuador*. For a contrasting celebratory take on the role of Noboa and other domestic elites in Ecuador's banana industry, see Roberts, *Empresarios ecuatorianos del banano*.
31. Chomsky, "Globalization, Labor, and Violence."
32. Chomsky.
33. Hough, "A Race to the Bottom?"; Chomsky, "Globalization, Labor, and Violence."
34. Chomsky, "Globalization, Labor, and Violence"; Hough, "A Race to the Bottom?"
35. Striffler, "El fruto del neoliberalismo."

11. HEALTHY RESISTANCE

1. Fallas, *Mamita Yunai*, 55.
2. Fallas, 250.
3. Anderson, "Where Is the Postcolonial History of Medicine?"
4. Brenner, Peck, and Theodore, "Variegated Neoliberalization."
5. Thrupp, "The Political Ecology of Pesticide Use"; Murray, *Cultivating Crisis*.
6. Swezey, Murray, and Daxl, "Nicaragua Revolution in Pesticide Policy," 30. Named after the early twentieth-century revolutionary Augusto Sandino, the Sandinistas instituted a variety of redistributive measures targeting the economic legacies of colonial exploitation, especially profound inequalities that Somoza had only deepened. In parallel to those economic efforts, the Sandinistas had responded to a Green Revolution–created pesticide treadmill crisis in the country's export-based cotton sector—which provided one of its few major sources of foreign currency—by stepping up programming in integrated pest management (IPM). IPM is an agricultural technique that involves "making maximum use of naturally occurring insect controls, using biological, environmental, cultural, and legal methods in a complementary fashion." The goal of IPM is to reduce pesticide use to a bare minimum, applied judiciously in ways that would rely on natural ecological checks and balances rather than brute-force pesticide use. The Sandinistas were aided in their IPM efforts by the non-governmental organization CARE's Safe and Rational Pesticide Use Project, funded by the Norwegian government, aimed at reducing indiscriminate and overall pesticide use via IPM and at documenting and reducing acute pesticide poisonings in the country. The pesticide safety public health efforts of the Sandinistas are described in Cole et al., "Pesticide Illness Surveillance."
7. Bourgois, *Ethnicity at Work*, 244.
8. Birn and Brown, *Comrades in Health*; Belli, *The Country Under My Skin*.
9. Brisbois, "Epidemiology and 'Developing Countries'"; Galvão et al., *Pesticides and Health*; Cole et al., "Pesticide Illness Surveillance"; Swezey, Murray, and Daxl, "Nicaragua Revolution in Pesticide Policy."
10. Castro-Gutiérrez et al., "Respiratory Symptoms."
11. Partanen et al., "Collaboration between Developing and Developed Countries."
12. Frundt, "Sustaining Labor-Environmental Coalitions"; Wesseling et al., "Cancer in Banana Plantation Workers."
13. Frundt, "Sustaining Labor-Environmental Coalitions," 104.
14. Barraza et al., "Social Movements and Risk Perception."
15. Frundt, "Sustaining Labor-Environmental Coalitions"; Clare, "El desarrollo del banano."
16. Bohme, *Toxic Injustice*.
17. Barraza et al., "Social Movements and Risk Perception."
18. Frundt, "Sustaining Labor-Environmental Coalitions."
19. Barraza et al., "Social Movements and Risk Perception"; Frundt, "Sustaining Labor-Environmental Coalitions."
20. Barraza et al., "Social Movements and Risk Perception."
21. Barraza et al.; Frundt, "Sustaining Labor-Environmental Coalitions."
22. Frundt, "Sustaining Labor-Environmental Coalitions."
23. Barraza et al., "Social Movements and Risk Perception."

24 Barraza et al.
25 E.g., Hofmann et al., "Mortality"; Wesseling et al., "Cancer in Banana Plantation Workers."
26 Barraza et al., "Social Movements and Risk Perception," 15.
27 Bohme, *Toxic Injustice*.
28 Keifer et al., "Solving the Pesticide Problem."

12. A LA COSTA

1 Larrea, *El banano en el Ecuador*, 104–5.
2 According to one Ecuadorian study, "almost all of the highways of the coastal region are banana highways because they cross similar zones or, in any case, are routes for the conduction of fruit to markets." Cueva, cited in Sylva Charvet, "Los Productores de Banano," 120.
3 Larrea, *El banano en el Ecuador*, 32.
4 Shiva, *The Violence of the Green Revolution*.
5 Larrea, *El banano en el Ecuador*, 104.
6 Locals hastened to inform me that a Canadian woman, Anna María Ezechiels, was crowned queen in 2004.
7 A vivid portrayal of how the flourishing of bananas is considered equivalent to or even more important than that of human life is found in *Viento Fuerte*, which describes the process of harvesting a banana bunch: "The movements of the harvest crew at the foot of the banana plant, which seemed like a green crucifix, were like Jews with ladders and lances trying to bring down a green Christ converted into a banana bunch, which descended between ropes and hands and was received with the care due to a supremely sensitive being, then transported in small cars to receive sacramental baths and be placed in a specially padded bag." See Asturias, *Viento Fuerte*, 25–26.
8 Zamora Acosta and Hernández León, "La agroindustria del banano"; Polo Almeida, "Relación territorio-salud."

13. TWENTY-FIRST-CENTURY SOCIALISM AND CONTEMPORARY FORMS OF SLAVERY

1 Pier, *Tainted Harvest*.
2 Striffler, "El fruto del neoliberalismo."
3 Striffler.
4 Quoted in Galarza Suárez, "Tierra, Trabajo y Tóxicos," 354.
5 Becker, "The Stormy Relations." Venezuela's Hugo Chavez and Bolivia's Evo Morales were other prominent "pink tide" representatives of such leftist responses to Latin America's neoliberal "lost decades."
6 Larrea and Greene, "Concentration of Assets."
7 Becker, "The Stormy Relations."
8 Herrera, "El 'vacío sindical.'"
9 Galarza Suárez, "Tierra, Trabajo y Tóxicos."
10 Herrera, "El 'vacío sindical.'"
11 Striffler, "El fruto del neoliberalismo"; Frundt, *Fair Bananas!*; Larrea, *El banano en el Ecuador*; Martínez Valle, "Trabajo flexible."
12 SIPAE, Broederlijk Delen, and Oxfam, "Prácticas de compra."

13 Brisbois, Harris, and Spiegel, "Political Ecologies."
14 Smith, "Fairtrade Bananas."
15 Martínez Valle, "Trabajo flexible"; Vitali, "Agroindustria y precarización laboral."
16 Larrea Maldonado, *Hacia una historia ecológica*.
17 Harari et al., *Producción Bananera*.
18 Harari et al.
19 Maldonado and Martínez, "Impacto de las fumigaciones aéreas," 9.
20 Herrera, "El 'vacío sindical.'" The Defensoría is an ombudsperson-type office with the mandate to investigate and intervene in cases of violations of the rights of Ecuadorians. The study originated in a 2007 formal complaint (Resolución 117-CNDHIG-2008) by a group of banana fumigation pilots. Led by former military pilot Jorge Acosta, the group of pilots was supported in their complaint by the *Red en Plaguicidas y sus Alternativas para América Latina* (RAPAL, or the Network on Pesticides and Their Alternatives in Latin America).
21 Szklo and Nieto, *Epidemiology*. Cross-sectional studies cannot establish whether the exposures in question preceded the outcomes, a key consideration in assessing possible causality.
22 Breilh, *Epidemiología*.
23 On the imperviousness of Ecuadorian pesticide policy to epidemiologic evidence, see Chapter 22 as well as Sherwood and Paredes, "Dynamics of Perpetuation."

14. A QUESTION OF CULTURE

1   Nading, "Living in a Toxic World."
2   Briggs, "Theorizing Modernity Conspiratorially"; Farmer and Good, "Illness Representations."
3   Harari et al., *Producción Bananera*, 15.
4   For a comparable ethnographic search for "authentic" traditional medical practices in coastal Ecuador, see Phillips, "Changing Health Moralities."
5   Barraza et al., "Pesticide Use"; Ríos-González, Jansen, and Sánchez-Pérez, "Pesticide Risk Perceptions"; Shattuck, "Risky Subjects."
6   Ríos-González, Jansen, and Sánchez-Pérez, "Pesticide Risk Perceptions."
7   Mera-Orces, "Paying for Survival"; see also Ríos-González, Jansen, and Sánchez-Pérez, "Pesticide Risk Perceptions."
8   Galt, "From *Homo economicus*"; Shattuck, "Risky Subjects."
9   Sellers, *Hazards of the Job*; Nash, *Inescapable Ecologies*. For more on the scientific and political problems with this belief, see Chapter 21.
10 Clark, "Racial Ideologies."
11 On such uses of "culture," see Mitchell, "There's No Such Thing as Culture."
12 Cf. Carrillo García, *Desarrollo rural*.
13 Ibarra, *Indios y cholos*; Roitman and Oviedo, "Mestizo Racism in Ecuador"; Whitten, "Symbolic Inversion."
14 Whitten. Insults such as *longo* or *cholo* capture this idea of *mestizos* lacking *cultura*, but can also—along with the terms *negro* and *negra*—be used in a semi-affectionate or mocking way that often subtly enforces *mestizaje*'s hierarchies by associating behaviours lacking *cultura* with such racialized categories. For example, I heard

a *mestizo* employee at the hotel where I lived in Machala affectionately address a female friend as *negra*.
15   Roitman, "Hybridity, Mestizaje, and Montubios."
16   Brisbois, "Bananas, Pesticides and Health"; Brisbois, Spiegel, and Harris, "Health, Environment and Colonial Legacies."

15. THE ILLNESS OF THE CENTURY

1   Such insights are consistent with the large and growing literature on affect in relation to politics, culture, environment, and health. See, for example, Ahmed, "Collective Feelings"; Nichols and Del Casino, "Towards an Integrated Political Ecology"; Sultana, "Emotional Political Ecology"; Brisbois, Harris, and Spiegel, "Political Ecologies of Global Health."
2   On the "acceleration" imposed on life for people such as Ecuadorian small farmers by the country's neoliberal integration into the global economy, see Breilh and Tilleria, *Aceleración global y despojo en Ecuador*.
3   Such individualizing narratives precede neoliberalism and have always been associated with capitalist ideology but have gained prominence in the neoliberal period. I am grateful to an anonymous reviewer for raising this point.
4   Brisbois, Harris, and Spiegel, "Political Ecologies of Global Health"; Nading, *Mosquito Trails*; Nichols and Del Casino, "Towards an Integrated Political Ecology." Political ecology of health has employed the term *entanglement* to express the interrelationships among social structures, relationships (both human and more-than-human), and bodies.
5   Shattuck, "Risky Subjects"; Galt, "From *Homo economicus* to Complex Subjectivities." These observations are generally consistent with an understanding of pesticide risk perception as reflecting embodied personal experiences and the "complex subjectivities" of pesticide users.

16. EL GRINGUITO

1   The effects of my positionality, as well as Pati's, on research with banana farmers and workers are explored in an article we co-authored: Brisbois and Polo Almeida, "Attending to Researcher Positionality." See also Sundberg, "Looking for the Critical Geographer"; Sundberg, "Ethics, Entanglement, and Political Ecology."
2   Haraway, "Situated Knowledges."
3   Deneault and Sacher, *Imperial Canada Inc.*
4   Natural Resources Canada, "Minerals and the Economy."
5   Birn et al., "Canada Kills, Inc."; Butler, *Colonial Extractions*; Mukhopadhyay et al., "Canada's Global Health Role." Mining has been a key part of Canada's national identity and economic prosperity since before 1867, when Confederation consolidated the various colonies France, and later Britain, had established on Indigenous lands. Resource extraction has been integral to both the development of settler-Canadian wealth, cities, and institutions, and the national ideologies that have accompanied and supported it.
6   Antonelli, "Canadá, entre la sed insaciable"; Gordon and Webber, *Blood of Extraction*. Consular services, financing through Export Development Canada, international development funding aimed to smooth over mining-associated conflicts, and

(neoliberalizing) bilateral trade agreements are a few of the mechanisms Canada has used to overcome community and national obstacles to profitable extraction of wealth.
7 For explorations of such links and their implications for health and environmental justice, see Brisbois et al., "Ecosystem Approaches to Health"; Brisbois et al., "Mining, Colonial Legacies and Neoliberalism."
8 Gordon and Webber, "Canadian Capital."

17. SAME JOKE, DIFFERENT CLOWN

1   Breilh, Campaña, and Maldonado, "Informe peritaje."
2   Vitali and Marega, "Investigación," 14.
3   Larrea and Greene, "Concentration of Assets."
4   Larrea and Greene, 108.
5   Larrea and Greene.
6   Larrea and Greene.
7   Larrea and Greene, 99.
8   Larrea and Greene, 100; cf. Latorre, "The Role of Ecuadorian Working-Class Environmentalism."
9   Galarza Suárez, "Tierra, Trabajo y Tóxicos."
10 Quoted in Isch López, "El extractivismo."
11 Quoted in Isch López.
12 Galarza Suárez, "Tierra, Trabajo y Tóxicos," 355.
13 Latorre, Farrell, and Martínez-Alier, "The Commodification of Nature"; Latorre, "The Role of Ecuadorian Working-Class Environmentalism."
14 Riofrancos, *Resource Radicals*.
15 Shade, "Sustainable Development or Sacrifice Zone?"; Arteaga-Cruz et al., "Connecting the Right to Health"; Latorre, Farrell, and Martínez-Alier, "The Commodification of Nature."
16 Isch López, "El extractivismo."
17 Isch López.
18 Martínez Novo, "Ventriloquism, Racism and the Politics of Decoloniality."
19 Herrera, "El 'vacío sindical.'"
20 Herrera; Polo Almeida, "Determinación social"; Vitali, "Agroindustria y precarización laboral"; Galarza Suárez, "Tierra, Trabajo y Tóxicos."
21 Macaroff, "El modelo bananero"; Larrea and Greene, "Concentration of Assets."
22 Herrera, "El 'vacío sindical.'"
23 Herrera.
24 Rubio et al., cited in Macaroff, "El modelo bananero."
25 Vitali, "Agroindustria y precarización laboral," 10.
26 Vitali.
27 Humbert and Brassel, "Sweet Fruit, Bitter Truth."
28 Humbert and Brassel, 25.
29 Humbert and Brassel, 31.
30 Humbert and Brassel, 31.
31 Polo Almeida, "Determinación social."
32 Galarza Suárez, "Tierra, Trabajo y Tóxicos."

33 Hutter et al., "Banana Pesticide Study."
34 Hutter et al., "Health Symptoms Related to Pesticide Use."
35 Zambrano-Ganchozo et al., "Neurotoxic Effects."
36 Galarza Suárez, "Tierra, Trabajo y Tóxicos."

18. PLAGAS

1 E.g., Giroux, "The Covid-19 Pandemic."
2 Riofrancos, *Resource Radicals.*
3 Herrera, "El 'vacío sindical.'"
4 Humbert, "The Plight of Pineapple and Banana Workers."
5 Macaroff, "El modelo bananero," 133.
6 Macaroff.
7 Hill, "Throughout South America."
8 Hill.
9 Badillo Salgado and Fischer, "Ecuador, COVID-19 and the IMF"; Iturralde, "The IMF's Role."
10 León Cabrera, "'Los que no aparecen.'"
11 Iturralde, "The IMF's Role."
12 Cuéllar et al., "Excess Deaths."
13 Acción Ecológica, "Serie Coronavirus #6."
14 Acción Ecológica.
15 Breilh, "SARS-COV2."
16 Ospina Peralta, "The Divided Left in Ecuador."
17 Green and Fernández-Flores, "Mexican Cartels."
18 Al Jazeera and News Agencies, "Who Was Fernando Villavicencio?"
19 "República Bananera del Ecuador."
20 Wallace et al., "COVID-19 and Circuits of Capital."
21 Ploetz, "Ploetz, "Panama Disease, Part 2"; de la Cruz and Jansen, "Panama Disease."
22 Paredes, "Experimental Science for the 'Bananapocalypse.'"
23 Paredes.
24 Martínez et al., "The Advance of Fusarium Wilt."
25 Naranjo et al., *Cosechas Bañadas en Tóxicos.*

19. THE BANANTHROPOCENE

1 Translated as "Sour Lake" and named after the Texas oil town of that name; the city's official name is Nueva Loja.
2 Ofrias, "Invisible Harms, Invisible Profits."
3 Maldonado and Martínez, "Impacto de las fumigaciones aéreas."
4 Maldonado Campos, "Una propuesta de reparación."
5 Clínica Ambiental Org, "Alianzas—Organizaciones Hermanas."
6 Tsing, *The Mushroom at the End of the World.*
7 Maldonado Campos, "Una propuesta de reparación."
8 Larrea Maldonado, *Hacia una historia ecológica.*
9 Maldonado Campos, "Una propuesta de reparación."
10 Larrea, *El banano en el Ecuador.*

11 Soluri, *Banana Cultures*; Larrea Maldonado, *Hacia una historia ecológica*; Thrupp, "The Political Ecology of Pesticide Use."
12 Hurtig et al., "Pesticide Use among Farmers."
13 Ofrias, "Invisible Harms, Invisible Profits."
14 San Sebastián and Hurtig, "Oil Development and Health."
15 Boix and Bohme, "Secrecy and Justice."
16 Davis et al., "Anthropocene, Capitalocene . . . Plantationocene?"
17 Soluri, *Banana Cultures*.
18 Soluri.
19 Soluri, "Bananas Before Plantations"; Bucheli, *Bananas and Business*.
20 Larrea, *El banano en el Ecuador*, 69.
21 United Nations Environment Programme, "Integrated Assessment of Trade Liberalization."
22 Arichábala, Flores, and Manasfi, "Buenos principios agrícolas."
23 Davis and Todd, "On the Importance of a Date"; Whyte, "Indigenous Climate Change Studies."
24 Moore, "The Capitalocene, Part I."
25 Davis et al., "Anthropocene, Capitalocene . . . Plantationocene?"; Tsing, *The Mushroom at the End of the World*.
26 For an insightful discussion of banana production in the Philippines in light of Plantationocene scholarship, see Paredes, "Experimental Science for the 'Bananapocalypse.'"
27 Mintz, *Sweetness and Power*.
28 Soluri, "Bananas Before Plantations"; Chomsky, *West Indian Workers*.
29 Davis et al., "Anthropocene, Capitalocene . . . Plantationocene?"
30 Tsing, *The Mushroom at the End of the World*. Tsing uses the term *salvage accumulation* to describe the ways in which aspects of life not initially intended to be commodities (like the sewing skills female maquiladora employees are assumed to have because they are female) are subsequently capitalized on in projects of capital accumulation.
31 Soluri, *Banana Cultures*; Marquardt, "'Green Havoc.'"
32 Moore, "The Capitalocene, Part I."
33 Brisbois and Ali, "Climate Change"; Hall and Sanders, "Accountability and the Academy."
34 Chung Tiam Fook, "Transformational Processes."
35 Elbehri et al., "Ecuador's Banana Sector under Climate Change"; Koeppel, *Banana*; cf. Holt-Giménez, Shattuck, and Van Lammeren, "Thresholds of Resistance."
36 Dunlap, "End the 'Green' Delusions"; Aronoff et al., *A Planet to Win*.
37 Soluri, *Banana Cultures*, 264.
38 Stein and Luna, "Toxic Sensorium," 100.

20. STORIES

1 Jordanova, *History in Practice*.
2 Jordanova; Miller, "The Dynamics of Framing Environmental Values."
3 Elías Caro, "La masacre obrera de 1928."

4 Coleman, "The Photos That We Don't Get to See"; Conejo Barboza, "Divisiones bananeras y memoria."
5 Quoted in Coleman, "The Photos That We Don't Get to See," 109.
6 Coleman.
7 Chiquita, "The Chiquita Story."
8 *Minions*, Universal Pictures, 2015.
9 *Despicable Me 2*, Universal Pictures, 2013.
10 Khrebtan-Hörhager and Avant-Mier, "Despicable Others."; *Despicable Me 2*, Universal Pictures, 2013.
11 Interestingly, the Disney/Pixar films used by Dole to promote its bananas also contain multiple instances of investors playing a similar role to those in *Despicable Me*. *Brave* (2012), *Onward* (2020), and *Monsters Inc.* (2001) all feature financial backers shaping business decisions, and therefore subsequent plot developments. Gru's identity as an offensive and politically significant Soviet stereotype is explored in Khrebtan-Hörhager and Avant-Mier, "Despicable Others."
12 The filmmaker subsequently documented his legal struggle with Dole in another film, entitled *Big Boys Gone Bananas!**, WG Films, 2011.
13 *A Bug's Life*, Walt Disney Studios Motion Pictures, 1998.
14 *Coco*, Walt Disney Studios Motion Pictures, 2017.
15 Wesseling et al., "Cancer in Banana Plantation Workers"; Bohme, *Toxic Injustice*.
16 Karnes, *Tropical Enterprise*. The founders of Standard Fruit also contributed to the Tulane School. For its part, UFC maintained a close relationship to the Harvard School of Tropical Medicine, whose founding director, Dr. Richard P. Strong, concurrently served as UFC's director of laboratories and of research work. As James Martin explains in *Banana Cowboys* (p. 111), UFC's Medical Division was an "important node within the wider, informally constituted world of North American tropical medicine during the first decades of the century."
17 Buekens, "From Hygiene and Tropical Medicine," S2.
18 Žižek, *The Sublime Object of Ideology*.

21. EVIDENCE I: REGULATING AND LITIGATING TOXICS

1 *Brave*, Walt Disney Studios Motion Pictures, 2012.
2 Federici, *Witches, Witch-Hunting, and Women*; Foucault, *The Birth of the Clinic*; McNally, *Monsters of the Market*.
3 Collard and Dempsey, "Accumulation by Difference-Making"; cf. Federici, *Caliban and the Witch*.
4 Cf. Moore, "The Capitalocene, Part I."
5 Denny, "Evidence-Based Medicine and Medical Authority."
6 Davis, *Banned*; Russell, *War and Nature*.
7 Rowe Davis, "On the Professionalization of Toxicology," 753–54.
8 Richter, Cordner, and Brown, "Producing Ignorance Through Regulatory Structure"; Murphy, "Chemical Infrastructures of the St Clair River."
9 Boudia, "Managing Scientific and Political Uncertainty"; Nash, "From Safety to Risk"; Sellers, "From Poison to Carcinogen."
10 Lanphear, "Low-Level Toxicity of Chemicals."

11. Vandenberg, "Low Dose Effects."
12. Morello-Frosch et al., "Understanding the Cumulative Impacts."
13. Richter, Cordner, and Brown, "Producing Ignorance Through Regulatory Structure"; Murphy, "Chemical Infrastructures of the St Clair River."
14. Beronius and Vandenberg, "Using Systematic Reviews."
15. Sellers, *Hazards of the Job*.
16. Sellers.
17. Nash, *Inescapable Ecologies*.
18. Galt, "From *Homo economicus*"; Soluri, *Banana Cultures*; Brisbois, "Bananas, Pesticides and Health"; Barraza et al., "Pesticide Use"; Hunt et al., "Balancing Risks and Resources"; Ríos-González, Jansen, and Sánchez-Pérez, "Pesticide Risk Perceptions"; Mera-Orces, "Paying for Survival"; Orozco et al., "Monitoring Adherence"; Aragón, Aragón, and Thörn, "Pests, Peasants, and Pesticides."
19. Sellers, *Hazards of the Job*; Nash, *Inescapable Ecologies*; Boudia, "Managing Scientific and Political Uncertainty"; Galt, "From *Homo economicus*."
20. Murray and Taylor, "Claim No Easy Victories."
21. Murray and Taylor.
22. Bohme, *Toxic Injustice*.
23. Bohme.
24. Bohme.
25. Bohme.
26. Bohme.
27. I spoke with a lawyer representing Ecuadorean plaintiffs in the lawsuits in Machala in 2011. She described how company efforts to pay off or intimidate workers who had been affected by DBCP, together with attrition as more and more of them died with each passing year, were weakening the power of class action lawsuits.
28. Bohme, *Toxic Injustice*.
29. Boix and Bohme, "Secrecy and Justice."
30. Liboiron, Tironi, and Calvillo, "Toxic Politics"; Murphy, "Alterlife and Decolonial Chemical Relations"; Pulido, "Geographies of Race and Ethnicity II"; Women's Earth Alliance and Native Youth Sexual Health Network, "Violence on the Land, Violence on Our Bodies."
31. Bohme, *Toxic Injustice*; Sawyer, "Crude Contamination"; Brisbois, "Communities, Controversy and Chevron."
32. Bohme, *Toxic Injustice*.
33. Dole, "DBCP Facts."
34. Bohme, *Toxic Injustice*.
35. Navas, "'If There's No Evidence, There's No Victim.'"
36. Fortun and Fortun, "Scientific Imaginaries."
37. E.g., Caron-Beaudoin et al., "Gestational Exposure"; for an example of such a toxicologist working with the Canadian environmental sector, see "Reena Sandhu."

22. EVIDENCE II: EPIDEMIOLOGY AND "DEVELOPING COUNTRIES"

1. Karnes's book, *Tropical Enterprise*, is written as a celebratory history of Standard Fruit.

2   Liboiron, Tironi, and Calvillo, "Toxic Politics."
3   Federici, *Witches, Witch-Hunting, and Women*. For a discussion of evidence-based approaches as "epistemological fascism," see Holmes et al., "Deconstructing the Evidence-Based Discourse."
4   McNally, *Monsters of the Market*.
5   Marx, *Capital, Volume 1*. Volume 1 of Marx's *Capital* makes similar points, and even compares capitalism to a vampire or a werewolf on several occasions.
6   Foucault, *The Birth of the Clinic*.
7   See also Breilh, *Epidemiología*; Turshen, "The Political Ecology of Disease."
8   Latin American scholarship in the social medicine tradition has perceptively documented such depoliticizing tendencies of mainstream Northern health sciences. See, for example, Breilh, *Epidemiología*.
9   Ecobichon, "Pesticide Use in Developing Countries," 29.
10 Ecobichon, 32.
11 Matthews, "Attitudes and Behaviours," 845.
12 Cf. Partanen et al., "Collaboration between Developing and Developed Countries"; Brisbois, "Epidemiology and 'Developing Countries.'"
13 Wesseling et al., "Cancer in Banana Plantation Workers," 1125.
14 Brisbois, "Epidemiology and 'Developing Countries.'"
15 Escobar, *Encountering Development*.
16 Barraza et al., "Social Movements and Risk Perception," 15.
17 For an analogous argument on the streamlined use of the "endangered other" trope to describe Indigenous peoples in research on the human dimensions of climate, see Hall and Sanders, "Accountability and the Academy."
18 See, for example Wesseling, Corriols, and Bravo, "Acute Pesticide Poisoning"; Barraza et al., "Social Movements and Risk Perception"; Cole, Crissman, and Orozco, "Eco-Health Projects."
19 Wesseling et al., "Hazardous Pesticides in Central America," 289.
20 Cole, Crissman, and Orozco, "Eco-Health Projects"; Sherwood and Paredes, "Dynamics of Perpetuation"; Orozco et al., "Monitoring Adherence." One of the Ecuadorian researchers involved in these efforts once described to me the Ministry of Agriculture's refusal to ban highly toxic insecticides despite being presented with literal stacks of peer-reviewed scientific evidence on their clear health impacts. The belief that such knowledge would actually translate into health-protecting government action was, she explained, a "very Canadian" one. For a comparable account of how banning highly toxic pesticides was rendered "unspeakable" in Honduras, see Jansen, "The Unspeakable Ban."
21 Hutter et al., "Health Symptoms Related to Pesticide Use," 2.
22 Wesseling et al., "Hazardous Pesticides in Central America," 292.
23 Wesseling et al., "Paraquat in Developing Countries."
24 Scott, "Testing Toxicity."
25 London, "Neurobehavioural Methods, Effects and Prevention."
26 Labonté et al., "Beyond the Divides."
27 Cf. Striffler, "El fruto del neoliberalismo."
28 Brisbois et al., "Mining, Colonial Legacies and Neoliberalism"; Shim and Thomson, "The End of the Epidemiology Wars?"

29 Tellez v. Dole Food Co.
30 Lanphear, "Low-level toxicity."
31 I analyze this controversy using discourse analysis in Brisbois, "Communities, Controversy and Chevron." An illuminating analysis of Chevron's use of corporate-funded toxicology studies in the legal proceedings is found in Sawyer, "Crude Contamination."
32 Liboiron, Tironi, and Calvillo, "Toxic Politics"; Nading, "Living in a Toxic World."
33 Tsing, *The Mushroom at the End of the World*.

23. SHOPPING

1 For an insightful analysis of problems with comparable campaigns in the US context, see Cousins et al., "Risky Business?"
2 Benson and Fischer, "Broccoli and Desire"; cf. Scott and Lewis, "Sex and Gender."
3 Hussey and Curnow, "Fair Trade."
4 Guthman, "The Polanyian Way?," 457.
5 Springer, "Fuck Neoliberalism," 289.
6 Soluri, "Accounting for Taste," 389.
7 Marquardt, "'Green Havoc'"; Marquardt, "Pesticides, Parakeets, and Unions."
8 Soluri, *Banana Cultures*.
9 Guthman, "The Polanyian Way?"
10 Barraza et al., "Social Movements and Risk Perception"; Hough, "A Race to the Bottom?"; Jansen, "Greening Bananas and Institutionalizing Environmentalism."
11 Taylor and Scharlin, *Smart Alliance*; Jansen, "Greening Bananas and Institutionalizing Environmentalism."
12 Jansen, "Greening Bananas and Institutionalizing Environmentalism."
13 Humbert and Brassel, "Sweet Fruit, Bitter Truth."
14 Smith, "Worker- and Small Farmer-Led Strategies."
15 Jansen, "Greening Bananas and Institutionalizing Environmentalism."
16 Cf. SIPAE, Broederlijk Delen, and Oxfam, "Prácticas de compra y condiciones sociales, laborales y ambientales."
17 Konefal, Mascarenhas, and Hatanaka, "Governance in the Global Agro-Food System"; Guthman, "The Polanyian Way?"
18 SIPAE, *Atlas sobre la tenencia de la tierra en el Ecuador*.
19 Cf. Martínez Valle, "Trabajo flexible en las nuevas zonas bananeras de Ecuador."
20 Melo and Wolf, "Ecocertification of Ecuadorian Bananas."
21 Carrillo García, *Desarrollo rural y cooperativismo agrario en Ecuador*.
22 Guthman, "The Polanyian Way?"
23 Frundt, *Fair Bananas!*.
24 Smith, "Fairtrade Bananas."
25 Brown, "Fairness for Whom?"
26 Brown.
27 Brown, 1.
28 Moberg, "Market's End."
29 Hussey and Curnow, "Fair Trade."
30 Shreck, "Resistance, Redistribution, and Power"; Guthman, "The Polanyian Way?"
31 Escobar, *Encountering Development*.

32 Menton et al., "Environmental Justice and the SDGs"; Brisbois et al., "Mining, Colonial Legacies and Neoliberalism."
33 Quoted in Hergesheimer, "Practical Mergers," 225, emphasis added.
34 Guthman, "The Polanyian Way?"
35 Humbert and Brassel, "Sweet Fruit, Bitter Truth."
36 Humbert and Brassel, 31.
37 Smith, "Worker- and Small Farmer-Led Strategies," 144.
38 Žižek, *The Sublime Object of Ideology*.
39 Kimmerer, *Braiding Sweetgrass*, 31.
40 Kimmerer.
41 Kimmerer, 29.
42 Taussig, *The Devil and Commodity Fetishism in South America*.
43 Grandin, *Empire's Workshop*.
44 Butler, *Colonial Extractions*; Gordon and Webber, *Blood of Extraction*.
45 McNally, *Monsters of the Market*, 116. One of McNally's stated intentions in detailing the relationships between zombies, vampires, and the monstrous nature of capitalism, inspired by the playwright Bertolt Brecht, is to "estrange us from the familiar." That is, his analysis furthers Karl Marx's efforts to denaturalize capitalist social relations by "defetishizing" commodities. A deeply unsettling shift in thinking is thus frequently required to appreciate the inherent monstrousness of capitalist social relations such as the ones linking Latin American banana workers to North American corporations.
46 Marx, *Capital, Volume 1*.

24. NOTICING

1 Liboiron, Tironi, and Calvillo, "Toxic Politics."
2 Tsing, *The Mushroom at the End of the World*.
3 Striffler, *In the Shadows of State and Capital*.
4 Carrillo García, *Desarrollo rural*; Carrillo García, "Historia agraria."
5 Striffler, *In the Shadows of State and Capital*.
6 Isch López, Rodríguez, and Carrión, "La ecología política"; Carrillo García, "Historia agraria."
7 Hutter et al., "Epidemiological Study."
8 Polo Almeida, "Relación territorio-salud," 62.
9 Moore and Velásquez, "Water for Gold."
10 Moore and Velásquez.
11 Quoted in Moore and Velásquez, 136.
12 Blaikie and Brookfield, *Land Degradation and Society*; Turshen, *The Political Ecology of Disease in Tanzania*.
13 Robbins, *Political Ecology*.
14 Cf. Peet and Watts, *Liberation Ecologies*; King, "Political Ecologies of Health."
15 Sultana, "Emotional Political Ecology"; Nading, *Mosquito Trails*; Shattuck, "Risky Subjects"; Galt, "From *Homo economicus*."
16 Cf. Goldman, Nadasdy, and Turner, *Knowing Nature*; Jackson and Neely, "Triangulating Health."

17 Brisbois, Spiegel, and Harris, "Health, Environment and Colonial Legacies"; cf. Harding, *Sciences from Below*.
18 Brisbois, "Epidemiology and 'Developing Countries.'"
19 Gonzalez Casanova, "Internal Colonialism and National Development."
20 Brisbois, Spiegel, and Harris, "Health, Environment and Colonial Legacies."
21 Cf. Breilh, *Epidemiología*.
22 *Innovating for Solutions*, 26. I had been involved with the IDRC-funded "Canadian Community of Practice in Ecosystem Approaches to Health" since the beginning of my PhD.
23 Saunders et al., "Who Will Publish Eulogies for the Victims of Barrick Gold?"; Hamilton, "Savoir, pouvoir et standpoint institutionnel."
24 Saunders, "The Munk School's Foreign Policy Agenda Is Showing"; Jeppesen and Nazar, "Beyond Academic Freedom"; Tannock, "Learning to Plunder."
25 Brisbois et al., "Mining, Colonial Legacies and Neoliberalism."
26 Escobar, *Encountering Development*.
27 Roy Grégoire, "Dialogue as Racism?"
28 Kirsch, *Mining Capitalism*; Butler, *Colonial Extractions*; see also Breilh and Tilleria, *Aceleración global y despojo en Ecuador*.
29 E.g., Cole, Crissman, and Orozco, "Eco-Health Projects"; Spiegel et al., "Social and Environmental Determinants"; Breilh, "Nuevo modelo de acumulación."
30 University of Toronto, "Miner's Lamp Award Dinner"; see also Velásquez, "The Science of Corporate Social Responsibility."
31 Gordon and Webber, *Blood of Extraction*.
32 Brisbois et al., "Mining, Colonial Legacies and Neoliberalism"; Hamilton, "Savoir, pouvoir et standpoint institutionnel"; Hall and Sanders, "Accountability and the Academy."
33 For a relevant discussion of contradictions between work within state structures and the achievement of environmental justice see Pulido, "Geographies of Race and Ethnicity II."
34 Sundberg, "Ethics, Entanglement, and Political Ecology," 120.
35 Neely and Nguse, "Research and Relationships," 141.
36 Haraway, "Situated Knowledges."
37 Nading, "Living in a Toxic World," 219.
38 Nading.
39 Gordon and Webber, *Blood of Extraction*.
40 Theriault and Kang, "Toxic Research"; see also Tuck, "Suspending Damage."
41 Brisbois, Spiegel, and Harris, "Health, Environment and Colonial Legacies," 7.
42 Castree and Sparke, "Introduction," 223.
43 Gramsci, *Selections from the Prison Notebooks*.

25. PLOTTING

1 Officially the Sovereign Military Hospitaller Order of Saint John of Jerusalem, of Rhodes and of Malta.
2 Order of Malta Canadian Association, "The Order in Canada."
3 Mintz, *Sweetness and Power*; Trischitta, "The Knights of Malta."
4 Grandin, *The Last Colonial Massacre*.

5   Studnicki-Gizbert, "Canadian Mining in Latin America (1990 to Present)," 96.
6   Dussel, *A History of the Church in Latin America*.
7   Pinto, "Tras montaje en la desaparición de los 43."
8   Rico Montoya, "Narrativas de violencia y resistencia."
9   Mondragón Ríos, "La producción social del miedo."
10 Rico Montoya, "Narrativas de violencia y resistencia."
11 Campos Navarrete, "Experiencing Buhts'An Qu'Inal."
12 Grandin, *The Last Colonial Massacre*; Hunter, "The Israeli Role in Guatemala"; Holt-Giménez, Shattuck, and Van Lammeren, "Thresholds of Resistance"; Mondragón Ríos, "La producción social del miedo."
13 Voltaire, *Candide*, 1.
14 Voltaire, 97.
15 Kimmerer, *Braiding Sweetgrass*. The sense of doing something wise also stemmed from the guidance provided by Robin Wall Kimmerer in her inspiring chapter on agro-ecological and Indigenous spiritual dimensions of Three Sisters gardens.
16 Davis et al., "Anthropocene, Capitalocene ... Plantationocene?"
17 Soluri, "Bananas Before Plantations"; Marquardt, "'Green Havoc.'"
18 Tsing, *The Mushroom at the End of the World*.
19 Weiler et al., "Food Sovereignty, Food Security and Health Equity."
20 Patel, "What Does Food Sovereignty Look Like?"
21 Wittman, "Reconnecting Agriculture and the Environment"; Latorre, "The Role of Ecuadorian Working-Class Environmentalism"; Clark, "Can the State Foster Food Sovereignty?"
22 Altieri and Nicholls, "Scaling Up Agroecological Approaches."
23 Weiler et al., "Food Sovereignty, Food Security and Health Equity."
24 Patel, "What Does Food Sovereignty Look Like?"
25 Belli, *The Country Under My Skin*.
26 Bohme, *Toxic Injustice*; Brisbois, Spiegel, and Harris, "Health, Environment and Colonial Legacies." This last legacy in fact implicates me, as one of the Northern epidemiologists involved in Nicaragua and later Ecuador, Donald Cole, would become my post-doctoral supervisor, mentor, and co-author on multiple publications.
27 Žižek, *The Sublime Object of Ideology*.
28 Brisbois, Harris, and Spiegel, "Political Ecologies of Global Health"; Nading, "Living in a Toxic World"; Nichols and Del Casino, "Towards an Integrated Political Ecology"; Theriault and Kang, "Toxic Research." These personal entanglements are consistent with political ecology analyses of how people such as banana farmers in Ecuador live stories about poverty, agriculture, pesticides, and political change in ways that reflect their relationships to land, to global markets, and to each other.
29 Gibson-Graham, *The End of Capitalism (as We Knew It)*.
30 Haraway, *Staying with the Trouble*.
31 Aronoff et al., *A Planet to Win*.
32 Kimmerer, *Braiding Sweetgrass*; Coulthard, *Red Skin, White Masks*.
33 Latorre, "The Role of Ecuadorian Working-Class Environmentalism," 287.
34 Jones and Jenkins, "Rethinking Collaboration."
35 Soluri, *Banana Cultures*. This closing sentence and other elements of this chapter are informed by the postscript to the second edition of John Soluri's illuminating

environmental history. In this chapter I am extending Soluri's call to explore stories about more diverse and marginalized food production and consumption practices. Suggesting that we should actually consume food while exploring such stories also evokes scholarship on transformative learning, inspired by Indigenous land-based learning traditions, that combines critical inquiry about injustice with food, physical activity, and building relationships to communities—human and more-than-human. Rather than academic citations to back up that point I will provide my recipe for banana bread, adapted from one in a well-known cookbook.

Flexible Banana Bread Recipe
Mix ⅓ cup melted unsalted butter or coconut oil with ⅓ cup sugar. Mix in 1–1¼ cups ripe mashed banana and 2 eggs. In a separate bowl combine 1¾ cups flour (including up to 1 cup whole wheat flour) with 2¼ teaspoons baking powder and ½ teaspoon of salt. Add the dry ingredients to the wet ones. Fold in any or all of the following: ½ cup walnut or other nut pieces; ¾ teaspoon grated lemon or lime rind; ¼ cup finely chopped apricots; ½ cup dark or white chocolate chips; 1 cup fresh or frozen raspberries (or other small fruit). Bake at 350°F (175°C) for approximately 1 hour in a greased loaf pan.

BIBLIOGRAPHY

Abram, David. *The Spell of the Sensuous: Perception and Language in a More-than-Human World*. New York: Vintage Books, 1997.

Acción Ecológica. "Serie Coronavirus #6: Los trabajadores de la maquinaria agroexportadora en tiempos de COVID-19." Serie Coronavirus, TLC Editoriales, Acción Ecológica, March 27, 2020. https://www.accionecologica.org/serie-coronavirus-6-los-trabajadores-de-la-maquinaria-agroexportadora-en-tiempos-de-COVID-19/.

Acosta, Alberto. *Breve historia económica del Ecuador*. 3rd ed. Quito: Corporación Editora Nacional, 2012.

Ahmed, Sara. "Collective Feelings: Or, the Impressions Left by Others." *Theory, Culture & Society* 21, no. 2 (2004): 25–42. https://doi.org/10.1177/0263276404042133.

Al Jazeera and News Agencies. "Who Was Fernando Villavicencio, Presidential Hopeful Shot Dead in Ecuador?" *Al Jazeera*, August 10, 2023. https://www.aljazeera.com/news/2023/8/10/who-was-fernando-villavicencio-presidential-hopeful-shot-dead-in-ecuador.

Aliano, David. "Curing the Ills of Central America: The United Fruit Company's Medical Department and Corporate America's Mission to Civilize (1900–1940)." *Estudios Interdisciplinarios de América Latina y El Caribe* 17, no. 2 (2006): 35–59.

Altieri, Miguel A., and Clara I. Nicholls. "Scaling Up Agroecological Approaches for Food Sovereignty in Latin America." *Development* 51, no. 4 (2008): 472–80.

Amaya Amador, Ramón. *Prisión Verde*. 3rd ed. Tegucigalpa: Baktun Editorial, 1983.

Anderson, Warwick P. "Where Is the Postcolonial History of Medicine?" *Bulletin of the History of Medicine* 72, no. 3 (1998): 522–30. https://www.jstor.org/stable/44445080.

Andreatta, Susan L. "Bananas, Are They the Quintessential Health Food? A Global/Local Perspective." *Human Organization* 56, no. 4 (1997): 437–49. https://doi.org/10.17730/humo.56.4.67827k23gx31wm2x.

Antonelli, Mirta. "Canadá, entre la sed insaciable de cordillera y la performance de democracia." In *Memoria Seminario Internacional—Extractivismo en América Latina: Agua que no has de beber . . .*, 94–110. Santiago, Chile: Observatorio Latinoamericano de Conflictos Ambientales and Observatorio de Conflictos Mineros de América Latina, 2014. https://www.ocmal.org/wp-content/uploads/2017/06/SEMINARIO-Internacional-EXTRACTIVISMO.pdf.

Aragón, Aurora, Cecilia Aragón, and Åke Thörn. "Pests, Peasants, and Pesticides on the Northern Nicaraguan Pacific Plain." *International Journal of Occupational and Environmental Health* 7, no. 4 (2001): 295–302.

Arichábala, Pablo, Johanna Flores, and Nadia Manasfi. "Buenos principios agrícolas en banano vinculados a la adaptación al cambio climático: Experiencias de productores en la provincia de El Oro." Quito: GIZ Ecuador, 2014.

Aronoff, Kate, Alyssa Battistoni, Daniel Aldana Cohen, and Thea Riofrancos. *A Planet to Win: Why We Need a Green New Deal*. New York: Verso Books, 2019.

Arteaga-Cruz, Erika, Baijayanta Mukhopadhyay, Sarah Shannon, Amulya Nidhi, and Todd Jailer. "Connecting the Right to Health and Anti-extractivism Globally." *Saúde Em Debate* 44, no. spe1 (2020): 100–08. https://doi.org/10.1590/0103-11042020s108.

Asturias, Miguel Ángel. *Viento Fuerte*. 2nd ed. Buenos Aires: Editorial Losada, 1955.

Badillo Salgado, Lucía, and Andrew M. Fischer. "Ecuador, COVID-19 and the IMF: How Austerity Exacerbated the Crisis." *bl*ISS (blog), April 9, 2020. https://issblog.nl/2020/04/09/covid-19-ecuador-covid-19-and-the-imf-how-austerity-exacerbated-the-crisis-by-ana-lucia-badillo-salgado-and-andrew-m-fischer/.

Barraza, Douglas, Kees Jansen, Berna van Wendel de Joode, and Catharina Wesseling. "Pesticide Use in Banana and Plantain Production and Risk Perception among Local Actors in Talamanca, Costa Rica."

Environmental Research 111, no. 5 (2011): 708–17. https://doi.org/10.1016/j.envres.2011.02.009.

———. "Social Movements and Risk Perception: Unions, Churches, Pesticides and Bananas in Costa Rica." *International Journal of Occupational and Environmental Health* 19, no. 1 (2013): 11–21. https://doi.org/10.1179/2049396712Y.0000000018.

Becker, Marc. "The Stormy Relations between Rafael Correa and Social Movements in Ecuador." *Latin American Perspectives* 40, no. 3 (2013): 43–62. https://www.jstor.org/stable/23466004.

Bell, Kirsten, and Judith Green. "On the Perils of Invoking Neoliberalism in Public Health Critique." *Critical Public Health* 26, no. 3 (2016): 239–43. https://doi.org/10.1080/09581596.2016.1144872.

Belli, Gioconda. *The Country Under My Skin: A Memoir of Love and War*. New York: Anchor Books, 2003.

Benson, Peter, and Edward F. Fischer. "Broccoli and Desire." *Antipode* 39, no. 5 (2007): 800–20. https://doi.org/10.1111/j.1467-8330.2007.00519.x.

Beronius, Anna, and Laura N. Vandenberg. "Using Systematic Reviews for Hazard and Risk Assessment of Endocrine Disrupting Chemicals." *Reviews in Endocrine and Metabolic Disorders* 16, no. 4 (2015): 273–87. https://doi.org/10.1007/s11154-016-9334-7.

Birn, Anne-Emanuelle, Mariajosé Aguilera, Nikisha S. Khare, and Ted Schrecker. "Canada Kills, Inc.: A Critical Political Economy of Health Analysis of Canadian Mining in Latin America and the Caribbean." *Canadian Journal of Latin American and Caribbean Studies / Revue canadienne des études latino-américaines et caraïbes* 48, no. 2 (2023): 301–27. https://doi.org/10.1080/08263663.2023.2193045.

Birn, Anne-Emanuelle, and Theodore M. Brown. *Comrades in Health: US Health Internationalists, Abroad and at Home*. New Brunswick, NJ: Rutgers University Press, 2013.

Blaikie, Piers M., and Harold C. Brookfield. *Land Degradation and Society*. London: Methuen, 1987.

Bohme, Susanna Rankin. *Toxic Injustice: A Transnational History of Exposure and Struggle*. Oakland: University of California Press, 2015.

Boix, Vicent, and Susanna R. Bohme. "Secrecy and Justice in the Ongoing Saga of DBCP Litigation." *International Journal of Occupational and Environmental Health* 18, no. 2 (2012): 154–61. https://doi.org/10.1179/1077352512Z.00000000010.

Boudia, Soraya. "Managing Scientific and Political Uncertainty: Environmental Risk Assessment in a Historical Perspective." In *Powerless Science? Science and Politics in a Toxic World*, edited by Soraya Boudia and Nathalie Jas, 95–112. New York: Berghahn Books, 2014.

Bourgois, Philippe I. *Ethnicity at Work: Divided Labor on a Central American Banana Plantation*. Baltimore: Johns Hopkins University Press, 1989.

Breilh, Jaime. *Epidemiología: Economía política y salud. Bases estructurales de la determinación social de la salud*. 7th ed. Quito: Universidad Andina Simón Bolívar, Corporación Editora Nacional, 2010.

———. "Nuevo modelo de acumulación y agroindustria: Las implicaciones ecológicas y epidemiológicas de la floricultura en Ecuador." *Ciência & Saúde Coletiva* 12 (2007): 91–104. https://doi.org/10.1590/S1413-81232007000100013.

———. "SARS-CoV2: Rompiendo el cerco de la ciencia del poder. Escenario de asedio de la vida, los pueblos y la ciencia." In *Posnormales*. Quito: Aislamiento Social Preventivo y Obligatorio, 2020.

Breilh, Jaime, Arturo Campaña, and Adolfo Maldonado. "Informe peritaje a la salud trabajadores de aerofumigación en plantaciones bananeras: Guayas, El Oro y Los Ríos (Ecuador)." Quito: Acción Ecológica, 2007.

Breilh, Jaime, and Ylonka Tilleria. *Aceleración global y despojo en Ecuador: El retroceso del derecho a la salud en la era neoliberal*. Quito: Universidad Andina Simón Bolívar y Abya-Yala, 2009.

Brenner, Neil, Jamie Peck, and Nik Theodore. "Variegated Neoliberalization: Geographies, Modalities, Pathways." *Global Networks* 10, no. 2 (2010): 182–222. https://doi.org/10.1111/j.1471-0374.2009.00277.x.

Briggs, Charles L. "Theorizing Modernity Conspiratorially: Science, Scale, and the Political Economy of Public Discourse in Explanations of a Cholera Epidemic." *American Ethnologist* 31, no. 2 (2004): 164–87. https://doi.org/10.1525/ae.2004.31.2.164.

Brisbois, Ben. "Bananas, Pesticides and Health in Southwestern Ecuador: A Scalar Narrative Approach to Targeting Public Health Responses." *Social Science & Medicine* 150 (2016): 184–91. https://doi.org/10.1016/j.socscimed.2015.12.026.

———. "Communities, Controversy and Chevron: Epidemiology in the Struggle over Contamination of the Ecuadorian Amazon." In *Case Studies on Corporations & Global Health Governance: Impacts, Influence and Accountability*, edited by Nora Kenworthy, Ross MacKenzie, and Kelley Lee, 213–26. London: Rowman & Littlefield International, 2016.

---. "Epidemiology and 'Developing Countries': Writing Pesticides, Poverty and Political Engagement in Latin America." *Social Studies of Science* 44, no. 4 (2014): 600–24. https://doi.org/10.1177/0306312714523514.

Brisbois, Ben, Andrés Burgos Delgado, Douglas Barraza, Óscar Betancourt, Donald C. Cole, Maya K. Gislason, Frédéric Mertens, Margot W. Parkes, and Johanne Saint-Charles. "Ecosystem Approaches to Health and Knowledge-to-Action: Towards a Political Ecology of Applied Health-Environment Knowledge." *Journal of Political Ecology* 24, no. 1 (2017): 692–715. https://doi.org/10.2458/v24i1.20961.

Brisbois, Ben, Mathieu Feagan, Bjorn Stime, Isaac Kukoc Paz, Marta Berbés-Blázquez, Juan Gaibor, Donald C. Cole, et al. "Mining, Colonial Legacies and Neoliberalism: A Political Ecology of Health Knowledge." *New Solutions: A Journal of Environmental & Occupational Health Policy* 31, no. 1 (2021): 48–64. https://doi.org/10.1177/1048291121001051.

Brisbois, Ben, and S. Harris Ali. "Climate Change, Vector-Borne Disease and Interdisciplinary Research: Social Science Perspectives on an Environment and Health Controversy." *EcoHealth* 7, no. 4 (2010): 425–38. https://doi.org/10.1007/s10393-010-0354-6.

Brisbois, Ben, Leila Harris, and Jerry M. Spiegel. "Political Ecologies of Global Health: Pesticide Exposure in Southwestern Ecuador's Banana Industry." *Antipode* 50, no. 1 (2018): 61–81. https://doi.org/doi:10.1111/anti.12340.

Brisbois, Ben, and Patricia Polo Almeida. "Attending to Researcher Positionality in Geographic Fieldwork on Health in Latin America: Lessons from La Costa Ecuatoriana." *Journal of Latin American Geography* 16, no. 1 (2017): 194–201. https://doi.org/10.1353/lag.2017.0005.

Brisbois, Ben, Jerry M. Spiegel, and Leila Harris. "Health, Environment and Colonial Legacies: Situating the Science of Pesticides, Bananas and Bodies in Ecuador." *Social Science & Medicine* 239 (2019): 112529. https://doi.org/10.1016/j.socscimed.2019.112529.

Brown, Sandy. "Fairness for Whom? Regulating Banana Production through Voluntary Certification and Labeling." PhD Thesis, UC Berkeley, 2012.

---. "One Hundred Years of Labor Control: Violence, Militancy, and the Fairtrade Banana Commodity Chain in Colombia." *Environment and Planning A:Economy and Space* 45, no. 11 (2013): 2572–91. https://doi.org/10.1068/a45691.

Brulle, Robert J., and David N. Pellow. "Environmental Justice: Human Health and Environmental Inequalities." *Annual Review of Public*

Health 27, no. 1 (2006): 103–24. https://doi.org/10.1146/annurev.publhealth.27.021405.102124.

Bucheli, Marcelo. *Bananas and Business: The United Fruit Company in Colombia, 1899–2000*. New York: New York University Press, 2005.

——. "Multinational Corporations, Totalitarian Regimes and Economic Nationalism: United Fruit Company in Central America, 1899–1975." *Business History* 50, no. 4 (July 2008): 433–54. https://doi.org/10.1080/00076790802106315.

——. "United Fruit Company in Latin America." In *Banana Wars: Power, Production, and History in the Americas*, edited by Steve Striffler and Mark Moberg, 80–100. Durham, NC: Duke University Press, 2003.

Buekens, Pierre. "From Hygiene and Tropical Medicine to Global Health." *American Journal of Epidemiology* 176, no. suppl 7 (October 2012): S1–3. https://doi.org/10.1093/aje/kws253.

Buse, Chris G., Jordan Sky Oestreicher, Neville R. Ellis, Rebecca Patrick, Ben Brisbois, Aaron P. Jenkins, Kaileah McKellar, et al. "Public Health Guide to Field Developments Linking Ecosystems, Environments and Health in the Anthropocene." *Journal of Epidemiology and Community Health* 72, no. 5 (2018): 420–25. https://doi.org/10.1136/jech-2017-210082.

Butler, Paula. *Colonial Extractions: Race and Canadian Mining in Contemporary Africa*. Toronto: University of Toronto Press, 2015.

Campos Navarrete, Marisol. "Experiencing Buhts'An Qu'Inal from sHachel Jwohc'a'Tel Through Sna'el Ya'beyel Stuc Te Bin Ay Ma'yuc: Fostering Local Economic Development in Tseltal Terms." PhD Thesis, Trent University (Canada), 2021.

Caron-Beaudoin, Élyse, Naomi Valter, Jonathan Chevrier, Pierre Ayotte, Katherine Frohlich, and Marc-André Verner. "Gestational Exposure to Volatile Organic Compounds (VOCs) in Northeastern British Columbia, Canada: A Pilot Study." *Environment International* 110 (2018): 131–38. http://dx.doi.org/10.1016/j.envint.2017.10.022.

Carrillo García, Germán. *Desarrollo rural y cooperativismo agrario en Ecuador: Trayectorias históricas de los pequeños productores en la economía global*. Ministerio de Agricultura, Alimentación y Medio Ambiente, 2014. https://digitum.um.es/digitum/handle/10201/45840.

——. "Historia agraria y organización social en la Costa Austral de Ecuador, 1950–2010. Estudio de caso de una cooperativa agrícola: La Unión Regional de Organizaciones Campesinas del Litoral, UROCAL." PhD

Thesis, Universidad de Murcia, 2013. http://dialnet.unirioja.es/servlet/tesis?codigo=38836.

Castillo, Luisa Eugenia, Eduardo Martínez, Clemens Ruepert, Candida Savage, Michael Gilek, Margareth Pinnock, and Efrain Solis. "Water Quality and Macroinvertebrate Community Response Following Pesticide Applications in a Banana Plantation, Limon, Costa Rica." *Science of the Total Environment* 367, no. 1 (2006): 418–32. https://doi.org/10.1016/j.scitotenv.2006.02.052.

Castillo, Luisa Eugenia, Clemens Ruepert, and Efrain Solis. "Pesticide Residues in the Aquatic Environment of Banana Plantation Areas in the North Atlantic Zone of Costa Rica." *Environmental Toxicology and Chemistry* 19, no. 8 (2000): 1942–50. https://doi.org/10.1002/etc.5620190802.

Castree, Noel, and Matthew Sparke. "Introduction: Professional Geography and the Corporatization of the University: Experiences, Evaluations, and Engagements." *Antipode* 32, no. 3 (2000): 222–29. https://doi.org/10.1111/1467-8330.00131.

Castro-Gutiérrez, Néstor, Rob McConnell, Kjell Andersson, Feliciano Pacheco-Antón, and Christer Hogstedt. "Respiratory Symptoms, Spirometry and Chronic Occupational Paraquat Exposure." *Scandinavian Journal of Work, Environment & Health* 23, no. 6 (1997): 421–27. https://doi.org/10.5271/sjweh.264.

Cepeda-Bastidas, Darío Alexander. "Ces mains qui font le régime: Dynamique et performances agro-économiques des systèmes de production bananiers en Équateur." PhD Thesis, Agro Paris Tech, 2009. https://pastel.hal.science/pastel-00819547/document.

Chiquita. "The Chiquita Story, 1944 Miss Chiquita." Accessed March 21, 2024. https://www.chiquita.com/the-chiquita-story/.

——. "Recipes." Accessed May 9, 2022. https://www.chiquita.com/recipes/.

Chomsky, Aviva. "Globalization, Labor, and Violence in Colombia's Banana Zone." *International Labor and Working-Class History* 72, no. 1 (2007): 90–115. https://www.jstor.org/stable/27673094.

——. *West Indian Workers and the United Fruit Company in Costa Rica, 1870–1940*. Baton Rouge: Louisiana State University Press, 1996.

Chung Tiam Fook, Tanya. "Transformational Processes for Community-Focused Adaptation and Social Change: A Synthesis." *Climate and Development* 9, no. 1 (January 2017): 5–21. https://doi.org/10.1080/17565529.2015.1086294.

Clare, Patricia. "El desarrollo del banano y la palma aceitera en el Pacífico costarricense desde la perspectiva de la Ecología Histórica." *Diálogos Revista de Historia* 6, no. 1 (2005): 308–46. https://doi.org/10.15517/dre.v6i1.6211.

Clark, A. Kim. "Racial Ideologies and the Quest for National Development: Debating the Agrarian Problem in Ecuador (1930–50)." *Journal of Latin American Studies* 30, no. 2 (1998): 373–93. https://www.jstor.org/stable/158530.

Clark, Patrick. "Can the State Foster Food Sovereignty? Insights from the Case of Ecuador." *Journal of Agrarian Change* 16, no. 2 (April 2016): 183–205. https://doi.org/10.1111/joac.12094.

Clínica Ambiental Org. "Alianzas—Organizaciones Hermanas." Accessed November 19, 2021. https://www.clinicambiental.org/alianzas/.

Cohen, Rich. *The Fish That Ate the Whale: The Life and Times of America's Banana King*. New York: Farrar, Straus and Giroux, 2012.

Colby, Jason M. "'Banana Growing and Negro Management': Race, Labor, and Jim Crow Colonialism in Guatemala, 1884–1930." *Diplomatic History* 30, no. 4 (2006): 595–621. https://doi.org/10.1111/j.1467-7709.2006.00570.x.

———. *The Business of Empire: United Fruit, Race, and U.S. Expansion in Central America*. Ithaca, NY: Cornell University Press, 2011.

Cole, Donald C., Charles C. Crissman, and A. Fadya Orozco. "Canada's International Development Research Centre's Eco-Health Projects with Latin Americans: Origins, Development and Challenges." *Canadian Journal of Public Health* 97, no. 6 (2006): 8–14. https://link.springer.com/article/10.1007/BF03405238.

Cole, Donald C., Rob McConnell, Douglas L. Murray, and Feliciano Pacheco Antón. "Pesticide Illness Surveillance: The Nicaraguan Experience." *Bulletin of the Pan American Health Organization* 22, no. 2 (1988): 119–32.

Coleman, Kevin. *A Camera in the Garden of Eden: The Self-Forging of a Banana Republic*. Austin: University of Texas Press, 2016.

———. "The Photos That We Don't Get to See: Sovereignties, Archives, and the 1928 Massacre of Banana Workers in Colombia." In *Making the Empire Work: Labor and United States Imperialism*, edited by Daniel E. Bender and Jana K. Lipman, 104–34. New York: New York University Press, 2015.

Collard, Rosemary-Claire, and Jessica Dempsey. "Accumulation by Difference-Making: An Anthropocene Story, Starring Witches." *Gender, Place*

& *Culture* 25, no. 9 (September 2018): 1349–64. https://doi.org/10.1080/0966369X.2018.1521385.

Conejo Barboza, Luis. "Divisiones bananeras y memoria: Un acercamiento al legado de las ciudades bananeras de la United Fruit Company en Centroamérica durante el siglo XX." *Revista de Historia*, no. 78 (October 2018): 95–118. https://doi.org/10.15359/rh.78.5.

Corkhill, David, and David Cubitt. *Ecuador: Fragile Democracy*. London: Latin America Bureau, 1988.

Coulthard, Glen Sean. *Red Skin, White Masks: Rejecting the Colonial Politics of Recognition*. Minneapolis: University of Minnesota Press, 2014.

Cousins, Elicia Mayuri, Lauren Richter, Alissa Cordner, Phil Brown, and Sokona Diallo. "Risky Business? Manufacturer and Retailer Action to Remove Per- and Polyfluorinated Chemicals from Consumer Products." NEW SOLUTIONS: *A Journal of Environmental and Occupational Health Policy* 29, no. 2 (August 2019): 242–65. https://doi.org/10.1177/1048291119852674.

de la Cruz, Jaye, and Kees Jansen. "Panama Disease and Contract Farming in the Philippines: Towards a Political Ecology of Risk." *Journal of Agrarian Change* 18, no. 2 (April 2018): 249–66. https://doi.org/10.1111/joac.12226.

CSDH. *Closing the Gap in a Generation: Health Equity through Action on the Social Determinants of Health. Final Report of the Commission on Social Determinants of Health*. Geneva: World Health Organization, 2008.

de la Cuadra, José. *El montuvio ecuatoriano: Ensayo de presentacion*. Quito: Libresa, 1996.

Cuéllar, Leticia, Irene Torres, Ethan Romero-Severson, Riya Mahesh, Nathaniel Ortega, Sarah Pungitore, Nicolas Hengartner, and Ruian Ke. "Excess Deaths Reveal the True Spatial, Temporal and Demographic Impact of COVID-19 on Mortality in Ecuador." *International Journal of Epidemiology* 51, no. 1 (February 2022): 54–62. https://doi.org/10.1093/ije/dyab163.

Davis, Frederick Rowe. *Banned: A History of Pesticides and the Science of Toxicology*. New Haven, CT: Yale University Press, 2014.

Davis, Heather, and Zoe Todd. "On the Importance of a Date, or, Decolonizing the Anthropocene." ACME: *An International Journal for Critical Geographies* 16, no. 4 (2017): 761–80. https://acme-journal.org/index.php/acme/article/view/1539.

Davis, Janae, Alex A. Moulton, Levi Van Sant, and Brian Williams. "Anthropocene, Capitalocene, ... Plantationocene?: A Manifesto for Ecological Justice in an Age of Global Crises." *Geography Compass* 13, no. 5 (May 2019): e12438. https://doi.org/10.1111/gec3.12438.

Deleuze, Gilles, and Felix Guattari. *A Thousand Plateaus: Capitalism and Schizophrenia*. Minneapolis: University of Minnesota Press, 1987.

Deneault, Alain, and William Sacher. *Imperial Canada Inc.: Legal Haven of Choice for the World's Mining Industries*. Vancouver: Talonbooks, 2012.

Denny, Keith. "Evidence-Based Medicine and Medical Authority." *Journal of Medical Humanities* 20, no. 4 (1999): 247–63. https://doi.org/10.1023/A:1022924404779.

Dole. "DBCP Facts." Accessed February 2, 2024. https://www.dole.com/en/about-us/dbcp-facts.

———. "Dole Delivers Original Recipes Inspired by Ariel and Moana as Part of Its Disney Princess Celebration." Accessed May 9, 2022. https://www.dole.com/en-ca/press/2021/20210608-dole-delivers-original-recipes-inspired-by-ariel-and-moana.

———. "Recipes." Accessed February 2, 2024. https://www.dole.com/en-ca/recipes.

Douglas, Mary, and Aaron Wildavsky. *Risk and Culture: An Essay on the Selection of Technological and Environmental Dangers*. Berkeley: University of California Press, 1983.

Dunlap, Alexander. "End the 'Green' Delusions: Industrial-Scale Renewable Energy Is Fossil Fuel+." *Verso* (blog), May 10, 2018. https://www.versobooks.com/blogs/3797-end-the-green-delusions-industrial-scale-renewable-energy-is-fossil-fuel.

Dussel, Enrique. *A History of the Church in Latin America: Colonialism to Liberation (1492–1979)*. Grand Rapids, MI: William. B. Eerdmans Publishing, 1982.

Ecobichon, Donald J. "Pesticide Use in Developing Countries." *Toxicology* 160, nos. 1–3 (2001): 27–33. https://doi.org/10.1016/S0300-483X(00)00452-2.

Elbehri, Aziz, Germán Carrillo García, Charles Staver, Almudena Hospido, and David Skully. *Ecuador's Banana Sector under Climate Change: An Economic and Biophysical Assessment to Promote a Sustainable and Climate-Compatible Strategy*. Rome: Food and Agriculture Organization, 2016.

Elías Caro, Jorge Enrique. "La masacre obrera de 1928 en la zona bananera del Magdalena-Colombia. Una historia inconclusa." *Andes* 22, no. 1 (2011): 99–134.

Elías Caro, Jorge Enrique, and Antonino Vidal Ortega. "The Worker's Massacre of 1928 in the Magdalena Zona Bananera-Colombia. An Unfinished Story." *Memorias: Revista Digital de Historia y Arqueología desde el Caribe*, no. 18 (2012): 22–54.

Ellis, Frank. *Las transnacionales del banano en Centroamérica*. Translated by Juan Mario Castellanos. San José, Costa Rica: Editorial Universitaria Centroamericana, 1983. https://cir.nii.ac.jp/crid/1130000797279728128.

Environmental Defence. "Reena Sandhu." Accessed August 29, 2023. https://environmentaldefence.ca/staff/reena-sandhu/.

Eschner, Kat. "The Story of the Real Canary in the Coal Mine." *Smithsonian Magazine*, December 30, 2016. https://www.smithsonianmag.com/smart-news/story-real-canary-coal-mine-180961570/.

Escobar, Arturo. "Displacement, Development, and Modernity in the Colombian Pacific." *International Social Science Journal* 55, no. 175 (2003): 157–67. https://doi.org/10.1111/1468-2451.5501015.

———. *Encountering Development: The Making and Unmaking of the Third World*. Rev. ed. Princeton, NJ: Princeton University Press, 2011.

Euraque, Darío A. *Reinterpreting the Banana Republic: Region and State in Honduras, 1870–1972*. Chapel Hill: University of North Carolina Press, 1996.

Fairtrade America. "Fairtrade Commits to a Better Future for Thousands of Banana Farmers." Accessed May 23, 2024. https://www.fairtrade-america.org/news-insights-fairtrade-commits-to-a-better-future-for-thousands-of-banana-farmers/.

Fallas, Carlos Luis. *Mamita Yunai*. 3rd ed. San José: Editorial Costa Rica, 2008.

Farmer, Paul, and Byron J. Good. "Illness Representations in Medical Anthropology: A Critical Review and a Case Study of the Representation of AIDS in Haiti." In *Mental Representation in Health and Illness*, edited by J. A. Skelton and Robert T. Croyle, 132–62. New York: Springer, 1991.

Federici, Silvia. *Caliban and the Witch*. Brooklyn, NY: Autonomedia, 2004.

———. *Witches, Witch-Hunting, and Women*. Oakland, CA: PM Press, 2018.

Ferguson, James. "The Uses of Neoliberalism." *Antipode* 41, no. s1 (January 2010): 166–84. https://doi.org/10.1111/j.1467-8330.2009.00721.x.

Forster, Cindy. "'The Macondo of Guatemala': Banana Workers and National Revolution in Tiquisate, 1944–1954." In *Banana Wars: Power, Production, and History in the Americas*, edited by Steve Striffler and Mark Moberg, 191–228. Durham, NC: Duke University Press, 2003.

Fortun, Kim, and Mike Fortun. "Scientific Imaginaries and Ethical Plateaus in Contemporary US Toxicology." *American Anthropologist* 107, no. 1 (2005): 43–54.

Foucault, Michel. *The Birth of the Clinic: An Archaeology of Medical Perception*. New York: Pantheon Books, 1973.

Frundt, Henry J. *Fair Bananas!: Farmers, Workers, and Consumers Strive to Change an Industry*. Tucson: University of Arizona Press, 2009.

———. "Sustaining Labor-Environmental Coalitions: Banana Allies in Costa Rica." *Latin American Politics and Society* 52, no. 3 (2010): 99–129. https://www.jstor.org/stable/40925587.

Galarza Suárez, Lucía. "Tierra, trabajo y tóxicos: Sobre la producción de un territorio bananero en la costa sur del Ecuador." *Estudios atacameños*, no. 63 (2019): 341–64. http://dx.doi.org/10.22199/issn.0718-1043-2019-0034.

Galarza Suárez, M.L. "Toxic Tropics: Gender, Nature and Capitalist Transformations in the Southern Coast of Ecuador." PhD Thesis, University of Amsterdam, 2020.

Galt, Ryan E. "From *Homo economicus* to Complex Subjectivities: Reconceptualizing Farmers as Pesticide Users." *Antipode* 45, no. 2 (2013): 336–56. https://doi.org/10.1111/j.1467-8330.2012.01000.x.

Galvão, Luiz Augusto, J.A. Escamilla, S. Henao, E. Loyola, C.S. Castillo, and P. Arbelaez. *Pesticides and Health in the Central American Isthmus*. Washington, DC: Pan American Health Organization, 2004.

García Márquez, Gabriel. *Living to Tell the Tale*. Translated by Edith Grossman. New York: Alfred A. Knopf, 2003.

Gibson-Graham, J.K. *The End of Capitalism (As We Knew It): A Feminist Critique of Political Economy*. Minneapolis: University of Minnesota Press, 2006.

Giroux, Henry A. "The Covid-19 Pandemic Is Exposing the Plague of Neoliberalism." In *Collaborative Futures in Qualitative Inquiry*, edited by Norman K. Denzin and Michael D. Giardina, 16–27. London: Routledge, 2021.

Goldman, Mara J., Paul Nadasdy, and Matthew D. Turner. *Knowing Nature: Conversations at the Intersection of Political Ecology and Science Studies*. Chicago: University of Chicago Press, 2011.

Gonzalez Casanova, Pablo. "Internal Colonialism and National Development." *Studies in Comparative International Development* 1, no. 4 (1965): 27–37.

Gordon, Todd, and Jeffery R. Webber. *Blood of Extraction: Canadian Imperialism in Latin America*. Halifax, NS: Fernwood Publishing, 2016.

———. "Canadian Capital and Secondary Imperialism in Latin America." *Canadian Foreign Policy Journal* 25, no. 1 (January 2019): 72–89. https://doi.org/10.1080/11926422.2018.1457966.

Gramsci, Antonio. *Selections from the Prison Notebooks of Antonio Gramsci*. Edited and translated by Quintin Hoare and Geoffrey Nowell-Smith. New York: International Publishers, 1971.

Grandin, Greg. *Empire's Workshop: Latin America, the United States, and the Rise of the New Imperialism*. New York: Henry Holt and Company, 2006.

———. *The Last Colonial Massacre: Latin America in the Cold War*. Updated ed. Chicago: University of Chicago Press, 2011.

Grant, Paul B.C., Million B. Woudneh, and Peter S. Ross. "Pesticides in Blood from Spectacled Caiman (Caiman Crocodilus) Downstream of Banana Plantations in Costa Rica." *Environmental Toxicology and Chemistry* 32, no. 11 (November 2013): 2576–83. https://doi.org/10.1002/etc.2358.

Green, Emily, and Miguel Fernández-Flores. "Mexican Cartels Are Turning Once-Peaceful Ecuador into a Narco War Zone." *Vice News*, April 17, 2023. https://www.vice.com/en/article/xgwxyn/ecuador-mexico-drug-war-cocaine.

Grossman, Lawrence S. *The Political Ecology of Bananas: Contract Farming, Peasants, and Agrarian Change in the Eastern Caribbean*. Chapel Hill: University of North Carolina Press, 1998.

Guthman, Julie. "The Polanyian Way? Voluntary Food Labels as Neoliberal Governance." *Antipode* 39, no. 3 (2007): 456–78. https://doi.org/10.1111/j.1467-8330.2007.00535.x.

Guthman, Julie, and Becky Mansfield. "The Implications of Environmental Epigenetics: A New Direction for Geographic Inquiry on Health, Space, and Nature-Society Relations." *Progress in Human Geography* 37, no. 4 (August 1, 2013): 486–504. https://doi.org/10.1177/0309132512463258.

Hall, Elizabeth F., and Todd Sanders. "Accountability and the Academy: Producing Knowledge about the Human Dimensions of Climate Change." *Journal of the Royal Anthropological Institute* 21, no. 2 (June 2015): 438–61. https://doi.org/10.1111/1467-9655.12162.

Hamilton, Karen. "Savoir, pouvoir et standpoint institutionnel: L'impact de la philanthropie minière sur la production du savoir dans les universités canadiennes." Master's Thesis, Université du Québec à Montréal, 2014. http://www.archipel.uqam.ca/6767/.

Harari, Raúl, Homero Harari, Natalia Harari, and Florencia Harari. *Producción Bananera: Impacto en la Salud y el Ambiente*. Quito: FENACLE, FOS, IFA, 2011.

Haraway, Donna. "Situated Knowledges: The Science Question in Feminism and the Privilege of Partial Perspective." *Feminist Studies* 14, no. 3 (1988): 575–99. https://doi.org/10.2307/3178066.

Haraway, Donna J. *Staying with the Trouble: Making Kin in the Chthulucene*. Durham, NC: Duke University Press, 2016. https://doi.org/10.1515/9780822373780.

Harding, Sandra. *Sciences from Below: Feminisms, Postcolonialities, and Modernities*. Durham, NC: Duke University Press, 2008.

Harrison, Jill. "Abandoned Bodies and Spaces of Sacrifice: Pesticide Drift Activism and the Contestation of Neoliberal Environmental Politics in California." *Geoforum* 39, no. 3 (2008): 1197–1214. https://doi.org/10.1016/j.geoforum.2007.02.012.

Henriques, William, Russel D. Jeffers, Thomas E. Lacher, and Ronald J. Kendall. "Agrochemical Use on Banana Plantations in Latin America: Perspectives on Ecological Risk." *Environmental Toxicology and Chemistry* 16, no. 1 (1997): 91–99. https://doi.org/10.1002/etc.5620160110.

Hergesheimer, Chris. "Practical Mergers: Export-Oriented Value Chains and Food Sovereignty Pathways in Haiti and Ecuador." PhD Thesis, University of British Columbia, 2017. https://doi.org/10.14288/1.0357229.

Heron, Barbara. *Desire for Development: Whiteness, Gender, and the Helping Imperative*. Waterloo, ON: Wilfrid Laurier University Press, 2007.

Herrera, Stalin. "El 'vacío sindical' como hegemonía empresarial en el sector bananero." Quito: Instituto de Estudios Ecuatorianos and Friedrich Ebert Stiftung, 2019.

Herrick, Clare. "Alcohol, Ideological Schisms and a Science of Corporate Behaviours on Health." *Critical Public Health* 26, no. 1 (January 2016): 14–23. https://doi.org/10.1080/09581596.2014.951313.

Hill, Dana. "Throughout South America, Structural Violence Is Showing Up as Street Violence." Foreign Policy in Focus, December 19, 2019. https://fpif.org/throughout-south-america-structural-violence-is-showing-up-as-street-violence/.

Hofmann, Jonathan, Jorge Guardado, Matthew Keifer, and Catharina Wesseling. "Mortality among a Cohort of Banana Plantation Workers in Costa Rica." *International Journal of Occupational and Environmental Health* 12, no. 4 (2006): 321–28. https://doi.org/10.1179/oeh.2006.12.4.321.

Holmes, Dave, Stuart J. Murray, Amélie Perron, and Geneviève Rail. "Deconstructing the Evidence-Based Discourse in Health Sciences: Truth, Power and Fascism." *International Journal of Evidence-Based Healthcare* 4, no. 3 (2006): 180–86. https://doi.org/10.1111/j.1479-6988.2006.00041.x.

Holt-Giménez, Eric, Annie Shattuck, and Ilja Van Lammeren. "Thresholds of Resistance: Agroecology, Resilience and the Agrarian Question." *Journal of Peasant Studies* 48, no. 4 (2021): 715–33. https://doi.org/10.1080/03066150.2020.1847090.

Hough, Phillip A. "A Race to the Bottom? Globalization, Labor Repression, and Development by Dispossession in Latin America's Banana Industry." *Global Labour Journal* 3, no. 2 (2012): 237–64. https://doi.org/10.15173/glj.v3i2.1121.

Humbert, Franziska. "The Plight of Pineapple and Banana Workers in Retail Supply Chains: Continuing Evidence of Rights Violations in Costa Rica and Ecuador." Oxford: Oxfam International, 2018.

Humbert, Franziska, and Frank Brassel. "Sweet Fruit, Bitter Truth: German Supermarkets' Responsibility for the Inhuman Conditions which Prevail in the Banana and Pineapple Industries of Costa Rica and Ecuador." Berlin: Oxfam Germany, 2016.

Hunt, Linda M., Rolando Tinoco Ojanguren, Norah Schwartz, and David Halperin. "Balancing Risks and Resources: Applying Pesticides without Using Protective Equipment in Southern Mexico." In *Anthropology in Public Health: Bridging Differences in Culture and Society*, edited by Robert A. Hahn, 235–54. New York: Oxford University Press, 1999.

Hunter, Jane. "The Israeli Role in Guatemala." *Race & Class* 29, no. 1 (1987): 35–54. https://doi.org/10.1177/030639688702900103.

Hurtig, Anna Karin, Miguel San Sebastián, Alejandro Soto, Angel Shingre, Diocles Zambrano, and Walter Guerrero. "Pesticide Use among Farmers in the Amazon Basin of Ecuador." *Archives of Environmental Health* 58, no. 4 (2003): 223–28. https://doi.org/10.3200/AEOH.58.4.223-228.

Hussey, Ian, and Joe Curnow. "Fair Trade, Neocolonial Developmentalism, and Racialized Power Relations." *Interface* 5, no. 1 (2013): 40–68. https://www.interfacejournal.net/wordpress/wp-content/uploads/2013/05/Interface-5-1-Hussey-and-Curnow.pdf.

Hutter, Hans-Peter, Michael Kundi, Helmut Ludwig, Hanns Moshammer, Peter Wallner, and Lucia Galarza. "Banana Pesticide Study: Epidemiological Study on Small-Scale Farmers and Farm Workers in Conventional and Organic Agriculture (Bananas) in Ecuador." Vienna: Austrian Doctors for a Healthy Environment, 2016.

Hutter, Hans-Peter, Michael Poteser, Kathrin Lemmerer, Peter Wallner, Michael Kundi, Hanns Moshammer, and Lisbeth Weitensfelder. "Health Symptoms Related to Pesticide Use in Farmers and Laborers of Ecological and Conventional Banana Plantations in Ecuador." *International Journal of Environmental Research and Public Health* 18, no. 3 (2021): 1126. https://doi.org/10.3390/ijerph18031126.

Hutter, Hans-Peter, Michael Poteser, Kathrin Lemmerer, Peter Wallner, Shifra Shahraki Sanavi, Michael Kundi, Hanns Moshammer, and Lisbeth Weitensfelder. "Indicators of Genotoxicity in Farmers and Laborers of Ecological and Conventional Banana Plantations in Ecuador." *International Journal of Environmental Research and Public Health* 17, no. 4 (2020): 1435. https://doi.org/10.3390/ijerph17041435.

Ibarra, Hernán. *Indios y cholos en la formación de la clase trabajadora ecuatoriana.* Quito: El Conejo, 1992.

"Innovating for Solutions." Ottawa: International Development Research Centre, 2015.

Isch López, Edgar. "El extractivismo como negación de la Constitución de la República." *La línea de fuego*, August 27, 2013. https://lalineadefuego.info/el-extractivismo-como-negacion-de-la-constitucion-de-la-republica-por-edgar-isch-l/.

Isch López, Edgar, Xavier Rodríguez, and Nancy Carrión. "La ecología política de la Producción bananera en la provincia de El Oro: Estudio comparativo de la producción orgánica y la producción convencional." Quito, Ecuador, n.d.

Iturralde, Pablo. "The IMF's Role in the Devastating Impacts of Covid-19—the Case of Ecuador." *Bretton Woods Project* (blog), July 16, 2020. https://www.brettonwoodsproject.org/2020/07/the-imfs-role-in-the-devastating-impacts-of-COVID-19-the-case-of-ecuador/.

Jackson, Paul, and Abigail H. Neely. "Triangulating Health: Toward a Practice of a Political Ecology of Health." *Progress in Human Geography* 39, no. 1 (2015): 47–64. https://doi.org/10.1177/0309132513518832.

Janes, Craig R. "Commentary: 'Culture,' Cultural Explanations and Causality." *International Journal of Epidemiology* 35, no. 2 (November 2005): 261–63. https://doi.org/10.1093/ije/dyi238.

Jansen, Kees. "Banana Wars and the Multiplicity of Conflicts in Commodity Chains." *European Review of Latin American and Caribbean Studies* 81 (2006): 97–113. https://www.jstor.org/stable/25676234.
———. "Greening Bananas and Institutionalizing Environmentalism: Self-Regulation by Fruit Corporations." In *Agribusiness and Society: Corporate Responses to Environmentalism, Market Opportunities and Public Regulation*, edited by Kees Jansen and Sietze Vellema, 145–75. London: Zed Books, 2004.
———. "The Unspeakable Ban: The Translation of Global Pesticide Governance into Honduran National Regulation." *World Development* 36, no. 4 (2008): 575–89. https://doi.org/10.1016/j.worlddev.2007.04.017.
Jeppesen, Sandra, and Holly Nazar. "Beyond Academic Freedom: Canadian Neoliberal Universities in the Global Context." TOPIA: *Canadian Journal of Cultural Studies* 1, no. 28 (2012). https://www.mediaactionresearch.org/wp-content/uploads/2019/05/jeppesen_nazar_neoliberal_university.pdf.
Jones, Alison, and Kuni Jenkins. "Rethinking Collaboration: Working the Indigene-Colonizer Hyphen." In *Handbook of Critical and Indigenous Methodologies*, edited by Norman K. Denzin, Yvonna S. Lincoln, and Linda Tuhiwai Smith, 471–86. Thousand Oaks, CA: Sage Publications, 2014.
Jones, Rhys, Papaarangi Reid, and Alexandra Macmillan. "Navigating Fundamental Tensions towards a Decolonial Relational Vision of Planetary Health." *The Lancet Planetary Health* 6, no. 10 (2022): e834–41. https://doi.org/10.1016/S2542-5196(22)00197-8.
Jordanova, Ludmilla. *History in Practice*. London: Arnold, 2000.
Kallet, Arthur, and Frederick John Schlink. *100,000,000 Guinea Pigs: Dangers in Everyday Foods, Drugs, and Cosmetics*. New York: Grosset & Dunlap, 1933.
Karnes, Thomas L. *Tropical Enterprise: The Standard Fruit and Steamship Company in Latin America*. Baton Rouge: Louisiana State University Press, 1978.
Keifer, Matthew C., Douglas I. Murray, Rafael Amador, Marianela Corriols, Diego Gonzalez, Jorge Jenkins Molieri, Ana Cecilia Rodriquez, Rudolf van der Haar, Catarina Wesseling, and Rob McConnell. "Solving the Pesticide Problem in Latin America: A Model for Health-Sector Empowerment." *New Solutions: A Journal of Environmental*

and *Occupational Health Policy* 7, no. 2 (1997): 26–31. https://doi.org/10.2190/NS7.2.f.

Khrebtan-Hörhager, Julia, and Roberto Avant-Mier. "Despicable Others: Animated Othering as Equipment for Living in the Era of Trump." *Journal of Intercultural Communication Research* 46, no. 5 (2017): 441–62. https://doi.org/10.1080/17475759.2017.1372302.

Kimmerer, Robin Wall. *Braiding Sweetgrass: Indigenous Wisdom, Scientific Knowledge and the Teachings of Plants.* Minneapolis: Milkweed Editions, 2013.

King, Brian. "Political Ecologies of Health." *Progress in Human Geography* 34, no. 1 (2010): 38–55. https://doi.org/10.1177/0309132509338642.

Kirsch, Stuart. *Mining Capitalism: The Relationship between Corporations and Their Critics.* Oakland: University of California Press, 2014.

Kish, Zenia, and Justin Leroy. "Bonded Life: Technologies of Racial Finance from Slave Insurance to Philanthrocapital." *Cultural Studies* 29, nos. 5–6 (2015): 630–51. https://doi.org/10.1080/09502386.2015.1017137.

Klein, Naomi. *The Shock Doctrine: The Rise of Disaster Capitalism.* Toronto: Knopf Canada, 2007.

Kleinman, Arthur, and Joan Kleinman. "Suffering and Its Professional Transformation: Toward an Ethnography of Interpersonal Experience." *Culture, Medicine and Psychiatry* 15, no. 3 (1991): 275–301. https://doi.org/10.1007/BF00046540.

Koeppel, Dan. *Banana: The Fate of the Fruit That Changed the World.* New York: Penguin, 2008.

Konefal, Jason, Michael Mascarenhas, and Maki Hatanaka. "Governance in the Global Agro-Food System: Backlighting the Role of Transnational Supermarket Chains." *Agriculture and Human Values* 22, no. 3 (2005): 291–302. https://doi.org/10.1007/s10460-005-6046-0.

Labonté, Ronald, Michael Polanyi, Nazeem Muhajarine, Tom McIntosh, and Allison Williams. "Beyond the Divides: Towards Critical Population Health Research." *Critical Public Health* 15, no. 1 (2005): 5–17. https://doi.org/10.1080/09581590500048192.

Lanphear, Bruce P. "Low-Level Toxicity of Chemicals: No Acceptable Levels?" PLOS *Biology* 15, no. 12 (2017): e2003066. https://doi.org/10.1371/journal.pbio.2003066.

Larrea, Carlos, ed. *El banano en el Ecuador: Transnacionales, modernización y subdesarrollo.* Quito: Corporación Editora Nacional, 1987.

Larrea, Carlos, and Natalia Greene. "Concentration of Assets and Poverty Reduction in Post-neoliberal Ecuador." In *Dominant Elites in Latin America: From Neo-liberalism to the Pink Tide* edited by Liisa L. North and Timothy C. Clark, 93–118. London: Palgrave Macmillan, 2018.

Larrea Maldonado, Carlos. *Hacia una historia ecológica del Ecuador: Propuestas para el debate*. Vol. 15. Quito: Corporación Editora Nacional, 2006.

———. *Pobreza, dolarización y crisis en el Ecuador*. Quito: Editorial Abya Yala, 2004.

Latorre, Sara. "The Role of Ecuadorian Working-Class Environmentalism in Promoting Environmental Justice: An Overview of the Hydrocarbon and Agricultural Sectors." In *The Palgrave Handbook of Environmental Labour Studies*, edited by Nora Räthzel, Dimitris Stevis, and David Uzzell, 271–94. London: Palgrave Macmillan, 2021. https://doi.org/10.1007/978-3-030-71909-8_12.

Latorre, Sara, Katharine N. Farrell, and Joan Martínez-Alier. "The Commodification of Nature and Socio-Environmental Resistance in Ecuador: An Inventory of Accumulation by Dispossession Cases, 1980–2013." *Ecological Economics* 116 (2015): 58–69. https://doi.org/10.1016/j.ecolecon.2015.04.016.

LeGrand, Catherine C. "Living in Macondo: Economy and Culture in a United Fruit Company Banana Enclave in Colombia." In *Close Encounters of Empire: Writing the Cultural History of US–Latin American Relations*, edited by Gilbert M. Joseph, Catherine C. LeGrand, and Ricardo D. Salvatore, 333–68. Durham, NC: Duke University Press, 1998.

León Cabrera, José María. "'Los que no aparecen': La búsqueda de los cuerpos extraviados en Ecuador durante la pandemia." *El País*, December 7, 2021, sec. Internacional. https://elpais.com/internacional/2021-12-07/los-que-no-aparecen-la-busqueda-de-los-cuerpos-extraviados-en-ecuador-durante-la-pandemia.html.

Liboiron, Max, Manuel Tironi, and Nerea Calvillo. "Toxic Politics: Acting in a Permanently Polluted World." *Social Studies of Science* 48, no. 3 (June 2018): 331–49. https://doi.org/10.1177/0306312718783087.

Lofters, Aisha, and Patricia O'Campo. "Differences That Matter." In *Rethinking Social Epidemiology: Towards a Science of Change*, edited by Patricia O'Campo and James R. Dunn, 93–109. Dordrecht, Netherlands: Springer, 2011. https://doi.org/10.1007/978-94-007-2138-8_5.

London, Leslie. "Neurobehavioural Methods, Effects and Prevention: Workers' Human Rights Are Why the Field Matters for Developing

Countries." *Neurotoxicology* 30, no. 6 (2009): 1135–43. https://doi.org/10.1016/j.neuro.2009.01.007.

Macaroff, Anahí. "El modelo bananero en el Ecuador como régimen de control sobre el territorio, las vidas y cuerpos de las mujeres." In *Asalariadas rurales en América Latina*, edited by Lorena Rodríguez Lezica, Julieta Krapovickas, Alicia Migliaro, Joaquín Cardeillac, and Matías Carámbula, 128–43. Montevideo, Uruguay: Grupo Investigación Acción sobre Desigualdades en el medio Rural, Universidad de la República, 2020. https://www.colibri.udelar.edu.uy/jspui/bitstream/20.500.12008/30005/1/Asalariadas%20rurales%20en%20AL_2020.pdf.

Macaroff, Anahí, Stalin Hererra, Santiago Chuquimarca, Victor Ávila, Christian Orozco, Patricia Polo, Alex Naranjo, Freddy Montenegro, Nancy Burneo, and María José Llerena. *Estado del banano en Ecuador: Acumulación, desigualdad y derechos laborales*. Quito: Friedrich-Ebert-Stiftung Ecuador, 2022.

Machado Aráoz, Horacio. "El auge de la minería transnacional en América Latina: De la ecología política del neoliberalismo a la anatomía política del colonialismo." In *La naturaleza colonizada: Ecología política y minería en América Latina*, edited by Hector Alimonda, 135–80. Buenos Aires: CLACSO, 2011.

Maldonado, Adolfo, and Ana Lucía Martínez. "Impacto de las fumigaciones aéreas en las bananeras de las Ramas-Salitre-Guayas." Quito: Acción Ecológica—FEDESO—Red Juvenil de Salitre, 2007.

Maldonado Campos, Adolfo. "Una propuesta de reparación socio-ecosistémica a los impactos del metabolismo de la actividad petrolera para la Amazonía ecuatoriana." PhD Thesis, Universidad Andina Simón Bolívar, Sede Ecuador, 2018. http://hdl.handle.net/10644/6827.

Marquardt, Steve. "'Green Havoc': Panama Disease, Environmental Change, and Labor Process in the Central American Banana Industry." *American Historical Review* 106, no. 1 (2001): 49–80. https://doi.org/10.2307/2652224.

———. "Pesticides, Parakeets, and Unions in the Costa Rican Banana Industry, 1938–1962." *Latin American Research Review* 37, no. 2 (2002): 3–36. https://www.jstor.org/stable/2692147.

Marston, Sallie A., John Paul Jones III, and Keith Woodward. "Human Geography without Scale." *Transactions of the Institute of British Geographers* 30, no. 4 (2005): 416–32. https://doi.org/10.1111/j.1475-5661.2005.00180.x.

Martin, James W. *Banana Cowboys: The United Fruit Company and the Culture of Corporate Colonialism*. Albuquerque: University of New Mexico Press, 2022.

Martínez, Gustavo, Barlin O. Olivares, Juan Carlos Rey, Juan Rojas, Jaime Cardenas, Carlos Muentes, and Carolina Dawson. "The Advance of Fusarium Wilt Tropical Race 4 in Musaceae of Latin America and the Caribbean: Current Situation." *Pathogens* 12, no. 2 (2023): 277. https://doi.org/10.3390/pathogens12020277.

Martínez, Luis Alfredo. *A la costa*. 2nd ed. Quito: Libresa, 2015.

Martínez Novo, Carmen. "Ventriloquism, Racism and the Politics of Decoloniality in Ecuador." *Cultural Studies* 32, no. 3 (2018): 389–413. https://doi.org/10.1080/09502386.2017.1420091.

Martínez Valle, Luciano. "Trabajo flexible en las nuevas zonas bananeras de Ecuador." In *Efectos sociales de la globalización: Petróleo, banano y flores en Ecuador*, edited by Tanya Korovkin, 129–56. Quito: Ediciones Abya-Yala, 2004.

Marx, Karl. *Capital, Volume 1: A Critique of Political Economy*. New York: Penguin Classics, 1992.

Matthews, Graham A. "Attitudes and Behaviours Regarding Use of Crop Protection Products—A Survey of More than 8500 Smallholders in 26 Countries." *Crop Protection* 27, nos. 3–5 (2008): 834–46. https://doi.org/10.1016/j.cropro.2007.10.013.

Mayer, Jonathan D. "The Political Ecology of Disease as One New Focus for Medical Geography." *Progress in Human Geography* 20, no. 4 (1996): 441–56. https://doi.org/10.1177/030913259602000401.

McClure, Elizabeth S., Pavithra Vasudevan, Zinzi Bailey, Snehal Patel, and Whitney R. Robinson. "Racial Capitalism Within Public Health—How Occupational Settings Drive COVID-19 Disparities." *American Journal of Epidemiology* 189, no. 11 (2020): 1244–53. https://doi.org/10.1093/aje/kwaa126.

McNally, David. *Monsters of the Market: Zombies, Vampires and Global Capitalism*. Leiden, Netherlands: Brill, 2011.

Melo, Cristian J., and Steven A. Wolf. "Ecocertification of Ecuadorian Bananas: Prospects for Progressive North-South Linkages." *Studies in Comparative International Development* 42, nos. 3–4 (2007): 256–78. https://doi.org/10.1007/s12116-007-9009-1.

Menton, Mary, Carlos Larrea, Sara Latorre, Joan Martinez-Alier, Mika Peck, Leah Temper, and Mariana Walter. "Environmental Justice and the SDGs: From Synergies to Gaps and Contradictions." *Sustainability Science* 15 (2020): 1621–36. https://doi.org/10.1007/s11625-020-00789-8.

Mera-Orces, Veronica. "Paying for Survival with Health: Potato Production Practices, Pesticide Use and Gender Concerns in the Ecuadorian Highlands." *Journal of Agricultural Education and Extension* 8, no. 1 (2001): 31–40. https://doi.org/10.1080/13892240185300061.

Miller, Clark A. "The Dynamics of Framing Environmental Values and Policy: Four Models of Societal Processes." *Environmental Values* 9, no. 2 (2000): 211–33. https://doi.org/10.3197/096327100129342047.

Mintz, Sidney W. *Sweetness and Power: The Place of Sugar in Modern History*. Harmondsworth, UK: Penguin, 1986.

Mitchell, Don. "There's No Such Thing as Culture: Towards a Reconceptualization of the Idea of Culture in Geography." *Transactions of the Institute of British Geographers* 20, no. 1 (1995): 102–16. https://doi.org/10.2307/622727.

Moberg, Mark. "Market's End: Fair-Trade Social Premiums as Development in Dominica." *American Ethnologist* 43, no. 4 (2016): 677–90. https://doi.org/10.1111/amet.12383.

———. "Review of *Globalized Fruit, Local Entrepreneurs: How One Banana-Exporting Country Achieved Worldwide Reach* by Douglas Southgate and Lois Roberts." *Agricultural History Review* 66, no. 1 (2018): 163–64.

Moberg, Mark, and Steve Striffler. "Introduction." In *Banana Wars: Power, Production, and History in the Americas*, edited by Steve Striffler and Mark Moberg, 12–30. Durham, NC: Duke University Press, 2003.

Mondragón Ríos, Rodolfo. "La producción social del miedo: Violencia política y terror en la zona Norte de Chiapas, México." *Intersticios: Revista Sociológica de Pensamiento Crítico* 1, no. 2 (2007): 140. https://www.intersticios.es/article/view/1089.

Moore, Jason W. "The Capitalocene, Part I: On the Nature and Origins of Our Ecological Crisis." *Journal of Peasant Studies* 44, no. 3 (2017): 594–630. https://doi.org/10.1080/03066150.2016.1235036.

Moore, Jennifer, and Teresa Velásquez. "Water for Gold: Confronting State and Corporate Mining Discourses in Azuay, Ecuador." In *Subterranean Struggles: New Dynamics of Mining, Oil, and Gas in Latin America*, edited by Anthony Bebbington and Jeffrey Bury, 119–48. Austin: University of Texas Press, 2013.

Morello-Frosch, Rachel, Miriam Zuk, Michael Jerrett, Bhavna Shamasunder, and Amy D. Kyle. "Understanding the Cumulative Impacts of

Inequalities in Environmental Health: Implications for Policy." *Health Affairs* 30, no. 5 (2011): 879–87. https://doi.org/10.1377/hlthaff.2011.0153.

Mukhopadhyay, Baijayanta, Lori Hanson, Klaudia Dmitrienko, Jannie Wing-Sea Leung, and Anne-Emanuelle Birn. "Canada's Global Health Role." *The Lancet* 392, no. 10162 (2018): 2349–50. https://doi.org/10.1016/S0140-6736(18)32759-4

Murphy, Michelle. "Alterlife and Decolonial Chemical Relations." *Cultural Anthropology* 32, no. 4 (2017): 494–503. https://doi.org/10.14506/ca32.4.02.

———. "Chemical Infrastructures of the St Clair River." In *Toxicants, Health and Regulation since 1945*, edited by Soraya Boudia and Natalie Jas, 103–16. London: Pickering & Chatto, 2013.

Murray, Douglas L. *Cultivating Crisis: The Human Cost of Pesticides in Latin America*. Austin: University of Texas Press, 1994.

Murray, Douglas L., and Peter L. Taylor. "Claim No Easy Victories: Evaluating the Pesticide Industry's Global Safe Use Campaign." *World Development* 28, no. 10 (2000): 1735–49. https://doi.org/10.1016/S0305-750X(00)00059-0.

Nading, Alex M. "Living in a Toxic World." *Annual Review of Anthropology* 49, (2020): 209–24. https://doi.org/10.1146/annurev-anthro-010220-074557.

———. *Mosquito Trails: Ecology, Health, and the Politics of Entanglement*. Oakland: University of California Press, 2014.

Naranjo, Alex, Elizabeth Bravo, Gabriela Villacís, and Patricia Polo. *Cosechas bañadas en tóxicos: Plantaciones agroindustriales y agrotóxicos en el Ecuador—El caso de las plantaciones bananeras*. Quito: Acción Ecológica, 2020.

Naranjo Márquez, Alexander. *El veneno llega por el aire: Informe sobre la situación del Mancozeb en la agroindustria del banano*. Quito, Ecuador: ASTAC and Acción Ecológica, 2023.

Nash, Linda. "From Safety to Risk: The Cold War Contexts of American Environmental Policy." *Journal of Policy History* 29, no. 01 (2017): 1–33. https://doi.org/10.1017/S0898030616000336.

———. *Inescapable Ecologies: A History of Environment, Disease, and Knowledge*. Berkeley: University of California Press, 2006.

Natural Resources Canada. "Minerals and the Economy." January 25, 2018. https://www.nrcan.gc.ca/our-natural-resources/minerals-mining/minerals-metals-facts/minerals-and-economy/20529.

Navas, Grettel. "'If There's No Evidence, There's No Victim': Undone Science and Political Organisation in Marginalising Women as Victims of DBCP in Nicaragua." *Journal of Peasant Studies* 50, no. 4 (2022): 1569–92. https://doi.org/10.1080/03066150.2021.2024517.

Neely, Abigail H. "Internal Ecologies and the Limits of Local Biologies: A Political Ecology of Tuberculosis in the Time of AIDS." *Annals of the Association of American Geographers* 105, no. 4 (May 2015): 791–805. https://doi.org/10.1080/00045608.2015.1015097.

Neely, Abigail H., and Thokozile Nguse. "Research and Relationships: Entanglements, Intra-actions, and Diffraction." In *The Routledge Handbook of Political Ecology*, edited by Tom Perreault, Gavin Bridge, and James McCarthy, 140–49. London: Routledge, 2015.

Neruda, Pablo. *Canto General*. 50th anniv. ed. Berkeley: University of California Press, 2000.

Neyra Ballestero, Bélgica. *Presencia de la etnia negra en la provincia de El Oro: Origen y trascendencia sociocultural*. Machala, Ecuador: Casa de la Cultura Ecuatoriana Benjamín Carrión, 2009.

Nichols, Carly E., and Vincent J. Del Casino. "Towards an Integrated Political Ecology of Health and Bodies." *Progress in Human Geography* 45, no. 4 (2021): 776–95. https://doi.org/10.1177/0309132520946489.

Ofrias, Lindsay. "Invisible Harms, Invisible Profits: A Theory of the Incentive to Contaminate." *Culture, Theory and Critique* 58, no. 4 (2017): 435–56. https://doi.org/10.1080/14735784.2017.1357478.

Order of Malta Canadian Association. "The Order in Canada." Accessed August 30, 2021. https://www.orderofmaltacanada.org/orderincanada/.

Orozco, Fadya A., Donald C. Cole, Greg Forbes, Jürgen Kroschel, Susitha Wanigaratne, and Denis Arica. "Monitoring Adherence to the International Code of Conduct: Highly Hazardous Pesticides in Central Andean Agriculture and Farmers' Rights to Health." *International Journal of Occupational and Environmental Health* 15, no. 3 (2009): 255–68. https://doi.org/10.1179/oeh.2009.15.3.255.

Ospina Peralta, Pablo. "The Divided Left in Ecuador." *Dissent*, April 9, 2021. https://www.dissentmagazine.org/online_articles/the-divided-left-in-ecuador.

Paredes, Alyssa. "Experimental Science for the 'Bananapocalypse': Counter Politics in the Mintz Plantationocene." *Ethnos* 88, no. 4 (2021): 837–63. https://doi.org/10.1080/00141844.2021.1919172.

Partanen, Timo J., Christer Hogstedt, Rabiul Ahasan, Aurora Aragón, Maria E. Arroyave, Jerry Jeyaratnam, Kari Kurppa, et al. "Collaboration between Developing and Developed Countries and between Developing Countries in Occupational Health Research and Surveillance." *Scandinavian Journal of Work, Environment & Health* 25, no. 3 (1999): 296–300. https://www.jstor.org/stable/40966901.

Patel, Raj. "The Long Green Revolution." *Journal of Peasant Studies* 40, no. 1 (2013): 1–63. https://doi.org/10.1080/03066150.2012.719224.

———. "What Does Food Sovereignty Look Like?" *Journal of Peasant Studies* 36, no. 3 (2009): 663–73. https://doi.org/10.1080/03066150903143079.

Peet, R., and M. Watts. *Liberation Ecologies: Environment, Development, Social Movements*. 2nd ed. London: Routledge, 2004.

Phillips, Lynne. "Changing Health Moralities in the Tropics: Ethics and the Other." In *Postmodernism and the Ethical Subject*, edited by Barbara Gabriel and Suzan Ilcan, 254–72. Montreal: McGill-Queen's University Press, 2004.

Pier, Carol. *Tainted Harvest: Child Labor and Obstacles to Organizing on Ecuador's Banana Plantations*. New York: Human Rights Watch, 2002.

Pinto, Ñaní. "Tras montaje en la desaparición de los 43, familiares se pronuncian contra la 'cuarta transformación.'" *Avispa Midia*, March 30, 2022. https://avispa.org/tras-montaje-en-la-desaparicion-de-los-43-familiares-se-pronuncian-contra-la-cuarta-transformacion/.

Ploetz, Randy C. "Panama Disease, an Old Nemesis Rears Its Ugly Head: Part 1, the Beginnings of the Banana Export Trades." *Plant Health Progress* 6, no. 1 (2005). https://doi.org/doi:10.1094/PHP-2005-1221-01-RV.

———. "Panama Disease, an Old Nemesis Rears Its Ugly Head: Part 2, the Cavendish Era and Beyond." *Plant Health Progress* 7, no. 1 (2006). https://doi.org/doi:10.1094/PHP-2006-0308-01-RV.

Polo Almeida, Patricia. "Determinación social de la salud en el territorio: Miradas de los trabajadores bananeros en Tenguel (Ecuador)." *Revista Ciencias de La Salud* 18 (2020): 1–22. https://doi.org/10.12804/revistas.urosario.edu.co/revsalud/a.9073.

Polo Almeida, Patricia Elizabeth. "Relación territorio-salud: Un análisis desde las representaciones sociales de los y las trabajadoras bananeras, recinto San Rafael, provincia del Guayas-Ecuador." PhD Thesis, Universidad Andina Simón Bolívar, Sede Ecuador, 2018. http://hdl.handle.net/10644/6431.

Pratt, Mary Louise. *Imperial Eyes: Travel Writing and Transculturation.* 2nd ed. London: Routledge, 2007. https://doi.org/10.4324/9780203932933.
Pulido, Laura. "Geographies of Race and Ethnicity II: Environmental Racism, Racial Capitalism and State-Sanctioned Violence." *Progress in Human Geography* 41, no. 4 (August 2017): 524–33. https://doi.org/10.1177/0309132516646495.
Raffles, Hugh. *In Amazonia: A Natural History.* Princeton, NJ: Princeton University Press, 2002.
"República Bananera del Ecuador." *Revista Crisis.* October 16, 2023. http://www.revistacrisis.com/editorial/republica-bananera-del-ecuador.
Richter, Lauren, Alissa Cordner, and Phil Brown. "Producing Ignorance Through Regulatory Structure: The Case of Per- and Polyfluoroalkyl Substances (PFAS)." *Sociological Perspectives,* 64, no. 4 (2020): 631–56. https://doi.org/10.1177/0731121420964827.
Rico Montoya, Angélica. "Narrativas de violencia y resistencia de las infancias zapatistas Educación autónoma y contrainsurgencia en Chiapas." *Argumentos* 29, no. 81 (2016): 13–35.
Riofrancos, Thea. *Resource Radicals: From Petro-Nationalism to Post-Extractivism in Ecuador.* Durham, NC: Duke University Press, 2020.
Ríos-González, Adriana, Kees Jansen, and Héctor Javier Sánchez-Pérez. "Pesticide Risk Perceptions and the Differences between Farmers and Extensionists: Towards a Knowledge-in-Context Model." *Environmental Research* 124 (2013): 43–53. https://doi.org/10.1016/j.envres.2013.03.006.
Robbins, Paul. *Political Ecology: A Critical Introduction.* 2nd ed. Malden, MA: Wiley-Blackwell, 2012.
Roberts, Lois J. *Empresarios ecuatorianos del banano.* Quito: Editorial CODEU, 2009.
Robinson, Cedric J. *Black Marxism: The Making of the Black Radical Tradition.* 3rd ed. Chapel Hill: University of North Carolina Press, 2020.
Roitman, Karem. "Hybridity, Mestizaje, and Montubios in Ecuador." University of Oxford, QEH Working Paper Series 165 (2008): 1–19. http://workingpapers.qeh.ox.ac.uk/RePEc/qeh/qehwps/qehwps165.pdf.
Roitman, Karem, and Alexis Oviedo. "Mestizo Racism in Ecuador." *Ethnic and Racial Studies* 40, no. 15 (December 2016): 2768–86. https://doi.org/10.1080/01419870.2016.1260749.
Rowe Davis, Frederick. "On the Professionalization of Toxicology." *Environmental History* 13 (2008): 751–56. https://doi.org/10.1093/envhis/13.4.751-a.

Roy Grégoire, Etienne. "Dialogue as Racism? The Promotion of 'Canadian Dialogue' in Guatemala's Extractive Sector." *Extractive Industries and Society* 6, no. 3 (2019): 688–701. https://doi.org/10.1016/j.exis.2019.01.009.

Russell, Edmund. *War and Nature: Fighting Humans and Insects with Chemicals from World War I to Silent Spring.* Cambridge, UK: Cambridge University Press, 2001.

Said, Edward W. *Culture and Imperialism.* New York: Knopf, 1993.

——. *Orientalism.* New York: Vintage Books, 1978.

San Sebastián, M., and A.K. Hurtig. "Oil Development and Health in the Amazon Basin of Ecuador: The Popular Epidemiology Process." *Social Science & Medicine* 60, no. 4 (2005): 799–807. https://doi.org/10.1016/j.socscimed.2004.06.016.

Sass, Robert. "Agricultural 'Killing Fields': The Poisoning of Costa Rican Banana Workers." *International Journal of Health Services* 30, no. 3 (2000): 491–514. https://doi.org/10.2190/PNKW-HAPB-QJBA-LLL4.

Saunders, Sakura. "The Munk School's Foreign Policy Agenda Is Showing." *Peter Munk OUT of UofT* (blog), September 9, 2015. https://munkoutofuoft.wordpress.com/2015/09/09/the-munk-schools-foreign-policy-agenda-is-showing/.

Saunders, Sakura, Anne-Emanuelle Birn, Ben Brisbois, Donald C. Cole, Paul A. Hamel, Lori Hanson, Jamie Kneen, and Baijayanta Mukhopadhyay. "Who Will Publish Eulogies for the Victims of Barrick Gold?" *Briarpatch*, April 24, 2018. https://briarpatchmagazine.com/articles/view/who-will-publish-eulogies-for-the-victims-of-barrick-gold.

Sawyer, Suzana. "Crude Contamination: Law, Science, and Indeterminacy in Ecuador and Beyond." In *Subterrannean Estates: Life Worlds of Oil and Gas,* edited by Hannah Appel, Arthur Mason, and Michael Watts, 126–46. Ithaca, NY: Cornell University Press, 2015.

Schenker, Marc B., Maria Stoecklin, Kiyoung Lee, Rafael Lupercio, R. Jorge Zeballos, Paul Enright, Tamara Hennessy, and Laurel A. Beckett. "Pulmonary Function and Exercise-Associated Changes with Chronic Low-Level Paraquat Exposure." *American Journal of Respiratory and Critical Care Medicine* 170, no. 7 (2004): 773–79. https://doi.org/10.1164/rccm.200403-266OC.

Schlesinger, Stephen, Richard Nuccio, and Jennifer Schirmer. "Preserving Bitter Fruit: Re-examining US Intervention in Guatemala." *Harvard International Review* 21, no. 4 (Fall 1999): 24–29. https://www.jstor.org/stable/43648969.

Scott, Dayna Nadine. "Testing Toxicity: Proof and Precaution in Canada's Chemicals Management Plan." *Review of European Community & International Environmental Law* 18, no. 1 (2009): 59–76. https://doi.org/10.1111/j.1467-9388.2009.00621.x.

Scott, Dayna Nadine, and Sarah Lewis. "Sex and Gender in Canada's Chemicals Management Plan." In *Our Chemical Selves: Gender, Toxics, and Environmental Health*, edited by Dayna Nadine Scott, 78–104. Vancouver: UBC Press, 2015.

Sellers, Christopher. "From Poison to Carcinogen: Towards a Global History of Concerns about Benzene." *Global Environment* 7, no. 1 (2014): 38–71. https://doi.org/10.3197/197337314X13927191904808.

Sellers, Christopher C. *Hazards of the Job: From Industrial Disease to Environmental Health Science*. Chapel Hill: University of North Carolina Press, 1997.

Shade, Lindsay. "Sustainable Development or Sacrifice Zone? Politics below the Surface in Post-neoliberal Ecuador." *Extractive Industries and Society* 2, no. 4 (2015): 775–84. https://doi.org/10.1016/j.exis.2015.07.004.

Shattuck, Annie. "Generic, Growing, Green?: The Changing Political Economy of the Global Pesticide Complex." *Journal of Peasant Studies* 48, no. 2 (February 2021): 231–53. https://doi.org/10.1080/03066150.2020.1839053.

———. "Risky Subjects: Embodiment and Partial Knowledges in the Safe Use of Pesticide." *Geoforum* 123 (July 2021): 153–61. https://doi.org/10.1016/j.geoforum.2019.04.029.

Sherwood, Stephen G., and Myriam Paredes. "Dynamics of Perpetuation: The Politics of Keeping Highly Toxic Pesticides on the Market in Ecuador." *Nature and Culture* 9, no. 1 (March 2014): 21–44. https://doi.org/10.3167/nc.2014.090102.

Shim, Janet K., and L. Katherine Thomson. "The End of the Epidemiology Wars? Epidemiological 'Ethics' and the Challenge of Translation." *BioSocieties* 5, no. 2 (2010): 159–79.

Shiva, Vandana. *Monocultures of the Mind: Perspectives on Biodiversity and Biotechnology*. London: Zed Books, 1997.

———. *The Violence of the Green Revolution: Third World Agriculture, Ecology, and Politics*. Lexington: University Press of Kentucky, 2016.

Shreck, Aimee. "Resistance, Redistribution, and Power in the Fair Trade Banana Initiative." *Agriculture and Human Values* 22, no. 1 (March 2005): 17–29. https://doi.org/10.1007/s10460-004-7227-y.

Siebert, Francisca. "U. de Chile lamenta el fallecimiento de Alejandro Rojas, ex presidente de la FECh y diputado de la República." *Noticias*, Universidad de Chile, April 16, 2018. https://uchile.cl/noticias/142609/fallecio-alejandro-rojas-ex-presidente-de-la-fech.

SIPAE. *Atlas sobre la tenencia de la tierra en el Ecuador*. Quito: SIPAE, 2011.

SIPAE, Broederlijk Delen, and Oxfam. "Prácticas de compra y condiciones sociales, laborales y ambientales en las plantaciones bananeras ecuatorianas que exportan a Alemania." Quito: SIPAE, 2011.

Slutsky, Morley, Jeffrey L. Levin, and Barry S. Levy. "Azoospermia and Oligospermia among a Large Cohort of DBCP Applicators in 12 Countries." *International Journal of Occupational and Environmental Health* 5, no. 2 (1999): 116–22. https://doi.org/10.1179/oeh.1999.5.2.116.

Slutzky, Daniel, and Esther Alonso. *Empresas transnacionales y agricultura: El caso del enclave bananero en Honduras*. 3rd ed. Tegucigalpa, Honduras: Editorial Universitaria, 1982.

Smith, Alistair. "Worker- and Small Farmer-Led Strategies to Engage Lead Firms in Responsible Sourcing." In *Rethinking Value Chains: Tackling the Challenges of Global Capitalism*, edited by Florence Palpacuer and Alistair Smith, 133–51. Bristol, UK: Policy Press, 2021.

Smith, Sally. "Fairtrade Bananas: A Global Assessment of Impact." Sussex, UK: Institute of Development Studies, University of Sussex, 2010.

Soluri, John. "Accounting for Taste: Export Bananas, Mass Markets, and Panama Disease." *Environmental History* 7, no. 3 (2002): 386–410. https://doi.org/10.2307/3985915.

———. *Banana Cultures: Agriculture, Consumption, and Environmental Change in Honduras and the United States*. 2nd ed. Austin: University of Texas Press, 2021.

———. "Bananas Before Plantations. Smallholders, Shippers, and Colonial Policy in Jamaica, 1870–1910." *Iberoamericana* 6, no. 23 (2006): 143–59. https://doi.org/10.18441/ibam.6.2006.23.143-159.

———. "Bananas, Biodiversity and the Paradox of Commodification." In *Territories, Commodities and Knowledges: Latin American Environmental History in the Nineteenth and Twentieth Centuries*, edited by Christian Brannstrom, 195–217. London: Institute for the Study of the Americas, 2004.

Southgate, Douglas, and Lois Roberts. *Globalized Fruit, Local Entrepreneurs: How One Banana-Exporting Country Achieved Worldwide Reach*. Philadelphia: University of Pennsylvania Press, 2016.

Spiegel, Jerry M., Mariano Bonet, Ana-Maria Ibarra, Nino Pagliccia, Veronic Ouellette, and Annalee Yassi. "Social and Environmental Determinants of Aedes Aegypti Infestation in Central Havana: Results of a Case-Control Study Nested in an Integrated Dengue Surveillance Programme in Cuba." *Tropical Medicine & International Health* 12, no. 4 (2007): 503–10. https://doi.org/10.1111/j.1365-3156.2007.01818.x.

Spiegel, Jerry M., Jaime Breilh, and Annalee Yassi. "Why Language Matters: Insights and Challenges in Applying a Social Determination of Health Approach in a North-South Collaborative Research Program." *Globalization and Health* 11, no. 9 (February 2015). https://doi.org/10.1186/s12992-015-0091-2.

Springer, Simon. "Fuck Neoliberalism." ACME: *An International Journal for Critical Geographies* 15, no. 2 (2016): 285–92. https://acme-journal.org/index.php/acme/article/view/1342.

Stein, Serena, and Jessie Luna. "Toxic Sensorium: Agrochemicals in the African Anthropocene." *Environment and Society* 12, no. 1 (2021): 87–107. https://doi.org/10.3167/ares.2021.120106.

Striffler, Steve. "El fruto del neoliberalismo: Organización laboral transnacional en el contexto de la industria bananera global, y el caso ecuatoriano." *Clío América* 2, no. 4 (2008): 179–94.

———. *In the Shadows of State and Capital: The United Fruit Company, Popular Struggle, and Agrarian Restructuring in Ecuador, 1900–1995*. Durham, NC: Duke University Press, 2001.

———. "Rebellion, Revolution, and Reversal in Ecuador's Countryside." In *Fifty Years of Peasant Wars in Latin America*, edited by Leigh Binford, Lesley Gill, and Steve Striffler, 50–70. New York: Berghahn Books, 2020.

———. "Wedded to Work: Class Struggles and Gendered Identities in the Restructuring of the Ecuadorian Banana Industry." *Identities: Global Studies in Culture and Power* 6, no. 1 (1999): 91–120. https://doi.org/10.1080/1070289X.1999.9962637.

Studnicki-Gizbert, Daviken. "Canadian Mining in Latin America (1990 to Present): A Provisional History." *Canadian Journal of Latin American and Caribbean Studies / Revue canadienne des études latino-américaines et caraïbes* 41, no. 1 (2016): 95–113. https://doi.org/10.1080/08263366 3.2015.1134498.

Sultana, Farhana. "Emotional Political Ecology." In *The International Handbook of Political Ecology*, edited by Raymond Bryant, 633–45. Cheltenham, UK: Edward Elgar, 2015.

Sundberg, Juanita. "Ethics, Entanglement, and Political Ecology." In *The Routledge Handbook of Political Ecology*, edited by Tom Perrault, Gavin Bridge, and James McCarthy, 117–26. London: Routledge, 2015.

———."Looking for the Critical Geographer, or Why Bodies and Geographies Matter to the Emergence of Critical Geographies of Latin America." *Geoforum* 36, no. 1 (2005): 17–28. https://doi.org/10.1016/jgeoforum.2004.03.006.

Swezey, Sean L., Douglas L. Murray, and Rainer G. Daxl. "Nicaragua Revolution in Pesticide Policy." *Environment* 28, no. 1 (1986): 6–36. https://doi.org/10.1080/00139157.1986.9929866.

Sylva Charvet, Paola. "Los Productores de Banano." In *El banano en el Ecuador: Transnacionales, modernización y subdesarrollo*, edited by Carlos Larrea, 111–86. Quito: Corporación Editora Nacional, 1987.

Szklo, Moyses, and F. Javier Nieto. *Epidemiology: Beyond the Basics*. 4th ed. Toronto: Jones & Bartlett Learning, 2018.

Tannock, Stuart. "Learning to Plunder: Global Education, Global Inequality and the Global City." *Policy Futures in Education* 8, no. 1 (March 2010): 82–98. https://doi.org/10.2304/pfie.2010.8.1.82.

Tansey, James. "Risk as Politics, Culture as Power." *Journal of Risk Research* 7, no. 1 (2004): 17–32. https://doi.org/10.1080/1366987042000151188.

Taussig, Michael T. *The Devil and Commodity Fetishism in South America*. Chapel Hill: University of North Carolina Press, 1980.

Taylor, J. Gary, and Patricia J. Scharlin. *Smart Alliance: How a Global Corporation and Environmental Activists Transformed a Tarnished Brand*. New Haven, CT: Yale University Press, 2004.

Taylor, Marcus. "Success for Whom? An Historical-Materialist Critique of Neoliberalism in Chile." *Historical Materialism* 10, no. 2 (2002): 45–75. https://doi.org/10.1163/156920602320318084.

Tellez v. Dole Food Co., BC312852 (Cal. Super. Ct. L.A. Cnty., Sep. 21–26, 2009). Video recording accessed May 27, 2024, at https://cvn.com/proceedings/tellez-v-dole-trial-2007-07-19.

Theriault, Noah, and Simi Kang. "Toxic Research: Political Ecologies and the Matter of Damage." *Environment and Society* 12, no. 1 (2021): 5–24. https://doi.org/10.3167/ares.2021.120102.

Thrupp, Lori Ann. "The Political Ecology of Pesticide Use in Developing Countries: Dilemmas in the Banana Sector of Costa Rica." PhD Thesis, University of Sussex, 1988.

Trischitta, Marcello Maria Marrocco. "The Knights of Malta: A Legend towards the Future." Rome: Association of the Italian Knights of the Sovereign Military Order of Malta, 1999.

Trostle, James A. *Epidemiology and Culture*. New York: Cambridge University Press, 2005.

Tsing, Anna Lowenhaupt. *The Mushroom at the End of the World: On the Possibility of Life in Capitalist Ruins*. Princeton, NJ: Princeton University Press, 2021.

Tuck, Eve. "Suspending Damage: A Letter to Communities." *Harvard Educational Review* 79, no. 3 (2009): 409–28.

Turshen, Meredeth. "The Political Ecology of Disease." *Review of Radical Political Economics* 9, no. 1 (1977): 45–60. https://doi.org/10.1177/048661347700900104.

———. *The Political Ecology of Disease in Tanzania*. New Brunswick, NJ: Rutgers University Press, 1984.

United Nations Environment Programme. "Integrated Assessment of Trade Liberalization and Trade-Related Policies: A Country Study on the Banana Sector in Ecuador." New York: United Nations, 2002.

University of Toronto. "Miner's Lamp Award Dinner Raises $600,000 for Mental Health Research." *The Campaign*, March 31, 2017. https://boundless.utoronto.ca/news/miners-lamp-award-dinner-raises-600000-for-mental-health-research/.

Vandenberg, Laura N. "Low Dose Effects Challenge the Evaluation of Endocrine Disrupting Chemicals." *Trends in Food Science & Technology* 84 (2019): 58–61. https://doi.org/10.1016/j.tifs.2018.11.029.

Velásquez, Teresa A. "The Science of Corporate Social Responsibility (CSR): Contamination and Conflict in a Mining Project in the Southern Ecuadorian Andes." *Resources Policy* 37, no. 2 (2012): 233–40. https://doi.org/10.1016/j.resourpol.2011.10.002.

Viales Hurtado, Ronny J. "Más allá del enclave en Centroamérica: Aportes para una revisión conceptual a partir del caso de la región Caribe costarricense (1870–1950)." *Iberoamericana* 6, no. 23 (2006): 97–111. https://doi.org/10.18441/ibam.6.2006.23.97-111.

Vitali, Sofía. "Agroindustria y precarización laboral en el sector bananero de Los Ríos, Ecuador." *Revista Economía* 68, no. 107 (2016): 153–70. https://doi.org/10.29166/economia.v68i107.2004.

Vitali, Sofía, and Magali Marega. *Investigación sobre las Afectaciones Psicosociales de la Explotación Laboral y sus Repercusiones en el Ámbito Reproductivo*

(Familiar, Comunitario, Territorial) en el Sector Bananero de Ecuador (Los Ríos y El Oro). Ecuador: ASTAC and Oxfam, 2023.

Voltaire. *Candide*. Electronic Scholarly Publishing Project, 1998. http://www.esp.org/books/voltaire/candide.pdf.

Wallace, Rob. *Dead Epidemiologists: On the Origins of COVID-19*. New York: Monthly Review Press, 2020.

Wallace, Rob, Alex Liebman, Luis Fernando Chavez, and Rodrick Wallace. "COVID-19 and Circuits of Capital." *Monthly Review* 72, no. 1 (2020). https://monthlyreview.org/2020/04/01/covid-19-and-circuits-of-capital/.

Watson-Verran, Helen, and David Turnbull. "Science and Other Indigenous Knowledge Systems." In *Handbook of Science and Technology Studies*, edited by Sheila Jasanoff, Gerald E. Markle, James C. Petersen, and Trevor Pinch, 115–39. Thousand Oaks, CA: Sage Publications, 1995.

Weiler, Anelyse M., Chris Hergesheimer, Ben Brisbois, Hannah Wittman, Annalee Yassi, and Jerry M. Spiegel. "Food Sovereignty, Food Security and Health Equity: A Meta-Narrative Mapping Exercise." *Health Policy and Planning* 30, no. 8 (2015): 1078–92. https://doi.org/10.1093/heapol/czu109.

Wesseling, Catharina. "Dole and DBCP." *Pesticides-I Digest*, n.d.

Wesseling, Catharina, Anders Ahlbom, Daniel Antich, Ana Cecilia Rodriguez, and Roberto Castro. "Cancer in Banana Plantation Workers in Costa Rica." *International Journal of Epidemiology* 25, no. 6 (1996): 1125–31. https://doi.org/10.1093/ije/25.6.1125.

Wesseling, Catharina, Aurora Aragón, Luisa Castillo, Marianela Corriols, Fabio Chaverri, Elba De La Cruz, Matthew Keifer, et al. "Hazardous Pesticides in Central America." *International Journal of Occupational and Environmental Health* 7, no. 4 (2001): 287–94. https://doi.org/10.1179/107735201800339236.

Wesseling, Catharina, Marianela Corriols, and Viria Bravo. "Acute Pesticide Poisoning and Pesticide Registration in Central America." *Toxicology and Applied Pharmacology* 207, no. 2 suppl. (2005): 697–705. https://doi.org/10.1016/j.taap.2005.03.033.

Wesseling, Catharina, Rob McConnell, Timo J. Partanen, and Christer Hogstedt. "Agricultural Pesticide Use in Developing Countries: Health Effects and Research Needs." *International Journal of Health Services* 27, no. 2 (1997): 273–308. https://doi.org/10.2190/E259-N3AH-TAIY-H59I.

Wesseling, Catharina, Berna Van Wendel de Joode, Clemens Ruepert, Catalina León, Patricia Monge, Hernán Hermosillo, and Timo J.

Partanen. "Paraquat in Developing Countries." *International Journal of Occupational and Environmental Health* 7, no. 4 (2001): 275–86.

Whitten, Norman E. "Symbolic Inversion, the Topology of *El Mestizaje*, and the Spaces of *Las Razas* in Ecuador." *Journal of Latin American Anthropology* 8, no. 1 (2003): 52–85. https://doi.org/10.1525/jlca.2003.8.1.52.

Whyte, Kyle. "Indigenous Climate Change Studies: Indigenizing Futures, Decolonizing the Anthropocene." *English Language Notes* 55, no. 1 (2017): 153–62. https://doi.org/10.1215/00138282-55.1-2.153.

Wiley, James. *The Banana: Empires, Trade Wars, and Globalization*. Lincoln: University of Nebraska Press, 2008.

Wittman, Hannah. "Reconnecting Agriculture and the Environment: Food Sovereignty and the Agrarian Basis of Ecological Citizenship." In *Food Sovereignty: Reconnecting Food, Nature and Community*, edited by Hannah Wittman, Annette Aurélie Desmarais, and Nettie Wiebe, 91–105. Halifax, NS: Fernwood Publishing, 2010.

Women's Earth Alliance and Native Youth Sexual Health Network. "Violence on the Land, Violence on Our Bodies: Building an Indigenous Response to Environmental Violence." 2016. http://landbodydefense.org/uploads/files/VLVBReportToolkit_2017.pdf.

Zambrano-Ganchozo, Gabriela, Andrea Rodriguez-Ramos, Kenny Escobar-Segovia, Luis Duque-Cordova, and Daniela Guzmán-Cadena. "Neurotoxic Effects on Banana Workers Exposed to Agrochemicals: Ecuador Case Study." In *Emerging Research in Intelligent Systems: Proceedings of the CIT 2021, vol. 1*, edited by Miguel Botto-Tobar, Henry Cruz, Angela Díaz Cadena, and Benjamin Durakovic, 327–37. Cham, Switzerland: Springer International Publishing, 2022. https://doi.org/10.1007/978-3-030-96043-8_25.

Zamora Acosta, Giannina, and Efraín Hernández León. "La agroindustria del banano en el litoral sur ecuatoriano: Una mirada crítica desde la coremática." *Revista de Investigación Talentos* 8, no. 1 (2021): 62–83. https://doi.org/10.33789/talentos.8.1.144.

Žižek, Slavoj. *The Sublime Object of Ideology*. New York: Verso, 1989.

INDEX

Page numbers with (f) refer to illustrations.

A

A la costa (novel), 21–23, 24, 28, 45
academic institutions
    about, 236–240
    academic extractivism, 231
    community participatory research, 239
    depoliticized research articles, 204–208, 211–213, 281n8
    entanglements of injustices and good intentions, 236–240, 251–252, 275n4
    funding by banana industries, 279n16
    funding by Canadian mining industries, 143, 234–235, 238–239
    global North/South colonialism, 143, 233–234
    "heroic" discourses, 35–36, 213
    journal article genre's limitations, 206–207, 211–213
    neoliberal capitalist structures, 212–213, 236–240
    Northern gaze, 246
    "objectivity," 10, 140, 191, 207, 211–213, 238–239
Acción Ecológica, 119, 157, 162
Acosta, Jorge, 145–146
Acteal massacre (1997), 244
aerial fumigation. *See* fumigation, aerial
affect. *See* emotions
Afro-descended peoples, 23, 26, 125–127, 233, 264n15, 265n20, 265n30
    See also West Indian workers
agroecology. *See* fairtrade and organic producers and organizations
Alianza País. *See* Ecuador
Allende, Salvador, 78–79, 81, 83, 98, 270n2
Alliance for Progress, US, 63, 80
Amaya Amador, Ramón, 67–68
Amazon region, Ecuador. *See* Ecuadorian regions, Amazon (*el oriente*); petroleum industry, Ecuador
Amisacho, Lago Agrio, 162–165
Andean plateau. *See* Ecuadorian regions, *serranos* (highlanders) and *la sierra* (plateau)
Anthropocene/Capitalocene/Plantationocene, 167–171, 188, 248–249, 278n26
Arauz, Andrés, 157
Árbenz, Jacobo. *See* Guatemala, Árbenz's government (1951–54)
Arévalo, Juan José, 40, 42
Argentina, 62, 82
AsoGuabo, 220, 231
ASTAC (banana worker organization), Ecuador
    global solidarity, 6

influence on public policy, 208–209
research facilitator, 6, 116–117, 119, 145–146, 149–151, 154, 213, 231
Asturias, Miguel Ángel, 31–32, 175, 273n7

B

Baker, Lorenzo Dow, 15, 179
BanaFair, 101
bananas
  biotechnology for, 171
  global bioprospecting expeditions, 34–35
  herb grown from rhizomes, 12
  in more-than-human world, 31
  pre-colonial history, 22
bananas, Cavendish variety
  about, 32, 44, 61–62, 68–70
  changes to agroecologies, 68–73
  characteristics, 32, 44, 61–62, 68–69
  chemical pesticides, 10, 64, 69–76
  contract production, 10, 44
  decline in labour needs, 89
  quality standards, 70
  shift from Gros Michel, 10–11, 34–35, 44, 48, 60–62, 68, 71
  technification, 61–62, 68–70, 165–166
  TR4 fungal disease, 158–159, 171, 259
  transportation and preparation, 61, 68–69, 73
  women workers, 69
bananas, diseases
  disease resistance, 34–35, 171
  red stain disease, 168
  TR4 fungal disease, 158–159, 171, 259
  See also fungi; fungi, Panama disease; fungi, sigatoka
bananas, Gros Michel variety
  about, 16, 32–35, 68–69
  characteristics, 16, 32, 44, 68–69
  consumer preferences, 16, 217
  Jamaican trade, 10–11
  Panama disease, 33–37, 44, 48, 61, 68, 217
  shift to Cavendish, 10–11, 34–35, 44, 48, 60–62, 68, 71
  UFC preference for, 16, 68, 217
  West Indian workers, 33

yield and productivity, 61
banana industries
  about, 1–4, 31–37
  complicity with injustices, 234–240
  historical overview, 60–62
  incomplete corporate control, 20, 43–44
  narratives of tropical poverty, 184, 226
  See also research project
banana industries, corporations
  monocultures of the mind, 77, 83
  narratives of tropical poverty, 184, 226
  neoliberal globalization, 85, 90, 136
  statistics on exports, 62
  supermarket suppliers, 91, 154, 218–219
  See also Del Monte Foods Inc.; Dole/Standard Fruit; Noboa Group; plantations; UFC/Chiquita (United Fruit Company)
banana industries, labour. See labour; labour unions and labour relations; West Indian workers
banana industries, large and small producers. See contract farms; fairtrade and organic producers and organizations; plantations; small farms
banana industries, marketing
  about, 7–8, 17
  banana stickers, 6, 7, 8, 69, 180, 182, 183, 218
  CSR efforts, 93–94, 98, 101–103, 226
  Disney/Pixar stories, 7–8, 180–184, 279n11
  fairtrade and organic bananas, 5–6
  nutrition and diet, 7–8
  quality standards, 70
  supermarkets, 218
  See also brands and labels
banana industries, pesticides and herbicides. See fungicides; herbicides; insects and insecticides; nematicides; pesticide industries; pesticides
banana industries, pests. See fungi; insects and insecticides; nematodes

banana industries, public health. *See* pesticides, application methods; pesticides, exposures and health effects; pesticides, health effects; public health
banana industries, research. *See* academic institutions; epidemiology; political ecology of health (PEH); social science research; toxicology
banana republics, 6–7, 17–18, 41, 263n27, 264n15
banana stalk borer, 70
Bananas! (film, Gertten), 181, 279n12
"Bananas of the world, unite!" (song), 7
Banana Queen competition, 112, 129, 170, 273n6
Barraza, Douglas, 101
benomyl, 71–72
benthic macroinvertebrates, 73
better ways to live. *See* everyday life
biomedical evidence, 188, 203–204, 209, 213
    See also evidence-based approaches; public health science
Black people. *See* Afro-descended peoples; West Indian workers
black sigatoka, 71–72, 88, 100, 112, 123, 153, 258
    See also fungi, sigatoka
blaming victims. *See* individualizing narratives (victim-blaming)
Bocas del Toro region, 23, 25, 53–54, 179, 266n32
Bohme, Susanna Rankin, 102, 193–194, 196–197
Bolivia, 3, 225
Bonanza (label), 110
Bonita (brand), 91, 109–110, 257
Bordeaux mixture (fungicide), 52–55, 67–68, 71, 73, 257
Borja, Rodrigo, 147
Boston Fruit Company (UFC), 15–17, 32
Bourgois, Philippe, 53–54, 99, 179, 265n21, 266n32
Braiding Sweetgrass (Kimmerer), 215, 224–225, 285n15
brands and labels
    about, 5–7
    banana stickers, 6–8, 69, 180, 182, 183
    Bonanza (label), 110
    Bonita (Noboa brand), 91, 109–110, 257
    DBCP nematicide, 193–194
    fairtrade and organic marketing, 5–6
    Miss Chiquita, 6–7, 17, 179–184, 257, 262n25, 279n11
    supermarket labels, 218
    See also banana industries, marketing
Brave (film), 187–188, 279n11
Bread for the World, 101
Breilh, Jaime, 119–120, 275n2
Bribri people, 23, 266n32
Brisbois, Ben
    early life, 241–244
    education and career, 1, 201–202, 215–216, 232–238, 242, 248
    entanglements of injustices and good intentions, 236–240, 251–252, 275n4, 285n26
    family connections to Guatemala, 241–242
    health, 245, 248, 251
    optimism, 247–252
    personal acts of care, 212–213, 238
    public health perspectives, 236–240
    researcher, ix, 1, 77, 121, 127
    sister (Marie Claire), 241–243, 245–246
    social position, 11–12, 137–144, 242–243, 275n1
    "tending our garden," 248–252, 285n15
    travels in Mexico and Central America, 242–246, 251–252
    See also research project
Britain. *See* United Kingdom
Brown, Sandy, 220
Bucheli, Marco, 43–44, 263n9
A Bug's Life (film), 8, 182, 184
buying bananas. *See* consumers

C

cacao
    Amisacho reforested farm, 162–165
    cacao boom (1860–1920), 24, 25, 27–28, 45–47, 126

Hacienda Tenguel, 46–47, 64
migrant labour, 24, 27–28, 45–46, 126
racial stereotypes, 27–28
UFC history, 46–47, 64
UROCAL history, 6, 230–231, 259
Canada
    academic funding by industry, 143, 234–237
    entanglements of injustices and good intentions, 236–240, 275n4
    gold mines, 246
    gringos, 138, 142–143
    Indigenous peoples, 188, 225, 249
    mining imperialism, 143, 225, 234, 236, 238–239, 242, 246, 275nn5–6
    neoliberal foreign policy, 235, 238–239
    resource extraction, 142–143, 275nn5–6
Canadian International Resources and Development Institute (CIRDI), 235–236
Candide (Voltaire), 247–248
capitalism
    about, 168–170, 184, 226
    Capitalocene, 168–169, 188
    commodification, 169–171
    early history, 203
    vs. gift economies, 215, 224–226, 285n15
    global interconnections, 168–169
    individualizing narratives, 121, 170, 204, 275n3
    poverty narratives, 184, 203–204, 226
    power relations, 5, 203–204
    racial capitalism, 29–30, 188, 266n37
    social and racial hierarchies, 188
    vampires and ideology, 202–203, 281n5, 283n45
    See also Anthropocene/Capitalocene/Plantationocene; neoliberalism
capitanes (labour subcontractors), 1, 18–19, 116–117, 148, 149–151
carbamates (pesticides), 59–60, 73
Caribbean labour. *See* West Indian workers
Carrillo García, Germán, 231
Carter, Jimmy, 195–196
Castle & Cooke, 75, 98–99, 194, 258
    See also Dole/Standard Fruit

Castree, Noel, 240
Castro, Fidel, 5, 78–79
Catholic Church, 100–101, 241–242
Cavendish. *See* bananas, Cavendish variety
Central America
    about, 10
    banana republics, 17–18
    black sigatoka, 88
    Bocas del Toro region, 23, 25, 53–54, 179, 266n32
    foreign-owned enclaves, 48
    Green Revolution, 80
    health research, 99–103, 119–120
    health-focused resistance, 98–100
    hurricanes, 88, 91–92, 167
    IRET studies, 102, 207, 258
    lawsuits, 196–197
    monocultural plantations, 32, 62
    neoliberalism, 82, 88, 94–95
    poverty narratives, 184, 226
    railways, 16–17, 22–25, 167
    shift to Cavendish, 61
    US imperialism, 17
    West Indian workers, 25, 249
    See also Costa Rica; Guatemala; Honduras; Nicaragua; Panama
Central American Institute for Studies on Toxic Substances (IRET), 102, 107, 258
certifications. *See* fairtrade and organic standards and certifications
chemical pesticide industries. *See* pesticide industries
Chevron/Texaco, 87, 162, 163(f), 166, 198, 212, 282n31
children
    child labour, xi, 7
    disabilities, 119, 145
    pesticide exposures, x, xi, 7, 118, 247
Chile
    Allende's presidency, 78–79, 81, 83, 98, 270n2
    coup (1973), 79, 94, 98, 270n2
    elite alliances, 98, 270n2
    nationalization of mines, 81
    neoliberalism, 79, 82, 83

Pinochet's presidency, 79–80, 82, 242–243
Chiquita, Miss, 6–7, 17, 179–184, 257, 279n11
Chiquita Brands International S.à.r.l.
　Disney/Pixar stories, 7–8, 180–184, 247, 279n11
　name changes, 179, 257, 262n25
　See also UFC/Chiquita (United Fruit Company)
chlorpyrifos, x, xi
Chomsky, Aviva, 266n34
Ciénaga massacre (1928), Colombia, 18–19, 25, 93, 158, 178–179, 250
CIRDI (Canadian International Resources and Development Institute), 235–236
class. See elites; social class
climate change
　Anthropocene/Capitalocene/Plantationocene, 167–171
　global interconnections, 161–162, 166–168
　petroleum industries, 166–167
　questioning of monocultures, 223–224
coastal people. See Ecuadorian regions, *costeños* (coastal people) and *la costa*
Coco (film), 182
Colby, Jason, 23–24, 263n9, 264n10, 265nn20–21
Cole, Donald, 285n26
Coleman, Kevin, 178
Collard, Rosemary-Claire, 188
Colombia
　about, 18–19, 92–95
　black sigatoka, 88
　CSR efforts, 93–94
　early history, 9, 10, 18–19, 22, 28
　elites, 18–19, 93
　Gros Michel bananas, 32
　labour relations, 18–19, 25–26, 93–95
　massacre in Ciénaga (1928), 18–19, 25, 93, 158, 177, 178–179, 250
　monocultural plantations, 32
　Panama disease, 46
　paramilitaries (AUC, FARC), 9, 93–94, 218

　racial stereotypes, 28
　TR4 fungal disease, 159
　UFC history, 18–19, 94–95
　US imperialism, 17, 19, 178–179
　workers, 18–19, 25, 92–93
colonialism
　about, 21–23, 27–28, 226
　banana research, 268n2
　"civilizing mission," 27–28, 55, 205
　corporate colonialism, 21, 44
　development and progress narratives, 35–37, 235–237
　financing of projects, 23–24
　gendered narratives, 27, 27(f)
　imaginative geographies, 27–29, 35, 205, 265n27
　PEH critiques of, 233–234
　poverty narratives, 184, 226
　power dynamics, 5
　pre-colonial history, 22
　racism, 21, 27–28
　See also Indigenous peoples, colonialism
COLSIBA (Latin American Organization of Banana Unions), 94, 252, 257
commodities. See petroleum industry, Ecuador
community health. See public health
community participatory research, 239
consumers
　about, 5–6, 215–217, 227
　conscious consumption, 5–6, 11, 215–216, 227
　fossil fuels in food systems, 167
　gift economies, 215, 224–226, 285n15
　market-based approaches to activism, 5–6, 215–217, 221–224, 227
　See also banana industries, marketing; everyday life
contract farms
　about, 44, 47–49, 90–91, 117–118, 149–150
　in Colombia, 18–19
　Del Monte, 89
　Dole/Standard Fruit, 88–89, 92
　economic precarity, 139

in Ecuador, 47–49, 51, 77, 88–89, 115–118, 129–136, 139
elites, 139, 181
emotional stress, 129–136, 275n1
fairtrade and organic farms, 117, 132–136
labour issues, 86, 90–91, 115–118, 149–150
neoliberal reforms, 90–91, 131, 154
pesticide use, 88–89, 117–118, 194
precarious employment, xi, 90–91, 117, 122, 139, 149, 157, 181
quality standards, 88, 117
shift to contract farms, 44–45, 47–49, 68, 77, 117–118, 181
technification, 88–89
transnational markets, 117–118
UFC history, 18–19, 44–45, 47–49, 68
workers, 86, 117–118, 149–150
contract workers for subcontractors (*capitanes*), 1, 18–19, 116–117, 148, 149–151
co-operative organizations
AsoGuabo co-op, 220, 231
everyday life, 129–136, 138
history of, 16
leadership, 220
research facilitators, 6, 127, 142
transnational solidarity, 132, 142
UROCAL co-op, 6, 222–223, 230–231
See also fairtrade and organic producers and organizations; social justice and environmental movements; UROCAL fairtrade and organic co-op, Ecuador
corm weevil, banana, 70
corporate social responsibility (CSR), 93–94, 98, 101–103, 226
Correa, Rafael, x, 109, 116, 145–156, 210, 231–232
Costa Rica
Bocas del Toro region, 23, 25, 53–54, 179, 266n32
DBCP use, 74–75, 100, 102, 195
Dole history, 195
early history, 17, 23–24
Foro Emaús, 101–103, 207, 208, 242
health effects, 73, 100, 102, 195

health research, 100–103, 119–120, 205, 211
Indigenous peoples, 23, 26, 53, 54, 266n32
industry influence on research, 211
IRET studies, 102, 207, 258
labour relations, 6, 26, 54–55, 97, 100
lawsuits, 100, 102, 196–197
liberation theology, 100–101, 242
neoliberalism, 100
Panama disease, 37, 267n31
pesticide use, 52–55, 69–70, 100–103, 205, 208
public health advocacy, 100–103, 208
racism, 37, 54–55
shift to Cavendish, 61
sigatoka fungus, 52–55, 71, 100
SITRAP union, 101, 258
solidarista associations, 100–101
strike (1934), 6, 26, 97
UFC history, 17, 23, 37, 52–55, 70, 100
US imperialism, 17, 99, 100
Costco, 115
costeños. *See* Ecuadorian regions, *costeños* (coastal people) and *la costa*
Coto, Alfonso, 100–101, 242
court actions. *See* laws and lawsuits
COVID-19
economic and social impacts, 210
in Ecuador, 156–158, 161
as *plaga*, 153, 156–158
CSR (corporate social responsibility), 93–94, 98, 101–103, 226
Cuba, 5, 17, 63
Cuenca, Ecuador, 141, 225
Cuyamel Fruit Company, 17, 18, 20, 41, 183

D

DBCP nematicide
about, 8, 74–75, 193–199, 257
application methods, 74–75
brands, 193–194
chemical plant workers, 194–195
Del Monte, 193–194
documentary film (*Bananas!*), 181
Dole history, 98–99, 193–196, 211
Dole's DBCP Facts, 8, 74, 181, 193

Dow and Shell production, 74, 193–195
health effects, 74, 75, 181, 193–195, 197
individualizing narratives, 194
ineffectiveness of PPE, 75
lawsuits, 75, 98, 181, 196–199, 210–211, 280n27
as nematicide, 8, 193, 257
research on, 75, 118, 193–194, 233–234
safe-use campaigns, 194
UFC history, 75, 193–195
US history, 75, 193–196
DDT, 69, 71, 73
Dead Sea Bromine Co., 193–194, 196
Defensoría del Pueblo (ombudsperson), Ecuador, 119, 145, 274n20
deforestation, 24, 33–34, 167, 217
Del Monte Foods Inc.
    DBCP use, 193–194
    ISO standards, 218
    Noboa's lobbying against, 87
    technification, 89
    UFC history, 9, 43, 68
    See also banana industries
Deleuze, Gilles, and Guattari, Felix, 12
Dempsey, Jessica, 188
Despicable Me (film series), 7, 180–184, 279n11
development narratives, 35–37, 235–237
diazinon, 71
dibromochloropropane. *See* DBCP nematicide
dieldrin, 70–72
diseases, banana. *See* bananas, diseases
diseases, human. *See* illness and disease
Disney/Pixar stories, 7–8, 180–184, 187–188, 247, 279n11
Dole/Standard Fruit
    about, 17, 88–89, 258
    Bananas! (film), 181, 279n12
    contract production, 88–89, 92
    corporate history of, 43, 48, 68, 98–99, 194, 258
    DBCP Facts, 8, 74, 181, 193
    DBCP use, 8, 74, 98–99, 181–182, 193–196, 211, 280n27
    Disney/Pixar stories, 7–8, 180–184, 279n11

early history, 17, 89
funding of educational institutions, 279n16
ISO standards, 218
lawsuits, 8, 181, 196–199, 211, 279n12, 280n27
more-than-human threats, 91
neoliberalism, 89
in Nicaragua, 98–99
Panama disease, 34, 43, 44
shift to Cavendish, 44, 61, 68
technification, 89
trade statistics, 88–89
See also banana industries
Dominica, 221
Dominican Republic, 17
Dow Chemical Company, 68, 74, 75, 109, 193–194, 280n27
Dracula (Stoker), 202–203

E

economy, capitalist. *See* capitalism; neoliberalism
Ecuador
    about, 60–62, 116, 146–157
    cacao boom (1860–1920), 24, 25, 45–46
    "Citizens' Revolution," 109, 146
    coalition of civil society groups, 116, 147–148, 152
    constitutional rights (2008), 116, 148
    Correa's government (2007–17), x, 109, 116, 145–156, 210, 231–232, 236
    COVID-19 response, 156–158, 210
    crime, 131–132, 157–158, 161
    currency, 92
    economic stresses, 91–92, 136, 156–158
    el paro uprisings (2019), 155–156, 157, 235
    elite alliances, 45–46, 48–49, 138–139, 146–148, 152
    extractivism, 147–148, 152, 153–154, 161, 232
    industry influence on public policy, 208–210, 281n20
    in *A la costa* (novel), 21–23, 24, 28, 45
    labour exploitation, 62, 145–152, 154
    land reforms, 146–147

Lasso's government (2021–23), 157–158
Mandate 8, 116–117, 148, 149–151
Moreno's government (2017–21), 109, 147–148, 153–157, 210
neoliberalism, 85, 89–91, 94–95, 131–132, 136, 153–156, 161
D. Noboa's government (2023–), 158
ombudsperson (Defensoría del Pueblo), 119, 145, 274n20
poverty, 24, 48, 157, 184, 226
in *Qué Tan Lejos* (film), 137–138
racism, 24, 27–28, 46, 125–127, 180, 264n15
"21st century socialism," x, 116, 154
Ecuador, banana industries
  about, 21, 44, 48–49, 60–62
  atmospheric events, 167–168
  banana boom (1948–65), 48–49, 108, 110
  capital flows to global North, 49
  corporate colonialism, 21, 44
  Dole/Standard Fruit, 48–49, 195
  global reserve supplier, 87–88, 91, 94
  historical overview, 60–62
  labour rights, 116–117, 148
  labour subcontractors, 90–91, 116–117, 148
  as leading exporter, 44, 48–49, 62
  local entrepreneurs, 48–49, 91
  minimum prices, 150
  more-than-human world, 167–168
  neoliberalism, 90–91, 94–95, 136
  Panama disease, 48, 54
  racist practices, 21
  shift from grower to marketer, 44, 47–49
  shift to Cavendish, 44, 48, 61–62, 68
  shift to contract producers, 44, 48–49, 61–62, 68
  supermarket supplier, 91, 115–116
  UFC history, 46–49, 60–62
  See also Noboa Group; research project; technification; UFC/Chiquita (United Fruit Company)
Ecuador, Indigenous peoples
  Alianza País coalition, 116, 146–148
  Amazon region, 155, 162, 164, 165
  Andean markets, 225
  CONAIE confederation, 155
  constitutional rights (2008), 116, 148
  el paro uprisings (2019), 155–156, 157, 235
  environmental justice, 148, 162
  individualizing narratives, 125–127, 142
  Kichwa, xii, 107, 116, 164, 225, 252
  lack of *cultura*, 125–127
  land reforms, 24, 146–147
  levantamientos uprisings (1990s), 91, 137, 147
  Pachamama (nature), 107, 116
  poverty, 125–126
  racism, 24, 125–126
  resistance to extractivism, 148, 155–156, 235
Ecuador, petroleum industry. *See* petroleum industry, Ecuador
Ecuadorian cities and provinces. *See* El Oro province, Ecuador; Guayas province, Ecuador; Los Ríos province, Ecuador; Machala, Ecuador; Quito, Ecuador
Ecuadorian regions, Amazon (*el oriente*)
  about, 162–167, 258
  Afro-Ecuadorians, 164–165
  Amisacho reforested farm, 162–165
  Chevron/Texaco, 87, 162, 163(f), 166, 198, 212, 282n31
  Correa era, 147–148, 155, 210, 232
  el paro uprising (2019), 155–156, 157
  environmental degradation, 162–167, 212, 232
  Indigenous peoples, 155, 162, 164, 165
  lawsuits, 162, 166, 212
  mushroom operations, 164
  petroleum industry, 87–88, 91–92, 165–167
  petroleum revenues, 146, 165, 210
Ecuadorian regions, *costeños* (coastal people) and *la costa*
  cacao boom (1860–1920), 24, 25
  certified farms, 219–220
  crime, 131–132
  emotional stress, 129–136, 275n1
  ethnographic fieldwork in, 122

floods, 92
future aspirations, 171–172
individualizing narratives, 121, 123–127, 129–132, 136, 233
lack of *cultura*, 123–127, 131–132, 233
land reforms, 63–64
organic and fairtrade farmers, 168
power relations, 123–124
racial and regional hierarchies, 125–127
research fieldwork in, 77–78, 121–122
stereotypes, 27–28, 122–127, 131–132, 234, 265n30
Ecuadorian regions, *serranos* (highlanders) and *la sierra* (plateau)
Indigenous peoples, 24
individualizing narratives, 125–127
landowners, 24, 46
mestizos, 24, 126–127
migration, xii, 24, 28, 46, 164, 230
potato farms, 125
poverty, 24
racial and regional hierarchies, 125–127
racism, 24, 125–127
serranos, 24, 126–127
stereotypes of migrants from, 27–28, 126–127, 265n30
Ecuaquímica, 109, 110
Efraín (participant), x, xii
El Niño–Southern Oscillation (ENSO), 167–168
el oriente. See Ecuadorian regions, Amazon (*el oriente*)
El Oro province, Ecuador
labour exploitation, 150–152
land reforms, 63–64
organic and fairtrade farmers, 168, 219
research fieldwork in, 77–78
See also Ecuadorian regions, *costeños* (coastal people) and *la costa*; Machala, Ecuador
El Salvador, 42, 82
Elías Caro, Jorge Enrique, 263n9
elites
alliances, 18, 22–23, 92, 94–95, 108, 152
banana booms, 108
cultured *mestizos*, 23
inequities and power relations, 122

land grants to US interests, 22–23
for modernization, 22–23
neoliberal governments, 86, 94–95, 156
Noboa, 63–64, 87, 92, 116, 271n30
racism, 235
white elites, 23
See also *specific countries*
emotions
discomfort, 252
hopefulness, 184
PEH approach, 233
power of stories, 9–10, 184, 251–252
stress, 129–136, 275n1
entanglement, as term, 275n4
environmental degradation
deforestation, 24, 33–34, 167, 217
petroleum industry waste, 162–167, 212, 232
plantation monocultures, 32–34, 52, 55, 69, 223–224
political ecology of health, 262n18
See also pesticides
environmental health sciences. See public health science
environmental movements.
See social justice and environmental movements
epidemiology
about, 2, 9, 201, 233–234
depoliticized research articles, 204–208, 211–213, 281n8
failure to impact pesticide use, 207–213
hierarchy of evidence, 201–202
human data from "developing countries," 203–205
PEH critiques of, 4–5, 233–234
research challenges, 2–3, 119–120
research methods, 81, 118, 119, 201–202
social determinants of health, 3, 11, 120, 210, 239
See also public health science
Escobar, Arturo, 206
Esmeraldas province, Ecuador, 46, 158, 265n30
ethnographic research and positionality, 137–144, 275n1
EurepGAP, 218–220

Europe
  fairtrade and organic solidarity, 6, 151, 222, 223
  gringos, as term, 138
  preferences for former colonies, 86, 221
  Rainforest Alliance, 218
  supermarkets, 154, 218
  witchcraft ways of knowing, 188, 281n3
everyday life
  about, 212–213, 229, 238
  acts of care, 212–213, 238
  food sovereignty, 11, 249–251
  gift economies, 215, 224–226, 285n15
  non-heroic everyday actions, 212–213, 229
  "noticing" life stories, 229–230
  "plotting" better stories, 11, 185, 248–252
  social knowledge as "non-scientific," 188, 190–191, 198–199
  tending our garden, 248–250, 285n15
  See also consumers
evidence-based approaches
  about, 187, 198–199, 207–213, 229
  depoliticized research articles, 204–208, 211–213, 281n8
  evidence, as term, 187, 198–199
  failure to impact pesticide use, 207–213
  human data from "developing countries," 203–205
  neoliberal contexts, 210
  "objectivity," 10, 140, 191, 207, 211–213, 238–239
  social determinants of health, 3, 210
  social knowledge as "non-scientific," 188, 190–191, 198–199
  See also epidemiology; social science research; toxicology
Exportadora Bananera Noboa, 48–49, 257
  See also Noboa Group
extractivism. *See* banana industries; mines and mining; petroleum industry, Ecuador
extractivism, academic, 231
Ezechiels, Anna María, 273n6

F

fairtrade and organic producers and organizations
  about, 132–136, 216–224
  AsoGuabo, 220, 231
  economic precarity, 219–220, 227
  environmental concerns, 133–134
  food sovereignty, 11, 249–251
  fundamental rights of workers, 6
  global solidarity, 5–6, 132–133, 136, 204–205, 216
  influence on public policy, 208–209
  integrated pest management, 98, 99, 272n6
  labour issues, 117
  market-based approaches, 216–217, 221–224, 227
  marketing, 5–6
  neoliberal models, 216–217, 221–223
  non-certified producers, 218–219
  North/South power relations, 221–224
  organic ambitions, 133
  social and emotional support, 132–136, 275n1
  social projects funding, 132
  worker health, 151
  See also consumers; co-operative organizations; UROCAL fairtrade and organic co-op, Ecuador
fairtrade and organic standards and certifications
  about, 5–6, 218–223
  affordability of improved practices, 219–220
  Banana Link, 222, 223–224
  bananas that exceed standards, 230
  EurepGAP and GlobalGAP, 218–220
  fairtrade certification, 117, 220–222
  GAP (good agricultural practices) standards, 218–220
  ISO standards, 218
  limited impacts, 220–222, 226
  neoliberal models, 221–224
  NGO funding, 219–220
  precarious labour, 220
  Rainforest Alliance, 101, 163–164, 218, 220
  small/large farms, 219–224

UFC history, 163–164
UN Sustainable Development
  Goals, 222
Fallas, Carlos Luis, 97
farm workers. *See* labour
Favorita (Wong's company), 91
Federici, Silvia, 188
females. *See* women
feminist scholarship, 138, 140, 213, 238, 252
FENACLE health research, 118
fertilizers, chemical, 61–62, 73, 80, 89, 109–110
films
  Bananas!, 181
  Brave, 187–188, 279n11
  A Bug's Life, 8, 182, 184
  Coco, 182
  Despicable Me (series), 7, 180–184, 279n11
  Inside Out, 8
  Minions, 180, 279n11
  Monsters Inc., 8, 279n11
  Qué Tan Lejos, 137–138
  Toy Story, 8
food
  Cuenca markets, 225
  food sovereignty, 11, 249–251, sss
  gift economies, 215, 224–226, 285n15
  recipe for banana bread, 286
  Three Sisters gardens, 248–249, 285n15
Foro Emaús, Costa Rica, 101–103, 207, 208, 242
Forster, Cindy, 42
Foucault, Michel, 203
Freire, Paulo, 78
Frundt, Henry, 91
fumigation, aerial
  lack of worker protections, 122
  operations, x–xi, xiii, 7, 70, 74, 110, 112, 118–119
  pilots' health complaints (2007), 119, 145, 274n20
  See also PPE (personal protective equipment)
fungi
  about, 32–33, 258, 259
  Fusarium epidemics, 33–35, 52, 258, 259

TR4 fungal disease, 158–159, 171, 259
  witches' broom, 45
fungi, Panama disease
  about, 32–37, 52, 71, 258
  abandoned and flooded plantations, 33–34, 40–41
  British bioprospecting expeditions, 34–35
  Cavendish resistance, 35, 44, 61, 69
  compared to sigatoka, 52
  cultivation shifts to avoid, 33–34, 68, 217
  deforestation, 33–34, 217
  Dole/Standard Fruit, 34, 43, 44
  Gros Michel susceptibility, 33–37, 44, 48, 61, 68
  names for, 33, 258
  progress narratives, 35–37
  TR4 fungal disease related to, 158–159, 171, 259
  UFC history, 33–37, 43–44, 249
fungi, sigatoka
  about, 51, 258
  black sigatoka, 71–72, 88, 100, 112, 123, 153, 258
  Bordeaux mixture (fungicide), 52–55, 67–68, 71, 73, 257
  compared to Panama disease, 52
  global diversity, 268n2
  impacts on banana industry, 54, 71
  resistance to fungicides, 72
  yellow sigatoka, 51, 71, 258
fungicides
  application methods, xi, 52–53, 54, 67, 71–72, 145
  benomyl, 71–72
  Bordeaux mixture, 52–55, 67–68, 71, 73, 257
  child exposures, xi, 7, 118, 247
  health effects, 53–55, 145
  more-than-human world, 72–73
  to prevent crown stem rot, 73
  resistance to, 70–72, 168, 268n2
  shift to synthetics (1960s), 52, 55
  for sigatoka, 71–72, 168
  spray workers ("parakeets"), 52–55, 67–68

for TR4 fungal disease, 158–159, 171, 259
UFC history, 52–55, 72
See also fumigation, aerial
Fusarium oxysporum, 33, 258, 259
See also fungi, Panama disease
Fusarium oxysporum, TR4 fungal disease, 158–159, 171, 259

G

Gaitán, Juan Eliécer, 93
Galarza Suárez, Lucía, 147, 150–152
García Márquez, Gabriel, 19, 177, 178, 184
gender
    Banana Queen competition, 112, 129
    colonial narratives, 27, 27(f)
    Green Revolution violence, 109
    masculinity of *mestizo* workers, 54
    witchcraft ways of knowing, 188, 281n3
    See also women
Gertten, Fredrik, 181, 279n12
gift economies, 215, 224–226, 285n15
GlobalGAP, 218–220
glossary, 257–259
gold mines. *See* mines and mining
government regulation. *See* regulation, government
Gramsci, Antonio, 240
Grandin, Greg, 81–82, 267n11
Green Revolution
    about, 80–82, 204
    benefits promoted by, 204, 249–251
    counter-movements, 249–250, 272n6
    "developing" countries narrative, 80, 125, 203–207, 212, 222
    health effects, 80–81, 204
    neoliberalism, 125
    PEH critiques of, 233–234, 249–250
    pesticide marketing, 109
    pesticide treadmill, 72, 80, 272n6
    petroleum products, 166
    poverty narratives, 184, 203–204, 226
    racist narratives, 121, 165, 235–236
    "safe" thresholds of exposures, 82, 125, 189–190, 192, 194
    scientific justification, 203–204
    technification, 147–148
    US military interventions, 81–83
    violence of, 109
    See also pesticide industries; technification
Greene, Natalia, 146–147
gringos, as term, 138
Gros Michel. *See* bananas, Gros Michel variety
Grupo Noboa. *See* Noboa Group
Guatemala
    about, 39–44, 246–247
    author's family connections, 241–243
    contract farms, 181
    dictatorships, 40, 42, 245
    elites, 26, 40, 42–43, 235
    hurricanes, 40, 44
    Indigenous peoples, 39–40, 43, 246
    labour organizing, 26–27
    ladinos (mestizos), 26
    massacres, 42, 242
    mining industry, 242, 246
    more-than-human world, 40, 43–44
    Panama disease, 37, 40–41, 43–44
    poverty, 40, 226, 245, 246
    racism, 26, 37, 40, 43
    safe-use campaigns, 192
    shift to Cavendish, 61
    UFC history, 17, 26–27, 37, 39–44, 179, 183, 235
    US imperialism, 82, 245
    in *Viento Fuerte* (novel), 31–32, 175, 273n7
    West Indian workers, 26, 37, 40
Guatemala, Árbenz's government (1951–54)
    about, 40–44, 181, 245
    as "communist threat," 42–43, 63, 178–179, 181, 192, 245, 250, 267n12
    coup (1954), 42–44, 63, 68, 179, 183, 250, 267n12
    land reforms, 40–43, 62, 81
    UFC role in coup, 42–44, 183, 267n12
    US imperialism, 17, 26, 42–44, 82, 250, 267n12
Guayaquil, Ecuador, 107–108, 126, 151, 156, 161, 234
Guayas province, Ecuador
    economic precarity, 135

health research, 118–119
  labour issues, 115–117, 150–151
  See also Hacienda Tenguel, Ecuador
Guevara, Ernesto "Che," 5, 244
Guthman, Julie, 216, 223

H

Hacienda Los Álamos (Noboa), 115–117
Hacienda Tenguel, Ecuador
  about, 46–49, 230–232
  agro-ecological farms, 230–232, 249
  cacao boom (1860–1920), 46–47, 64
  descendants of protesters, 230–232, 249
  environmental degradation, 231–232
  gold mines, 230, 232, 269n15
  labour unrest, 47, 230
  land reforms, 62–64, 230, 269n15
  military occupations, 62–64, 230, 231, 250
  occupation by workers (1962), 230
  Panama disease, 47
  shift to contract production, 48, 49, 68
  social infrastructure, 46–47
  UFC history, 46–49, 63
  UROCAL co-op, 230–232
  workers, 46–47, 49, 269n15
Haiti, 17
  See also West Indian workers
Harding, Sandra, 265n28
Harvard School of Tropical Medicine, 279n16
health
  constitutional rights (2008), 116
  COVID-19, 156–158
  emotional stress, 129–136, 275n1
  health as ability to work, 122
  political ecology of health, 275n4
  precarity of health, 122, 157
  traditional practices, 111, 122, 274n4
  women's labour, 131–132
  See also individualizing narratives (victim-blaming); pesticides, health effects; public health
herbicides
  health effects, 99
  paraquat, 1, 73, 99, 209, 211
  research on, 99, 209, 211

toxicity, 73, 209
  uses on plantations, 69, 72–73, 163, 209
Hergesheimer, Chris, 222–223
highlanders. *See* Ecuadorian regions, *serranos* (highlanders) and *la sierra* (plateau)
Honduras
  black sigatoka, 71, 74
  coup (1911), 41–42, 183
  Cuyamel Fruit Co., 17–18, 20, 41–42, 183
  DBCP use, 74, 193–195
  demographics, 17
  Dole/Standard Fruit, 17, 20, 195
  early history, 16–17, 20
  hurricanes, 88
  industry influence on public policy, 281n20
  labour unrest, 20, 42
  migration of workers, 54
  Panama disease, 33–34, 217, 267n31
  in *Prisión Verde* (novel), 67–68
  shift to Cavendish, 61
  UFC history, 16–17, 20, 33–34, 41–42, 217–218
  US imperialism, 17–18, 41–42, 99
Human Rights Watch report (2002), xi, 7, 115, 118, 141
hurricanes and cyclones
  banana industry impacts, 167–168
  Central America, 91, 92, 167
  Guatemala, 40, 44
  Honduras (1974), 88
  Jamaica (1898), 32
  Pacific cyclones, 167

I

IDRC (International Development Research Centre), 232, 234, 236, 284n22
IFA health research, 118, 121
illness and disease
  lack of *cultura*, 123–127, 131–132, 233
  malaria, 36
  tuberculosis, 5, 53, 67
  West Indian workers' immunities, 36
  yellow fever, 36

See also individualizing narratives (victim-blaming); pesticides, health effects
illness and disease, prevention. *See* public health; public health science
imaginative geographies, 27–29, 35, 205, 265n27
IMF (International Monetary Fund), 89–90, 155–156, 161, 210, 221
imperialism
    Canada's mining industries, 143, 225, 234, 236, 238–239, 242, 246, 275nn5–6
    historical overview, 60–62
    imaginative geographies, 27–28
    PEH critiques of, 233–234
    poverty narratives, 184, 226
    See also United States
Indigenous peoples
    banana varieties, 35
    gift economies, 215, 224–226, 285n15
    healing practices, 111, 122, 188
    ideals of well-being, 225, 244, 285n15
    land-based learning, 285n35
    pre-colonial bananas, 22
    Quechua language family, xii
    traditional knowledges, 35, 165, 188, 267n20
    traditional territories, 23, 164–165
    See also Ecuador, Indigenous peoples
Indigenous peoples, colonialism
    as banana workers, 26, 28, 37, 180
    difference-making processes, 188
    lack of *cultura*, 24, 125–127
    land dispossession, 23–24, 244, 266n32
    levantamientos uprisings (1990s), 91, 137, 147
    petroleum industry, 162
    poverty, 125–126
    progress narratives, 35–37
    racial and class hierarchies, 23–24, 27–28, 126–127, 264n15
    stereotypes, 180
    US imperialism, 225
    See also Anthropocene/Capitalocene/Plantationocene
individualizing narratives (victim-blaming)
    about, 121, 123–124, 129–132, 136, 170, 212–213, 233
    capitalist ideology, 121, 130, 275n3
    educational aspirations, 129–130
    lack of *cultura*, 123–127, 129–132, 170, 191–192, 233
    neoliberalism, 125, 132, 136, 275n3
    PEH's critique of, 233
    pesticide exposures, 3, 64–65, 123, 129–130, 136, 191–192, 194, 233
    racial stereotypes, 125–127, 129–130, 170
    social and racial hierarchies, 123–127, 129–130, 142
    toxicology studies, 191–192, 212
    ubiquity of, 136, 142, 275n3
insects and insecticides
    about, 69–73
    application methods, x, xi, 69–71, 166
    banana corm weevil, 70
    banana stock borer, 70
    health effects, 150, 281n20
    insecticides, x, xi, 69–73, 166, 209
    more-than-human world, 31, 70
    mosquitoes and malaria, 36–37, 54
    refusal to ban, 209, 281n20
    thrips, 70–72, 168
    UFC history, 70–71
Inside Out (film), 8
integrated pest management (IPM), 98, 99, 272n6
International Development Research Centre (IDRC), 232, 234, 236, 284n22
International Monetary Fund (IMF), 89–90, 155–156, 161, 210, 221
interviews. *See* research project
IRET (Central American Institute for Studies on Toxic Substances), 102, 207, 258
Isch, Edgar, 231

J

Jamaica, 15–16, 25–26, 32–34, 179, 249
    See also West Indian workers
Jansen, Kees, 68–69, 218
Janssen Pharmaceuticals, 110, 111(f)
Jordanova, Ludmila, 178
journals, scientific, 10, 204–208, 211–213

See also academic institutions

K

Karnes, Thomas L., 201, 280n1
Keith, Minor, 16–17, 22–25, 32
Kennedy, John F.., 63
Kichwa people, xii, 107, 116, 164, 225, 252
Kimmerer, Robin Wall, 215, 224–225, 285n15
Klein, Naomi, 83
Knights of Malta, 241–242
Kuna Nation, 26

L

la costa (coast). *See* Ecuadorian regions, *costeños* (coastal people) and *la costa*
la sierra (plateau). *See* Ecuadorian regions, *serranos* (highlanders) and *la sierra* (plateau)
labels. *See* brands and labels; fairtrade and organic standards and certifications
labour
   about, 89–91, 97, 149–152
   flexible labour, 90–91, 154, 157
   industry moves to less-protected jurisdictions, 2
   minimum wage, 115, 149–150
   neoliberalism, 90–91
   pay equity, 154
   precarious employment, xi, 157
   premature aging, 89
   racist practices, 25–26, 28–29
   research on, 149–152
   social security systems, 115, 116, 149–151
   subcontractors (*capitanes*), 1, 18–19, 116–117, 148, 149–151
   technification impacts, 69, 89
   women, 69, 149–150, 154–155
   See also West Indian workers
labour, organizations. *See* ASTAC (banana worker organization), Ecuador; social justice and environmental movements; UROCAL fairtrade and organic co-op, Ecuador
labour, public health. *See* pesticides, application methods; pesticides, exposures and health effects; pesticides, health effects; public health
labour, small and large banana producers. *See* contract farms; fairtrade and organic producers and organizations; plantations
labour unions and labour relations
   about, 28–29, 89, 151–152
   blacklists, 117, 141, 146, 150, 151
   COLSIBA (regional organization), 94, 252, 257
   as "communist threat," 42–43, 63, 80, 178–179, 181, 192, 245, 250
   early history of organizing, 18–20, 26, 28–29
   el paro uprising (2019), 155–156, 157, 235
   labour law agreements, 89
   Noboa Group conflicts (2002), 115–117
   SITRAP (Agricultural Plantation Workers' Union), 101, 258
   strikes, 6, 26, 97, 115–117
   suppression strategies, 117, 141, 146, 150, 151–152, 154–155
   women's issues, 149–150, 154–155
Lago Agrio, Ecuador, 162–165
Larrea, Carlos, 49, 62, 87, 88–92, 108, 110, 146–147, 268n2
Las Ramas, Guayas, 118–119, 162
Lasso, Guillermo, 157–158
Latin American Organization of Banana Unions (COLSIBA), 94, 252, 257
laws and lawsuits
   about, 1, 187, 190–192, 196–199, 210–211
   DBCP effects, 75, 98, 181, 196–199, 210–211, 280n27
   Dole, 8, 181, 196–199, 211, 279n12, 280n27
   evidence, as term, 187–188, 190–191, 198–199
   exports of banned pesticides, 195–196
   individualizing narratives, 191–192
   "kill step" strategy, 166, 181, 197–198, 210–211
   limitations of, 166, 196–198, 210–212, 280n27
   "not convenient" principle, 196–197
   "objectivity" in proceedings, 191, 211, 212

petroleum companies, 162, 166, 212, 282n31
social knowledge as "non-scientific," 188, 190–191, 198–199
solidarity partnerships, 198–199
subcontracting ban, 1, 116–117, 148, 149–151
See also social justice and environmental movements
lived experience. *See* everyday life
Living to Tell the Tale (autobiography), 177
Los Ríos province, Ecuador
female worker exploitation, 154
labour exploitation, 135, 146, 149–150, 154
school for children with disabilities, 145

M

Machala, Ecuador
about, ix, 45, 110–113
banana boom (1948–65), 108, 110
"banana capital of the world," ix, 45, 110–113
research project base, xiii, 137, 140–141
UFC Chiquita mural, 27, 27(f), 129
urban life, 140–142, 202, 265n30, 274n14
wealth accumulation, 126, 234
World Banana Fair, 112
Mahuad, Jamil, 92
Make Fruit Fair, 151, 222, 223
malaria parasite, 36–37, 54
malathion, 71
Maldonado, Adolfo, 119, 162, 165
Mamita Yunai (novel), 97
market-based approaches
about, 11, 216–217, 221–224
climate change, 171, 223–224
conscious consumption, 11, 215–216, 227
entanglements of injustices and good intentions, 217
mechanisms for activism, 216–217, 221–224
as neoliberal, 216–217, 221–223
North/South power relations, 221–224
Marlin Mine, Guatemala, 246

Marquardt, Steve, 52–54, 263n9, 266n12, 267n10
Martin, James, 21, 279n16
Martínez, Luis, *A la costa*, 21–24, 28, 45
Marx, Karl, 226, 281n5, 283n45
massacres
Ciénaga, Colombia (1928), 18–19, 25, 93, 158, 177, 178–179, 250
Guatemala, 42, 242
Mexico, 243, 244
McNally, David, 202–203, 283n45
medical care. *See* health
mestizos
Afro-descended, 125–126, 164–165
early history, 23–24
elite cultured *mestizos*, 23
Indigenous-descended, 23, 126, 264n15
individualizing narratives, 36–37
in *A la costa* (novel), 21–22, 28, 45
lack of *cultura*, 123–127, 265n30, 274n14
ladinos in Guatemala, 26
land reforms, 164–165
racism, 23, 25–26, 46–47, 126, 264n15
serranos, 24, 126–127
social hierarchies and categories, 23, 126–127, 264n15, 274n14
stereotypes, 28, 54, 126–127, 180, 265n30
UFC history, 26, 46–47
as workers, 25–26, 54
methamidophos, 209
Mexico
Chiapas, 124–125
Disney/Pixar stories, 180, 182
drug cartels, 158
early history, 17
elites, 244
Indigenous peoples, 244
individualizing narratives, 124–125, 191
liberation theology, 242
massacres, 243, 244
pesticide exposures, 124–125, 191, 195
US imperialism, 17
Zapatistas, 242–244
mines and mining
Canadian mining industry, 143, 225, 234–236, 238–239, 242, 246, 275nn5–6
Correa's support, 148, 232

INDEX | 337

funding for academic institutions, 143, 234–237
gold mines, 230, 232, 234, 236, 246
Indigenous resistance, 235
Minions (film), 180, 279n11
Miss Chiquita, 6–7, 17, 179–184, 257, 262n25, 279n11
Moberg, Mark, 5, 221
monocultures, plantations as, 32–34, 52, 55, 69, 223–224
   See also plantations
Monsters Inc. (film), 8, 279n11
Moore, Jason, 168, 169
Moreno, Lenín, 109, 147–148, 153–157, 210
more-than-human world
   about, 31, 37, 55, 88, 92, 251–252
   aquatic ecosystems, 72–73
   atmospheric actors, 167–168
   banana industry impacts, 55, 70–72, 91–92, 133, 167–168
   constitutional rights in Ecuador, 116, 148
   emotional relationships, 133–134, 275n1
   entanglements of injustices and good intentions, 236–240, 275n4
   natural predators, 70, 72
   sentience, 252
   toxicology experiments, 189
   See also bananas; fungi; hurricanes and cyclones; insects and insecticides; pesticides
movies. See films
Munk School of Global Affairs, Toronto, 235
Murray, Douglas L., 80–81, 272n6
mushrooms, 164
Mycosphaerella fijiensis, 258
   See also black sigatoka
Mycosphaerella musicola, 258
   See also yellow sigatoka

N

Nading, Alex, 238, 285n28
narratives
   about, 170–171
   competing narratives, 178–179
   development and progress narratives, 35–37, 235–237
   framing of issues, 170, 178–179
   Green Revolution, 80, 121
   illness narratives, 3, 8–9, 122
   of inequities, 121
   of mental stress, 129–136
   political ecology of health, 262n18
   of power relations, 121
   racist narratives, 121, 165, 235–236
   social processes as contexts, 170–171
   See also individualizing narratives (victim-blaming); stories
Nash, Linda, 191
nature. See more-than-human world
Neely, Abigail, 237
nematicides, 8, 69, 74–75, 181, 193–194
   See also DBCP nematicide
nematodes, 8, 71, 74, 182, 257
neoliberalism
   about, 82–83, 85, 94–95, 136, 153–156, 226
   academic institutions, 234–237
   austerity budgets, 83, 90–91, 155–157
   bananas as "fruit of neoliberalism," 87, 94–95
   commodity production, 236
   COVID-19 responses, 156–158
   dehumanizing effects, 85
   deregulation, 83, 216
   in Ecuador, 89–91, 94–95, 131–132, 136, 153–156
   global model, 82–83, 85, 94–95, 136, 216–217
   IMF approach, 89–90, 155–156, 161, 210
   labour exploitation, 82, 87, 153–156
   local particularities, 83, 94–95
   market-based mechanisms, 216–217, 221–224
   mental health effects, 131–132
   as *plaga*, 153–156
   poverty narratives, 184, 226
   resistance to, 82–83, 85, 91
   US imperialism, 64–65, 81–83, 94–95
   See also capitalism; individualizing narratives (victim-blaming)
Neruda, Pablo, 15

Ngäbe (Guaymí) Nation, 26, 53, 54
Nguse, Thokozile, 237
Nicaragua
    about, 98–103, 272n6
    DBCP use, 74, 195–198, 211, 250
    Dole/Standard Fruit, 195
    elites, 98–100
    health research, 99–103, 250, 272n6
    integrated pest management, 272n6
    lawsuits, 196–198, 211
    mestizo workers, 54
    Panama disease, 267n31
    Sandinista revolution, 82, 88, 94, 98–99, 250, 272n6
    Somoza regime (1979), 98, 272n6
    US imperialism, 17, 42, 82, 94, 98–100
Noboa, Álvaro, 116, 158
Noboa, Daniel (Álvaro's son), 158
Noboa Group
    about, 48–49, 63–64, 87–88, 92, 258
    Bonita brand, 91, 109–110, 257
    corporate history, 48–49, 63–64, 87, 165
    elites, 63–64, 87, 92, 116, 271n30
    government support, 87–88
    Hacienda Los Álamos, 115–117
    hurricanes, 91–92
    labour conflicts (2002), 115–117
    leading exporter of bananas, 92, 257
    neoliberalism, 87
    non-traditional markets, 88
    as reserve supplier, 91–92
    statistics, 87
    supermarket supplier, 91, 115–116
    vertical business model, 49, 110
    working conditions, 92, 115–116
"noticing" in social science research, 11, 185, 229–230, 239–240, 248
    See also everyday life
novels and poetry
    Dracula, 202–203
    A la costa, 21–23, 24, 28, 45
    Mamita Yunai, 97
    One Hundred Years of Solitude, 19, 178, 184
    Prisión Verde, 67–68
    "La United Fruit Co.," 15
    Viento Fuerte, 31–32, 175, 273n7

O

O. Henry, 41, 264n15
"objectivity," 10, 140, 191, 207, 211–213, 238–239
occupational health sciences. *See* public health science
oil industry. *See* petroleum industry, Ecuador
One Hundred Years of Solitude (novel), 19, 178, 184
organic and fairtrade producers. *See* fairtrade and organic producers and organizations; fairtrade and organic standards and certifications
organophosphates, 73, 151, 194, 209
Orrego, Elena, 79, 270n5
Oxfam research, 149–150, 154, 223

P

Pachamama (earth-mother), 107, 116
Panama
    Bocas del Toro region, 23, 25, 53–55, 179, 266n32
    Indigenous people, 26, 266n32
    Panama Canal, 17, 25, 48
    Panama disease, 33–34, 37, 267n31
    shift to Cavendish, 61
    UFC history, 23, 25, 33–34
    West Indian workers, 25
Panama disease. *See* fungi, Panama disease
pandemic, COVID-19. *See* COVID-19
Panzós, Guatemala, massacre (1978), 242
"parakeets" (spray workers), 52–55, 67–68
paraquat, 1, 73, 99, 209, 211
PEH. *See* political ecology of health (PEH)
Pérez, Yaku, 157
personal protective equipment. *See* PPE (personal protective equipment)
Peru, 91, 159
pesticide industries
    about, 55, 64–65, 69, 208–213
    advertising, 109–110, 111(f)
    chemical and petroleum industries, 55, 68, 74–75, 166
    Dead Sea Bromine Co., 193–194, 196
    exports of banned pesticides, 195–196

INDEX | 339

influence on public policy, 208–213, 281n20
local companies, 109
power relations, 210, 221–224
"safe" thresholds of exposures, 82, 125, 189–190, 194
Syngenta, 109, 110, 111(f), 204, 211
transnational companies, 109, 110, 111(f)
See also Dow Chemical Company; Shell Chemical Company
pesticides
about, 51–52, 69–70
carbamates, 59–60, 73
colloquial terms for, 153
DDT, 69, 71, 73
diazinon, 71
dieldrin, 70–72
historical overview, 10–11, 69–70
impact on ecosystems, 70, 72–75
management decisions on, 70
more-than-human world, 55, 70, 72
organophosphates, 73, 151, 194, 209
pesticide resistance, 70–72
pesticide treadmill, 72, 80, 272n6
research challenges, 2–3, 119–120
See also DBCP nematicide; fungicides; insects and insecticides; nematicides
pesticides, application methods
aerial fumigation, x–xi, xiii, 7, 70, 74, 110, 112, 118–119, 122
backpack sprayers, xi, 110, 111
plastic bags on bananas, x, 74, 166
pesticides, exposures and health effects
about, 3, 73–75, 193–195, 233
child exposures, x, xi, 7, 118
individualizing narratives, 3, 64–65, 123, 129–130, 136, 191–192, 194, 233
lack of *cultura*, 124–127, 233
pilots' health complaints, 119, 145, 274n20
plant worker exposures, 194–195
"safe" thresholds, 82, 125, 189–190, 194, 272n6
scalar reasoning, 262n14
See also individualizing narratives (victim-blaming); pesticides,

application methods; PPE (personal protective equipment)
pesticides, government roles. *See* laws and lawsuits; regulation, government
pesticides, health effects
about, 73–75
cancers, 73, 75, 119, 151, 205
cardiac problems, 119
congenital malformations, 119, 145
nausea, 119
neurological problems, 73, 151
reproductive impacts, 73, 75, 133, 193–195, 197, 211
respirator problems, 73
skin irritations, 73
as *veneno*, xi
vision problems, 73, 119
pesticides, health effects research. *See* epidemiology; public health science; toxicology
petroleum industry, Ecuador
about, 87–88, 91–92, 165–167
Chevron/Texaco, 87, 162, 163(f), 166, 198, 212, 282n31
Correa era, 147–148, 155, 210, 232
el paro uprising (2019), 155–156, 157
environmental degradation, 162–167, 212, 232
Indigenous peoples, 155, 162, 164, 165
lawsuits, 162, 166, 212
revenues from, 146, 165, 210
Philippines, 88, 195, 278n26
Pinochet, Augusto, 79, 82, 235, 242–243
Pixar. *See* Disney/Pixar stories
plagas. See COVID-19; neoliberalism; TR4 fungal disease (Tropical Race 4)
planes, fumigation. *See* fumigation, aerial
plantations
about, 32–33, 168–169
Correa's supports, 147–148
drainage systems, 72–73
early history, 16
global interconnections, 168–169
labour exploitation, 122–123, 149–152
land reforms, 63–64
as monocultures, 32–34, 52, 55, 69

more-than-human world, 31, 72–73, 163–164, 167–168, 175
Plantationocene, 168–171, 188, 229, 248–249
power relations, 122–123
sigatoka overview, 52–53
TR4 fungal disease, 158–159, 171, 259
vertical integration, 16
in *Viento Fuerte* (novel), 31–32, 175, 273n7
See also Anthropocene/Capitalocene/Plantationocene; banana industries; technification
Plaza Lasso de la Vega, Galo Lincoln, 46, 47
"plotting" better stories, 11, 185, 248–252
See also everyday life
political ecology of health (PEH)
 about, 4–5, 233–239, 262n18
 defined, 262n18
 emotional and relational ways, 184, 233
 entanglements of injustices and good intentions, 236–240, 251–252, 275n4, 285n28
 history's impacts on environment, 233
 as political ecology subset, 262n18
 See also environmental degradation; social science research
Polo Almeida, Patricia, 231, 275n1
popular culture
 "Bananas of the world, unite!" (song), 7
 Disney/Pixar stories, 7–8, 180–184, 187–188, 247, 279n11
 Miss Chiquita, 6–7, 17, 179–184, 257, 279n11
 vampires and capitalism, 202–203, 281n5, 283n45
 violence of Green Revolution, 109
 See also films; novels and poetry
poverty
 about, 184, 203–204, 226
 COVID-19's impacts, 157–158
 depoliticized research articles, 204–208, 211–213, 281n8
 "developing" countries, 80, 125, 203–207, 212, 222
 imperialist narratives, 184, 226
 individualizing narratives, 24, 121, 125–127, 129–130, 136, 204, 233
 lack of *cultura*, 24, 123–127, 131–132, 233
 political ecology of health, 233–234
 racist exploitation, 126–127, 226
 social determinants of health, 3, 210
power relations
 about, 121–123, 203–204
 of capitalism, 203–204
 contract farms, 134–135, 139
 in environmental injustice, 5, 121, 139
 fairtrade and organic standards and certifications, 221–224
 gringos, 139–140
 political ecology of health, 5, 233–234
 precarious employment, 122–123, 157
 research participant observations, xiii–xiv
 resistance to structural inequities, 122–123
 See also capitalism
PPE (personal protective equipment)
 on contract farms, 118
 equipment, 118
 individualizing narratives, 123–124, 141, 142, 191–192
 ineffectiveness, 75
 labour exploitation, 149
 misuse and lack of *cultura*, 123–124, 233
 narratives of misuse or refusal to use, 118, 194
 safe-use campaigns, 124, 192, 194, 206
 on small farms, 110
precarious, as term, 261n5
Prisión Verde (novel), 67–68
progress narratives, 35–37, 235–237
Pseudocercospora fijiensis, 258
 See also black sigatoka
Pseudocercospora musae, 258
 See also yellow sigatoka
public health
 about, 4, 37, 184
 emotional stress, 129–136, 275n1
 human need for hope, 184
 progress narratives, 35–37
 racial capitalism impacts, 29–30, 266n37

social determinants of health, 3, 11, 120, 210, 239
  See also COVID-19
public health science
  about, 118–120, 187–188, 212–213
  banana industry relations, 183–184
  biomedical evidence, 188, 203–204, 209, 213
  depoliticized research articles, 204–208, 211–213, 281n8
  difference-making processes, 188
  early research, 203–204
  evidence, as term, 187–188, 191, 198–199, 281n3
  hierarchies of science and folklore, 188
  human data from "developing countries," 203–205
  individualizing narratives, 191–192
  influence on public policy, 208–213, 281n20
  Northern gaze, 246
  "objectivity," 10, 140, 191, 207, 211–213, 238–239
  poverty narratives, 184, 226
  See also epidemiology; evidence-based approaches; pesticides, exposures and health effects; social science research; toxicology
Puerto Rico, 17

Q

Qué Tan Lejos (film), 137–138
Quetzaltenango (Xela), 245
Quito, Ecuador
  geography, 107
  health research, 118–119, 121
  Indigenous protests, 155
  wealth accumulation, 126, 234

R

racism
  about, 21–27, 126–127, 264n15
  as difference-making, 188
  early history, 23–24, 28, 46, 264n15
  global interconnections, 169
  hierarchies, 24, 26, 27–28, 188, 264n15, 265n20
  historical overview, 60–62
  imaginative geographies, 27–28
  Indigenous peoples, 125–127
  individualizing narratives, 24, 123–127, 142, 191–192, 233
  in *A la costa* (novel), 21–24, 28, 45
  lack of *cultura*, 123–127, 233, 265n30, 274n14
  ladinos (mestizos), 26
  mestizo categories, 126
  PEH critiques of, 233–234
  progress narratives, 35–37, 235–237
  racial capitalism, 29–30, 266n37
  social and racial hierarchies, 123–124, 126–127, 264n15
  stereotypes, 22, 27–28, 108, 141, 180, 265n30
  West Indian workers, 25–27, 37, 40, 266n32
  white supremacy, 24–26, 29, 126, 262n16, 265n20
railways, 16–17, 22–25, 167
Rainforest Alliance, 101, 163–164, 218, 220
Ramón (doctor in Machala), ix–x, xiv
Reagan, Ronald, 195–196
recipe for banana bread, 286
red stain disease, 168
reforestation, 162–165
Regional Union of Peasant-Farmer Organizations. *See* UROCAL fairtrade and organic co-op, Ecuador
regulation, government
  about, 11, 187, 189–190, 195–196
  DBCP exposures, 193–195
  devolution to consumers, 215–216, 227
  evidence, as term, 187, 198–199
  exports of banned pesticides, 195–196
  human data from "developing countries," 203–205
  industry influence on public policy, 189, 208–213, 281n20
  neoliberal deregulation, 83, 195–196
  risk assessment model, 189–190, 209
  "safe" thresholds of exposures, 82, 125, 189–190
  toxicology evidence, 189–191

research project
  about, xi–xii, 263n40
  author's approach, xi–xii, 11–12, 177–178
  author's positionality, 10, 12, 137–144, 275n1
  ethics terms, x, 59–60
  ethnographic fieldwork, 140–141, 263n40
  la costa, xii, 263n40
  limitations, 11–12, 119
  Machala as base, ix–x, 1, 6, 140–142, 202
  methodology, 119, 121, 263n40
  narratives and stories, 3, 8–12, 121, 251–252
  participants, ix–xiii, 140, 261nn1–2, 263n40
  political ecology of health, 4–5
  related projects, xi
  rhizomatic approach, 12
  Spanish language, x, 141, 142
  UROCAL's support, 6, 231
  See also Brisbois, Ben
Rodas, Hernán, 230, 242
Rojas, Alejandro, 77–80, 78(f), 83, 270n5
Roldós Aguilera, Jaime, 89
Roman Catholics, 100–101, 241–242
Rothman, Kenneth, 212

S

salvage accumulation, 169, 249, 278n30
Sandinistas, 82, 88, 94, 98–99, 250, 272n6
Sandino, Augusto, 272n6
Schenker, Marc, 211
science. *See* epidemiology; evidence-based approaches; public health science; toxicology
scientific journals, 10, 204–208, 211–213
  See also academic institutions
Sellers, Christopher, 191
serranos (highlanders). *See* Ecuadorian regions, *serranos* (highlanders) and *la sierra* (plateau)
Shell Chemical Company, 68, 74–75, 193–194, 196–197, 280n27
Shiva, Vandana, 77, 109
shopping for bananas. *See* consumers

sigatoka. *See* fungi, sigatoka
SITRAP (Agricultural Plantation Workers' Union), 101, 258
slavery
  abolition in British Empire (1834), 15, 25
  contemporary forms, 115–117
  legacies of, 169, 265n20, 266n37
  in *Mamita Yunai* (novel), 97
  racial capitalism, 29–30, 266n37
  salvage accumulation, 169, 249, 278n30
small farms
  about, 64, 90, 129–136, 219–224
  certified fairtrade and organic farms, 219–224
  competition with large farms, xiii, 220
  decline of, 61–62, 64, 90
  diversity of, 77
  economic precarity, xiii, 130–136, 138–139, 210, 219–220, 275n2
  emotional stress, 129–136, 275n1
  future aspirations, 171–172
  individualizing narratives, 129–132, 136
  labour exploitation, 150–152, 222
  land reforms, 64, 90
  market-based approaches, 216–217, 222–224
  technification demands, 61–62
  women's labour, 131
  See also contract farms; fairtrade and organic producers and organizations
social class
  divisive labour management, 25–29
  elites overview, 108
  imaginative geographies, 27–29, 35, 205, 265n27
  intersection of *cultura* and race, 27–30, 126–127
  in political ecology, 4–5
  stereotypes overview, 27–28
  See also elites; stereotypes; West Indian workers
social justice and daily life. *See* everyday life
social justice and environmental movements
  about, 1–4, 98

challenges, 9
constitutional rights (2008), 116, 148
critiques of individualizing narratives, 233
entanglements of injustices and good intentions, 236–240, 251–252, 275n4
evidence-based supports, 213
Foro Emaús, 101–103, 207, 208, 242
global solidarity, 6–7, 198–199, 210, 230
human need for hope, 184
influence on public policy, 208–209, 281n20
IRET research institute, 102, 207, 258
non-heroic response in everyday life, 229
racial capitalism, 29–30, 266n37
strategies, 11
See also ASTAC (banana worker organization), Ecuador; everyday life; fairtrade and organic producers and organizations; UROCAL fairtrade and organic co-op, Ecuador
social science research
about, 229, 237–240
emotions in, 9–10, 184, 238
entanglements of injustices and good intentions, 236–240, 275n4
feminist scholarship, 138, 140, 213, 238, 252
Northern gaze, 246
"noticing," 11, 184–185, 229–230, 239–240, 248
"objectivity," 10, 140, 191, 207, 211–213, 238–239
political ecology of health, 4–5, 237–240
power relations, 121
social location of researcher, 10, 12
societal causes of harms, 3
See also evidence-based approaches
social science research facilitators. See ASTAC (banana worker organization), Ecuador; UROCAL fairtrade and organic co-op, Ecuador
Soluri, John, 27, 34–35, 171, 217, 263n9, 271n2, 285n35

Somoza Debayle, Anastasio, 98, 272n6
Spanish language, x, 261n3
Sparke, Matthew, 240
Spiegel, Jerry, xi, 77
Springer, Simon, 217
Standard Fruit. See Dole/Standard Fruit
standards, agricultural. See fairtrade and organic standards and certifications
stereotypes
about, 27–28
costeños (coastal people), 27–28, 122–127, 131–132, 234, 265n30
imaginative geographies, 27–29, 35, 205, 265n27
individualizing narratives, 125–127, 129–130, 170
mestizos, 28, 54, 126–127, 180, 265n30
racism, 22, 27–28, 108, 141, 180, 265n30
serranos (highlanders), 27–28, 126–127, 265n30
West Indian workers, 28, 180
Stoker, Bram, 202–203
stories
about, 9–10, 170–171, 184, 251–252
alternative stories, 250–252
devils and capitalism, 3
emotional power, 9–10, 184, 252
emotional stress, 129–136, 275n1
framing of issues, 170, 178–179
human need for, 184, 251–252
as ideologies, 251
social processes as contexts, 170–171
vampires and capitalism, 202–203, 281n5, 283n45
See also everyday life; films; narratives; novels and poetry
Striffler, Steve, 5, 47, 49, 231, 263n9, 269n15
subcontractors, labour (capitanes), 1, 18–19, 116–117, 148, 149–151
sugar plantations and markets, 3, 15, 168–169, 242, 248–249
Sundberg, Juanita, 237
supermarkets, 91, 154, 218–219
Syngenta, 109, 110, 111(f), 204, 211

T

Taussig, Michael T., 3, 225

technification
  about, 61–62, 68–69, 77
  certification and standards, 221–222
  chemical fertilizers, 61–62, 73, 80, 89
  decline in labour needs, 89
  Green Revolution overview, 80–82
  on-farm facilities, 68–69
  petrochemicals, 166
  shift to Cavendish, 61–62, 68–69, 165–166
  women workers, 69
  See also Green Revolution
Tenguel, Ecuador, 150
  See also Hacienda Tenguel, Ecuador
Texaco, 87–88, 162, 166
  See also Chevron/Texaco
thrips, 70, 72, 168
Thrupp, Lori Ann, 69–70, 72
Torrijos, Omar, 81
toxicology
  about, 189–191, 198–199, 212–213, 233–234
  animal experimentation, 82, 189, 247
  DBCP research, 75, 193–194, 198–199
  depoliticized research articles, 204–208, 211–213, 281n8
  evidence in, 187–188, 191, 198–199
  failure to impact pesticide use, 207–213
  Green Revolution, 82–83, 125
  herbicides, 73, 209
  human data from "developing countries," 203–205
  individualizing narratives, 191–192
  IRET research institute, 102, 207, 258
  "objectivity," 10, 140, 191, 207, 211–213, 238–239
  PEH critiques of, 233–234
  "safe" thresholds, 82, 124–125, 189–190, 192, 194
  social knowledge as "non-scientific," 188, 190–191, 198–199
  solidarity partnerships, 198–199
  "Tox Lab" (U of Chicago), 82–83, 189
Toy Story (film), 8
TR4 fungal disease (Tropical Race 4), 158–159, 259, 271
trade, global
  bananas as "fruit of neoliberalism," 87, 94–95, 136
  distribution networks, 16
  Ecuador as reserve supplier, 87–88, 91, 94
  preferred sources with lowest costs, 86
  statistics, 62
  tariffs, 81, 86, 87, 259
  vertical integration, 16
  WTO rules, 86
trade unions. See labour unions and labour relations
transportation networks
  highways, 108, 273n2
  railways, 16–17, 22–25, 167
  refrigeration, 167
Tropical Race 4 (TR4 fungal disease), 158–159, 171, 259
Tsing, Anna, 164, 169, 213, 229, 278n30
tuberculosis (TB), 5, 53, 67
Tulane School of Hygiene and Tropical Medicine, 183, 279n16
Tzeltal people, Mexico, 244

U

UBC. See University of British Columbia
Ubico, Jorge, 40, 42
UFC/Chiquita (United Fruit Company)
  about, 15–20, 43–44, 179–184, 259
  cacao farms, 46–47, 64
  certifications, 101, 163–164, 218
  Chiquita brand, 6–7, 15, 17, 179–184, 257, 262n25, 279n11
  competing narratives, 178–184
  corporate colonialism, 21
  corporate history, 15–18, 32, 41, 43–44, 257, 259
  Disney/Pixar stories, 7–8, 180–184, 247, 279n11
  early history, 10, 15–20, 25–26, 33–34, 205, 279n16
  as el pulpo, 15
  fungicides, 52–55, 72
  image control, 178–184, 218
  incomplete corporate control, 20, 43–44
  Keith as co-founder, 16–17, 22–25, 32

medical departments, 53, 279n16
more-than-human world,
　44–45, 48, 167
nematicides, 75, 193–195
Panama disease, 33–37, 43–44, 249
racism, 21–22, 25–28, 36–37, 40
research departments, 33–37
scholarship on, 263n9
shift from Gros Michel to Cavendish,
　44, 48, 61, 68
shift from grower to
　marketer, 44, 47–48
shift to contract producers, 18, 44, 47,
　61, 68, 86
symbol of US imperialism, 179–180
United Brands, 75, 100, 193–194, 257
US anti-trust actions, 18, 41, 43, 68
See also banana industries; Hacienda
Tenguel, Ecuador; *and specific countries*
Union Association of Agricultural
　and Peasant Workers. See
　ASTAC (banana worker
　organization), Ecuador
Union of Banana Exporting Countries
　(UPEB), 81, 86, 87, 259
Unión Regional de Organizaciones
　Campesinas del Litoral. See
　UROCAL fairtrade and organic
　co-op, Ecuador
unions. See labour unions and
　labour relations
United Brands, 75, 100, 193–194, 257
See also UFC/Chiquita (United
　Fruit Company)
"La United Fruit Co." (poem, Neruda), 15
United Kingdom
　abolition of slavery (1834), 25
　Banana Link, 222, 223–224
　bioprospecting for banana
　　varieties, 34–35
　financing of colonial projects, 23–24
　progress narratives, 35–37
United Nations
　slavery investigation, 116–117
　Sustainable Development Goals, 222
United States

about, 17–18, 41–42, 86, 178–
　180, 184, 226
Alliance for Progress, 63, 80
alliances with elites, 41–42
anti-trust actions, 18, 41, 43, 68
banana republics, 17–18
chemical plant worker
　exposures, 194–195
Cold War politics, 42–43, 63,
　178–179, 181
"communist threats," 42–43, 63, 80,
　178–179, 181, 192, 245, 250, 267n12
competing narratives, 178–180
debt leveraging, 264n10
economic imperialism, 17, 264n10
exports of banned pesticides, 195–196
fairtrade global solidarity, 6–7
Green Revolution overview, 80–82
gringos, as term, 138
incomplete control, 41, 43–44
Indigenous peoples, 225
military interventions, 5, 17, 22,
　42–44, 63, 81–83
neoliberal models, 64–65, 238
PEH critiques of, 233–234
poverty narratives, 184, 226
progress narratives, 35–37
racism, 22, 27–28, 43, 265n21
"Tox Lab" (U of Chicago), 82–83, 189
UFC as symbol of imperialism, 179–180
See also capitalism; Green Revolution;
　neoliberalism; *and specific countries*
United States, banana industries. See
　banana industries; Del Monte
　Foods Inc.; Dole/Standard Fruit;
　pesticide industries; UFC/Chiquita
　(United Fruit Company)
United States, petroleum industries. See
　petroleum industry, Ecuador
United States Agency for International
　Development (USAID), 80–81
Universidad Andina Simón Bolívar, 119
Universidad Nacional, Costa Rica, 101–102
University of British Columbia, xi,
　201, 235–237
University of Chicago, 82–83, 189
University of Toronto, 232–233, 234–237

UPEB (Union of Banana Exporting
    Countries), 81, 86, 87, 259
upper class. *See* elites
UROCAL fairtrade and organic
    co-op, Ecuador
  history of, 6, 220, 222–223,
    230–232, 242
  influence on public policy, 208–209
  "progressive" bananas, 230
  research facilitator, 145, 151, 208–
    209, 230–231
  transnational solidarity, 6, 230
Uruguay, 62, 82

V

vampires and capitalism, 202–203,
    281n5, 283n45
Vasquez, Joaquín, 222–223, 231–232
Velasco Ibarra, José María, 47
Venezuela, 158, 159, 262n18
victim-blaming narratives. *See*
    individualizing narratives
    (victim-blaming)
Vidal Ortega, Antonino, 263n9
Viento Fuerte (novel), 31–32, 175, 273n7
Voltaire, *Candide*, 247–248

W

Wesseling, Catharina, 102, 207–209
West Indian workers
  about, 25–26
  agro-ecological knowledge, 25, 33, 34,
    169, 249, 266n12
  Bocas del Toro region, 23, 25, 53–54,
    179, 266n32
  early history, 25–26
  as English-speaking British
    subjects, 26, 29
  global interconnections, 169
  health problems, 36–37
  land ownership, 28–29, 266n32
  railway construction, 24–26, 37
  resistance by, 28–29, 266n32
  stereotypes, 28, 180
  UFC racism, 25–27, 37, 40, 266n32
  See also labour
witch hunts and ways of knowing,
    187–188, 198
witches' broom fungus, 45
women
  Banana Queens, 112, 170
  burden of care work, 216
  colonial narratives, 27, 27(f)
  feminist scholarship, 138, 140,
    213, 238, 252
  labour exploitation, 149–150, 154–155
  mental health, 131–132
  technification using, 69
  ways of knowing, 187–188, 198, 281n3
  See also gender
Wong, Segundo, 49, 91
workers. *See* labour; labour unions
    and labour relations; West
    Indian workers
World Trade Organization
    (WTO), 86, 271n5
worms. *See* nematodes

Y

yellow fever, 36
yellow sigatoka, 51, 71, 258
  See also fungi, sigatoka

Z

Zapata Petroleum, 5
Zapatistas, 242–244, 246, 250
Zemurray, Samuel, 18, 41–42, 183,
    264n16, 267n5

BEN BRISBOIS is an Assistant Professor in the Department of Social and Preventive Medicine of the Université de Montréal's School of Public Health. He lives in Montréal.

ABOUT THE SERIES
DIGESTIONS

Publishing established and emerging scholars and writers, *Digestions* is a book series that considers the history of food, the culture of food, and the politics of what we eat from both a Canadian and a global perspective.

OTHER BOOKS IN THE *Digestions* SERIES:

Bread & Water: Essays
by dee Hobsbawn-Smith

Uncertain Harvest: The Future of Food on a Warming Planet
by Ian Mosby, Sarah Rotz, and Evan D.G. Fraser

Speaking in Cod Tongues: A Canadian Culinary Journey
by Lenore Newman

Arab Cooking on a Prairie Homestead
by Habeeb Salloum

FOR MORE INFORMATION ABOUT
PUBLISHING IN THE SERIES, PLEASE CONTACT:

URP Acquisitions
University of Regina Press
3737 Wascana Parkway
Regina, Saskatchewan s4s 0A2 Canada
uofrpress.acquisitions@uregina.ca
www.uofrpress.ca